THE SHOGUN'S PAINTED CULTURE

Fear and Creativity in the Japanese States, 1760–1829

TIMON SCREECH

REAKTION BOOKS

This book is dedicated to Zoo:

. . . iro o mo ka o mo shiru hito zo shiru

Published by Reaktion Books Ltd
79 Farringdon Road
London EC1M 3JU, UK

www.reaktionbooks.co.uk

First published 2000

国際交流基金
The Japan Foundation

The Shogun's Painted Culture was published with the assistance of The Japan Foundation.

Colour printed by BAS printers Ltd, Over Wallop, Hampshire
Printed and bound in Great Britain by Biddles Ltd,
Guildford and King's Lynn

British Library Cataloguing in Publishing Data

Screech, Timon
The Shogun's painted culture: fear and creativity in the Japanese states, 1760–1829
1.Sadanobu, Matsudaira – Influence 2.Art, Japanese – Edo period, 1600–1868 3.Art, Political aspects – Japan – History – 18th century 4.Art and state – Japan – History – 18th century 5.Japan – Civilisation – 18th century – 1600–1868
I. Title
709.5'2'09033

ISBN 1 86189 064 8

Contents

Acknowledgements

My first debt is one of thanks. The research necessary for writing this book was undertaken during the academic year 1994–5 at Keio University, where I was a guest of the Department of Art History. Kawai Masatomo ensured that I had every facility there and I am profoundly grateful to him. I was financially supported during that period by an Asahi Fellowship.

Development of the ideas presented here and completion of the manuscript that became this book were immensely aided by discussions with Chino Kaori, Timothy Clark, Stephen Dodd, Kasuya Hiroki, Kobayashi Tadashi, John Rosenfield, Henry Smith, Takayama Hiroshi, Tanaka Yūko and others too numerous to mention. Inception, gestation and fruition were assured by Kazuhiro Murayama and Nicole Rousmaniere, and the small measure of success here attained is due to them. I would also like to thank Andrea Belloli and all at Reaktion Books. All errors remain my own.

Chronology

1603 Investiture of Tokugawa Ieyasu as first shogun
1616 Death and deification of Ieyasu
1617 Kano Tan'yū nominated first shogunal artist-in-waiting
1629 Shujo Kotohito (posthum. Go-Mizunoo) resigns in favour of daughter Okiko (posthum. Meishō)
1657 Great Fire of Edo
1689 Matsuo Bashō embarks on 'narrow road to deep north'
1704 Invention of 'Prussian Blue' pigment
1716 Birth of boy later known as Itō Jakuchū
1727 Engelbert Kaempfer's *History of Japan* published (London)
1730 Birth of boy later known as Kano Eisen-in
1731 Qing-period painter Shen Nanpin arrives in Japan
1733 Birth of boy later known as Maruyama Ōkyo
1743 Closing of Dutch station in Siam
1745 Birth of boy later known as Shimazu Shigehide, daimyo of Satsuma
1748 Chosŏn embassy arrives
1753 Birth of boy later known as Kano Korenobu
1754 Birth of boy later known as Sumiyoshi Hiroyuki
1758 Birth of boy later known as Matsudaira Sadanobu
1760 Investiture of Tokugawa Ieharu as tenth shogun; George III crowned King of England; second Great Fire of Edo
1763 Kano Eisen-in made 'inner painter'; birth of boy later known as Tani Bunchō
1764 Chosŏn embassy arrives; Dutch threaten cancellation of embassy
1765 Maruyama Ōkyo meets the prince–abbot Yūjō
1774 Matsudaira Sadanobu adopted by daimyo of Shirakawa; publication of *Kaitai shinsho (New Anatomical Atlas)*
1775 Carl Peter Thunberg arrives
1778 Appearance of malevolent star; Kubota Castle burns; Hendrik Duurkoop dies en route to Japan
1779 Investiture of Tomohito as shujo (posthum. Kōkaku); Tokugawa Iemoto dies falling from horse
1780 Fourth Anglo-Dutch War (to 1784); Akizato Ritō publishes *Miyako meisho zue (Complete Illustrated Places of the Capital)*; Isaac Titsingh gives Tokugawa Ienari a mouth-organ
1781 Promulgation of the Tenmei ('heavenly brilliance') era
1782 Both Dutch ships fail to arrive

1783 Matsudaira Sadanobu becomes daimyo of Shirakawa; Shiba Kōkan produces first copperplate print; eruption of Mt Asama; Daikoku-ya Kōdayū shipwrecked; death of Yosa Buson
1786 Assassination of Tanuma Okitomo; death of Tokugawa Ieharu
1787 Investiture of Tokugawa Ienari as eleventh shogun; Matsudaira Sadanobu becomes chief councillor
1788 Matsudaira Sadanobu becomes regent; Shibano Ritsuzan nominated shogunal Confucian expert; Great Fire of Keishi (Kyoto)
1789 Promulgation of the Kansei ('lenient government') era
1790 Death of Kano Eisen-in; Tomohito returns to the new Dairi
1791 Matsudaira Sadanobu holds poetry test; English word 'panorama' neologized
1793 Matsudaira Sadanobu resigns principal posts; Daikoku-ya Kōdayū repatriated; Tani Bunchō produces 'realistic' coastal views
1794 Tani Bunchō made attendant to Matsudaira Sadanobu; Chōbusai Eishi begins study with Kano Korenobu
1795 Death of Maruyama Ōkyo; French invasion of Netherlands; Carl Peter Thunberg's *Travels* published (London)
1796 Chosŏn embassy mooted
1797 Air pump manufactured in Japan; Matsudaira Sadanobu commands survey of Mt Fuji
1798 Burning of Great Buddha; death of Gijsbert Hemmij; promulgation of Kansei Calendar
1799 Motoori Norinaga writes *E no koto (On Pictures)*; *Shūko jusshū (Collected Antiquities in Ten Categories)* completed
1800 Females allowed on to Mt Fuji; death of Itō Jakuchū
1802 Jippensha Ikku publishes first instalment of *Tōkaidōchū hizakurige (Down the Tōkaidō on Shank's Pony)*
1805 Doi Tsudayū repatriated by Nicolai Rezanov
1807 Eitai Bridge disaster
1808 Death of Kano Korenobu; arrival of *HMS Phaeton*
1810 Death of Sumiyoshi Hiroyuki
1811 Chosŏn embassy arrives
1812 Matsudaira Sadanobu retires from daimiate of Shirakawa
1822 Isaac Titsingh's *Illustrations of Japan* published (London)
1823 Death of Ōta Nanpo
1829 Death of Matsudaira Sadanobu
1833 Death of Shimazu Shigehide
1837 Death of Tokugawa Ienari
1840 Death of Tani Bunchō
1845 Death of Tomohito (posthum. Kōkaku)
1854 Burning of Dairi

Introduction

This book is about building a boundary to construct a centre. The term for the centre was either *wa* or *nihon*. Both terms overlapped, and in English we can render them 'Japan'. The former stressed an autonomy from – and hence a parallelism with – north-east Asian Continental cultures, while the latter appealed more to a trans-historical sense of an indigenous enlightenment in isolation. The concrete core of this came to be seen as the city of Kyoto. All three toponyms – *wa, nihon, kyoto* – were old and by the latter part of the eighteenth century had at least one thousand years' standing. But none was the necessary recipient of the huge load of meaning it began to assume. In the pages that follow I attempt to study the invention, formalization and fixing of a 'Japan' supported by its nodal city and canopied by a presence that was to be defined as tangible 'Japanese culture'.

Thinkers had planted philosophical markers around 'Japan' before this time. Attempts to stake out a zone from within extending Continental norms had begun at least in the early part of the century, if not earlier. It was only from the 1760s, I contend, that this space became object-based, and the manner in which a 'Japanese culture' was *materialized* is our theme. What was willed then continues to be influential, perhaps even fundamentally disciplines our sense of what Japan is, to this day. Those who work in the field of Japanese cultural history today are, I think, often unaware of how many of their assumptions derive from an enclosure established just two centuries ago, and part of my intention is to bring this issue to the fore.

The contention that the quintessence of Japan was bedded in the city of Kyoto is now the truism of tourist brochures, but it emerged at this time. 'Kyoto' was not in fact known by that name for most of its history. Until the mid-seventeenth century it was more often called Miyako, and thereafter Kyō or Keishi. This last is the name I shall use below. Keishi as a real entity was wiped out in 1788 by a devastating fire and its antique purity honed through reconstruction; the resurrected space was given the ancient, largely defunct, name Kyoto.

Selections made or proposed for compass within 'Japanese culture', like the survivals from Keishi's horrendous fire, were arbitrary. They were not, however, thoughtlessly decided on, and many were astutely culled. The agenda behind selection needs to be carefully examined: as some things were included, others were left out.

At that time the Japanese islands were not yet a unified country but were ordered as a confederation under some 280 hereditary regional rulers, or daimyo (properly *daimyō*), a term that is variously rendered in English; Europeans who visited Japan in the period covered here likened them to the German petty monarchs of the Holy Roman Empire. Most daimyo were independent, with their own currencies, weights and measures, laws, privileges and linguistic and behavioural norms, although few had outright autonomy. Above this echelon was a bicephalic royalty, one half of the hydra being the shogun (properly *shōgun*), whose office, since 1603, had been passed on by heredity in the house of Tokugawa and whose capital was Edo (modern Tokyo). Shoguns formed an executive base for all the Japanese states, and daimyo, whose overlords they were, resided intermittently at their court. Power was cephalized also in the shujo (properly *shujō*), usually rendered in English as 'emperor'; his pedigree went further back as ancestral high priest, cultural mediator and sometime potentate, but his role was less well defined. (Note also that as terms such as daimyo, shujo and shogun are now commonly known in English, they will not be italicized or given macrons on their long vowels in this book.) After the collapse of the Tokugawa shogunate in 1868, the shujo would become a Western-style monarch under the titles *mikado* and *tennō*. He is the ancestor of the emperors of Japan in the present day. But before that he was pontifical rather than sovereign. It is important to note that in the eighteenth century, when Westerners referred to the 'emperor of Japan' (or *keizer* in the Dutch more common in the East Indies), they meant not the shujo but the shogun. The shujo lived in Keishi as the guest of the shogun, who personally ruled the city. The shogun, indeed, controlled all the main metropoles directly or through Tokugawa collaterals, and around a third of the archipelago was accounted his privileged territory, known as Ten'ryō ('lands of heavenly command') – not unlike the *Erblanden* of the Habsburg emperors. The shujo had no terrestrial sway. This Japanese collectivity was called the Tenka ('all under heaven') – another term that will be left untranslated below. It is necessary to emphasize these points, for I am aware they may not match other scholars' interpretations. They nevertheless inform my analysis that follows. Homogenization and tightening of the loose strands that made up the diverse cultures of this Tenka were part of establishing a shared 'Japanese' culture; the 280 or so daimyo states were all but foreign countries to each other.

Natural evolutions occurred within this political and social system, and these led ultimately to a sense of cultural urgency at the end of the eighteenth century. Slippage meant patterns of life were being forgotten and material forms erased in a rising tide of memory loss. There was also an external menace with the intrusion of outside nations, principally Russia and Great Britain, whose ships were increasingly seen from the 1770s. The Qing empire (China) or the Chosŏn kingdom (Korea) had long been known, and the United Provinces (Holland) had enjoyed trading rights since the establishment of the Tokugawa regime. But the new foreignness was too great to be accommodated. International communities had been sequestered in the city of Nagasaki since the early seventeenth century, but now they broke out. Constraint was no longer an option. The motivation of much of the late eighteenth-century reification of 'Japanese culture' was the establishment of a real entity to counter a belligerent Other. It was fear-led.

Central to my narrative is the persona of the shogun's chief councillor at this time, Matsudaira Sadanobu. He has already been the subject of much writing, though his character remains elusive. Much of this writing was by himself and was contradictory, which I see as part of a deliberate construction of equivocality. Sadanobu's diaries and jottings are diffuse, and it is hard to pin him down. Analogously, they are often hard to parse and grammatically fragmented. As the ultimate author of 'Japanese culture', Sadanobu found it useful to hide his aims in a profusion of secondary documentation. By extinguishing the possibility of grasping the figure of a *him*, the self-evidence of what Sadanobu dictated appeared all the more convincing. The result of his *bricolage* is not seriously contested. Nevertheless, it would be absurd to claim that Sadanobu was alone in this or that he had a prior blueprint. Although he was chief councillor, he lacked the capacity or will to fabricate 'Japanese culture' single-handedly. But I find him the most conscious actor in the processes with which I deal in this book, and I shall refer to a 'Sadanobu process'. Sadanobu's writings on culture are a crucial record. His final years were spent in retirement but were his most productive. If his councillorship had been vital to establishing his authority, his removal to an off-centre position allowed him an apparently dispassionate stance. I shall use Sadanobu as the peg on which to hang the contents of this book, but always with the recognition that he is something of a cypher for larger events. Much of his thinking was derivative and shared, but his public role ensured him higher exposure.

Chapter One will attempt to locate this Sadanobu, or rather 'Sadanobu', the personage that wanders within circles of his own devising. His writings are investigated, as are those of others whom he influenced positively or adversely. His concept of culture and of the shogun's person within it are discussed.

Chapter Two will identify the features of later eighteenth-century life that were evinced as symptoms of the collapse which was the premise for a regeneration of culture. Without what I shall call a 'discourse of disaster' the radical work of transformation could not have been pushed through. All periods have unease and decriers, but, unusually, this was a time when decline became the dominant rhetoric. It is not my purpose to weigh up the truth or error of the contentions put forward (although a series of bad harvests, floods and eruptions did seem to lend a firm empirical base) but to show the manner in which evidence was again and again adduced about how the dispensation of the Tenka was egregiously awry. The central figure in Chapter Two is Sugita Genpaku, an anatomical physician of a distinctly modern bent, who kept a now little-read journal of the grievous happenings of the age. To him, the present was the worst that history had ever known.

Chapter Three will look at the tasks of official cultural shoring-up. Sadanobu dominates, but he had colleagues. Action was taken vis-à-vis the official painting school of the Kano, which furnished the government with its icons. The rebuilding of the city of Keishi, which would re-emerge as Kyoto, was germane too; Sadanobu was able to configure it more or less at will. We will consider the rebuilding of the shujo's mansion, the Dairi ('inner rear'), for which official artists were very much required. This Dairi was totally unlike any other that had existed before but was touted as a 'revival' (*fukkō*) of antique architectural style. Sadanobu made his only trip to Keishi/Kyoto at this time to see the reality of the loss of medieval and early-modern cityscapes and to oversee the new rhetoric of antiquity. In the next year, 1789, the shogunate declared the beginning of a new calendrical era (*nengō*), calling it year one of Kansei (literally, 'lenient government'); Sadanobu formalized a series of Kansei Reforms, centring them on the revival of shogunal power and the positioning of the Tokugawa at the core of 'Japanese culture'.

In this rebuilding of the Dairi a trap was set for the shujo, whose name was Tomohito, and who was young but already ten years into a long incumbency. His mansion was 'revived' most gloriously, whereas the shogunal castle, which had also fallen victim to the flames, was not rebuilt. This undercut Tomohito, according to the pivotal Confucian concept of princely modesty or 'lenience' – the very word built into the era itself.

Chapter Four looks in detail at the most singular artist of the period, both before and after the fire: Maruyama Ōkyo. He was regarded as the foremost painter of his own – and perhaps of all – time. He made sensational pictures in a style he called his 'new concept' (*shin'i*). This manner spread to a wide social spectrum, and it is no exaggeration to say that Ōkyo was the first to create a stylistic unity to serve a totalized 'Japan'. Previously, all pictorial manners had been class-dependent (unless overtly eccentric), but Ōkyo's were generally obtainable. He was an independent artist who managed to step out beyond the academies in which he had been initially trained and to create a style that purported to do no more than replicate nature itself. His new concept was just, he claimed, an artless copying of what he saw. But his themes were ideologically dense. The power of his images was locked into a pretension of transparency that totally disarmed critics of his hegemonic endeavour.

Ōkyo's persona is as important to my argument as is the evidence of his paintings themselves. He guarded and refined his aura. Although the two men never met, Ōkyo's concept meshed with Sadanobu's projects; the councillor kept a pocket-sized portrait of the artist always with him. Ōkyo signed himself 'Ōkyo of Heian', reviving the name for Keishi that pre-dated even Kyoto. He asserted himself as master of the depictional order that emanated from that historic (though actually now new) city.

Chapter Five will address moves towards drawing a more formal boundary around the purview of this 'Japanese culture' and by extension, therefore, relegating what was not part of it. This was a delicate task, since the late eighteenth century was precisely a time of Japanese territorial expansion. It is crucial that Sadanobu himself emerged from the margins of the Tenka, being the daimyo of Shirakawa, a buffer zone between culture and 'barbarity', and the historic symbol of the 'edge'.

The real eighteenth-century borders were further off, in Ezo (modern Hokkaido) in the north-east, the final home of the humiliated Ainu people, and in Nagasaki, where Europeans and Chinese were. Geographical studies and cartography of the ends of the Tenka were made. The posited culture of the interior was put out for view, newly equipped with an edge. The period saw the rise of leisure tourism by those taking stock of a culture that was now becoming theirs. Poetically inspired, often sedentary, notional travel by cultivated spirits had once been the standard expression of love of landscape, but this gave way to people who really went somewhere, who wanted information when they got there and who wanted the sites they visited to look good. Rebuilding of monuments was extensively practised, and with it the past was condensed and rendered unproblematic and appealing.

Renovation merged into surrogacy and pastiche. All the colours of these three *modi operandi* were used to make revivalism work at ground level. By the second quarter of the nineteenth century, where this book closes, the shogunate no longer felt itself under threat. We will consider this last harmonization, appropriately enough I hope, in a final coda taking the metaphor, or case study, of music – always important in Confucian states where melody symbolized the regulation of humanity with the dancing heavens. Not all nations rang their bells in the same way, but the shogunate was confident enough, when it welcomed an embassy from the Chosŏn court in 1811, to give parting gifts that are telling: paintings of the survival of ancient music among members of the Japanese military elite. These were executed by members of the reformed official school, billed as 'revivalist' but done in a novel manner. Here, for sure, was the shogun's painted culture.

For nearly half a century after the end of the period covered by this book the several Japanese ethnic groups would continue to speak mutually incomprehensible tongues, to calibrate differently and to vow loyalty to different rulers. Things were not the same all across the Tenka. Yet a definitive move towards a single culture is recognizable as beginning in the latter part of the eighteenth century, and the period coincides with Sadanobu's control. There are those who will see something akin to state formation here, and it is an interesting chance that the Kansei era began in the year of that defining moment of nationhood, the French Revolution. The shogunate was aware of many political events and attendant cultural transformations in Europe and North America, and as the Tenka shifted from a rather amorphous and unbelted extension of polities crossing dozens of islands, mountain ranges and ethnic groups, not so much terminating as fading out, and became something more solid, they knew that this was happening elsewhere too. Sadanobu and others used the old term *kokka*, 'family of states', in a way that does seem to prefigure its modern usage of 'nation'. One of Sadanobu's acts in building his 'Japanese culture' was the compilation of a book to standardize political terms, *A Correction of Names (Seimeiron)*, published in 1791, which deals with the nomenclature of apportionment of authority between shogun, daimyo and shujo, and he was also interested in foreign political labels. I am not yet ready to give the name of nation to what emerged under Sadanobu, and so I shall keep Japan in the plural as 'states'.

The language of return infiltrates much discourse and stands in marked contrast to the flagged 'innovations' that have punctuated more overt Japanese revolutions. When the Tokugawa assumed the shogunate, they said they had 'begun the states' (*kokusho*), and when they lost it, the shujo took over and made a 'new bond' (*ishin*). Sadanobu was much more temperate. His orbit was the cultural rather than the legislative. Many elements of this ‘culture’ would have perplexed people of a generation earlier for whom even ‘Japan’ was barely a recognizable concept. But, for good or ill, his formulations defined Japan and continue to do so.

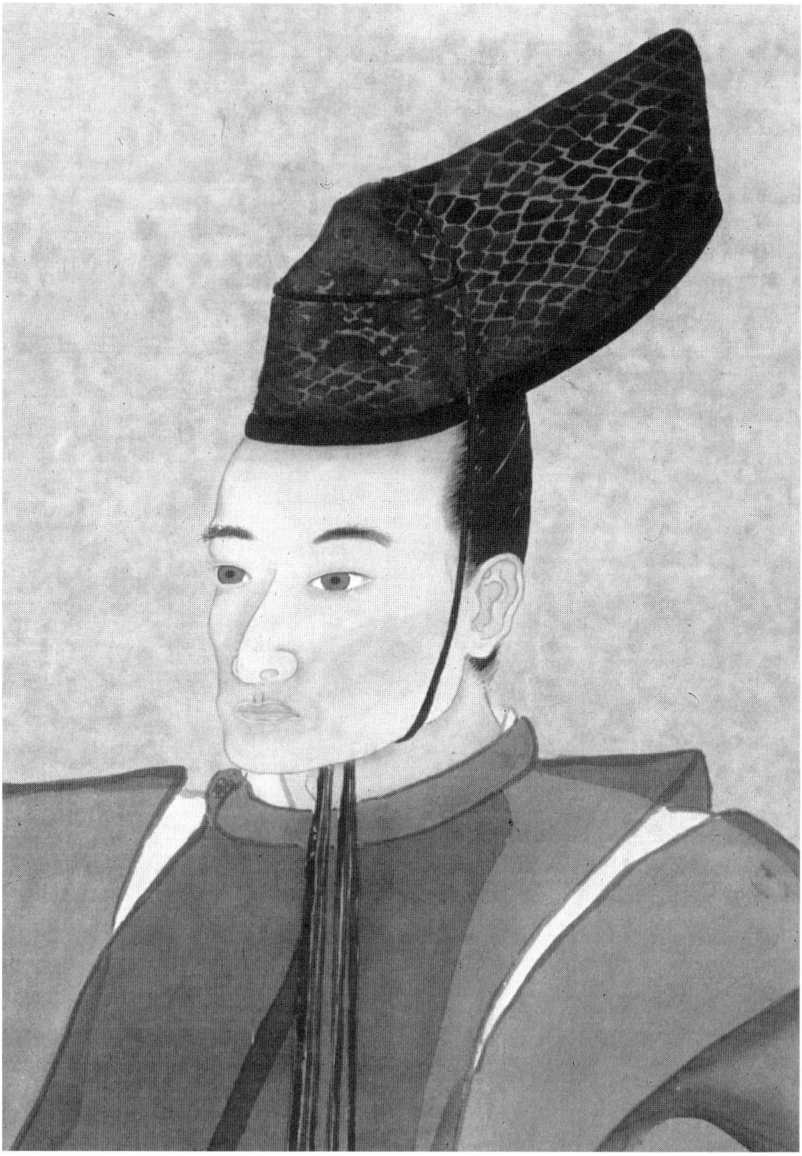

1 Detail of illus. 16.

1 Matsudaira Sadanobu and the Domestic Dilemma

How can one govern a country which has five hundred cheeses?
– Charles de Gaulle

In governing a country of eight thousand provinces,
one must have regard to the tenor of the times.
– Matsudaira Sadanobu

Central to the activities of the artists, politicians and thinkers that figure in this book was, I propose, the construction of an entity that could meaningfully be called 'Japanese culture'. This was the first time such an artifice had been made consciously, or certainly concretely. The central figure was Matsudaira Sadanobu, a man of some 25 years of age when he appeared forcefully on the central shogunal stage of Edo (now Tokyo), in the early 1780s.[1] Although not alone in his sense of a dilemma facing the Japanese states, he was among the most active in addressing it. Sadanobu was acutely aware that certain elements in the disparate societies overseen by the shogunal house of Tokugawa had become so problematical that they would have to be neutralized if the collectivity was long to retain its delicate balance. Without restabilizing, the shogunal regime would fall. It seemed about to, indeed, in a resurgence of the civil wars that had been the normal condition for a good century of pre-Tokugawa history. The means of averting this was to fabricate gloriously a shared bond that would hold space culturally together. This creation is what I call the 'shogun's painted culture'.

In the early 1780s the incumbent shogun was Ieharu, tenth in a line that stretched back to Tokugawa Ieyasu, the 'divine ancestor' (*shinsō*) who had established his shogunate in 1603. That monumental event was referred to as the 'beginning of the states' (*kokusho*). In office since 1760, Ieharu was not admired, was unable to assert authority and was presiding over (thought those such as Sadanobu) a backslide into ruin.

In 1787, through string-pulling and blood right, Sadanobu became the shogunal chief councillor (*ryōjū shūza*). He had already enjoyed two years in the junior post of adviser in the antechamber (*tamari-no-ma zume*). In 1788 he was elevated to a post so high it was usually left unfilled: shogunal regent (*shōgun hosa*). However unlikely it would have seemed during the 1780s that the shogunate would survive into its third century, by 1829, when Sadanobu died, the Tokugawa were snug in a reformulated garb which they were to wear for a further four generations. It was Sadanobu who engineered this revival. He did not work alone, but even in the areas he did not personally manipulate (and technically he retired in 1793) the dynamo of a 'Sadanobu process' can be felt, grinding on. Sadanobu was not disinterested in the revival of Tokugawa fortunes, for he was their close relative. His grandfather was the last but one (eighth) shogun, Yoshimune. Some thought Sadanobu likely to become shogun himself, on Ieharu's death, although that did not transpire. The 'Sadanobu process' was not just about rearrogating power, it was about the formation of convincing cultural patterns.

From the standpoint of today we may observe continuums within the structural problems that brought the shogunate down in the mid-nineteenth century, going back to the eighteenth. The shogunate never successfully grappled with many of its bloated bureaucratic practices. But a marked breakage, and a reformation, is to be detected during the years from about 1785 to about 1810, and these denote a definitive rupture. This book is concerned with the conception of culture that emerged and with the senses of security that artistic and literary enterprise was able to impart. In the second decade of the nineteenth century the alarums of the 1780s had fallen silent. They were not necessarily to stay so for long, and another story exists to be told of how the Tokugawa met their final demise in the 1860s. But even within the later trajectory of collapse, the 'Sadanobu process' had lodged a sense of the reality of a 'Japanese culture' which survived more or less intact and, I would argue, is still with us.

At the beginning of our period, then, anxiety over the survival of inherited norms, disparate and diffusely scattered though they were among the 280 or so states into which the Japanese archipelago was divided (or united), was every thinking person's overriding emotion. By the end, it was no longer so. A 'Japanese people' had also been postulated to receive this culture, which, though, was not said to be new but always to have been there. The construction outlasted the shoguns for whose aggrandizement it was made.

At the ascent of Ieharu in 1760, almost every institution considered itself trammelled and constrained by its history; sclerosis had compromised the ability to move. Many centres of learning, creativity or honour looked moribund. The economy was doing well, but this was perceived as part of the problem, not the cure, for wealth had moved from an older to a newer elite, whose purchasing strategies were different. The consistency of debate about decline, loss of meaning and the wrong apportionment of goods peppers the writings of the period to an extent that cannot be gainsaid. To contemporaries, even the new beneficiaries, these interpretations had the status of truth, and they caused anxiety. Collapse was the dominant discourse, and to fail to see it was to appraise superficially. Despite the joy of modern historians in celebrating 'the rise of the merchant' during this period, thinkers were likely to be aghast at the depredation of civil norms in Edo's rampaging urban culture.

Scholars now hail the welter of differences that emerged in art and literature from the mid-eighteenth century as signs of freedom and energy and are wont to side with the forces of alterity and unrest. The parting of the ways between the populace and their betters is taken as democratic – an analysis which reaches its apogee when, as happens, the predatory consumerism of the popular *demi-monde* (or Floating World, *ukiyo*) is selected as prime representative of the epoch's cultural excellence.

This book is not deluded by those who spoke up for sobriety, for their voices were often self-serving. Figures who moved to restrain social structures from pulverizing and the power of art from reaching the wrong hands may have been looking mostly to their own privileges. But I do take seriously the protestations of the shogunal class. Their elite aim was not just to shore up a 'Venice preserv'd' but to avoid waste and warfare. They were educated in an intellectual mould that told them a severe and moral rulerhood was the only surety of harmony with the Heavenly Way (*tendō*).

The Past, and Other Foreign Countries

The first day of 1784 saw a particularly sorry event. The New Year's festivities were supposed to reiterate the bond between the shogun, the realm above and the states below, but they went wrong.[2] One of the rites was for the shogun to fly a kite from the castle ramparts. Flying a kite was an established metaphor for directing the state, and in fact just two years later the shogunal chief councillor, Matsudaira Sadanobu, was to base his celebrated treatise on government around the analogy.[3] On this occasion the shogun was Tokugawa Ieharu. He had a fittingly magnificent kite, four metres across and emblazoned with the auspicious designs of cranes and pine-trees, skilfully executed by the head of the official painting academy, Kano Eisen-in Michinobu. Ieharu's handling was a matter of some importance. Being the man he was, his attention wandered, and a sudden gust made him lose his grip. The kite lurched, and four members of the shogunal household staff lunged to hold it steady. As they clung to the rope, they were all yanked into the air. Letting go amid gasps of fear, they fell. Three died on impact, one

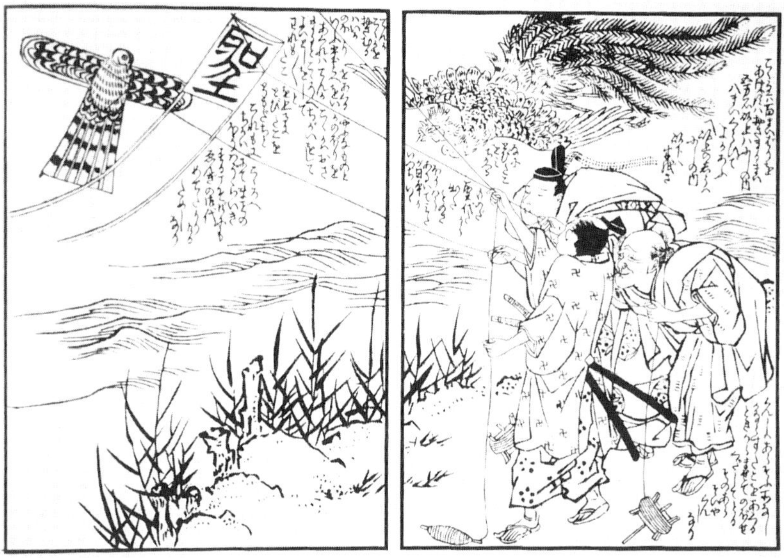

2 Kitao Masayoshi, Pages from Koikawa Harumachi, *Ōmu-gaeshi bunbu no futamichi*, 1789, monochrome woodblock prints. Foolish samurai fly kites, and a *hōō* bird miraculously appears.

survived. Hotta Bingo-no-kami, a favourite of Ieharu, grabbed the whipping rope, wound it around his arm and tugged, until he too was lifted high before falling and smashing his bones on a wellhead. The kite wheeled and plummeted, just missing a direct hit on Ieyasu's sacred shrine set in the castle precincts. In response to this event a council of state was called, and it was determined that the ritual should be abandoned. Nature could no longer be relied upon to aid the display of shogunal statesmanship, nor the shoguns to behave circumspectly.

The scurrilous comments directed at Ieharu show that scorn was the principal reaction he provoked. This levity was recorded by those out of personal danger. Foreign commentators are useful here. Jan Crans, head of the Dutch East India Company factory in Japan, noted in 1768 that Ieharu was written off and 'depicted as a lazy, lustful, stupid man'. A later Company head, Isaac Titsingh, who was unusual in that he spoke Japanese and read Chinese, recorded that Ieharu did not improve with age and to the last had 'little sense'.[4]

In 1786 Ieharu died. He was succeeded by the eleventh shogun, Tokugawa Ienari. With exquisite rudeness Kurahashi Itaru, a senior samurai who represented the daimyo of Suruga-Ojima at the shogunal court, wrote a comic story parodying the kite-flying incident and also offering a dig at the title of Sadanobu's new treatise that had used the kite metaphor. Sadanobu's book was called *The Words of a Parrot (Omu no kotoba)* – or, as we might say, words 'on one's hobby-horse'. Itaru gave his book the title *That Parrot Keeps Squawking: 'Twin Paths of Arms and Letters' (Omu-gaeshi bunbu no futamichi)*. The second phrase identified the two main constituents of culture, used as the slogan of Sadanobu's revivalist programme. *Bunbu* ('arms and letters') had a rather silly ring to it, even to a native speaker, and Itaru was not the only one to spoof Sadanobu's 'parrot cry' that sounded like an irritating insect buzz.[5]

At one point in the story, two provincial samurai arrive in Edo and decide to buy a book to learn the ways of their new city. The bookseller recommends to them, with tongue-in-cheek enthusiasm, what is clearly intended to be Sadanobu's treatise. The samurai make their purchase and 'desirous of putting My Lord's recommendations into practice' proceed to try some kite-flying. This lumpen response to Sadanobu's rhetorical turn is further milked, as Itaru unnecessarily expounds:

> From the simile of flying a kite as ruling a state, they derived the misprision that so long as a kite was in the air the government would be sound. 'Us too', they cried, 'we'll help to put matters to right!'[6]

Itaru's illustrator for this book was the famous Floating World artist Kitao Masayoshi; the two had worked on many collaborative comic projects. In the picture accompanying the episode Masayoshi showed two paper rigs, one ornamented with the word 'sagehood' (another of Sadanobu's much-used terms) and hovering alongside a *hōō*, the mythical bird said to appear when rule is virtuous; the Kano School made paintings of *hōō* to furnish elite chambers, but here the bird's jubilant presence is utterly ironic (illus. 2). The book broke all known records by selling 15,000 copies.[7] Sadanobu was incensed. Itaru had written under the pseudonym Koikawa Harumachi, but his identity was not thereby adequately concealed. Although Sadanobu had no legal right to interrogate a daimyo's minister, he demanded Itaru's presence at Edo Castle. Wisely perhaps, the latter did not go.

The use of precedents to point to how government should be properly conducted was deeply ingrained in Tokugawa thinking. The past was a pool from which to fish examples of how the present should be. Sometimes the difference between this and actuality could be rasping. If the problems faced by the shogunate at this time had many roots, an inability to control the iconography of its own institutional legitimation was a major one. The impoverishment of symbols was a result of the long span of Tokugawa rule, but it was exacerbated by the new encounter with foreign regimes whose systematics of state were challengingly different. The Chosŏn kingdom on the Korean peninsula and the Qing dynasty in China had emblems not too far removed from Japan's, but as the monarchies of Europe came into view alternatives were discussed and noted. It became clear that political representation was highly variable and that other options than those in play might be better. Foreignness had formerly been a source of mild interest, gift-wrapped as desired, not wholly credited, for no Western polity was strong enough to impose itself or its iconic system. The United Provinces (Holland) traded via its East India Company, but it had no royal link. In the mid-eighteenth century the Western monarchies forced themselves provocatively on to the shogunal consciousness. An expanding Russian empire and a now-unified Great Britain were assessed by scholars for what help or hindrance they might offer for the construction of political authority. The ability to *contain* foreignness was terminated.

If this was true for the shogunate, it was also so at the other pole of Japan's twin imperium. One who thought hard and long about the foreign, and the possibility of belligerence with it, was Tomohito (posthumously known as Kōkaku), who had become shujo in 1779.[8] In 1801 Tomohito attempted to pre-empt what he saw as imminent invasion by sending a legate with gifts to his family shrine at Ise.[9] This was a bravura display. No shujo had directly invoked the gods since Yohiyo (posthumously, Go-Uda) had done so when the Korean admiral Hong Tagu lay off the coast, in command of Khubilai Khan's armada, poised to incorporate the Japanese islands into the Mongol empire over five centuries earlier. Before that, invocation had been attempted only once, in 939, when Yutaakira (posthumously, Suzaku) sought to counter the rebel Taira no Masakado. In short, now was a time matched in urgency by only two others in the history of the Japanese states. Tomohito sent two sculpted lion-dogs, one sumptuously worked in gold, the other in silver. The two previous invocations had resulted in magical delivery and, in extremis, it was hoped the spells might work again.

The immediate cause of alarm was the approach of the British-made vessel the *Liander*, which had recently been sold to the Russian navy, who renamed it *Nadezhda* ('Hope') and sent it to compel Japan to open its coasts. Thanks to Tomohito, the ship was struck by a *kamikaze* (divine gale). The terrifying effects of this miracle were recorded by an eminent German naturalist who was on board, Georg Langsdorff. Although unaware of the portents, he wrote of the blasts in eschatological phrases:

The raging of the elements was frightful beyond expression: all nature appeared in commotion and uproar [. . .] The sea, rising into mountains seemed united with the heavens. It was impossible to trace the boundaries between the air, the clouds, and the water.[10]

The ship did not sink, but it could offer no aggression on arrival.

Shogun and shujo, and their staffs, were not always in accord and animosity was recurrent, but it was in the interests of both to maintain the status quo. On the shogunal side, Sadanobu wrote of Europe:

Their lands they are perpetually at war and their soldiers are necessarily skilled at handling weaponry. When you hear that in their primitive countries they rear soldiers expressly in advance, how can you imagine our table-top military tactics will be equal?[11]

The Shogun's Chief Councillor

The agents in the various programmes mentioned above were too many and diverse to be construed as operating according to a single brief, although there was a shared agenda. Sadanobu's name is a useful peg on which to hang a collective enterprise. He was neither the most original nor the most consistent thinker involved, but he was the most powerful. His office allowed him to cast his often second-hand notions far across the states. In the present book he functions as something of a synecdoche for the anxieties of late eighteenth-century cultural life and for the creativity that they engendered. Sadanobu wrote voluminously, leaving copious evidence of himself across many reams of paper. Much of the corporate effort of what occurred during and after his tenure of the chief councillorship is known via the medium of his brush and hence via the controlling filter of his own mind.

Sadanobu was born in 1758 to Tayasu Munetake, one of the most senior members of the shogunal entourage. The Tayasu were top of the 'three princes' (*sankyō*), making them fifth in the overall pecking order, after only the 'three noble houses' (*go-sanke*), or shogunal collaterals, and the shogun himself. The Tayasu held a permanent seat on the council of Tokugawa elders (*karō*).[12]

At the age of fifteen Sadanobu was adopted out of this illustrious line to become heir to the daimyo of Shirakawa, Matsudaira Sadakuni. This was not an unusual practice nor an undesirable one for, as a younger son, Sadanobu could not hope for the Tayasu headship. He thus gained more clout in the admittedly lower Matsudaira family. (The Matsudaira clan-name denoted a distant Tokugawa relation.) Then his older brother died. The Tayasu house was without a successor. Protocol

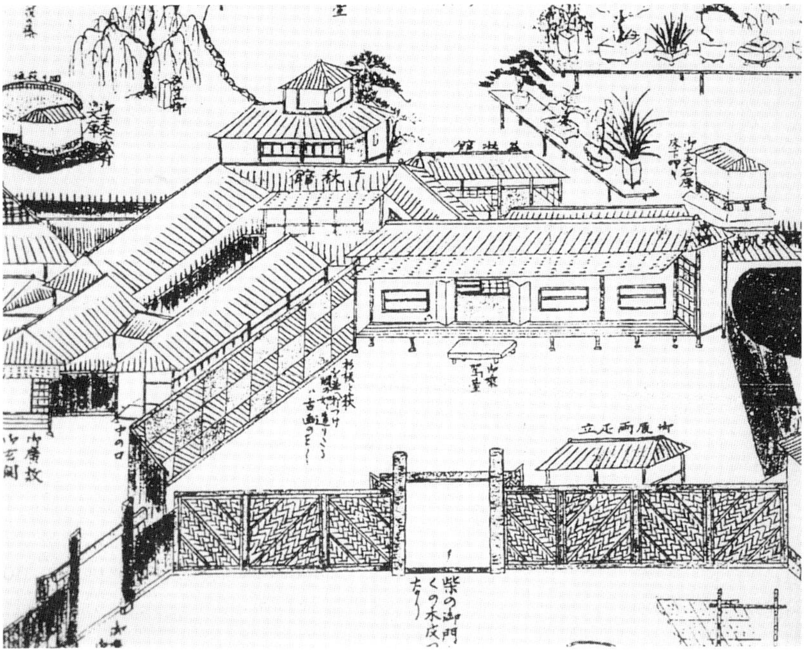

3 Detail of illus. 14.

forbade Sadanobu's moving back. This was a galling eventuality. In 1772 he inherited in his new line, becoming daimyo of Shirakawa.

He was thirty (by the inclusive Japanese count) when he took over the shogunal chief councillorship six years later. Attainment of power was not his aim, rather he sought to control something more profound: culture, and the means of representation. Sadanobu's 'revival' coincides with a wholesale monopolization of the instruments for fashioning and interpreting knowledge. From the learned societies of Confucianism, historiography and medicine to the artistic schools, everything was drawn tightly in. When he surrendered his offices, he kept the less bureaucratic, and hence more efficient, role of behind-the-scenes dirigiste. His writings are generally silent about issues of overt policy. They dwell on one only: the defending of borders. The rest of his literary energies went on incessant discussion, weaving through all his output, of the systematics of cultural representation.

Sadanobu's conceptualization of the elements proper to 'Japanese culture' was refined in his retirement villa, the Turret of a Thousand Autumns (Senshū-kaku), built in Edo's Tsukiji district. The land was donated to him by a grateful shogunate in 1792, and from here there streamed forth injunctions and recommendations which, because

Sadanobu was no longer councillor or regent, seemed usefully decentred from the government itself. The villa was nicely named, for autumn is the season of aging, but at a thousand years Sadanobu saw no immediate end, either for himself or for the Tokugawa lineage. Surrounding the turret was a sumptuous park laid out to Sadanobu's own designs and called the Garden of Bathing in Obligation (Yokuon-en). It was here that he enlivened the past, repaid his debts to the regime and to history and reified culture anew (illus. 3, 14).

The villa and surrounding garden were reduced to ashes in a fire that swept through Edo in 1829. All that is known of its appearance is a depiction by Sadanobu's loyal retainer, an amateur painter called Okamoto Jishō.[13] Just months after this Sadanobu died, no doubt deeply saddened. And yet the conflagration had a beneficial effect. It erased the axis of generation of 'Japanese culture'. With the garden gone, an intangibility was imparted to the process of fabrication. The site where heads were knocked together, brains thrown about, documents copied and collated, and facts recorded or excised could no longer be visited. This lent (and lends) Sadanobu's construction its final measure of persuasiveness, by eradicating all sight of his 'process'.

The park has since become Tokyo's fish market. The staff of material sustenance for a modern Japan, rich enough to empty the world's seas, is now brokered there. Nothing remains of the waterfront that abutted Sadanobu's garden and from which he looked askance at the heaving sea; all around now is reclaimed land. The Tsukiji district is now criss-crossed by roads and covered by offices and, ironically perhaps, the headquarters of *Asahi Shimbun*, the quality newspaper that circulates information to inculcate into the modern Japanese nation its sense of the world and of itself, looms over the former garden area. Asahi (via an Asahi Fellowship) also sponsored the research that prefigured this publication. Plants and buildings have been transformed, but much of what Sadanobu conceptualized within the garden is still in place.

Sadanobu was loathed while in power. Afterwards he took the name Rakuō-kō ('merry old prince'), but not much changed. His domineering judgements, excessive punishments and pusillanimity in the face of objection were greatly despised. But ambivalence was also a key to his make-up. His strongest actions were followed by retractions, even before any complaint was heard. He listened to the echos of the past, trying to determine how they should be amplified to resonate within the present, but was never entirely confident he heard the sounds aright. He caught snatches and (to continue the metaphor) he synthesized. Sadanobu wrote a list of things he considered 'sad wastes' (in itself a revivalist act, since 'literary lists', *monotsukushi*, were an eleventh-century genre), and he included the following three:

– Going off into the mountains and experiencing a purification of heart, but then finding there is a temple nearby and having to put up with the din of voices.
– An old incised slab on which only a couple of characters in the inscription can be discerned.
– A person of scholarly aptitude who develops new theories about classic texts.[14]

The clamour of the present, the recessiveness of the past and the waywardness of those to whom the task of keeping history alive was entrusted all boded ill. The voices of the past were woefully faint and everywhere needed help. Yuasa Akiyoshi, an otherwise little-known samurai from Okayama, estimated enthusiastically in his chronicle of this period that 'nine tenths of [Sadanobu's] policies were aimed at revival'.[15] But others had other notions and sniffed obsessive politicking. With the institutions of record in his hock, Sadanobu's voice was the loudest heard. He paid scrupulous attention to rituals and paraphernalia, many of which had disappeared centuries before; several were refabricated or revived. Citing Confucius's epigram 'Govern the land according to ritual', he noted:

If we put things back into force now, in the present time, and each state, according to its particular assets, took to heart the rituals of former kings in the orders of religion, commemoration, court behaviour, and military requisitioning, or the rites of weddings, funerals, thanksgiving and prophylaxis, or the proprieties of dress, food and drink, or the use of tools, and if from the ruler down to the populace all treated laws as firm, then we could say that we had restored the rituals of former kings in the present day!

This was important because:

Ritual clothing has been devised, from headwear, belts and sashes, to dress for use in the open air and indoors, and it is because we have these things in their prescribed shapes that we are able to align our inner selves with creation [. . .] Formal rituals and leisure activities are the external aspects of the person, but we should be aware that they permeate to the interior.[16]

But was it so simple? Forcing outward compliance was easier than breeding the right mental state in a recalcitrant population. Dissidents in the 'Sadanobu process' were many. Ever-increasing restrictions on thought and behaviour provoked malcontents. Even those who recognized the need for buttressing mistrusted Sadanobu's approach. Revivalism highlighted the degree to which past and present were split and how unworkable the former was in the world of the present. New theories were needed for new readers; inscriptions always fade. Sadanobu also wondered:

> But then, do we really need to pretend that following the rituals of former kings means riding about in the royal carriages of the [sixteenth-century BC] Yin, or wearing the headdresses of the [twelfth-century BC] Zhou?[17]

The degree of latitude permissible in this depended on the individual.

Knowledge of history came from scholarly investigation, and so the checking of reading was one of his important acts. Sadanobu is famous for his controls on 'heterodox interpretations' (*igaku*). He told his own retainers that study was 'to understand the past', and he condemned those who let their bookishness run riot: 'when people's reading is like boiling water or tangled thread, who can control their minds?'[18] Mental ebullition was the instrument of social collapse. 'He mostly wished', wrote an admiring Yamada Shinsuke (later Sadanobu's biographer), 'to hand on the physical appearance of things so as to assist ministers in times to come'.[19] That is, the project was to block the past, dam up time and prevent all further erosion.

Contradicting the juggernaut of Sadanobu's policies or pointing out their internal inconsistencies was not advisable. Traces of popular objection can only be found today in the diaries of those with little to fear. In practice this meant those writing in scripts that could not be read, i.e. foreigners. Members of the Dutch East India Company are useful here too, for they captured whisperings and committed them to paper, without which our knowledge of the period would be seriously incomplete. Casper Romberg, intermittently leader of the European factory from 1784 to 1794, noted how the 'hated and strict' or 'feared and hated' governance of Sadanobu was so disliked it seemed about to precipitate the end of the Tokugawa regime rather than delay it.[20] When Sadanobu mooted retirement in 1790, the then Company leader, Johan, Baron van Reede, noted, 'all the citizens are rejoicing at this'; prematurely, as it turned out, for Sadanobu did not quit. When the 'gratifying communication' of his exit finally came, it made little difference as he continued his work backstage, first in his own state capital of Shirakawa, then in his Edo turret.[21]

Sadanobu's name is indissolubly linked to a spate of reforms he enacted on assuming the councillorship and which can be seen as his first foray into cultural reconstruction. This raft of legislation is known as the Kansei Reforms, although anachronistically, since the era of that name was not promulgated until 1789. The Reforms are generally given an economic spin: the depressed condition of the shogunal finances, the impoverishment of the samurai and of many daimyo, and the general passing of wealth from nobles to successful merchants are duly cited and are undeniable. Inflation was biting hard at samurai who lived on fixed stipends and whose government wages were anyway left unpaid, unilaterally cut or disbursed late. But I take issue with the economic reductionism of those who see in the Reforms an aim to right only monetary problems. More important was the requirement to right the displacement of *symbols*. It is better to consider what occurred in the language of art than of finance. The shogunate did need to claw back money, but more crucial was restitution of its visual base.

Sadanobu's efforts to enhance shogunal authority were aided by the death of Ieharu in 1786. By all accounts this was a happy event. It triggered the shake-up by which he made his entrance into the shogunal high command. Not every Tokugawa progeny was of fine mettle, and there had been bad shoguns as well as good before Ieharu. But he alone had presided over a pulling out of shape of the entire shogunal iconography. The remark of Jan Crans, quoted above, may be repeated: Ieharu was 'depicted as a lazy, lustful, stupid man'. Importantly, Crans does not so much impugn the shogunate's character, which, given a good council, was not decisive, but his capacity for self-representation: it is the *depiction* that is condemned.[22]

Since Sadanobu was seeking restoration of shogunal authority, he had to tread lightly with Ieharu's reputation, and he could not chide the apex of the regime without further degrading the entire edifice, whose faltering self-representation was the nub of concern. In a well-tried manner he displaced vilification on to the shogun's advisers, and especially on to Ieharu's chief councillor, Tanuma Okitsugu, whom Sadanobu was to replace. Okitsugu, after two decades in office, had Ieharu in thrall, or so it was 'depicted'. Titsingh reiterated this line, observing that Ieharu's errors were great but were due to his being 'wholly guided' by Okitsugu, a man 'held in low esteem'.[23] Another samurai commentator from Sadanobu's camp was Yoshida Shigefusa, who called Okitsugu 'truly unparalleled in past generations for pomposity'.[24] Under Sadanobu, demonization of Okitsugu became the official line. The latter was cast as the one who had pulled the stones from the shogunal foundations and begun the transfer of authority from the central elite to new men – of whom he was himself one – and thence out to the urban masses at large. In no wise could cultural and political disjunction be blamed on the Tokugawa house itself.

Okitsugu's ouster came rapidly after the death of his patron Ieharu. This would probably have happened whatever his probity, but he had too many enemies.[25] Okitsugu had not recovered politically, nor perhaps emotionally, from the fatal stabbing of his son Okitomo in 1784 in the shogunal castle itself – which compounded the affront.[26] The event is worth considering. No one had intervened as the assailant, Sano Zenzaemon, lunged and, as Titsingh informed the European reader, the shogunal guard arrived 'but so leisurely that there was every reason to believe it to have been their intention to give the assassin time to escape'.[27] Okitomo, then in his thirty-fifth year, had been elevated far beyond the acceptable degree, this too being 'truly unparalleled in past generations', according to Shigefusa.[28] Okitomo's coffin was stoned as it passed through the streets, while Zenzaemon was accounted a hero.[29] It was taboo to report serious crimes, particularly ones implicating the ruling class, and Edo sources reveal little. But scurrilous poems were circulated indicating pleasure at the murder, making use of the punning potential of the Japanese language that can submerge real meaning in a sugared coating. There was much play on the somewhat incoherently labelled Edo office of 'young elder' (*waka-doshiyori*), held by Okitomo, with 'stupid old fool' (*baka-toshiyori*), or with the state ruled by the Tanumas, Yamashiro, of which the latter part, *shiro*, was homophonous with 'white', the colour of costumes worn by senior ministers but which contrasted with Okitomo's bloodied robes ('Better call him the red minister', they said). More extended was a poem with a triple pun involving the murderer's family name, Sano, and the famously poetic Sano Bridge, Tanuma and its literal meaning 'paddy marsh', and Yamashiro with its literal meaning 'mountain castle':

In the Eastern lands [Edo]
The Sano crossing
Overflows with water
Cutting through the paddy marsh
And overthrowing the mountain castle.[30]

The East India Company officers tried to discover more facts. Caspar Romberg sent home a report that 'on entering the palace [Okitomo] had been slashed so badly with a sword, by a young officer of the guard, Sano Zenzaemon, that he died a couple of days later, and the offender has slit his belly'; but, he had to add, 'the reasons are not yet clear'. Perhaps because his linguistic advantages provided him with a

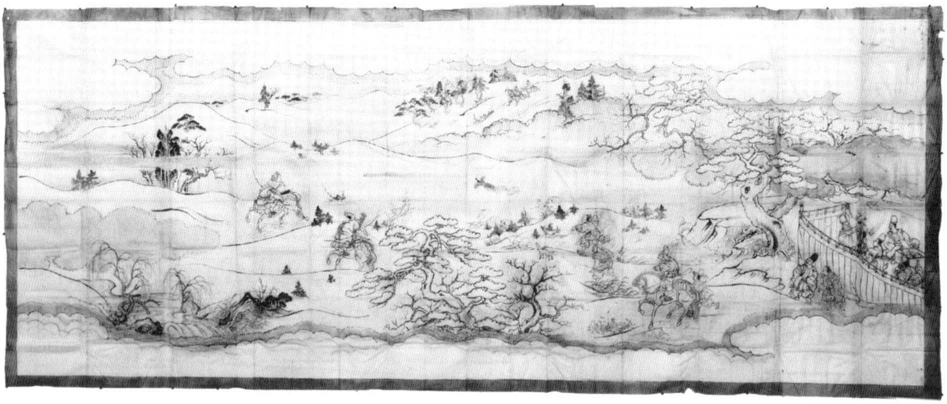

4 Sumiyoshi Hiroyuki, *Courtiers Hawking in Spring [and Winter] (Shun[tō] dōjō hōyō)*, 1808, preparatory sketch for pair of folding screens, ink on paper. The left-hand (winter) scene is lost; the finished works were sent to the Chosŏn kingdom as diplomatic gifts for Sunjo *wang*.

network of confidants in Japan, Titsingh (briefly out of the country at the time), claimed 'several persons of the highest distinction were privy to [the murder], and encouraged it'.[31] If this is true, then by the mid-1780s the shogunal circle believed it was time to rework the multifoliate wonder of the Tenka, root and branch.

With Okitsugu and Ieharu gone, Sadanobu had *carte blanche* to reposition the principal players. The shogunal heir apparent (*seishi*), Ienari, aged fourteen, took over. But the succession proved no cure-all and was tinctured with dubiety about Ienari's entitlement (he was an adopted, not a biological, son). It was unhelpful for Ienari that he was initially denied full honours, ostensibly on account of age, but certainly for other reasons, and was addressed as Great Minister of the Centre (*naidaijin*) – high, to be sure, but below the shogunal due of Great Minister of the Right (*udaijin*). Popularly he was referred to as His Loftiness (*uesama*) but was not, immediately, by the proper title, *shōgun-sama*.[32]

Moriyama Takamori, a minor official throughout these times, was propelled to prominence by Sadanobu for reasons that will become clear below. After his elevation he served Sadanobu as his willing gauleiter and wrote an autobiography in 1798, outlining how he perceived the 'Sadanobu process' to have taken shape. Takamori entitled his book *Told Around a Diver's Weed Fire (Ama no takumo no ki)*. This was a conscious imitation of the well-known work of Ara Hakuseki, adviser to the sixth shogun, Ienobu, which was called *Told Around a Brushwood Fire (Oritaku shiba no ki)* and completed over 80 years earlier.[33] Hakuseki too had dealt with a period of rot, which he saw as cured by the master he served and achieved by restoration of norms, emblematically, those of ritual and law. On his accession, Ienobu had reviewed every recent criminal conviction and given nearly 10,000 amnesties, so that 'there is no act of lenient administration to be likened to this over the whole course of this regime's existence'.[34] Good government stabilized values as an act of mercy towards a people oppressed by arbitrariness and by enslavement to spiralling fashions which they could ill afford. Takamori's recollection of Hakuseki's paean of praise was value-laden, for he wished Sadanobu to be seen in no other light. Kansei, the era promulgated in 1789, means 'lenient government'. Takamori drew this conclusion:

> When the prince of Shirakawa [Sadanobu] governed the Tenka as regent, appointments were made on the merit or demerit of the individual, not on grounds of personal likes or snobbery. Those who would mature were retained, those with no promise were let go.[35]

Unlike the situation under Okitsugu. This epitome of good rule rippled down to all those below, making the states quiescent and content.

Takamori's attempts to present a bullish tale find several challenges, most strangely in his choice of title. His allusion to Hakuseki conspicuously fails to conjure up that author's happy sense of warmth. A story 'told around a brushwood fire' is a feast of words at a hearth made from any thicket – a rousing tale commonly told. But Takamori's story is harder to come by, for his fuel is of dangerous procurement. By 'weeds' (*takumo*) he meant water plants, which were indeed used for heating, but they had to be dragged up by swimmers sent breathlessly down to the bottom of the sea to fetch them – a skilled and hazardous occupation that damaged the lungs in the long term. Moreover, weed divers were always female so, as a man, Takamori could have no knowledge of the arduous harvest, nor of how it was dried so that the stalks could be ignited. Crucially, then, Takamori's fire could not be made by himself nor by anyone he might have known.

Takamori believed a shared culture had once existed but had been lost. It had to be hauled back against the odds, as if from submersion, and his book is the narrative of how this was done. There are three legs to the tale: former glory, near loss and restoration. All cultural modes are discussed and the 'arms and letters' comprehensively covered. But, interestingly, Takamori places centrally within this trajectory the vicissitudes of *painting*, that is, representation. In one episode he tells of a conversation held with a notable artist, Sumiyoshi Hiroyuki, then head of the Sumiyoshi Academy, one of the senior Edo schools and specialists in classical literary themes (illus. 4). Not coincidentally, Hiroyuki was a protégé of Sadanobu and the headship of his school had been secured for him among competing claims by direct government intervention.[36] Like Takamori, Hiroyuki was a stout pillar of 'revived' culture who owed Sadanobu a great deal.

Takamori's talk with Hiroyuki took the form of a glum assessment of culture. 'We talked until dark of how things used not to be like this, and how the visual, literary and martial arts had all turned, everywhere you looked, into trivia.'[37] The two men went on to discuss the wise restorative actions that Sadanobu was taking, and Takamori then made his own contribution by asking Hiroyuki to train his grandson, Moritoshi, in painting. Mastery of the brush was part of expected education among the ruling class and Takamori, we are told, 'had previously bitten off a little skill in that direction and stored it away'. More concerted effort was now demanded, so Takamori enlisted Hiroyuki's professional tuition. Note that Hakuseki had also mentioned painting, stating that his father, for one, had excelled and that, in common with the stalwart samurai of those days, he would only paint in black, 'disliking the use of colours', because his character was so austere.[38] But people could no longer respond to such prickly imagery, Takamori felt, and so he wanted Moritoshi to learn to make pictures that would seduce first, charmingly, and then elevate. This was indeed the orbit of the Sumiyoshi, which hybridized a variety of lineages and produced pictures that were comfortable to look at but also compelling because of their historic, ennobling themes. They were neither starchily academic nor free-wheelingly loose. This was the school on which Sadanobu most relied. By the time of writing, Takamori noted with delight, Moritoshi, though 'not yet proficient', was working at his pictures, poor boy, 'from morning through to night'.

Sadanobu's Defensive Posture

Rectification of culture and a return to precedent was one mode of defence. More concrete steps were also taken. There was a new discourse of the sea. Sadanobu's governmental policies sought to deal with overseas menace. He revived the Tenka by drawing a line around it, isolating the space that pertained to 'Japanese culture' and relegating that which lay outside. Under Okitsugu, work had begun on an incipient shogunal navy, but this was now thrown into doubt.[39] Even coastal ships made the in/out border fuzzy. Sadanobu wished for a boundary

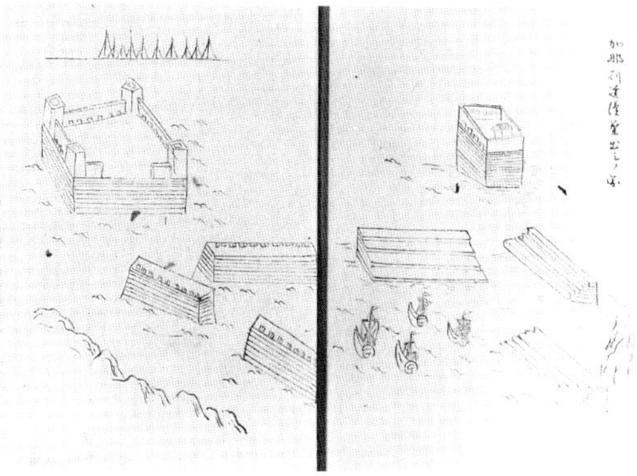

5 Illustration showing Russian coastal fortifications, from Ōtsuki Gentaku, *Kankai ibun* (1807), *c.* 1830, colour on paper. The shogunate provided nothing similar in its ports.

defended by a stout inside, not by a roving outer police, and although experiments in deep-sea naval building continued intermittently, with Sadanobu not implacably opposed to all shipwrighting, no navy was ever formalized. Naming was one option: a ship destined for the investigation of Ezo (modern Hokkaidō) was named the *Kamikaze*, as if to smother the fact that it was destined for exploratory expansion.[40] Many of Sadanobu's attendants, Takamori among them, condemned even this shipbuilding: 'What avails it to construct such things? [. . .] Are these really the recommendations of loyal ministers?'[41] There was no idiom in which naval vessels could be represented or, more literal-mindedly, in which ships could be built. To equip the shogunate with European- or Chinese-looking ships was self-defeating, and yet it was vain to attempt any local style, for there was none. Instead, Sadanobu began planning the erection of coastal fortifications. The sea was turned into a clean line of departure between 'Japanese' ways and elsewhere, with the inner sector commensurately homogenized.

Takamori's post within the shogunal bureaucracy was that of senior bombardier *(senpō hōgeki-rō)*.[42] Gunnery was not a usual career path, for it was regarded as inferior to swordsmanship. Guns were largely limited to coastal defence. This was marginal, but calculated to appeal to Sadanobu. It lay to Takamori's charge to prevent an altogether different sort of combustion on the seashore from the one he cites in his autobiographical title.

Sadanobu was Takamori's patron and, in 1792, enlisted him in an important exercise of coastal defence installation. According to Takamori, this project was plagued by inefficiency and he was irked by the leadership of Nagagawa Kenzaburō, a senior shogunal bureaucrat, but inept; Takamori felt 'a girl could have done the job better'.[43] But the infirmity of purpose surrounding the coastal defence team was part of

Sadanobu's ambivalence, and it reveals much. The objective was to select sites for forts aimed at keeping the Russians and British out, but, in essence, the policy was rhetorical. Representation and iconography were more crucial. A problem resided in the fact that any publicly visible bastions would advertise insecurity. Forts looked like a regression from the days when admiration for the Japanese polity alone had secured safety and overseas nations were not inclined to challenge and meddle. To fortify boundaries was to acknowledge the exhaustion of moral suasion within. By erecting forts and fitting them with guns, Sadanobu would announce that the shogunate was down to its final argument – that of force. In Europe cannon were known as *ultima ratio regis* ('the king's last argument'), which words might be inscribed on the barrels, a fact of which Sadanobu could have been aware, for he read widely in Western military books and commissioned a seventeen-volume compilation of them.[44] There was no tradition of mounting batteries in Japan, nor a mythology to justify their presence.

Writers were not behindhand in pointing out that it was the building of stockades by European nations, especially on coasts, that marked them as culturally inferior and betrayed their deficiency in mutual respect and trust. The shogunate received detailed pictures and explanations of Russian harbour walls, rendered unassailable through brutal encastellation (illus. 5); it was also pointed out that European ships were like marauding fortresses, built to sail into such places, and were even called *wowatoru kasuteiru* ('water castles').[45] The brief handed to Nagagawa Kenzaburō was that a stronghold should be positioned 'on every off-shore isle and headland'.[46] Yet not a single one was actually built. While making all aware how conscientious he was in defence of the shogunal soil, Sadanobu permitted no building to besmirch the ethical claim of the Tenka. It was a clever double-posture and exemplary of Sadanobu's sensitivity to the form of material things and of the need for continuity of appearance between past and present.

Sadanobu upgraded the Magistracy for Distant Countries (*enkoku bugyō*), which had generally been a dead-end office; he picked wardens to run his forts although, since the forts were non-existent, the nominees stayed in Edo.[47] Sadanobu himself marched with the inspection team, despite his press of affairs, although, if Takamori's record is to be trusted, he repeatedly suspended operations to view places of poetic or historical interest and spent as much time examining ancient artefacts in temples along the way as plotting the foundations of walls. Revivalism won the day. Discovery and advertisement of antique objects scattered along the coast was a finer proof of shogunal right to the land, and so a higher form of protection, than the brutish bombas of castles.[48]

The coastal survey resulted in no tangible changes to the coast, but it produced an interesting result in the form of a series of paintings. Sadanobu arranged for an artist to accompany the team. Sumiyoshi Hiroyuki might have been asked, but his lyrical historicizing style would have been defective in rendering empirical landscape views. Instead Sadanobu selected Tani Bunchō, a figure similarly part of the world of official art but more closely linked to Sadanobu than to his academic masters. Bunchō had begun training in the main shogunal academy, the Kano School, but had left to become independent. Hailing from a family of hereditary retainers of the Tayasu family (Sadanobu's natal house), he had personal ties to Sadanobu, and in 1794 Sadanobu took advantage of this to make him a personal attendant (*tsuke*) – an honour that was unusual for a painter.[49] Bunchō worked as a kind of universal practitioner, or encyclopaedist of style, turning himself into a conduit for the provision of a variety of manners old and new. He could replicate all work of past and modern times and was much employed by Sadanobu to this end. With Bunchō around, nothing died out. In the case of the coastal commission, he was selected for his skill in landscape realism. The coastal commission was to produce empirical vistas of the seaboard. A set of one dozen paintings emerged, done in a positivist style that was not unprecedented in Japan but which derived from Europe and had yet to make significant inroads (see illus. 15).

The paintings were passed about in copies, and copies of copies, for years to come. Five years after Bunchō's production the great literatus from Keishi, Minagawa Kien, came into possession of a set.[50] The bald exposure of the style, and the very fact of depicting landscapes that had no overlay of history or poetry, made viewers quizzical. The pictures were devoid of the expected narratives and would not answer, in any known language, the question of why they were made. Notwithstanding the impressive realism and the stated utilitarian aims, the pictures smothered, within their own representational space, any realization of the motives for their production. They were enigmatically athwart two ideologies of coasts: the one held that the beauty and morality of the inner polity was all the defence required, and the other enjoined knowledge of every bluff and scarp in case of attack. The pictures do not conspicuously concentrate on 'isles and headlands' or on flat areas where forts could sensibly be built, nor do they identify vantages and prospects. They make the coasts look outstandingly fine; Mt Fuji repeatedly offers its sacral presence to vouchsafe the Tenka's place near the summit of the world's cultural clusters. Only one image shows the survey team at work, pacing and measuring within the landscape, and this was apparently dropped when the sets were reproduced, perhaps because it constituted an official secret or perhaps just to withhold evidence of the rationale for the commission.[51] Bunchō's paintings, like Sadanobu's inspection tour itself, heightened a general consciousness of the coastline but did not propose that any fleet might sail in – or out – or how one would be repulsed. The paintings nevertheless single out the perimeter of the Japanese states, in and of themselves, as places of importance.

Sadanobu's Looking

It was necessary above all for Sadanobu to believe in the authenticity of the culture being constructed ('restored') behind these coastal edges of the Tenka. This precluded anyone's owning up to a role in its confection. This effacement was partly due to the *ad hoc* nature of the project but was also, I believe, a ploy that became part of Sadanobu's construction of himself as the reviver who made nothing. One of his most complete journals, entitled *Leisure Jottings (Taikan zakki* – the dismissive casualness is itself indicative), is useful in analysis of Sadanobu's thinking during his latter years in power and immediately afterwards. Sadanobu would have been aware that this work would circulate in manuscript copies and so, even though not explicitly intended for publication, it exists midway between private memoire and public justification, with both genuine and staged revelations. The first lines offer an observation that cannot but be metaphorically intended:

> When cutting a pane of glass, put a metal ruler or similar object into a fire. Remove it when red-hot and apply it along the line you wish to incise. Immerse the cut edge of the glass in a small quantity of cold water. This is how to do the job.[52]

Glass was a new material; it opened up an uncoloured vista, because of the premise that the glass was being looked through, not at. In Sadanobu's text, he is cutting a pane to make a window to see a beyond that is held like an empirically correct landscape picture. These self-abnegating claims made glass, in a way, similar to Bunchō's transparent style.

Sadanobu pulls the reader up at the opening of his book to assure them of the objectivity of the representations that will follow. Windows reveal, but they forbid touching of what lies beyond. Winds will not blow in, dust does not collect and sound is shut out, and Sadanobu thus affirms his disengagement from his own text. A jamming of personal involvement prefigures his analyses of the Tenka, its customs and conditions, and of all the panoply of cultures whose process of 'restoration' is the meat of his book.

The lines on the cutting of glass would have recalled to literate readers the close (rather than opening) of the famous journal of Yanagisawa Kien, composed about the same time as Hakuseki's autobiography in 1715. Yanagisawa Kien (not to be confused with the Confucian scholar Minagawa Kien) was a fiery young intellectual of twenty; his uncle was Yanagisawa Yoshiyasu, chief minister – some said lover – of the shogun Tsunayoshi, whose miscreancy made Hakuseki's master's 'leniency' necessary.[53] Yanagisawa Kien was later to have much impact on painting through his adoption of the *nanga*, or Continental 'southern' manner, which was highly heterodox and deplored by Sadanobu.[54] Somewhat radically, in light of where his uncle slept, Kien entitled his book *Sleeping Alone (Hitorine)*. He was his own man, and not much impacted on him outside his own thoughts and tastes. Kien's character and his intent were the opposite of Sadanobu's, and this is demonstrated by the latter's borrowing and then inverting his metaphor of glass. Kien's book ran over 175 pages until he closed with reference to a glass bottle.[55] The thoughts of the written-out author tumble higgledy-piggledy into a handily placed receptacle which, being glass, leaves them visible. The world can view them on a 'take it or leave it' basis. Sadanobu was the reverse: his journal was still to come when he invoked the window, which he is imagined preparing with care so as to give him passivity towards what is beyond.

The connection between Sadanobu and the neutralizing force of windows may be further pursued. The top floor of his Turret of One Thousand Autumns, in the Garden of Bathing in Obligation, was his study. It is said to have been Edo's first fully glazed room (see illus. 3).[56] The objective feel that glass conferred, with the exposure of the outside to view and the disallowance of collusion in it, would have been Sadanobu's thrilling and rare experience daily as he worked. His construction of the shogun's culture is built on this metaphor, acquiring an air of simple viewing and recording. Of course, the landscape Sadanobu saw through the glass had been planted out by himself, for it was his park and made to his own plans.

Glass bottles of the sort Kien referred to were sometimes domestically made and were not hard to find. But windows were almost unknown and could not be manufactured in Japan.[57] The panes through which Sadanobu looked must have been imported. They too, then, were like Bunchō's style, which was noiseless but also reverberated with Europe. The equation of windowed seeing with the objectively captured view was a crucial European artistic myth. Sadanobu possessed Egbert Buys's encyclopaedia of 1768–73, the *Nieuw en volkomen woordenboek*, which had several entries related to pictures and propounded the notion of how accurate depiction meant 'the representing of objects on plain surfaces, after the same manner as they would appear to our sight, if seen through that plane, which is supposed as transparent as glass'.[58] There was certainly a dilemma in using Western materials and myth to bolster the Tenka against Western aggression. But the co-opting of elements of the Other in the construction of the self ought not to surprise us, for it is ever thus. Insinuation of the foreign permitted, as well as necessitated, a remaking of the past. Exposure to other patterns of culture demanded a reconstitution of the home space.

The abruptness of visions taken through foreign glass was reported by many. Sadanobu did not expound on his windows at any greater length, but a parallel case may be cited. In about 1740, no less a person than the *huangdi* ('emperor') of China's Qing dynasty, Qianlong (posthumously, Gaozong), wrote a poem on the glass windows installed in the baroque palace in his park, the Garden of Perfect Brightness (Yuanming Yuan). Every educated Japanese knew Qianlong's verses.[59] I have translated the verse fully elsewhere, but it opens 'In Europe they lack for nothing in amazing goods!' and one relevant couplet reads that, thanks to glass, 'All things enter my field of vision, becoming clear and distinct; / All phenomena display themselves to me in their beauty or ugliness'.[60] This is what Sadanobu also found, although the visions in his garden at least did not come to him by chance. Importantly, the records suggest that it was in 1789, the first year of the Kansei era, that Ienari, two years in office, installed the first glass windows in Edo Castle.[61] The restoration of the Tenka's splendid historic residue took place beyond their sheen.

Windows were prized enough to be worth a great effort to obtain. The year before Ienari procured his, some panes were stolen from the Dutch East India Company offices in Nagasaki (complete with frames and leading). Arrest of the thieves was swift and they were tortured to death appropriately horribly.[62] Importation of glass is attested in a fragmentary way at least a century before this time, so that why it became so sought after only in the late eighteenth century needs explaining. Glass was improving, but more likely it was the monstrous upheavals in the states that led to the call for more of it, to satisfy psychological needs. Glazed viewing empowered. This might be self-serving, and the ease with which objectivity could melt into spuriousness is apparent in the case of the daimyo of Kaga, Maeda Narinaga, richest of all regional princes, who installed Dutch panes in his palace but had them engraved with auspicious birds.[63] He looked out on to his territory, seemingly permanently stocked with omens of happy rule.

Sadanobu's Study

Indicative of the search for objectivity was the establishment of 'Japanese studies' as a discipline. Sadanobu set up an institute to define this field. Private scholars were working on issues of national identity, as Sadanobu knew since his blood father, Tayasu Munetake, had been involved.[64] The general tendency had been to isolate indigenous strata to place against imported Continental norms and call the exercise *kokugaku*, 'study of the states'; in English this is rendered as 'Nativism'. The term *kokugaku* had a relativist ring, for it was non-viable epistemologically without the alterity of an overbearing Continent. It sought to sift out two strands that had been shaken together for over a millennium. Sadanobu instead used the term *wagaku*, 'study of *wa*', where *wa* meant the Tenka as an entity that included digested portions of Chinese, Korean and even Indian cultures. *Wagaku* ruled out Chinese, Korean or Indian civilizations as objects of its interest *per se* but accepted that they infused Japan. Sadanobu allowed *wa* maximum absorbency. It was the choicest fruit of ages of grafting.

It was to be expected that Sadanobu should seek to co-opt and bend the scholarly practices of *kokugaku* for shogunal use, as he did with all areas of academic endeavour. But he was not on good terms with *kokugaku*'s most outspoken proponent, Motoori Norinaga, and did not respond to Norinaga's overtures to be drafted into government service.[65] Norinaga was virulently anti-Continental and espoused a kind of 'Japan' that was so pruned as to almost expose the shogunal polity to blight. Sadanobu preferred to use Furukawa Koshōken, who in 1793 became head of the new institute. Koshōken was a scholar, geographer and some-time Sadanobu spy, as well as a successful pornographer (although Sadanobu may not have been aware of this last activity).[66] Under Koshōken the institute went through several manifestations but was transformed in 1795, made bigger than before, now with an impressive library of 1,273 titles.[67] The name was changed from the original Wagaku Lecture Room (Wagaku kōdan-jo) to the more dedicated-sounding School of Difficult Questioning (Kakuken-kō). Sadanobu came up with another, poetic, title for the place, the

Hall of the Warm Past (Onkō-do), which he also used for his private library–studio in his garden.[68] Was this past really still warm, or merely reheated? With admirable lack of prejudice, though uneasy symbolism, Sadanobu appointed as first rector Tamotsu Kiichi, a man who had 'published anthologies of many things' and was a noted collator of historical detail but who was blind.[69]

With 'revival' established as the exclusive modality, Sadanobu encouraged concrete endeavour. What collected in the pool behind the dam he erected to stop the ebbing of the past was 'Japanese culture'. The obsessive nature of Sadanobu's personal commitment to this can be told in his engagement with the eleventh-century novel *The Tale of Genji (Genji monogatari)*, a celebrated book and a trove of accounts of ancient life and ritual, but long and hard to follow and, as with most vernacular classics, no one actually read it. The *Genji* had become a disembodied string of anecdotes, mistold, encrusted with error and known from secondary retellings in delectuses, précis and commentaries, or via pictures. It was printed only nine times during the 250 years of Tokugawa rule, eight times in the seventeenth century and then not again until 1749.[70] Those minded to read the book would be hard-pressed. It was Norinaga who had parsed the text in a revolutionary manner, corrected scribal errors and, importantly, argued for an emotional focus to the meaning, whereby antiquity and modernity could be brought together through responses to the story's sentimental pathos (*mono no aware*).[71]

Sadanobu was to pick up on this, but here as elsewhere he was concrete. Norinaga was exegetic; Sadanobu made text. In 1803 Sadanobu began to copy the entire work (2,000 pages in a modern edition), starting, symbolically, the day after New Year; he downed brush exactly one year later on the first day of 1804.[72] He had reified the historical value that the book contained, while 'making' nothing, and had soldered past and present together. It was unexceptional for members of the elite to enhance their cultural capital by copying texts, but Sadanobu was extreme. Less than two years later he began a second copy, starting on the 28th of the 8th month and finishing on the last day of the next second month. That autumn he began a third copy, writing over the ensuing eleven months, and completing on the 21st of the 9th month, 1808. A fourth copy was begun in 1811 and finished in under three months, rushed, perhaps, in order to meet the auspicious eighth day of the eighth month of the eighth year of that era. In the spring of 1815 he commenced a fifth transcription, terminating about as quickly as the fourth. 1818 saw the making of another, completed in eight months, while a seventh was begun in the middle of the first

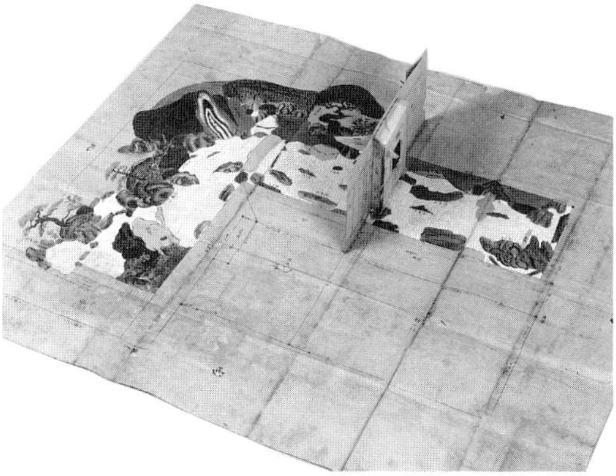

6 *Pop-up of Stone Garden at Daisen-in*, *c*. 1700, colour on paper. This model of one of Kyoto's most famous gardens was in Sadanobu's collection and may have inspired his own cultural 'paperizations'.

month of 1822 and finished on the ninth of the eighth. No one had ever done so much before.

Sadanobu expended labour on the multiplication of known literary texts and also on the collecting and inventorizing of written and manufactured objects. He dispatched others to replicate on his behalf when he was busy. The scope of his interests is visible in the preamble to a five-volume report submitted in 1792 by the painters Sumiyoshi Hiroyuki and Tani Bunchō and Sadanobu's favourite Confucian expert, Shibano Ritsuzan, and others, after they had inspected ancient temple holdings. *Genji* was a part of the *kokugaku* concern, but Sadanobu's *wa* also embraced Continental transmissions. The team was instructed:

> . . . to check Buddhist images, relics, wooden sculptures of the patriarchs and of learned monks, any treasured item or book, the titles on the covers and boxes to be verified against the testimony of temple monks [. . .] Every object is to be copied on this occasion and then identified by a triangular seal affixed [to the original]. Items previously copied for government use [. . .] are to be copied again.[73]

The tour took the men to Yamashiro and Yamato (the Nara–Kyoto region). At the compound of the wealthy and historic Eastern Temple (Tōji), for example, Hiroyuki (here called Daiki) spent six days with Ritsuzan in the storehouses, digging out artefacts. A typical log entry reads:

> Folding Screen with Landscape: one pair held. Gift of the Tang ruler Yuanhe [r. 806–821]. Seal in vermilion. Left of pair does not appear the work of a Continental artist, and Daiki's associate Shōki surmised it to be by Chinkai, a student of Tosa Motomitsu who lived in the time of Go-

Sanjō-in, that is, in the Enkyū era [1069–73]. In Kano Einō's *Painting of this Realm* [*Honchō gashi*] it says the Temple of Daigo-ji possesses a study of Manjuśri by Chinkai, on the back of which is the date Kennin 2 [1202]; note also there is conflicting attestation that Chinkai lived in the Zenna-in sub-complex of the Daigo-ji, and later at the Great Eastern Temple [Tōdai-ji], and that he was well known at the time of Tsuchimikado-in [1198–1210]. On the other hand, the appearance of the work would suggest the earlier date.[74]

No investigative effort is spared as the men pore over the screens, aided by reference materials, date charts and memories of what they have seen elsewhere. Provenance, date and divergence of the present state from the original intent are all assessed, as are past restorations and earlier errors of judgement. The work is then brought back to Edo in the form of a copy and the original put back, untouched.

This was government work, but it was directed by and accountable to Sadanobu. The archives of copies became mountains. But they remained pieces of paper. Sadanobu did not attempt to *acquire* the treasures he gathered in mimic. The requisition of historical vessels, or works of art, was standard practice among the elite. Tanuma Okitsugu had been an arrant accumulator of other people's treasures, so notorious for acquisitiveness it was said the gateway to his residence resembled the entrance to a bazaar.[75] Sadanobu's sense of the friability of culture disinclined him to remove any part of it.

He opined materialistically. He never read an old book but he fell to wondering about weights and masses, shapes and sizes, how long lances had been in the past, how far arrows had been able to fly, or how people had cut their hair.[76] Beneath all was the master narrative of 'Japanese culture'.

Sadanobu also built up a collection of architectural models. He may have been prompted by finding a late seventeenth-century, three-dimensional pop-up of the ancient garden at the Daisen-in, a sub-complex of the Temple of Great Virtue (Daitoku-ji) (illus. 6). He commissioned other similar ones, all of paper.[77] Sadanobu did not seek to relocate the actual buildings, although it would have been possible and was often done, there being a practice in Japanese architecture of dismantling and rebuilding famous halls and pavilions on a new site. Viewers could not enter his quivering buildings, and the models were only tremulous pointers to real presences flung across the landscape of the shogun's realm, to which the devoted student should repair.

Sadanobu's paper museum was intended for open access, and this was the point – to compensate for the distance and inaccessibility of the originals. He did not envisage his copies tucked away in his own

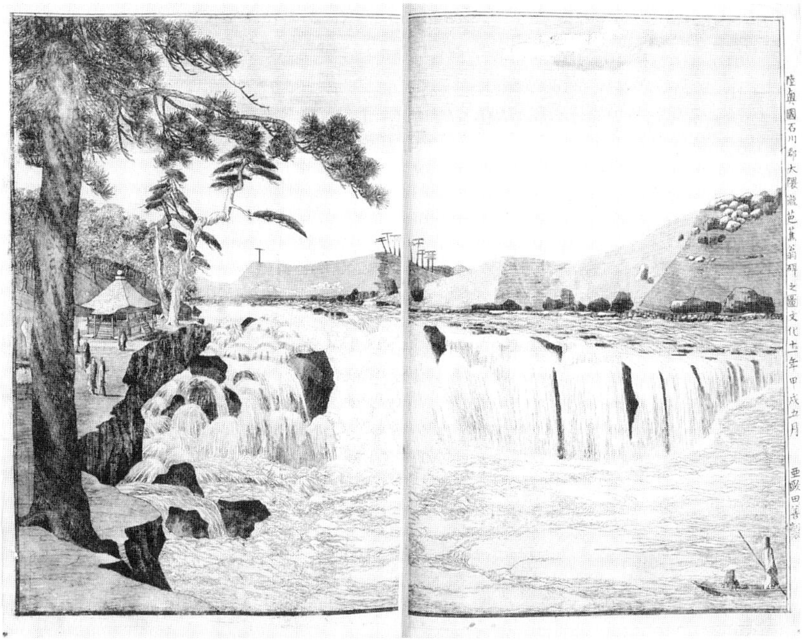

7 Aōdō Denzen, *Monument to Bashō at Ōtsumi Falls in the Village of Ishikawa, Mutsu*, 1814, copperplate etchings. Denzen was one of the first to produce local scenes in the copperplate medium.

mansion but intended them for multiple printing and sale among the citizenry. Each person could buy the summary of the material deposit of 'Japanese culture' and keep it at home.

Sadanobu was an enthusiast for printing, and the School of Difficult Questioning became a centre for the publication of texts.[78] He also fostered technological innovations, prime among them copperplate etching, by which pictures could be better replicated. From 1765 colour printing was possible in Edo, as it was not yet in Europe, but the material from which the impressions were taken was wood. By the standards of copperplate technology, the wood block was exiguous and its lines thick and necessarily rather few on the page. Since no presses were imported, copperplates had to be hand-rubbed, which was not ideal, but knowledge of etching circulated. The first successful etcher was Shiba Kōkan, who cracked the secret in 1783, working from books such as Buys's or less up-to-date works, like Abbé Noël Chomel's *Dictionnaire oeconomique* of 1709.[79] Kōkan was unpalatable to Sadanobu for social and personal reasons, and he soon wrested the breakthrough away from him and sidelined the artist, entrusting his own commissions to Nagata Zenkichi. Zenkichi was a samurai, unlike Kōkan, and also unlike him he was from Sadanobu's own state of Shirakawa.[80] Sadanobu chided Kōkan for being both no good at etching and for refusing to share the technology.[81] As late as 1794 Kōkan was billing himself as 'first exponent in Japan' (*nihon sōsei*), but his monopoly had been broken.[82] Monopoly of a multiplication medium was, of course, an intellectual oxymoron, albeit a serviceable business scheme.

Sadanobu called Zenkichi a man 'fixated by painting', unable to stop churning pictures out. He first had him study a range of styles with Bunchō and then move into copperplate, in which he soon became the acknowledged master. Zenkichi took the artistic sobriquet 'Denzen', combining the last element in his family name, Naga*ta* (here read as *den*), with the first of his given name, *zen*; Sadanobu awarded him a studio label, 'Aōdō', meaning 'Euro-Asian', and so the artist became known as Aōdō Denzen (illus. 7).[83] Etched multiplication of images – even if rarely undertaken – began a discursive ripple that allowed the conceptualization of 'Japanese culture' as a thing papered for circulation to a multitude of viewers.

Like glass, copperplates had been known for decades, but an interesting transformation in the value attached to them took place at the end of the century. In 1799 Kōkan told how 'some years ago' the Dutch East India Company had brought 'several hundred' etched prints, but that these had been politely declined and 'all handed back' to the Europeans.[84] The situation began to change, and extant imports (and copies of imports) from the 1780s are numerous. Again, theft shows desirability: Titsingh was angered at having a large illustrated book stolen from him in Nagasaki and returned with 'all the prints [. . .] torn out'.[85] As with many cultural shifts, the new-found admiration of copperplates was projected back on to Yoshimune, the long-ruling and admired eighth shogun at mid-century, who, it was said, was the first to realize the importance of etching and its utility in the Tenka.[86]

Sadanobu continued this. The high-ranking samurai Morishima Chūryō was taken into Sadanobu's service in 1792, and this may have been partly in response to his studies in etching. In 1786 Chūryō had conducted a public demonstration of aqua-forte and the following year had published this event, together with an extended treatment of copperplate technology and all Western picture-making, in a popularizing book entitled *A European Miscellany (Kōmō zatsuwa)*.[87] Chūryō told how the acid used in etching 'will recreate an image perfectly, and far more cleanly than is possible with a chisel', and that 'the liquid is manufactured in Europe, but I have some in my family storehouse'.

Kōkan limited himself to the topographical views done with exaggerated vanishing points that were then popular in Europe. Denzen did

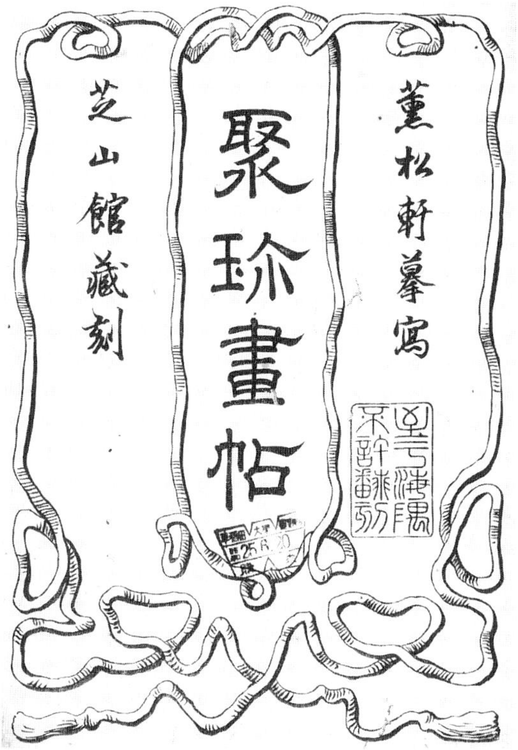

8 Ishikawa Tairō, Title page of Morishima Chūryō *et al.*, eds, *Shūkin gachō*, 1803, monochrome woodblock print. Although a woodblock, this print was made to look like copperplate and follow the conventions of a European title page.

not. Although he produced topographies, he put etching to much wider service, using it for illustrations in scholarly writings and the reproduction of old and new pictures on a variety of themes. He did not attempt to put Sadanobu's collection of copies of old objects in copperplate, perhaps because, in the continuing absence of a press (the need for which Chūryō does not even mention in his account), the ability to create images whose accuracy was actual rather than notional was compromised. No book illustrations were fully etched until 1806.[88] But the centrality of the technology to a vocabulary of open 'Japanese culture' is increasingly evident.

In 1803 some works by Kano Tan'yū were published. Tan'yū was regarded as a great painter and had been the first to work officially for the Tokugawa, becoming their artist-in-waiting (*goyō eshi*) in 1617. In this capacity he enjoyed unparalleled access to collections of artistic treasures, many of which he had reproduced as sketches (*shukuzu*). These were not the careful copies that Sadanobu ordered, but rapid *aides-memoires* for a practising artist; they did, however, constitute the fullest corpus of painting (Japanese and Continental) available in the Tenka. Many of the originals from which Tan'yū's sketches were taken were lost or held in secret, so publication of his copies was the best way to make generally available a body of pictures crucial to cultural history but otherwise doomed to languish unseen. Tan'yū's sketches were prepared for printing by a samurai directly in the shogunal employ, Ishikawa Tairō. Tairō was also respected as an amateur painter and held distinctly Europeanizing leanings, as can be told from his use of the Dutch 'Tafel Berg' (Table Mountain, in Cape Town) as his artistic sobriquet.[89]

The book contained no copperplates in fact, but Tairō made the title page into a mock-up etching, complete with shadows done in hatch-lines (illus. 8). The whole page, indeed, was made to look like that adorning a European book, so that Tairō simulated not only the medium but the conventions of the frontispiece plate, with a rope swag wound about the title in a kind of design that would be unfamiliar to his audience. Again something Western is made to hang about the impetus to define old artefacts, and again, it poses something to be seen through, not looked at. The persons chosen to write the prefaces to the collection were Chūryō and another Sadanobu associate, Yashiro Hirokata. Chūryō expressed regret that too few people were able to see good works of old art, whether for their delight or for training, which was vitiating current practice.[90] Accordingly, he and his colleagues were putting the images into the public domain. They offered to pull Tan'yū's privileged grasp on the history of painting back from oblivion.

A far more comprehensive attempt to collect and circulate antique work was undertaken by Tani Bunchō. He made reproductions of some 1,100 old masters on the grounds that:

> . . . most famous works are exceptionally difficult to gain sight of, which I, for one, think a great pity. That is why each time I see a historic piece I copy it down, regardless of how I might myself estimate its artistic merit, and keep the copy carefully, or else I might just sketch it in brief on a few leaves of paper.[91]

Little was known of Western art itself, and the most familiar European painter in shogunal circles was Gérard de Lairesse. Although neglected today, de Lairesse was celebrated in his own time and most particularly was known as an enthusiastic advocate of etching. He may have acquired his penchant for reproducibility from Rembrandt, with whom he was associated (Rembrandt painted his portrait).[92] De Lairesse went blind and, unable to work, he devoted himself to producing a manual, the *Groot schilderboek*, published in 1707, which was imported to Japan in many copies; it was used by Chūryō, Bunchō, Denzen and

Kōkan (among others).[93] Engraving, de Lairesse wrote, was:

> . . . to the sight what fame is to the ear. Painting has but one original, but engraving hundreds. Fame can tell the many wonders of painting in its absence; but engraving makes itself everywhere present; flying over the universe, as well as the sounding trumpet of fame. It keeps an eternal register of everything that is praise-worthy.[94]

De Lairesse's dedication to the medium extended to personally etching his own paintings – a laborious task that few artists of stature bothered with. To him, the etching was not autonomous, but a means of circulating good art.

Sadanobu was not involved with the Tan'yū project directly, although it probably had his blessing. His own attitude can be told more clearly from his reaction to another work, the famous pictorial biography of the prelate Hōnen (or Enkō) called *Encomium on the Great Teacher Enkō (Gyōjo Enkō daishi)*; the original dated to some time after Hōnen's death in the early thirteenth century, but it had recently been published in woodblock. Sadanobu applauded the new edition and examined it minutely, using his power to borrow the original and compare the two. He ultimately detected a fault: one section, showing 'a fine illustration of the inner precincts of the Temple of Taima', was unaccountably left out. This was surely just oversight, but Sadanobu was perturbed as it falsified the copy. The Taima temple was a hugely important place in Buddhist history but had structurally been altered over time, so that its antique form ought to be circulated. He personally rectified the omission, getting out his brush and 'putting the absence right by copying the segment in'.[95] Reproduction was a serious and necessary task, but it was the truth of the original that had to fly 'over the universe'.

Gathering the past ought not to be for self-aggrandizement but to bind the present back into historical time. The lucky few could immerse themselves in classical reading or ownership of antiques. The commonality used simpler primers or prints. The daimyo of Okayama, one of the pampered, when he felt his links to antiquity growing intolerably loose, would don antique clothes and literally dress himself in a robe of history, improving, he would have hoped, his cultural grasp and the 'leniency' of his rule.[96] Sadanobu singled out for praise his adoptive father, Sadakuni, who 'took an interest in antiques' and constantly viewed his pieces. To historicize himself via his collection, he historicized the collection itself and rehung his pictures in an old-fashioned way.[97] Sadakuni looked at antiques, and he looked *antiquely*. He had noticed how old scrolls showed elite interiors with painting edges 'flat to the architecture', whereas by the eighteenth century the practice was to hang the tops away from the walls, angled downwards. The old positioning looked odd to contemporaries and 'people refused to accept it', doubting whether Sadakuni's faith in the old scroll illustrations was valid. Then, after Sadanobu had sent Bunchō and the rest on one of their temple tours, Bunchō 'was able to certify that in the Southern Capital [Nara] the framed works in the pagodas of the Temples of Fukū-in, Hōki-ji and Kōfuku-ji, as well as in all other places that have them, are indeed fixed flush to the walls'. In short, 'Lord Sadakuni's contention was entirely correct'. The mechanics of artistic appreciation were likely to fall out of step in Edo, as the city was new, while Nara was the Tenka's most ancient city. But through accurate pictures all could be informed.

Sadakuni's scholarly integrity allowed him to enjoy paintings hung in this manner, but it did not suit the many, and it was also obvious that loitering in a reverie of pastness was not easy in the modern world. People needed help. Under Sadanobu, those who possessed treasures were encouraged to bring them out of store and relate properly to them, but the requirement that culture be reachable led Sadanobu to tolerate the needs of the moment even when they parted company with historical norms. His emphasis on reproduction in fact defetishized possession and, by furthering multiple possession, he inevitably allowed for multiple ways of viewing.

Sadanobu's Heart

Sadanobu's own collecting took a rather special turn. His unwillingness to remove objects from their settings was an impediment to building up a large array of pieces. He seems actively not to have wanted the storehouses full of treasures that most daimyo took as the reasonable adjunct to their suzerainty. Sadanobu's preference was to amass either paper or just disjointed and broken parts. He acquired a storehouseful of remnants, too worn or useless to be restituted to their former sites. His collection was the detritus of culture that few but he would value. His idiom was of salvage, and he enlisted his objects to remind him about the lost wholes from which they derived.

Sadanobu installed his cache of items in his other Edo park, located in the hilly outskirts at Ōtsuka. The compound was a series of six interlocking spaces, each on a separate theme, and was accordingly known as the Six Gardens (Mutsu-no-sono).[98] There were spring and autumn gardens, a bamboo grove and a flower garden – all quite normal. Then came two stranger zones: a garden of 'collected antiquities' (*shūko*) and a spinney of 'selected sites' (*sanshō*). The former was where he kept his relics and was studded with the fragments of disappearing historical loci, brought out and disposed about as the mood took him. Three storehouses of broken things were built to the side, containing, for example, lintels of temples, bits of stone lantern, tiles from temple roofs, and a section of old palace.[99] The latter zone contained plants cut from places where significant past events, or stories of events, had unfolded. These fifth and sixth gardens negotiated connections with olden times, the one referring to structures, the other to sites. One showed the creativity that had kept the generations ethically true, the other how this had taken place in the real spaces of the Tenka. Any heady optimism was stunted by the fact of the plants being reflections of places and the objects being degraded. The future was not secure.

Information on the Six Gardens is scant, but in one of the sections (the Garden of Collected Antiquities seems likely) was a pavilion called the Hall of Good Responses (Zen'ō-dō). This was a replica of the Phoenix Hall (Hōō-dō), the only surviving structure of the Temple of Equality (Byōdō-in), founded in 1052 and perhaps the most sublime ancient monument.[100] The splendid original was in Uji, far from Edo, and in good condition, having recently been restored.[101] Sadanobu sent an unspecified 'famous painter from Kyō' to study and depict the sublime hall prior to replication, for he determined that his version should be no different from the real one 'by even so much as a drop of dew'.[102] A carpenter, Sugiura Zenzō, did a marvellous job and the resemblance was said to be exact. Except in one regard: Sadanobu's replica was on a ratio of one *shaku* to the *bu*, that is 1:10. As the original frontage was (or is, the building being extant) 50 m long, the resulting garden ornament was shrunk to a few steps. The Six Gardens covered an area of 30,300 square metres, and there was ample space for a larger model or even a full-scale copy. But Sadanobu wanted his hall to be too diminutive to admit a living person.

Cultivating good responses required diligence. Past items were viewed not just for their loveliness (there is rarely any appeal to beauty in Sadanobu's writings) but to conjure back the higher sentiments of antiquity. The painter then said by many to be foremost in the land, and personally admired by Sadanobu, worked under the name of 'Ōkyo', which might be paraphrased as 'my project is correct responses'.[103] Cultivating an ability to respond was the role of education. It meant allowing the modern person into the embrace of the past. To those who knew 'good responses' belonged the right to control others. Feeling correctly in front of artefacts betokened the assimilation of mind and body with history. This was the objective of study, and it accorded the status of rulerhood. Sadanobu emphasized to his samurai that learning was a two-part twinned process: 'to rectify the mind [*seishin*] and school the body [*shushin*], and to govern the states [*jikoku*] and pacify the people [*anmin*]'.[104]

Upon coming to power, Sadanobu instituted a series of examinations to raise the professionalism of the administration.[105] Less well known is another test he set for all samurai in the shogunal employ, held in 1791, to examine their cultural levels and particularly their ability to 'respond'. The event was colourfully recorded by Moriyama Takamori, author of the autobiography, who might well wish to remember it, since he took first place, which may have assured his rise to prominence. Entrants were to compose a verse on the topic of 'An Autumn Moon at Night' (*ryōya*) – a conservative theme, not particularly taxing and well within familiar parameters. The sinuosity with which the hackneyed subject could be turned into a vehicle for genuine emotional expression was the key. Takamori recorded:

On the 15th day of the 8th month of that year, he had Lord Tōe-no-kami Hisachika circulate the title to be worked on, 'An Autumn Moon at Night'. [Sadanobu] stipulated that from the most senior on downwards, all ranks would come forward and proffer their verses, each according to his ability. This would be done in the Central Chamber, and the process would continue for as many days as it took.[106]

So,

One after another people submitted their verses. Even when the result was less than perfect, everyone thought it was bound to do, and fell to analysing the composition, until they realised the verse was not going to be good enough.

Takamori's turn arrived.

One night as I was in waiting at the Castle this verse came to me:

Its motions all
Unseen,
Tonight too it appears.
I think of those eyes
Looking with ardour at the moon.[107]

I wrote it down and sent it in, then went before Lord Shirakawa [Sadanobu] thinking to hear his opinion. Among all the good poems they had received on the 'Autumn Night', he felt, mine was the most interesting, for it possessed the capacity to move people.

Takamori imagined a person looking in longing at the moon, whose brilliance illumines the pathway of a lover who does not come; the moon is both dependable and changeable. His verse was best because it brought 'living sentiment' (*kanshō*) to the hearer, within the old-style prosody and wording, knotting the present and the past. The compositions were gathered in an anthology made available in the major cities, and the Confucianist Shibano Ritsuzan read it, sending a message of congratulation to Takamori:

He told me how the *Book of the Autumn Moon at Night (Ryōya no itchō)* was on everybody's lips, being praised all about, and that according to people where he was, the verse going 'Its motions all/Unseen' was best of all!

It was not chance that inclined Sadanobu to take the ability to handle poetry as the subject of his test. The verses demanded were in the 5-7-5-7-7 metre of the *waka* (*wa* poem), or vernacular verse, and not that of the Chinese *kanshi*. The latter were reckoned good for hortative exposition, whereas the former, it was thought, better grasped the fullness of sentiment which alone was the tractor of 'response'. *Waka* were prevalent at court, and Titsingh had been struck by how the shogunal entourage 'suffer no event at all worthy of remark to pass without making it a subject for exercising their passion for poetry'.[108] But 'passion for poetry' was not quite the point: verses in Japanese were phonetically recorded and so sounded the same in every age, while ideographic Chinese shifted. *Waka* articulated in the sounds of history and, by observing prosodic rules, allowed moderns to speak like the ancients. The problem was that the modern heart had hardened into unresponsiveness, and modern poets were poor.

Sadanobu's Image

When Sadanobu quit Shirakawa to assume membership of the shogunal council, he left behind a self-portrait to be used in veneration. He inscribed it 'Dispense with insurrection and return to right; prize goodness and hate wrong-doing' (see illus. 16). The work has an uneven appearance. A carefully rendered head seems to sit ill on the neglected trunk. The body and outfit are formal and denote only rank, not person, while the head compels attention.

A number of portraits of Sadanobu survive, and his jutting jaw, high

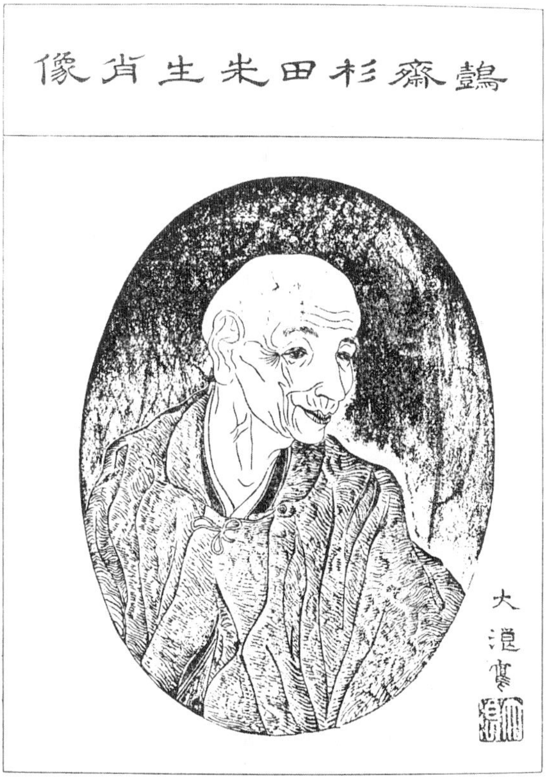

9 Ishikawa Tairō, Frontispiece of Sugita Genpaku, *Keiei yawa*, 1802, monochrome woodblock print. The old doctor appears as a reflection in an imported mercury mirror.

forehead and long nose appear in other contexts and presumably were recognized as his. But to know them himself, he must have inspected his features in a mirror. The north-east Asian copper-alloy mirror went back to prehistory, and it offered a good reflective surface. It was fast being supplanted, however, by the looking-glass imported, along with glass itself, by the Dutch East India Company. Both were, in fact, important items in trade and also in smuggling.[109] The process by which mercury was applied to the rear of glass was complex and it intrigued Sadanobu. On more than one occasion he wrote of the efforts required to transform a pane into a reflective surface.[110] His interests in glass mirrors and in glass windows were linked, as was also the case for Qianlong, the Qing emperor, who had written a verse on seeing his face in a mercury mirror composed to be linguistically similar to his one on glass window panes. The mirror poem had concluded with the lines:

Beautiful people appear in their beauty, and the ugly in their ugliness.

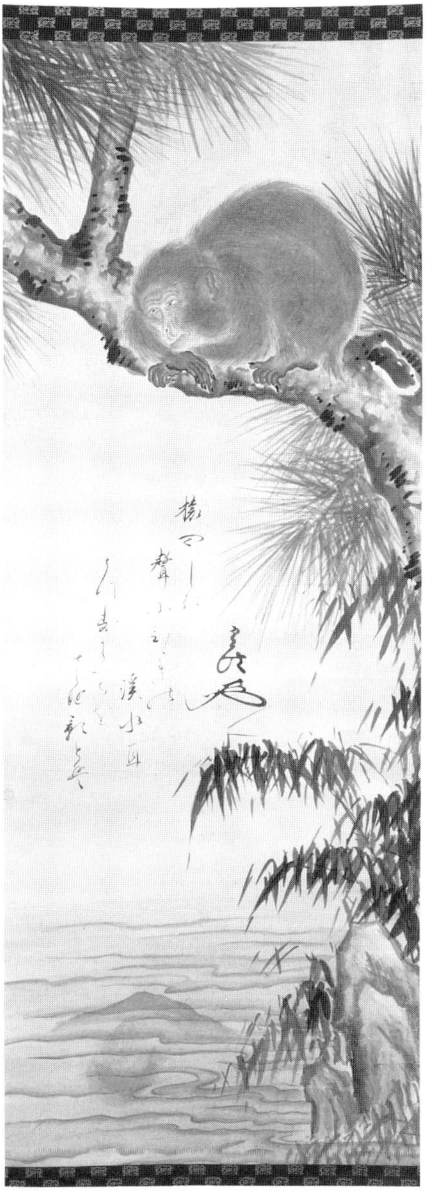

10 Matsudaira Sadanobu, *Monkey*, *c*. 1800, hanging scroll, colour on paper. This work parodies the Zen parable of the monkey who broke the moon's reflection by trying to grasp it.

Sitting on my fine bed and gazing at the mirror
All the multifarious influences of karma are stilled,
And then I commune with myself for a long while.[111]

Sadanobu probably knew this verse too and understood how the nothingness of glass could be turned on to the self, to expose objectively the onlooker's face.

Sadanobu's use of a mercury mirror (or any mirror) in the creation of his portrait is no more than presumptive, but others industriously involved with new ways of perception and representation certainly did so. Sugita Genpaku, the scholar we shall encounter in Chapter Two, wrote of the hours he spent meditating on his face in a mirror and turned his musings into a book entitled *Night Talks by a Reflected Shadow (Keiei yawa)*. The publishers placed Genpaku's image on the frontispiece, borrowed from Ishikawa Tairō's portrait of him made some years before, but they cut the full body down to just the head, and enclosed this in an oval (illus. 9). The result suggests Genpaku's reflection in a European looking-glass (Japanese mirrors are round), with its suggestively darkened hinterland behind.

Portraits – other than posthumous ones – are fairly rare in all north-east Asian art. In the late eighteenth century the genre underwent something of a surge. Imported instruments of vision were spurs, as was the realization that the portrait was central to Western art.[112] The European compound in Nagasaki, for example, was dripping with them.[113] It was Bunchō who pioneered redefinition of the genre. According to his pupils, he refused to paint sitters under 30, probably feeling the power of the portrait was too great and would tempt the young into pride.[114] Sadanobu had not yet befriended Bunchō when he made his own self-portrait, but that year, 1787, was indeed his thirtieth. The young councillor emerged into full adulthood, relocated himself to the shogunal seat and began his construction of the Tenka, leaving his true face lying caught on paper at the periphery.

At the other end of his span, Sadanobu painted his face again (see illus. 17). The year was 1812 and he was 55. A text preserved with the painting explains that Sadanobu did the face but had the rest done by a professional artist, Kano Osanobu, then head of the Kano School and grandson of the famous Eisen-in Michinobu, who had painted the unlucky kite. An element of context is given with the fresh new tatami mat, which raises the sitter in a dignified way above the viewer. At 30, Sadanobu had been perfunctory about his flesh, but now it is careworn and jowly, with a mouth that has sagged and a body perhaps shorter of wind and infirmer of step. He does not engage with it himself but entrusts it to Osanobu, who keeps it largely obfuscated by the hieratics of costume. But the doing part of the body is now included, and the hands are seen. Perhaps, at the end of his life, Sadanobu is beginning to admit to the active role he had played.[115]

These images can be seen against a third, painted at some time between the others and again by Sadanobu himself. A monkey crouches, looking down from a tree (illus. 10). It is staring at its face in a pond. This is an adaptation of a Zen parable that likened a monkey trying to catch the moon reflected in water to humanity grasping at Buddhist truths. We are unaware that all we see are reflections and that the act of seizing shatters the hope of comprehension. Sadanobu made two small but salient alterations to this standard theme. First, it is itself that the monkey inspects, not the moon, and, secondly, its paws are folded, not outstretched. It views its face but does not seek to touch. Self-knowledge comes from quiescence and meditation, not from action. The levels of ontological distance multiply, as the monkey reflects on a reflection of itself, and the viewer sees in a picture that reflection's reflection. In the wilderness of mirrors, all depends on representation. Sadanobu inscribed a poem on the painting:

Its cry reverberates
Through the valley.
But what is this reflected shape,
That will not go away?[116]

If the monkey leaves, its face will disappear too. But via the painting it can be held forever in place. The verse is a pun on *saru*, meaning both 'monkey' and 'to depart'; a non-departing monkey is thus an internally unsustainable pun. The verb *utsusu*, also used, means 'to reflect' and 'to depict': a good picture is a kind of reflection pinned down. Materials are not substantial, but they are our only expediencies against ruin. Cease the clamour, Sadanobu enjoins, and let imagery do its job of interim, tentative, *ad hoc* compelling.

2 Sugita Genpaku and the Dismemberment of the Present

Let them eat cake.
– Marie-Antoinette, *c.* 1788

Let them eat crake.
– Son of the daimyo of Nakatsu, *c.* 1788[1]

Sugita Genpaku, whose wizened portrait we saw in Chapter One, was a learned samurai in the service of the Kohama state in Wakasa, although he resided in Edo (see illus. 9). In 1787 he compiled a three-volume account of his times, bringing the narrative up to the moment of writing.[2] His end-stop was just weeks into Sadanobu's appointment. Genpaku assigned this work the title *Essays in Hindsight (Nochi-migusa)* and in its preface explained what this meant: looking back, to the acute investigator, past and present were little different. The notion might offer comfort in a world-view where history was proposed as a trajectory of diminution, but Genpaku intended no such solace. He limited his stories to disasters, showing that the present equalled even the most hideous precedents of the last century or so.

Genpaku opened his *Essays* with the colossus of hopelessness that had occurred since the beginning of the Tokugawa regime in 1603. This did not allow for much historical depth, but that date was identified as the 'foundation of the states' (*kokusho*) and the present's most decisive juncture. Genpaku's 'past' was not far removed, but the brevity of his chronological sweep had the advantage of collapsing events into something graspably near at hand. The book did not treat legendary tales and saws, but dealt in nothing but actualities, many of them lingering within recall. Genpaku was careful to unfold his stories among known spaces and via known organs and institutions, and to use a nomenclature that was still familiar.

Volume one dealt with the Great Fire of Edo in 1657. The conflagration had obliterated all life in the city and fundamentally altered the shogunal polity for ever. Genpaku had apparently found a lost eyewitness account of this disaster and decided to use it to prefigure his account of the present.[3] This was an extraordinary literary decision gratuitously bringing the fire back into the public mind as the archetypal forebear of the here and now. This is followed by a jump to the period of Genpaku's own adulthood, volume two covering 1753 to mid-1772 and volume three the period from late 1772 to the time of writing, 1787. The later sections are written as a rolling continuum, in journal mode, as if kept at the time, which perhaps they were. The *Essays* is not a long book – some 50 pages in the modern edition – but grim recollection succeeds grim recollection so powerfully that the reader is beaten down until the complete cessation of civilized life is reached. Genpaku asserts he was living in the very couch of horror, or, in his own simile, in the crushed grass on which a wolf had made its bed.[4]

Some events stand out with particular force. 'A certain person told me', Genpaku wrote, 'how at about this time [1773] when he was crossing a bridge in the country of Dewa, he noticed corpses lying exposed beneath; these were the bodies of those who had died of hunger'. Famine was a recurrent woe, but Genpaku makes this special:

> . . . he saw a traveller in religious guise down amongst the bodies slicing off thighs and stuffing them into hampers. When asked why, he said he intended to mash them with leaves and grasses, and sell them as dog meat.[5]

This was not degeneracy of a normal kind. It was emblematic of a downgrading of humanity to the animal state. Consumers thought they were digesting dog and bitch, bad enough in a vegetarian Buddhist context and often cited as the harshest index of hunger, but actually it was human flesh that infused their bodies, wrecking their karmic links and propelling them on a slide towards the bottom. A short way into Genpaku's narrative, which began in fire, the reader is in Hell.

Discourse and Diagnosis

The period covered by Genpaku is remembered today for the extravagance of life. Urban centres fostering the hedonism of the 'floating world' (*ukiyo*) are applauded for creating marvellous artefacts in fabric, personal accessories, and the famous multi-coloured woodblock print. In many media, this was a Golden Age. But to Genpaku the time was one of sudden or lingering death. Society was being systematically erased. 'When Heaven conveys disaster', he wrote, 'there is little humanity can do to withstand it'.[6] Much of the culture now so admired was, to him, culpably escapist. Misery did not come by chance but was part of an organized onslaught from Heaven, and flight from this was a refusal to read Heaven's warnings. Each event recorded by Genpaku is projected as a portent to be deciphered. The art of divination relied on observations grounded in time and place, not on general impression, and Genpaku records details to arrest the present and force readings – an eclipse, a monster birth, an unseasonal precipitation. Portents took on meaning insofar as they mismatched inductive expectations. Genpaku's book offers symptoms for diagnosis. Far from the arbitrary swipes of a disjointed world, 'these are signs', he thought, from an integrated system, 'perfectly easy to interpret for those with the mind to understand'.[7]

Old men are apt to decry the collapse of what they knew as youths, but this was not Genpaku's case. He was just 20 when he began the *Essays*, and although he was 54 by the time he completed them, he was still vigorous and was to live for another 30 years.[8] Anguish coloured not his dotage but his prime.

Genpaku was a sober man of high analytic credibility. Some years before embarking on the *Essays* he had inherited his father's position as private physician to the daimyo of Kohama, in which capacity he attended at the Kohama compound in Edo. He enjoyed a reputation as a scholar of empirical temperament and radical calibre, as proven in 1774 when he startled the intellectual world by publication of the *New Anatomical Atlas (Kaitai shinsho)*. This elegantly illustrated volume was intended to provoke a new kind of thinking, not only among specialist doctors, for there was not much room for anatomy, or its sister, surgery, in the Sino–Japanese medical tradition (*kanpō*), but also among generally educated persons. The book was predicated on a novel epistemology of exposure and probing, which came prior to any attempt at cure.[9]

The *New Anatomical Atlas* was a collaborative work, and Genpaku's team included Maeno Ryōtaku, Nakagawa Jun'an and Katsuragawa Hoshū – all senior samurai physicians located in Edo. Ryōtaku was doctor to the daimyo of Nakazu and Jun'an, like Genpaku, was in the service of Kohama. Hoshū, brother of Morishima Chūryō (later to write the preface to Tan'yū's published sketches), was still in his teens, though soon to inherit the post of shogunal physician. The four worked for three years on the book, which was in fact a translation, derived largely from the *Anatomische Tabellen* of the Danzig doctor Johannes Kulm (or Kulmus), published in German in 1725, but known to them in the Dutch version of 1734, *Ontleedkundige tafelen*. Kulm's book was a good choice, as it too was intended for the lay reader rather than the professional anatomist.[10] Anatomy was a new and Western-derived thing, and it fitted into the emerging domain of knowledge called 'Dutch learning' (*rangaku*). Just a few short years after the pilgrim had been seen flesh-slicing under the bridge, members of informed circles were provided with access to an anatomically based assessment of the body. De luxe complimentary copies were sent to major figures in the shogunal and shujo courts, and the team spared no effort to ensure that the book looked appealing.[11] It was published by one of Edo's most prestigious houses, the Suhara-ya. Copperplate illustrations were culled from Kulm and other European books (by Paré, Bartholin and Palflyn) to ensure a visual panache second to none, and these were transposed to woodblock to accompany the new work – a meticulous job undertaken by Odano Naotake, a young samurai from the sub-state of Kakunodate in Akita (illus. 11).[12] The authors repeatedly stressed the 'value to the states' (*kokuyō*) of their project and, as not a soul was ever healed by the book (new anatomical knowledge was rarely put into practice), the utility lay by extrapolation in moral, rather than clinical, lessons. The ligaments, nerve-trees and skeletons offered revised epistemic grids.

The *Atlas* was not without its critics, even among those who admired its agenda. Shiba Kōkan condemned it as 'awfully mixed up' and 'careless'; he also condemned its elitism. Kulm was not translated into the vernacular but into scholarly pseudo-Chinese (*kanbun*), which, Kōkan claimed, meant commoner readers 'have a terrible job

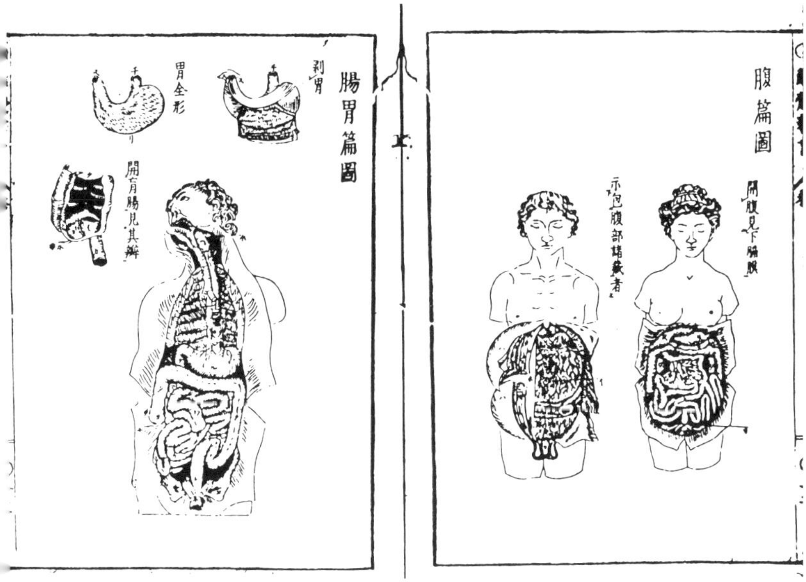

11 Odano Naotake after Adam Kulm, Illustrations from Sugita Genpaku *et al.*, trans., *Kaitai shinsho*, 1774, monochrome woodblock prints. The first almost integral translation of a Western book; plates were culled from celebrated medical texts.

trying to understand it, as the sentences are just too difficult to fathom'.[13] But this was the point: anatomy was a discourse directed to the Tenka's rulers. The book was certainly perused by them. Takatsukasa Sukehira, the shujo's regent, sent back thanks for his free copy, expressing himself in the form of a *waka* poem.[14]

When in later life Genpaku summed up his achievements (which he felt were huge, modesty not being his forte), he praised himself most for fathering Japanese anatomy. This was not quite accurate, but it was how he wanted to be seen. He claimed to have invented the word 'anatomy' (*kaibō*, literally 'cutting asunder' or 'dissection') to replace the older, and to him mistakenly nuanced, term 'dividing the viscera' (*fuwake*). Mythologization of corporeal intrusion by simple 'division' is ousted in favour of the scalpel and the knife.[15] Genpaku, however, never performed an autopsy. Being a samurai he was too nice to cut up bodies, whether living or dead. It was in ideological terms that he was an anatomist. Such a man was, then, the compiler of the *Essays*. His horror journal clove the sealed skin of the state to delve into the abdominal matter and identify its maladies.

Medical language was consistent with an analysis of rule, and Genpaku was not the first to use it. Precedents can be found in early writing, and something akin to 'bodies politic' is known in East Asia.[16] Significant examples are found shortly after Genpaku's time. One was Yuasa Genzō's *Treatise on the Curing of States (Kokui-ron)* of 1793, which expounded the continuing social unrest in terms of disease and its end as a healing;[17] Genzō identified Matsudaira Sadanobu as the attending physician. But only Genpaku made diagnostic claims that specifically emanated from anatomy. He proposed himself alone as the one who unabashedly cut through opacity, revealing the ailment to hand and eye and thereby, finally, knowing it. His cure was not arrived at by an oesophagal swallowing of physic, but by ripping apart the surface and probing deep beneath.

Genpaku's support for the Tokugawa was absolute. He dismissed *in toto* the canopy of metaphysical reasoning that European doctors erected over their discipline. He scorned the philosophical language in which imported books, including all medical tomes, were steeped. Genpaku sought to justify anatomy by neither the imported dictates of the Christian notion of the similarity of man's body to God's nor the pagan injunction to 'know thyself'. Such sections were deleted from the Kulm translation. The whole team would have determined this approach, but Genpaku particularly went out of his way to deny any interest in such Western stances: 'it is fruitless to inquire into their false creeds, and I always avoid debating them', he announced.[18] The fascinating workings that could be detected in the opened body, and the empirical obviousness of malfunctionings so revealed (Genpaku was optimistic about how clearly one can see inside a dissected body), were to him justification enough. The morbid body of the shogunal confederacy was ripe for investigation.

Illness was not hard to find. Edoites were dying at the rate of 2,000 per day.[19] Other cities were similarly hit. In Nagasaki, wrote Casper Romberg, a dozen people were succumbing per street – a total of thousands. In 1783 and 1784, the Dutch East India Company found itself in the anomalous position of having to import rice to keep famine at bay as the shogunate defaulted on its most basic duty to nourish its people's bodies. (On the later voyage the bags were badly sealed, and the rice spoiled before delivery.)[20] People were left with bark or leaves to eat – even the dogs were already slaughtered. 'Some', wrote Genpaku, 'took to hacking the heads off children, peeling their faces away and barbecuing them on fires'. Others 'broke open infant skulls, stuck in skewers and dug out the brains'.[21] Cannibalism may have occurred, although Genpaku reports it as hearsay. Primarily this functions as a narrative construction, giving the clue to a larger dilemma: this is a society in its death-throes.

Genpaku's civic body's malfunctioning is tied to that of the macrocosm of the universe itself. In 1778 a 'malevolent star', one metre across when viewed from the ground, shone out. It looked like Mercury (called the 'Water Star'), but, inversely, it sucked moisture from the earth until the wells went dry. In Keishi they dug into the Kamo riverbed in search of subterranean trickles; in Odawara they rationed water (one *shō* per person, three for a horse).[22] The star reappeared the following year and for a third time two years later. Then two moons came into the sky. 'Could there be', Genpaku pondered, 'a more agonizing thing?'[23] The world was losing its cosmic poles of orientation. Healthy categorization became impossible. 'Sardines proper to the east coast were found breeding in the north, and south sea bonito appeared in the east.' In sum, 'what should be in one place was not there, while what should not be there was present instead'.[24] Phenomena pulled apart like ruptured organs, and matter haemorrhaged through the gaps.

The power of this discourse was such that even routine menace was accorded a tincture of cosmic crisis. Burglars seemed to enter and steal with preternatural impunity, no matter how firmly doors were locked. One, Hamajima Shōbei, although finally caught, transfixed Edo for months with a mystique that expanded the relevance of his petty crimes. When sickness is acute, trivial ailments bring great fears.

Shōbei was able to make his escapes in eight-metre bounds to front, back or sides, like a hero from Chinese legend turned to the bad. The populace called him ironically 'Nihon'emon' ('Jack Japan').[25] In a world-view that conjoined rule with planetary order, this anthropomorphic form of the cultural cluster that was Nihon boded ill.

Sadanobu recorded the general public unease. 'The like of this is seldom seen', he affirmed, then continued:

> All over the city, people had only to hear a dog bark to think a thief had come upon them and so have the bells rung. This caused panic to all who heard it and prevented anyone from getting rest at night.[26]

Countervailing voices of calm were not believed. The shogunal councillor Matsudaira Nobuaki glumly noted, like some about-face Cassandra, 'ill rumour, even if untrue, will be believed if it seems in keeping with the times'.[27]

Like customary crime, the customary supernatural, which people were equipped to deal with as a reasonable response to reasonable events, relocated, inducing unexpected fears. A ghost appeared in the palace of the daimyo of Kazusa and wailed there for fourteen consecutive nights in a voice so loud that all were sleepless for blocks around. 'Of course', analogized Genpaku, 'ghosts are known to appear in far-flung mountain villages with few inhabitants', but this was in Edo's premier residential neighbourhood of Sakarada, right beside the castle, 'in the very centre of this busy city, and at the house of a military gentleman at that, which has never happened before'.[28]

A pivotal event came in 1783. This takes up far more space than any other episode in Genpaku's *Essays*. The occurrence amounted to a direct assault on the hinterland which Edo relied on for its psychological and nutritional needs: Mt Asama, a 2,500 m peak some 200 km to the north-west of the city, erupted. Its lava flow spilled through the writings of almost every diarist of the time, and its 'incredible mischief' was even heard of in Europe.[29] It is one of the only concrete events mentioned by Yuasa Genzō as needing political medicine, and Sadanobu dwelt at length on it too.[30] It was the final attempt on life in the Edo area. Many years later Aōdō Denzen was to depict Asama's scarred summit, by then cold but still entirely bare (illus. 12).[31]

The facts are easily pieced together.[32] A mighty noise was heard throughout Edo on the eighth day of the seventh month. The sky turned black. For the next three days there was total silence. On the fourth, bodies with mutilated or severed limbs began floating down the river into Edo, jostling with the corpses of horses and cattle. Only later

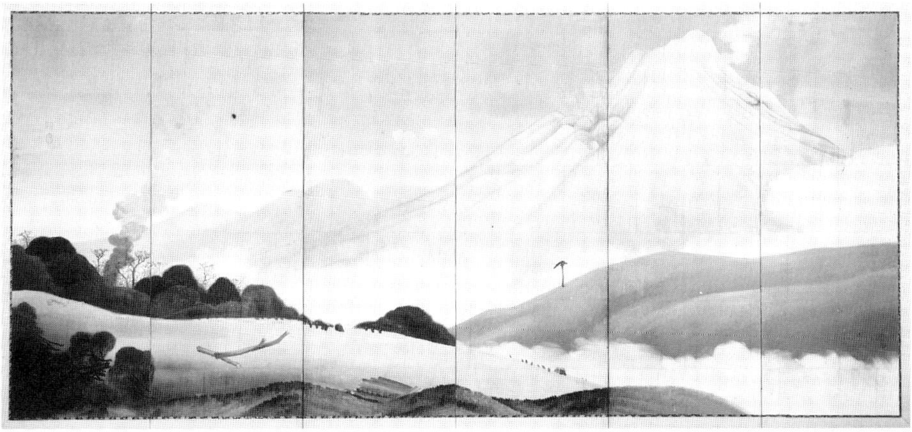

12 Aōdō Denzen, *Mt Asama*, after 1804, single six-fold screen, colour on paper. The mountain remains denuded of vegetal life twenty years after erupting.

did survivors straggle in, telling stories that were barely imaginable – 'terrifying even at second hand', wrote Genpaku:

Affected areas were from the foothills of Asama to the banks of the Yone, a distance of some 40 *ri* [160 km]. All became a sea of molten rock. Not a house, not a tree, not a blade of grass remained. Everything was buried in sand and stifled under mud. The number of livestock killed cannot be reckoned. As for people, old, young, men, women, clerical and lay, all in all, more than 2,000 perished. The flow of the Old, the New and the Lower Yones were bank to bank in the bones and bodies of humans and horses.[33]

The Japanese archipelago is volcanic and eruptions are to be expected. But this upheaval was more than seismic, and more than any of the other disasters it perplexed the authorities with anxieties greater than the numbers of dead among people and livestock. It was an indication that the bond between Heaven and earth had snapped. Asama's eruption was spoken of in terms of unparallelability and of contradiction. One man brought to Edo larval lumps that were 30 cm across, but light as feathers.[34] The landscape was made absurd as rocks – 'the bones of the earth' – liquefied and were transformed into nondescript matter, like a body after exquisite torture. This was apocalypse here, now, in Edo.

The eloquence of the disorder at Asama was not forgotten. Looking back at the age of 80, the venerable chronicler Saitō Hikomaro wrote in 1846 how the eruption he had experienced as a boy of 16 remained the greatest 'abnormality' of his incident-studded life. Asama erupted again that year (prompting Hikomaro's remarks), but it was never to be so destructive or, more to the point, it was never again to lock so firmly into a wider discourse of horror.[35]

Sadanobu and the Stars

The charge of lese-majesty to the shogunal court was a serious one to incur, and this obliged commentators to avoid any direct apportioning of blame for cosmic turmoil and its repercussions in the human realm. But it was rulers who mediated with Heaven, and only their insufficiency could lead to cataclysm. Members of the shogunate were imbued with a sense of their awesome task of regulating the spheres and were as traumatized by events as the lower orders, who at least had recourse to riot to vent their anxiety. Senior bureaucrats could not but doubt the validity of the regime they themselves constituted. The year before the eruption Tanuma Okitsugu, then chief councillor, had erected a government observatory in the Kanda district of Edo, equipping it at considerable expense (illus. 13). It was a kind of *New Anatomical Atlas* for the planets, and its scholars pored over the latest Western books and theories, notably Joseph Lefrançois de Lalande's

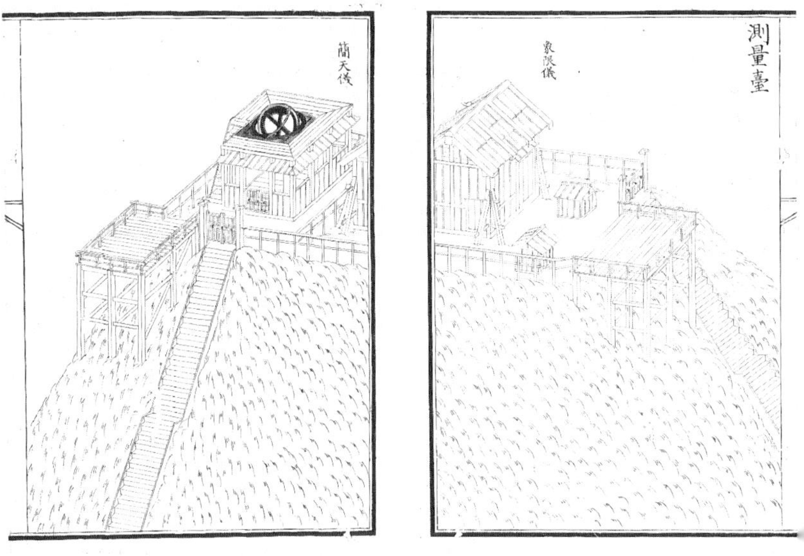

13 Illustration from Shibukawa Kagesuke *et al.*, eds, *Kansei rekisho*, 1853, ink drawing. Edo's splendid new observatory.

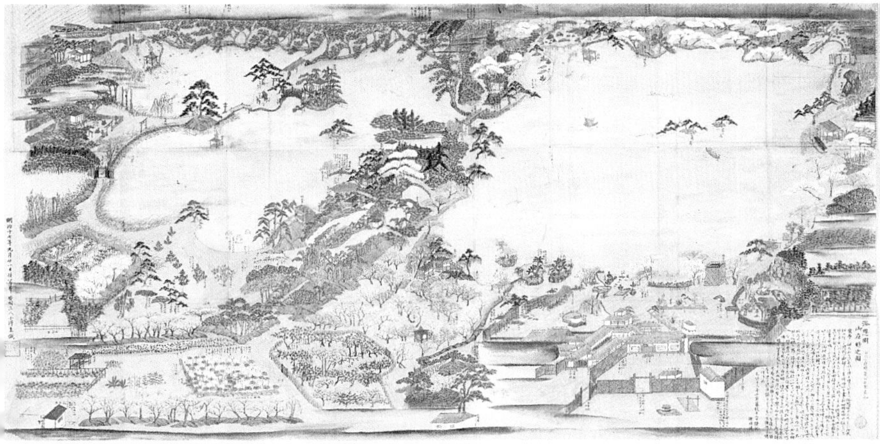

14 Copy of Okamoto Jishō, *Yokuon-en gozaiji no zu* (1842), 1884, colour on paper. Sadanobu's garden and mansion, planned to his own designs on land donated by the shogunate.

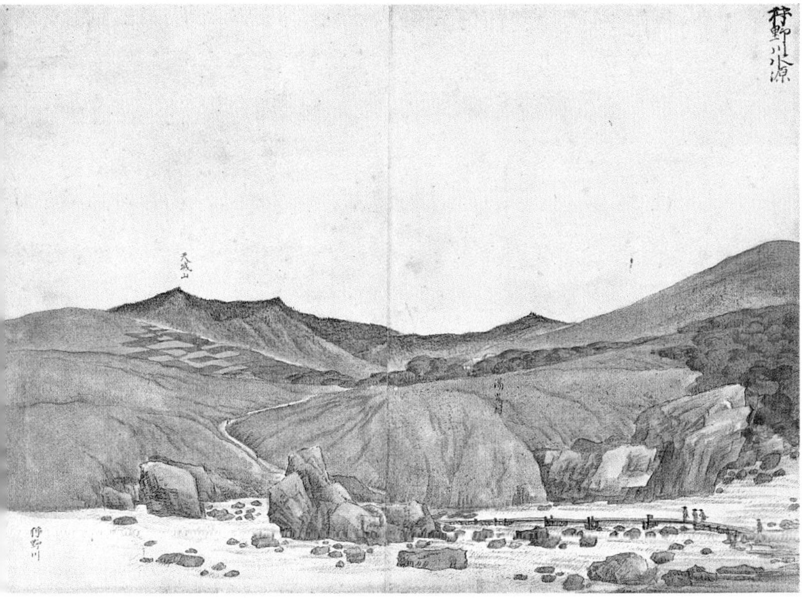

:5 Tani Bunchō, 'The Source of the River Kano', 1793, from *Kōyo tanshō-zu*, handscroll remounted as an album, colour on paper. Sadanobu's inspection team tours Edo's coastline.

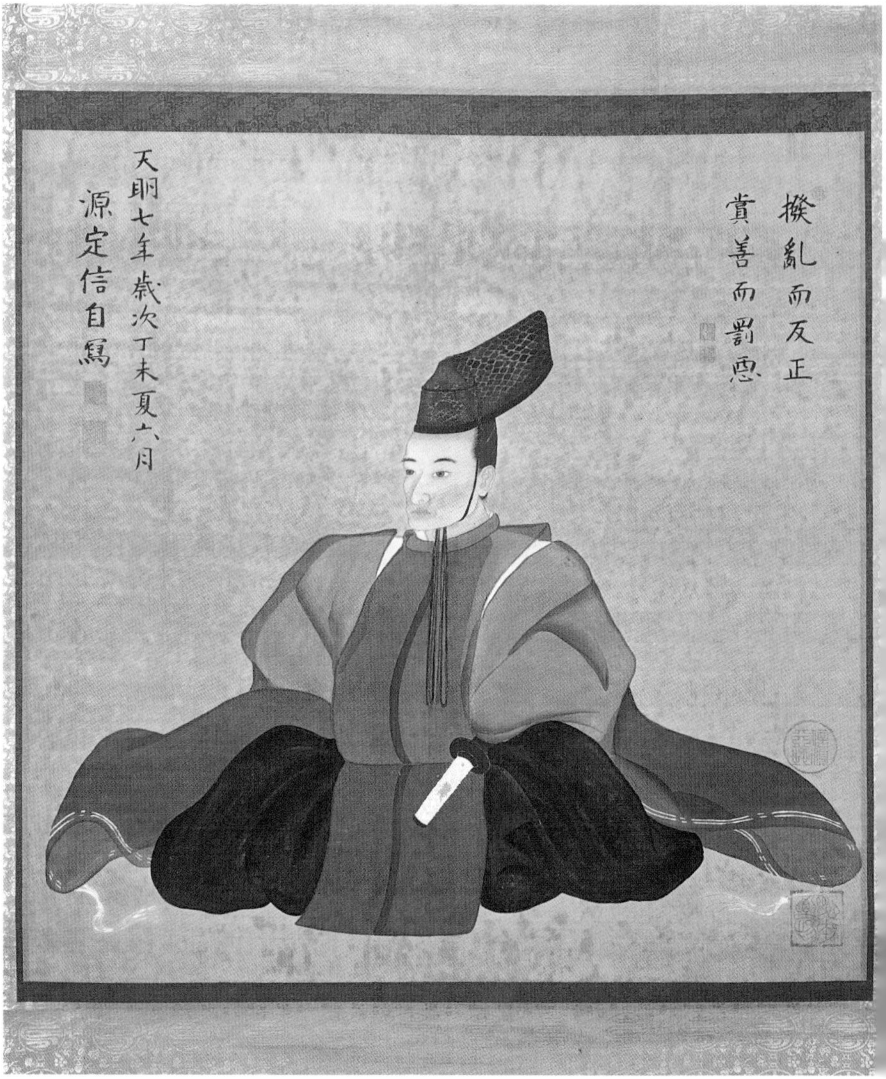

16 Matsudaira Sadanobu, *Self-portrait*, 1787, hanging scroll, colour on paper. Sadanobu left this image behind when he moved to Edo.

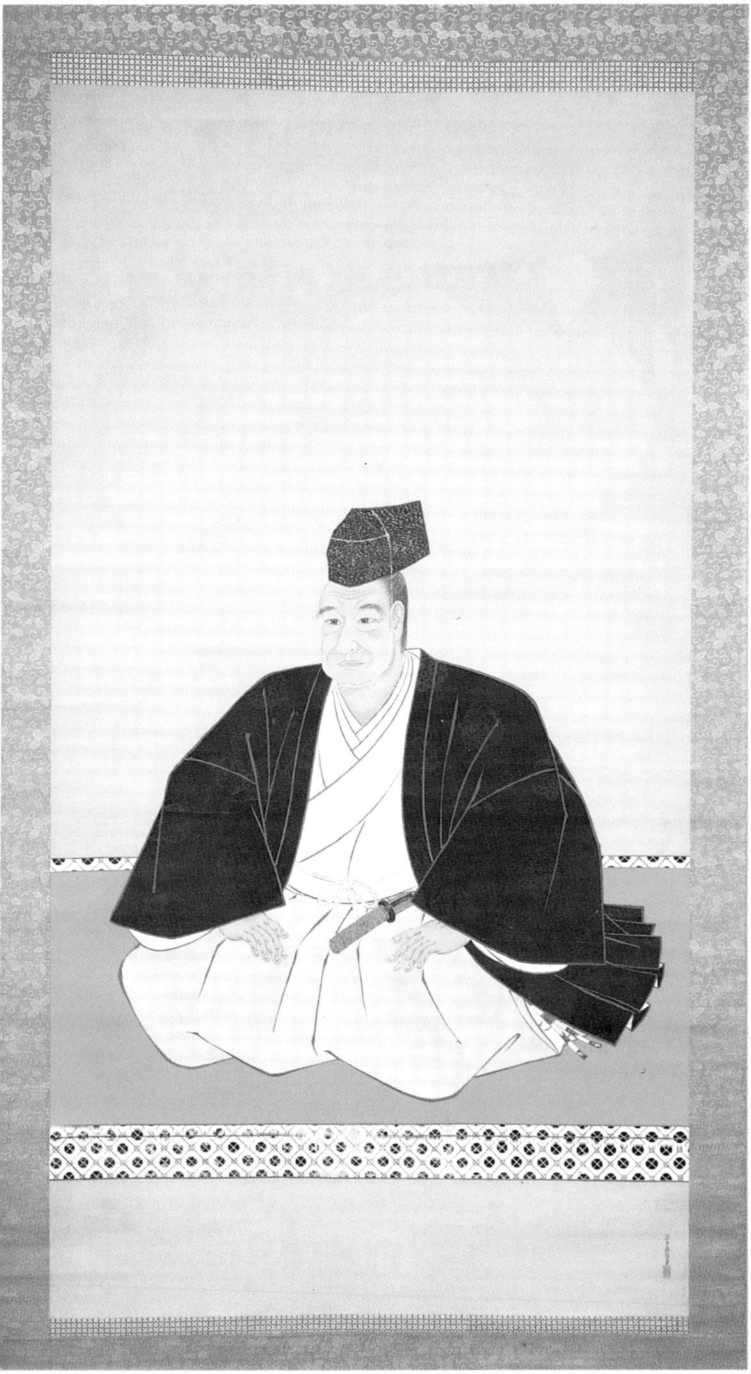

17 Matsudaira Sadanobu (with Kano Osanobu), *Self-portrait*, 1812, hanging scroll, colour on silk. Sadanobu rendered his own face and had the head of the government's painting academy do his body.

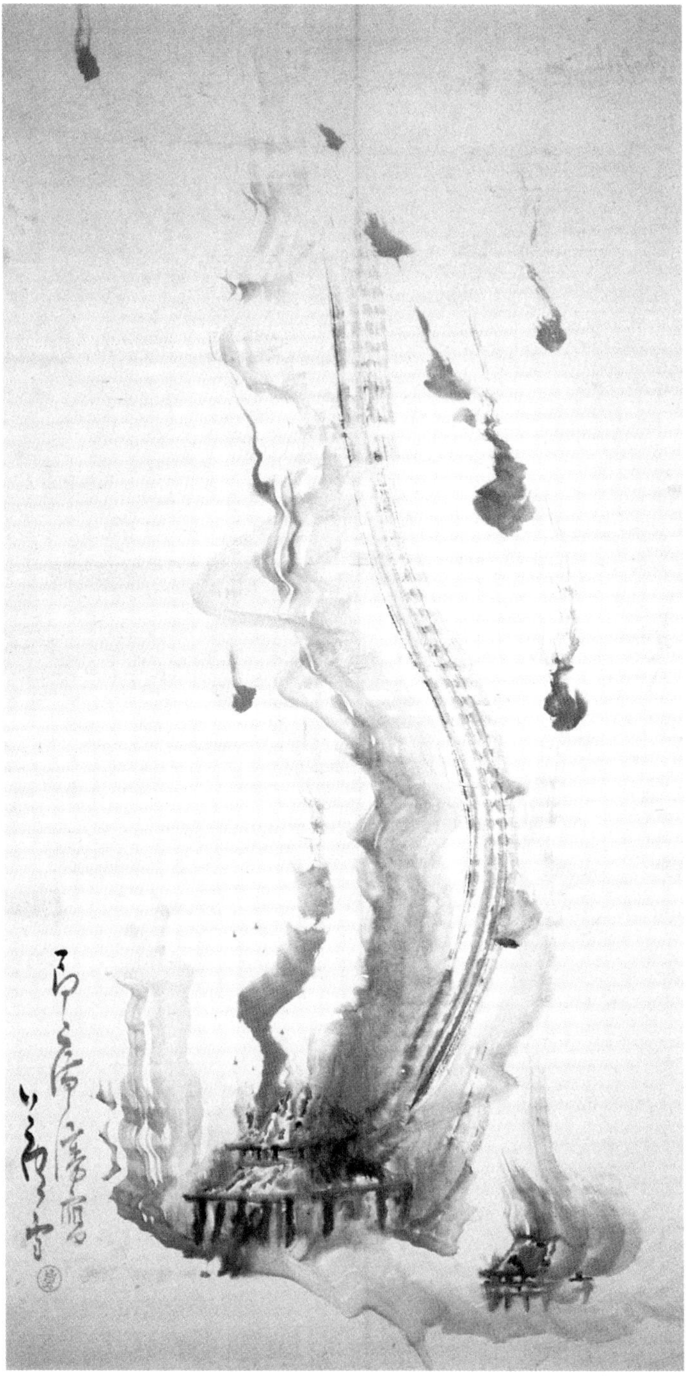

18 Nagasawa Rosetsu, *Destruction of the Great Buddha Hall by Fire*, 1798, hanging scroll, colour on paper. Japan's greatest temple (and the largest wooden building on earth) goes up in flames.

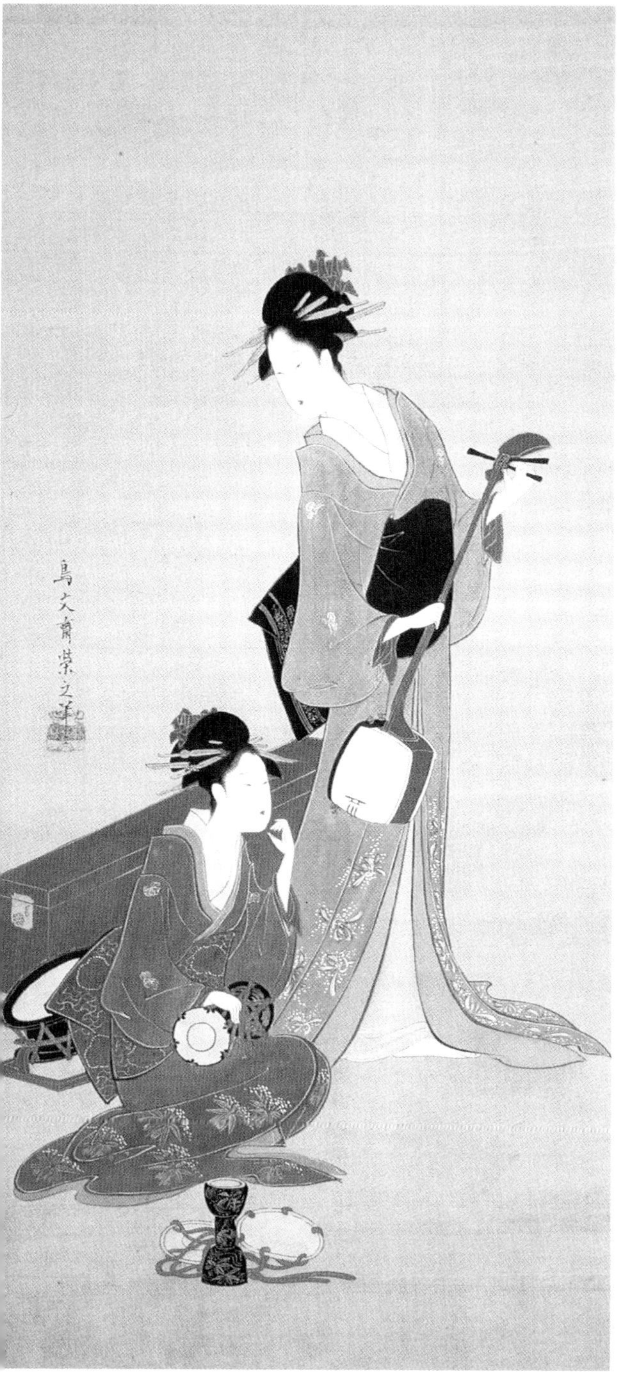

9 Chōbunsai Eishi, *Two Beauties with Musical Instruments*, mid-1780s, anging scroll, colour on paper. This picture captures the flamboyant roticism of the Tenmei era.

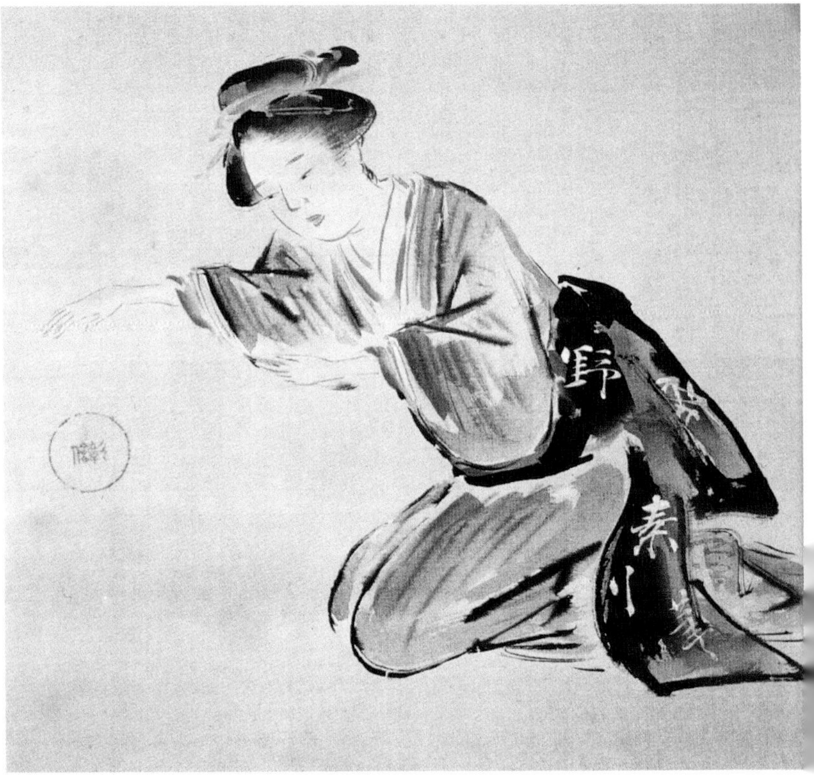

20 Kano Sōsen Naganobu, *Woman Playing with a Ball*, *c.* 1830, hanging scroll, colour on paper. The woman's sash is inscribed 'painted by Kano Sōsen', while the ball, which reads 'Naganobu', is the artist's seal.

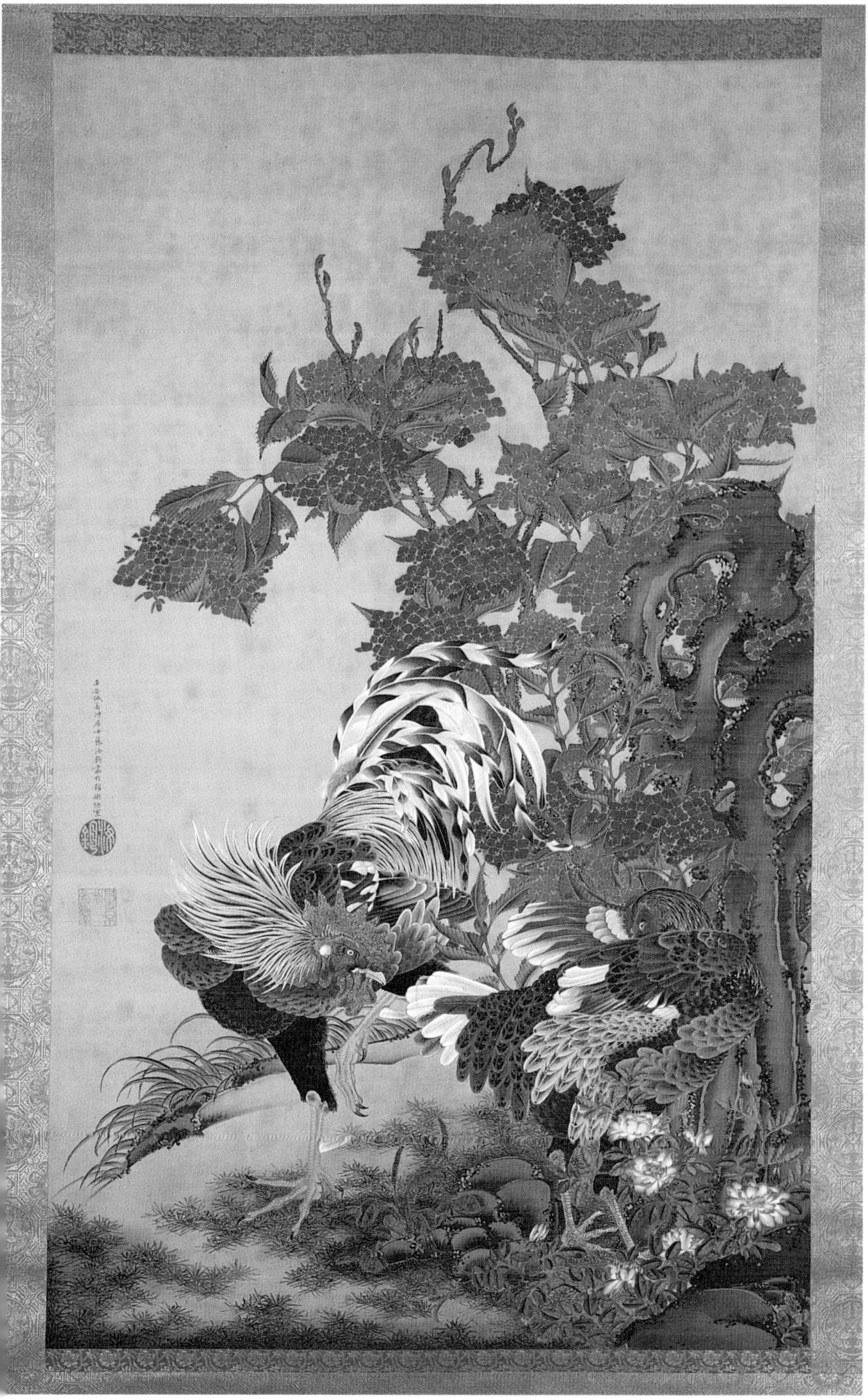

1 Itō Jakuchū, *Cock and Hen among Hydrangeas*, c. 1765, hanging scroll, olour on silk. Jakuchū kept a chicken run outside his atelier.

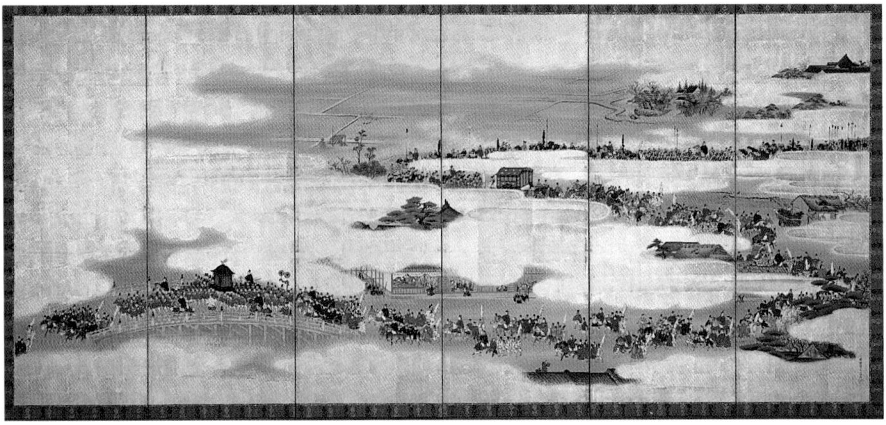

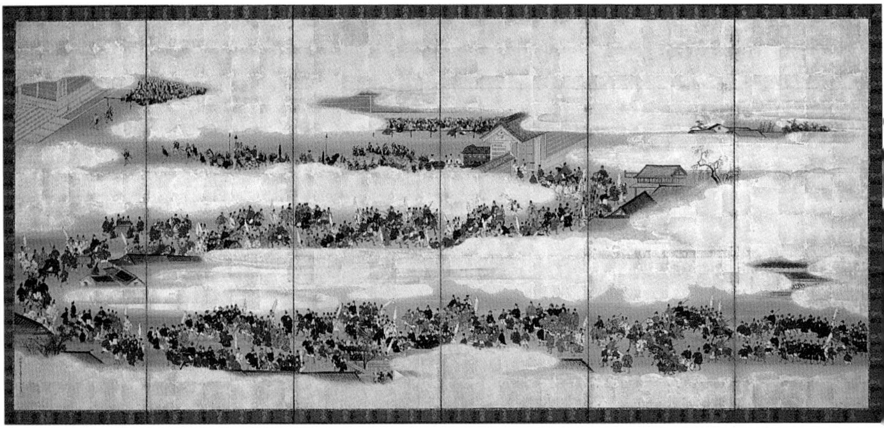

22, 23 Yoshimura Shūkei, *Tomohito Returning to the Capital over Sanjō Bridge*, 1790, pair of six-fold screens, colour on paper. The shujo processed magnificently back to the Dairi on the 22nd of the 11th month 1790.

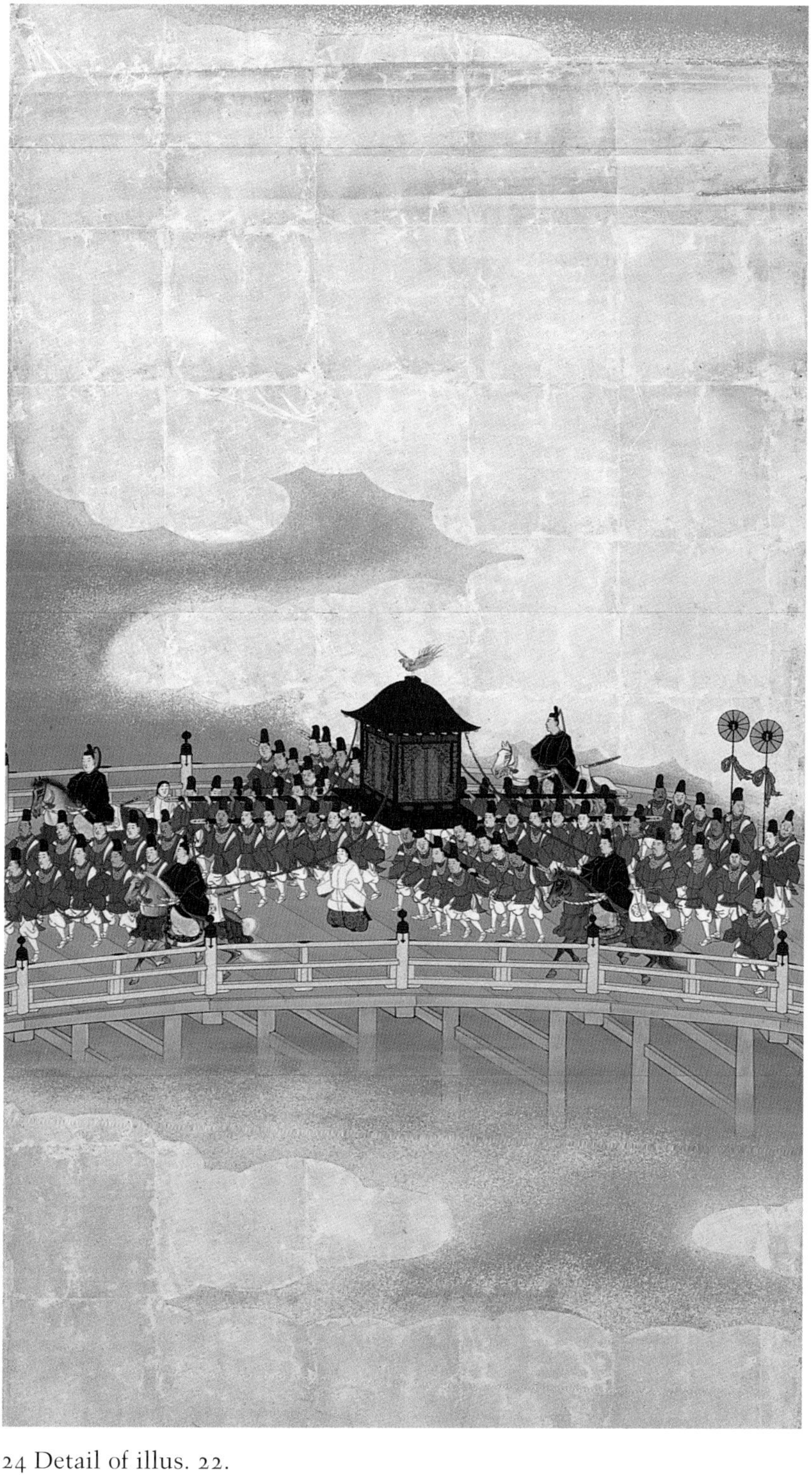

24 Detail of illus. 22.

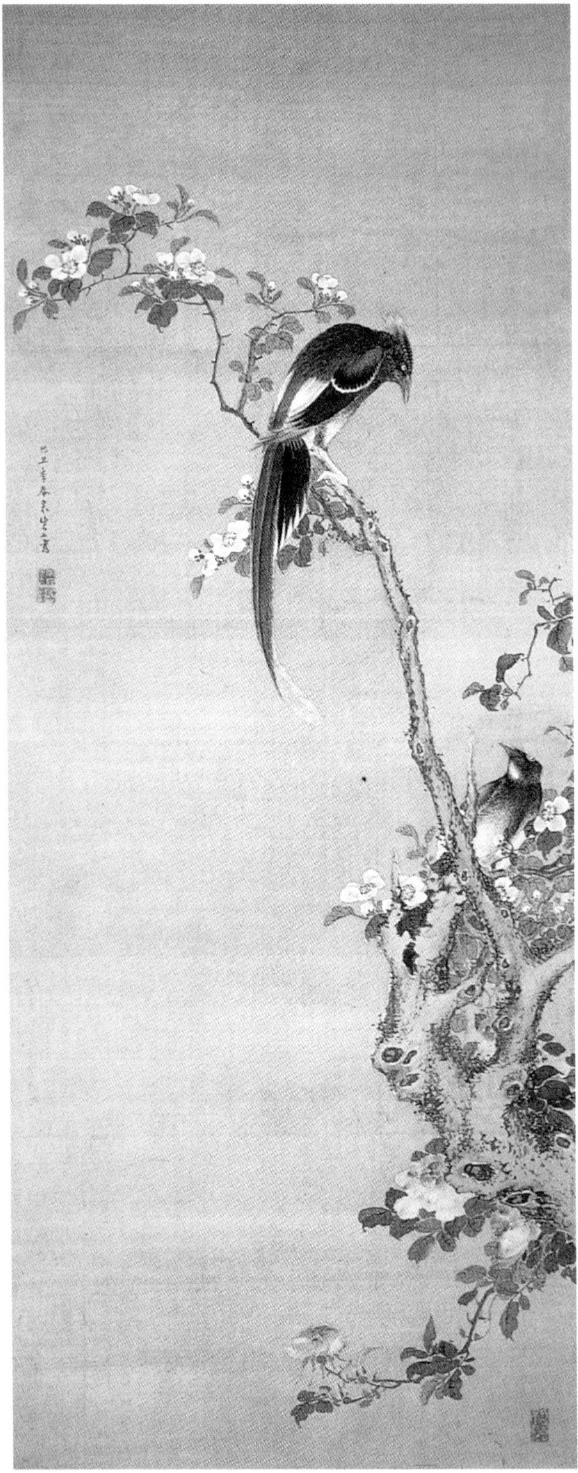

25 Sō Shiseki, *Small Birds on a Rosebush*, 1769, hanging scroll, colour on silk. To some, the detail of the brushwork was vitiated by inconsistencies of scale.

26 Kishi Ganku, *Crane in Snow*, *c.* 1790, hanging scroll, colour on silk. Precision of brushwork is coupled with attention to material forms.

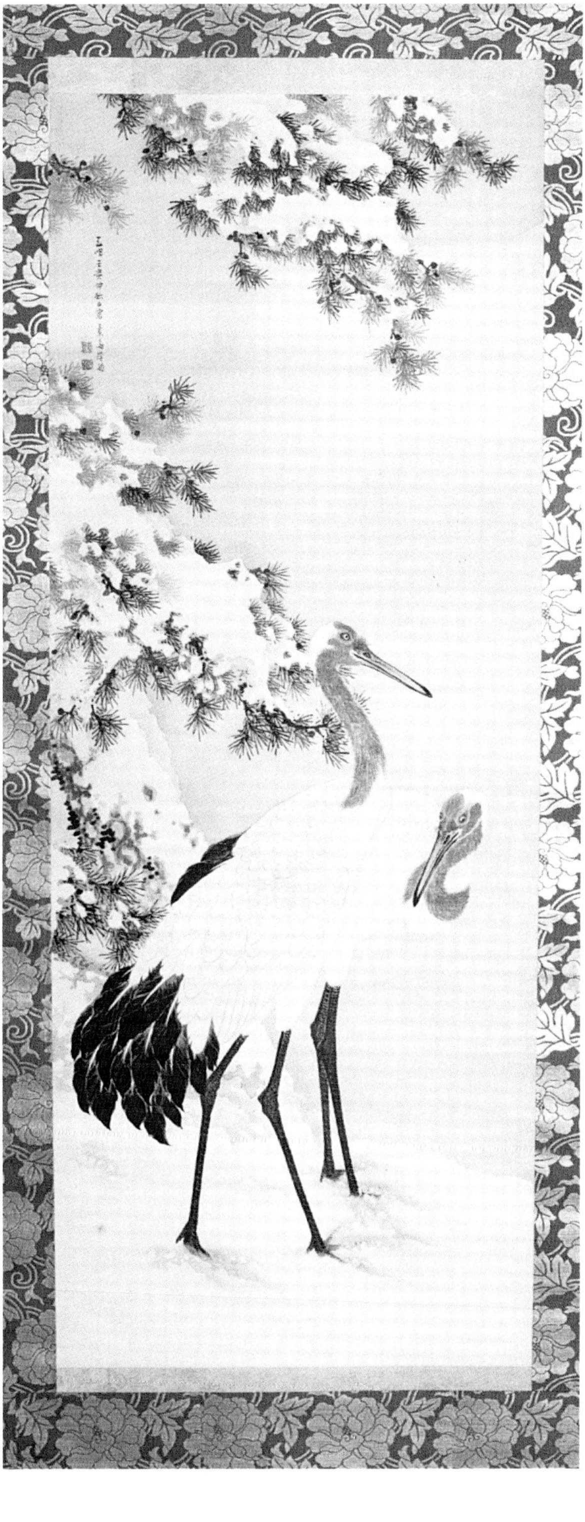

27 Detail of illus. 26.

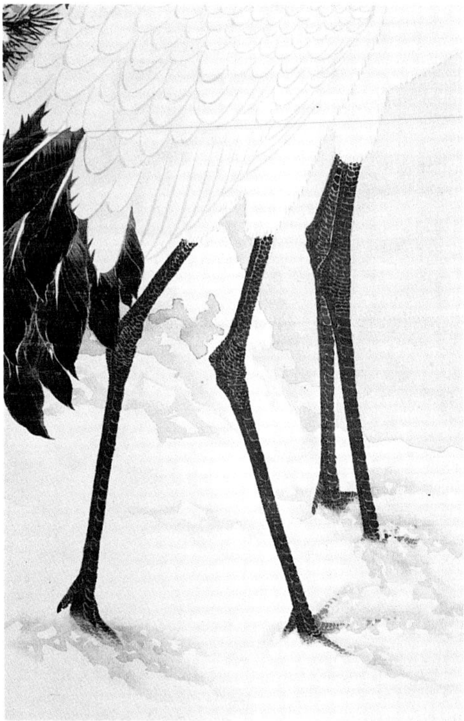

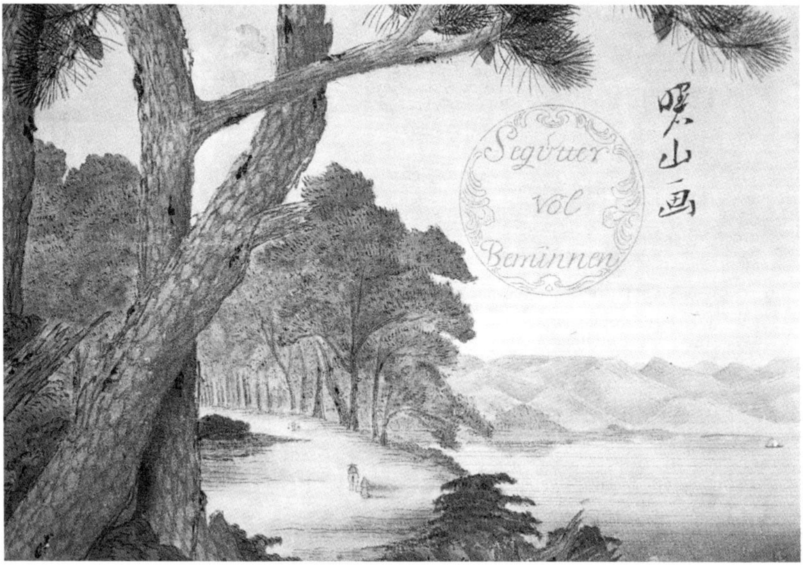

28 Satake Yoshiatsu, *Western Landscape*, c. 1780, hanging scroll, colour on paper. The daimyo of Akita began Westernist painting *c.* 1775, often using Dutch formats and seals; the figure with a yoke indicates that this is intended to be a European scene.

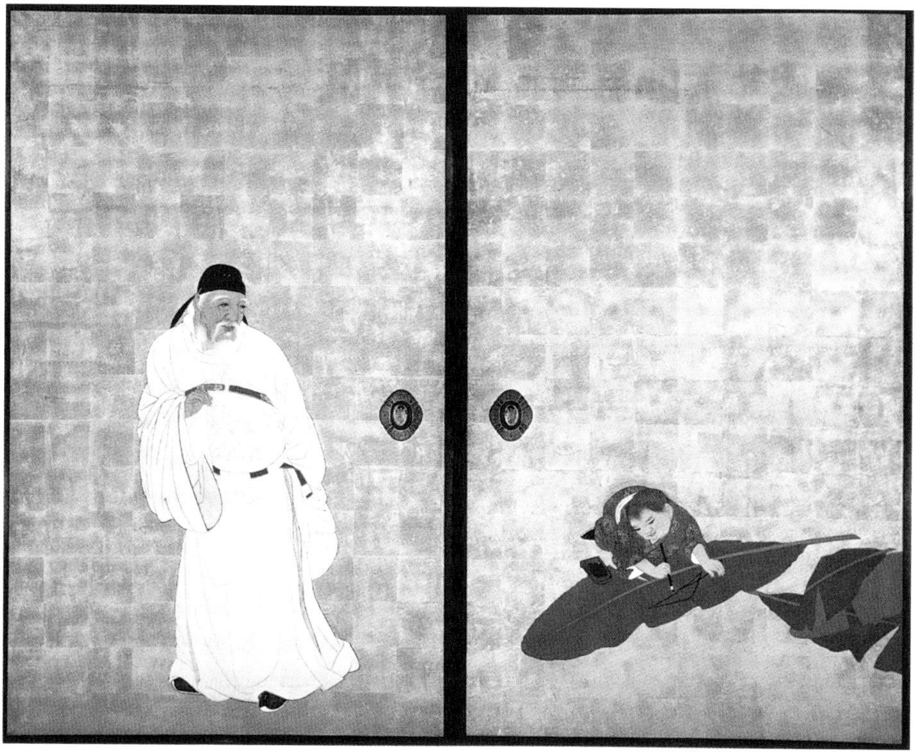

29 Maruyama Ōkyo, Section of *Guo Ziyi and his Grandchildren*, 1787, sliding doors, colour on paper. Formal works which nevertheless aspire to capture the bodily form of antique personages.

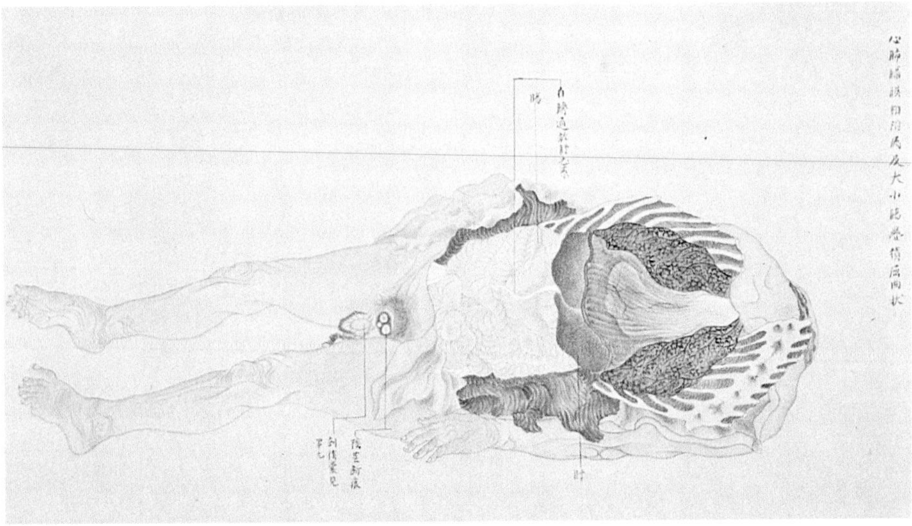

30 Yoshimura Ranshū, Section from *Heijirō zōzu*, 1783(?), handscroll, colour on paper. One of the fullest and most influential renditions of an autopsy in progress; the viewer winds through the scroll seeing the body in increasing states of dismemberment.

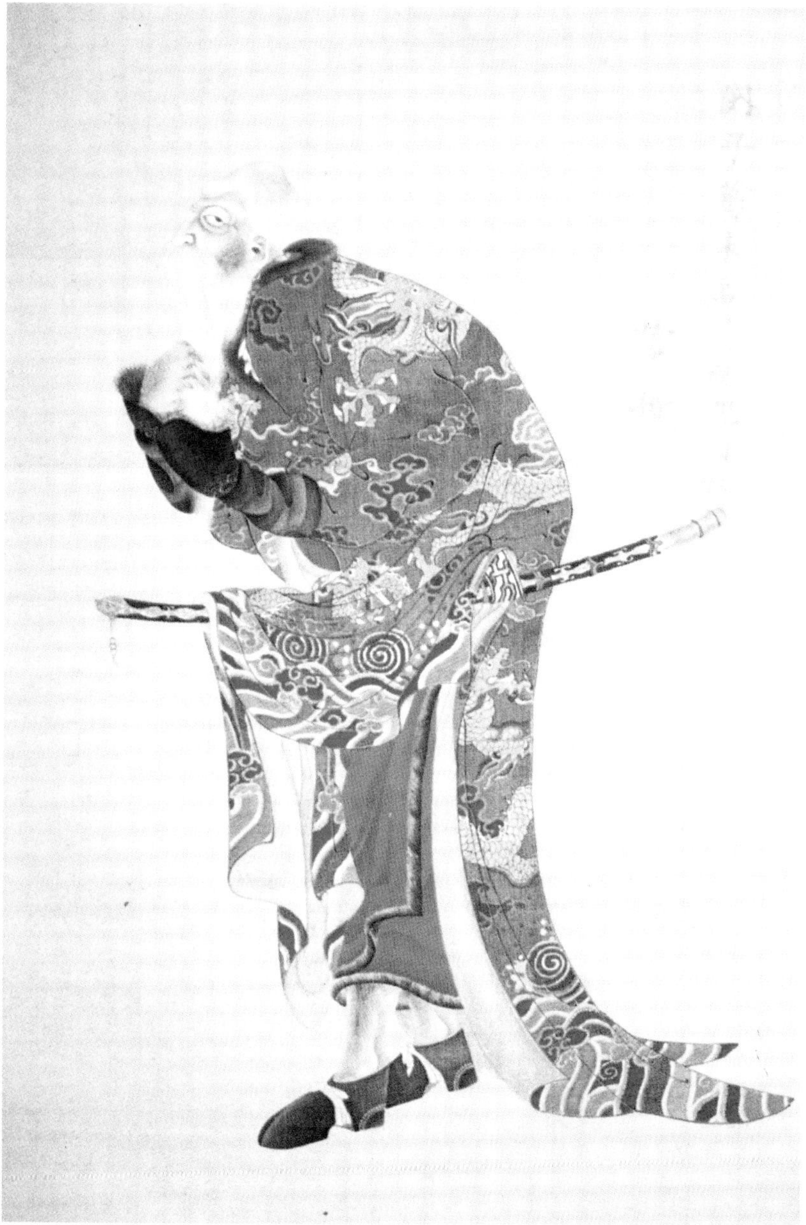

31 Kakizaki Hakyō, *Ainu Chief, Shonko*, 1790, hanging scroll, colour on silk. One of a series of portraits of Ainu leaders who fought on the Japanese side.

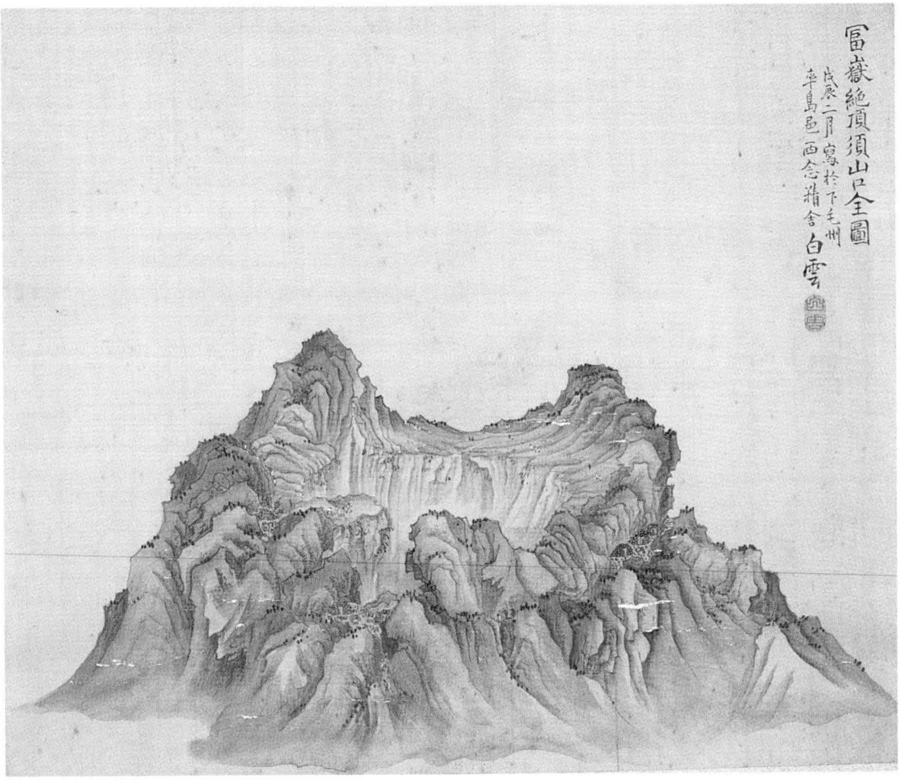

32 Hakuun, *Peak of Mt Fuji*, 1808, hanging scroll, colour on silk. Fuji seen with an unwonted close-up gaze.

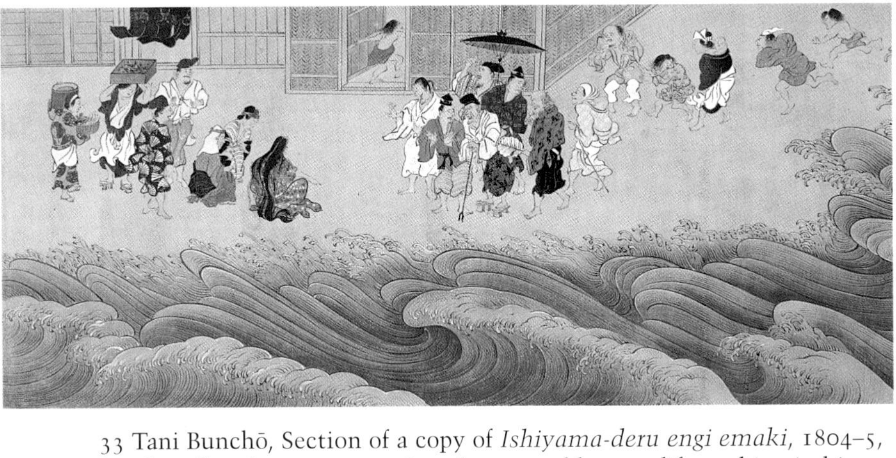

33 Tani Bunchō, Section of a copy of *Ishiyama-deru engi emaki*, 1804–5, handscroll, colour on paper. Bunchō was told to modify nothing in his copy.

Astronomie; the latest European astronomical equipment was procured, as well as Chinese and Japanese pieces.[36] The building was ritually protected and so declared off-limits to women, and it was lit at night by hundreds of oblatory candles, supplied as the shogun's personal gift. Being lunar, the calendar had to be reset frequently and had become highly wayward through the 1770s, prompting calls for a general reparation. But the new observatory reaped little reward, and the disjointedness of Heaven and earth grew more apparent. Civic rituals were mismatched or thwarted, even agricultural practices did not sit where they calendrically should. In 1786, faults hit a tension that made the regime nearly snap apart. A near total eclipse occurred on New Year's day, which meant that the sun of the 'triple morning' (*mitsu no asa*, i.e. dawn of the year, month and day) declined to shine.[37] This preluded a year that saw a fire in which most of Edo was laid waste. When Baron van Reede (who had noticed the eclipse in Nagasaki) arrived in Edo in early spring, he was able to ride in his palanquin for almost an hour through total ruin; he reported loss of half the city, with a seven-mile strip burned out, including the shogunal palace.[38] Any renewal of efforts to interpret Heaven and calibrate it better was met with an equal and opposite force of heavenly recalcitrance. The calendar was finally reworked in 1798, based on Lalande, but the planets slid again, unlocked themselves, and within a decade the much-touted 'Kansei Calendar' was out.

Sadanobu's ousting of Okitsugu, which, as we have seen, was made easier by the assassination of the latter's son Okitomo, was at least partly possible also because of this mishandling of forecasts. The reverse peristalsis of the earth seen at Asama continued, and rain and flood, heat and cold came and went without let or stay, escaping prediction and resisting preemptive steps unpredictably. One may wish to see the influence of El Niño here, which also affected Europe, provoking, it has been argued, the hunger that sparked the French Revolution.[39] But the mythical constructs of the shogunal states gave a clear obligation to rulers to lessen such blows by virtuous conduct and careful performance of rites. Headship of the shogunal council could be given to Sadanobu because of his clever projection of himself as the sole ruler exonerated by Heaven: his state of Shirakawa had avoided the awful series of events.[40] Whether or not this was fact is unsure, but it was much bruited and served to construct Sadanobu as a 'virtuous prince' (*meikun*), one divinely mandated to rule.

Shirakawa had actually been hit as badly as anywhere, but Sadanobu's wise interventions had averted all loss of life. Heaven pulled its punches for good kings or, otherwise put, good rule absorbed the occasional jolts that Heaven inevitably gave. Sensitivity to suffering and avoidance of loss of common life were measures of a prince's fitness. The name of the new era, Kansei, declared in 1789 after Sadanobu came to power, means, as we have seen, 'lenient rule'. Lenience implies care and attention to underlings, including sparingness in doling out punishment and avoidance of anything harsh. Samurai were educated in such mythologies. The daimyo of Yonezawa issued a memorandum in similar vein, which also seems to demonstrate the elite's absorption of anatomical language. 'It is right that there should be degrees of high and low', he wrote, 'and yet everyone's guts and vital organs are the same', and so he made a public show of having his son and heir eat peasant gruel; the straitened people, on hearing this, 'wept tears of gratitude', which was certainly better than having them riot.[41] Scapegoats were singled out too, like the son of the daimyo of Nakatsu, quoted in the epigraph to this chapter, who when told that the farmers were starving riposted, amid peals of laughter, that they could surely eat field birds.[42] The 'virtuous ruler' mythology was easily wheeled in for fraudulent show. The governor of Nagasaki, for example, while hoarding the best for himself, built a few token granaries for public distribution and, although he stocked them inadequately, sited them with maximum visibility. This purely iconic gesture was dismissed as done 'to curry favour with the authorities'; the Nagasaki governorship was one of the most lucrative in the shogunal bureaucracy and no incumbent wished to be relieved of it prematurely.[43]

International Prestige

The cynical remark about the Nagasaki granaries was made by the Dutch East India Company's leader, Petrus Chassé. His debunking was based on his understanding of the quite different European configurations of state. It is possible some Nagasakiites were fooled, and probable that faraway Edo allowed itself to be. What few of the Europeans meditated on was how their presence in the Tenka was dovetailed into similar symbolic purposes. They too functioned as emblems of supply as they seemed to promise a flow of goods from the ends of the earth. There was also more for, in Confucian theory, virtue attracts. Lesser breeds were pulled to the citadels of the righteous by the magnet of virtue. The coming of Europeans, and also of Chinese, Koreans and Ryūkyūans, was essential for trade but was also part of the Tokugawa propaganda of moral worth. Real cycles of trade fluctuated, but the symbolic value of foreign peoples remained generally high. In practical terms, copper was the export item that drew the Europeans, who had little desire to participate in emblematics they did not understand and saw as tiresome and expensive.[44] But from the Tokugawa point of view these were crucial. Even the basic trading commodity copper, precious seams of which coursed under the soil, could be proposed as Heaven's gift to the shogunate, as elements in the economy of virtue that drew the foreigners near. Possession of natural wealth was not merely of minerological importance, and it outweighed in signification its monetary worth. The superfluity of metals was a sign of goodness and also a sign of peace, for it meant weapons were not being forged. The mythical *baku* which eats metals was said to become dormant in times of war, and the Tokugawa nodded at this by riddling their architectural monuments with sculptures of *baku*.[45] But without virtue, metal would not only be put to the wrong uses, it would sink into the ground and become elusive. It is not hard to imagine the horror felt from the mid-eighteenth century when miners found themselves turning up only unworkable slag. In the late 1760s copper veins were already declared to be on the point of exhaustion.[46] The Europeans mooted pulling out of Japan. They persisted for another dozen years until in 1782, Isaac Titsingh, then leader, wrote that as profits had now 'virtually petered out', trade must cease.[47] (In the event, the Company persisted more.)

An intriguing coincidence had occurred about a decade before in Akita, the main mining region. Hiraga Gennai was summoned there in 1773 to advise on deep-shaft pumping, about which he had learned in Nagasaki from the Dutch.[48] The yield of his trip was ultimately zero for copper extraction (Heaven cannot so easily be manipulated) but significant for painterly representation. It was in Akita that Gennai met Odano Naotake, and since he knew Genpaku and was aware he was looking for a likely artist to produce the illustrations for the *New Anatomical Atlas*, Gennai took Naotake back to Edo with him. Satake Yoshiatsu, Naotake's prince, gave permission for this unusual alteration to his hereditary duties and became interested in the Western mode himself, leading to the wider phenomenon of the Akita Western-style school of art, *Akita ranga*, that Yoshiatsu also practised, working under the name of Shozan (see illus. 28).

Still, Akita's finances became parlous. Its copper dwindled and the evidence of travellers to the region was of ever crueller conditions. People were warned not to tread its paths at night in case they stepped in the mulch of the unseen dead, rotting at the wayside; the air was filled with continual stenches.[49] In 1778, as if in cosmic plaint, the command centre of the Akita copper-belt, Kubota Castle, was struck by lightning and burned to the ground, forcing Satake Yoshiatsu to flee for his life.[50]

Loss of copper meant destitution for Akita and for the shogunal finances which relied heavily on it, but it was more importantly an assault on a pillar of Tokugawa iconography. If the land were no longer precious, the shogunate could not welcome the international community or ensure the rhetoric of virtue continued. Exhaustion of copper would render the Tenka an unvisited tundra on the edge of the world, as exhaustion of silver had already threatened to do in the early seventeenth century. In 1764, following a scare about copper shortages, the East India Company cancelled its annual diplomatic visit to Edo in protest. This would have been the first time the shogun was not greeted in springtime by foreign peoples for a century and a half. The Company was finally persuaded to come, so the citizenry were spared the inference that Heaven had declined to supply their errant rulers. Although the 1764 procession went ahead, the rituals hid the grim reality that only 6,000 piculs of copper were available for export: barely half the former sum. Chinese traders, who did not send legates to Edo but who bought copper, had their allocation slashed to 5,000 piculs.[51]

Threat and counter-threat continued, centred around availability of copper. In 1782 no scheduled East Indiaman docked in Nagasaki, causing consternation that the Dutch had made good their threat to abandon Japan as economically (and hence ritually) worthless. In 1783 and 1784, only one of the two expected ships came. Non-arrival was due to adverse weather in the China Seas and British aggression (the Fourth Anglo-Dutch War spanned the years 1780–84), but this was not how the situation was read locally. Profit continued to slump even when peace returned, until Titsingh suggested sending two ships every three years rather than annually – a proposal roundly rejected by the shogunate, even though it had little to sell.[52] The population of Nagasaki got wind of these discussions and went *en masse* to their parochial temples for three solid days of prayer that the European traders would remain amongst them.[53]

The Company kept quiet about its own political problems, but the domestic troubles of the Japanese states had parallels beyond their confines. That some larger danger was stalking the outside world became increasingly clear. In 1788, for the first time ever, Chinese junks arrived in Nagasaki with cannon on deck (owing to the Formosan War).[54] A major power shift was underway in Europe and its Asian colonies, which required fighting. The Anglo-Dutch wars were admitted, but Europe's greatest *débâcle* – the French Revolution – was not mentioned in Japan until 1794.[55] In 1795, the French Armée du

Nord invaded the Netherlands and annexed them. The stadholder, William V, fled to England; he commended his overseas possessions, colonies, ports, harbours and ships to the British Crown in the Circular Note of Kew, which had far-reaching implications for the Company and for Japan.[56] The Dutch East India Company was nationalized and its network went into shock; three years later it was terminated. The next head of the Dutch station, Willem Wardenaar, was obliged to travel to Japan aboard a borrowed US ship, the *Massachusetts*, and had to clear up the mess left by his thieving, and probably murdered, predecessor, Gijsbert Hemmij (see below); Wardenaar left in 1803.[57] In 1806 Louis Bonaparte became 'King of Holland'. Two years later the British man-o'-war *HMS Phaeton*, one of the strongest craft in the Royal Navy, being a ship of the first rate, took advantage of the entitlement received at Kew and entered Nagasaki brandishing its multiple cannon.[58] The *Phaeton* made to seize the Company's concession in the name of George III, with 'all kinds of warlike engines, balls made of crooked iron nails hammered together, copper balls to be fired red-hot, etc, etc', as the Nagasaki magistrate's diary reported; this put everyone's 'loins out of joint' from fear.[59] The British intended to sink any Dutch ships in port, although sickness among the crew and the absence of any Dutch vessel in dock at the time curtailed this vainglorious venture, and they withdrew after inflicting only minor insults on the city and liberating the Dutchmen they had unlawfully arrested.[60]

The Dutch could not hold their own. In 1797 a US ship, the *Eliza*, 'a small strange ship, manned by an unfamiliar sort of black people', arrived and was met by 'an extraordinary display' of official anger when it was discovered to be falsely flagged with the Dutch tricolour and worse – an indication of how seriously rituals and myths were taken – to be carrying no auspicious gifts for the shogun.[61] The Americans tried again in 1799 with the *Eliza*, in 1800 with the cheekily-named *Emperor of Japan* (i.e. the shogun), and the *Franklin*, also giftless, which 'caused much muttering at court' (four watches were produced impromptu from the last ship, but the shogunate brusquely refused them).[62] The exclusivity that had characterized international trade for 150 years started to crack. Hemmij had colluded to erode this on the Japanese side by opening secret negotiations to trade directly with the daimyo of Satsuma, Shimazu Shigehide (whose daughter had married Ienari). This flagrant breach was likely to go ahead until the shogunate began preparations for war on Satsuma (Ienari and Shigehide being estranged), leading the daimyo to back down. Some relevant people were impaled, others decapitated.[63] Titsingh had already been in secret communication with this same Shigehide and remained in contact after his departure from Japan, corresponding effortlessly thanks to the daimyo's excellent command of Dutch. These letters and their contents are lost, but when British officials in India were made aware of them they offered Titsingh fully £20,000 to divulge this chink in Japan's isolationism. He declined.[64] Even before this, the shujo, Tomohito, had felt things might go his way and put out feelers to trade directly with Europe, circumventing the shogunate.[65] It was surely not mere chance that Tomohito laid on one of his great charitable acts (the distribution of cash prizes to anyone publicly encircling his mansion as an act of veneration) on the day that the Dutch contingent led by Romberg arrived in Keishi.[66] It was on his return from a visit to Edo that Hemmij died in suspicious circumstances, some said poison, some said suicide, leaving massive debts incurred by his high-level finaglings.[67] Wardenaar then took a leaf out of the same book and conspired to undermine from the European side; he joined the British, returning to Japan in 1813 with Stamford Raffles (bringing the shogun an elephant, although Wardenaar had evidently forgotten that Nagasaki's wharf facilities could not handle large cargoes without transshipping or else did not know that no elephant would jump overboard, so the beast was returned).[68]

The point was, notwithstanding sabre-rattling, that whether Japanese ports were visited or not, which ones, by whom and what the foreigners did there, were matters over which the shogunate exercised a disintegrating degree of control.[69]

Ritual Roadways

The main path for transit within the Japanese states was the Tōkaidō. It was famous for its well-tempered regulation and its celebrated and often-depicted 53 stations, or official check-points (Hemmij was at the 26th, Kakegawa, when he died). The Tōkaidō was functional but was also used for all ritualized traffic, whether international or daimyo bodies. The road joined Edo with Keishi, and then Osaka, and was the spine through which the cords of the Tokugawa system passed. Without it, nothing circulated. The normal route from Nagasaki was by water up to Osaka and then along the Tōkaidō to Edo. The Tōkaidō was probably the most excellent highway anywhere in the world, far superior to any at that time in Europe. The well-travelled Swedish physician Carl Peter Thunberg said when he took it in 1776 he had 'never made so pleasant a journey as this'.[70] (Thunberg – though he did not yet know it – was bound for an encounter with Jun'an and Hoshū, who had shortly before brought out the *New Anatomical Atlas*.'

Thunberg noted the speed of movement along the Tōkaidō but also the choreography of it all. People kept scrupulously to the correct side (the left, as was not yet common in Europe), and he felt it 'would be of the greatest utility' to copy the system, since Europeans 'frequently travel upon the roads with less discretion and decorum'. The Tōkaidō was a prize shogunal possession, built and regulated by them, carved extraterritorially out of the states through which it passed, and pulsing along its length with regular distance-markers – a hillock topped by a pine-tree.

Social hierarchy was respected on the Tōkaidō and it was not a place where travel liberated one from established codes. Lodgings and horses went to those of highest status first, and all passage stopped when an important person went past. Diplomats were carefully treated. In 1764, when the *wang* of the Chosŏn (i.e. the king of Korea) sent an embassy to congratulate Ieharu on the latter's elevation to shogun four years earlier (the received practice), they necessarily took the Tōkaidō. Such a ritual had not occurred since after the investiture of Ieshige as ninth shogun in 1748. In preparation, hostels of a splendid kind were prepared and fords were bridged, turning the Tōkaidō into a scintillating ribbon of easy transit, unwinding across the landscape. The Koreans made fine progress and were no doubt impressed. While they were in Edo, however, before they had availed themselves of the facilities on their return, the highway was hit by furious gales. Every single bridge was washed away and most of the hostels wrecked.[71] Human depravity then coupled with heavenly disaster to make the embassy a fiasco: the Koreans' hostel in Edo was burned down while they were in it, probably through carelessness, and on their way back their belongings were stolen in Osaka and the deputy ambassador, Tae Ch'onzong, was murdered in his bed. This last crime met appropriate punishment, with the nails and teeth of the proclaimed perpetrator (not necessarily the real guilty party) being pulled out before he was beheaded in view of the ambassador; the criminal's brother suffered the same treatment, although it was conceded he had played no role.[72] The shogunate had intended to mount an exhibition of the sophistication of the Tenka but ended up showing how lightly they were regarded by Heaven and how uncouth were their people. When the next embassy was proposed for 1788 to congratulate Ienari on succession, it was repeatedly delayed through fractiousness on both sides. Finally, the Koreans seemed likely to arrive in 1796, and the shogunate commanded the best European glassware and cloth to deck their halls of state as if Japanese products, which had formerly been used, were too crude.[73] They then demanded first refusal on all top-grade items from the next in-coming Dutch ship

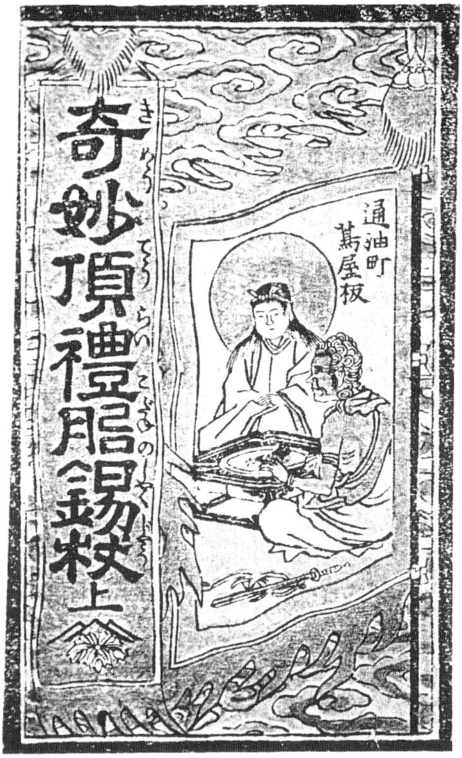

34 Cover of Jippensha Ikku, *Kimyō chōrai kodane no shakujō*, 1795, monochrome woodblock print. The Tsutaya publishing house gave several comic books the running cover of a Korean ambassadorial flag.

('100 pieces of silk cloth and as many rarities as the ship might [carry]'). Alas, the vessel failed to arrive because, the Dutch stated, 'the war with France has still not come to an end', making the seas deadly, and 'the poor exports from here [Nagasaki] could not satisfy the markets in Europe', making Japan not worth the trouble.[74] The Chosŏn court aborted the trip anyway. After 1764 the Koreans stayed away until 1811, and even then concluded their protocols on the isle of Tsu without landing in Japan proper.

Dutch parades were inherently less stately than the Korean ones since the East India Company did not represent the Dutch stadholder. They were also more routine because they were held annually rather than only after each shogun's investiture. But similar lapses began to dog the rituals. In 1778 the Company leader, Hendrik Duurkoop, died on board ship while still bound for Japan, annulling the disembarkation rituals, which was thought so baleful that the Europeans were requested to dress up another of their number to impersonate the deceased until after a decent interlude, so as not to impugn the shogunate. The Edo visit that spring had to be performed by Arend Feith and

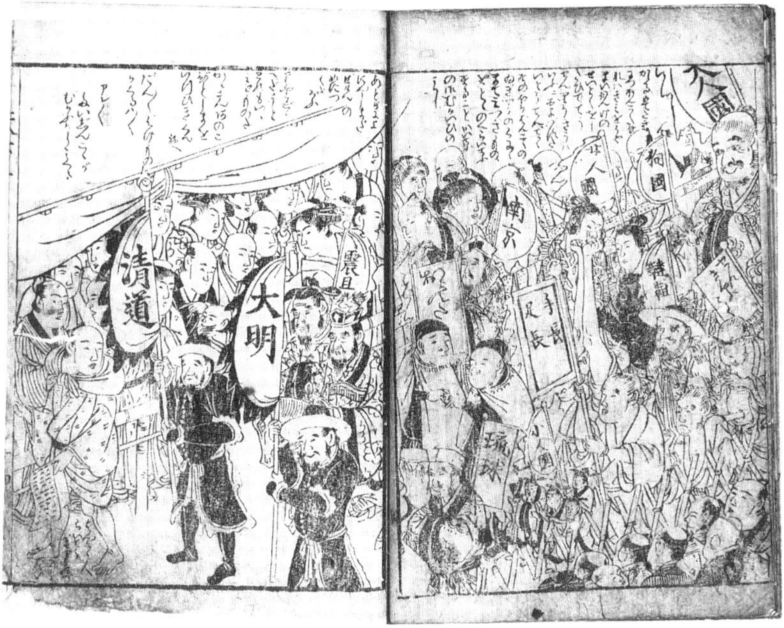

35 Eishōsai Chōki, Pages from Tōrai Sanna, *Tenka ichimen kagami umehachi*, 1789, monochome woodblock prints. Ambassadors of the 'ten thousand nations' throng the Tokugawa court.

Caspar Romberg as stand-ins.[75] The death of Hemmij at Kakegawa was a far more serious blemish. Covering up the evidence seemed the best response. Duurkoop's burial in distant Nagasaki did not arouse too much attention (although Shiba Kōkan published a picture of the odd Western-shaped grave after his trip there), but Kakegawa was on the Tōkaidō itself. Hemmij's body was therefore interred some way off the highway in a temple called the Tennen-ji, which kept the relic of international friction away from the general tourist trail; it was not advertised to travellers, although the more intrepid did visit the grave.[76] Again, Heaven struck at attempts to mitigate its auguries and, four days after Hemmij's quiet burial, the Dutch entourage learned by runner that their activities in Japan had been further assaulted and all their buildings in Nagasaki entirely lost to fire.[77]

Unlucky coincidences vitiated several European embassies about this time. The worst deserves special attention. In 1779 the Company arrived with a fine present for Ieharu's son, Iemoto: a Persian horse.[78] Iemoto, who was sixteen, was the heir apparent (*seishi*). He took the horse out but fell off it, and it then fell on him, and the boy pumped

36 Shiba Kōkan, *Dutchmen at Edo Castle*, c. 1790, hanging scroll, colour on silk. The Dutch walk around the shogunal seat in wonder; the inscription reads 'You must eat to live not live to eat.'

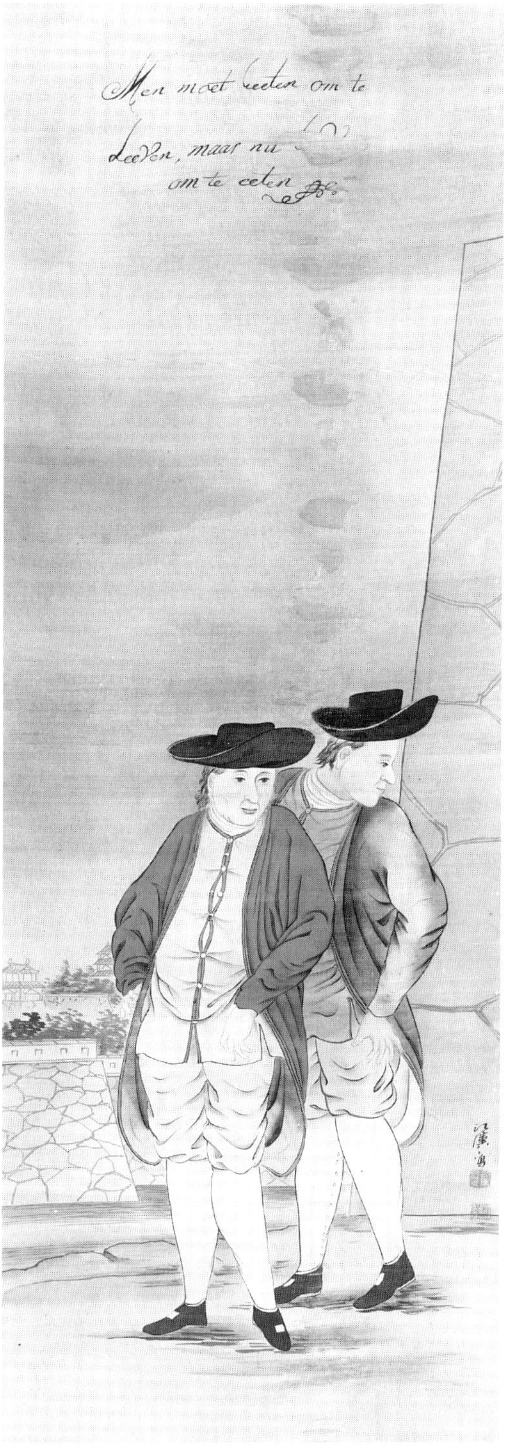

two pints of blood into the soil before he could be brought home. Every government temple was required to pray for him, but to no avail, for Iemoto died. The Company record states, 'the emperor [shogun] is completely overcome with grief. In his anguish he has slain several high officials with his sword and other high officials have had to cut open their bellies'.[79] Foreigners wrote what others could only whisper. Feith, in Edo, won admiration for stripping the accessories off his clothes and donning simulated European mourning dress for the next week.[80] But even this hardly met the enormity of the fact. Tactlessly, for years to come, the Dutch continued to press the shogun for a 'reciprocal present' to match their wretched horse until, after fifteen years of nagging, they were politely advised to desist.[81]

The Tokugawa battened down. Daimyo processions to Edo were called 'alternate attendance' (*sankin kōtai*) and generally made every other year, so that the regional princes spent half their time in the shogunal capital and half in the capital of their own state. In 1789 these were cut, and daimyo were told they need only attend one third as often.[82] The Company was similarly asked to visit only every third year, and on the first of these reduced showings, 1794, they were told they need come only once in five years.[83] The Chosŏn embassy, as already stated, was cancelled. It was Sadanobu who took the final decision, feeling that, in this climate, the visual impact was counterproductive before a rancorous people and was not dependable either. The Tokugawa forewent their pageantry. Rather than being seen amiss, they preferred not to be seen at all.

Curtailing expenditure was one reason for reducing the embassies, and to do so fitted in with a rhetoric of 'virtuous' modesty. But the real issues related to pride and symbol. It was argued that the Chosŏn mission was well done without, since the Tokugawa had never dissuaded the Koreans from carrying banners reading 'Clean and Fresh' (*reirei*) (i.e. we are and you are not), 'Purify our Path' (*seidō*) and 'Regional Tour of Inspection' (*junshi*), as if the Tenka were just a dirty outpost in their own state. Precedent allowed for these flags, but they rankled and, with the shogunate on the defensive, Sadanobu wanted them done away with. The Osaka scholar Nakai Chikuzan submitted to him the tart suggestion that as the slogans 'amply demonstrate what they think of our states', and as 'they deem it immensely necessary for us to clear the roads for them, imagining the diplomatic gifts [*chōkō*] they leave for us in Tsu will make us delirious with enthusiasm',[84] the embassies should be ended. Sadanobu agreed. He was also uneasy at how the Koreans wore their court crowns, even in front of the shogun himself, without doffing them, and how their ritual dress on the whole looked more noble than the Japanese equivalent.[85]

The people mocked. As preparations were beginning for the (already delayed and subsequently abandoned) Korean arrival of 1796, the Edo publishing house operated by the energetic Tsutaya Jūzaburō issued a series of comic books with a running-cover depicting the embassy, taunting the shogunate with a vision of the political uplift they had failed so long to enjoy (illus. 34).[86] Already in 1789, after the initial postponement, this publishing house had ridiculed the authorities for diplomatic ineptitude in a more sustained parody. The house had put out a book by Tōrai Sanna spoofing the shogunate's down-graded international profile under the title *The Mirror of the Tenka: the Plum Pot (Tenka ichimen kagami umehachi)*. The title left no one in doubt, for a plum pot was Sadanobu's family crest. In the story, a bumbling minister called 'Lord Suga' attempts to order the states; although the overt reference is to the tenth-century bureaucrat and plum fancier Sugawara no Michizane, it is evident that this figure is Sadanobu in disguise.

Topsy-turvily, Sanna has the whole world thronging to the shogunal castle to bask in its moral sunshine. A veritable 'procession of ten-thousand states' (*bankoku gyōretsu*) descends on the gates: not only Koreans, Ryūkyūans and Dutch, but Ming, Nanking and Mongolian emissaries, as well as representatives of the lands of giants, midgets, long-arms and long-legs, dog-heads, delegates from the island of women and from the 'land of people with holes in their chests' (illus. 35). Sanna's illustrator, Eishōsai Chōki, depicted the motley crew headed by a banner indeed reading 'Purify our Path'. Sanna claimed, 'Japan was in so felicitous a condition they all came to her courts, bearing tribute, to witness the adulation secured for authority by my Lord Suga'.[87] To wit, Sadanobu was a fool. The shogunate had the book suppressed, and Sanna and Chōki were lucky to escape with no severer punishment.[88]

More congenial to Sadanobu, perhaps, would have been Shiba Kōkan's treatment of the same diplomatic theme. An undated painting of about this period shows two Europeans walking in the lee of Edo's castle walls, towers seen vaguely in the background (illus. 36). The men have alighted in the place, like birds of bright plumage, to take refuge in its guardian ethical force. An inscription above removes all hint of recent incompetence and stresses the modest virtue of the regime. Translated it reads, 'One must eat to live, not live to eat'. The two men are dressed as befits ambassadors, but Edo is not a place of extravagance or feasting; if regalement is not what it once was, this is because the shogunate is lenient to its people and spares expense. The motto is written in Dutch but was understood in Edo, as it had been published in 1783 by Ōtsuki Gentaku, the shogunal adviser on Western affairs, which gives a *terminus post quem* for this painting.[89]

Forcing Heaven's Hand

If problems began in the second half of the eighteenth century, this coincided with the reign of Ieharu, who became the tenth in the Tokugawa line in 1760. By chance, this was the year that an equally incomplete monarch ascended the English throne as George III. And of Ieharu it might with equal justice have been said, 'He ought never to have occurred / One can only wonder / At so grotesque a blunder'. George and Ieharu at least had the advantage over their predecessors of speaking the native language clearly: George II had been more comfortable in German, while Ieshige was nigh on incomprehensible because of speech impediments and was anyway 'almost an idiot'.[90] But Ieharu was not much to be proud of, neither robust nor intellectually promising, derided, often ill, and petulant. He has been defined as a 'pallid nonentity'; Jan Crans called him 'a lustful, lazy, and stupid man'; Titsingh said he had 'little sense'.[91] Ieharu rose late, snacked between meals and never went outside. Sadanobu tried to force him out of bed, to get him to leave off eating sweets and spend at least two hours each morning practising the martial arts. To make his point, Sadanobu banned the import of sugar (with severe consequences for the East India Company).[92]

Ieharu could neither motivate the present nor fulfil his debts to the past. When a once-in-a-lifetime visit was planned for him to Ieyasu's mausoleum in Nikkō, three days north of Edo, farmers came out and prevented his progress.[93] This was sad for a man whose official title included the phrase Subduer of Wild Peoples (*seii*). Ieharu could not get to Nikkō for the next three years and when he did accomplish the pilgrimage, in 1776, although he made the accompanying daimyo spend some 15,000 *ryō* apiece (making a grand total of 1,680,000 *rixdollars* by the European estimate – although the two currencies cannot be satisfactorily aligned) to ensure a fanfare, his preparations were inadequate, and the shelter he was staying in burned down.[94]

The trip to Nikkō was a sober chance to pay homage to the founder of the Tokugawa line. Few shoguns actually took it for want of time, so this ought to have been a high moment. The trip was necessitated, though, by Ieharu's inadequacy: Iemoto's death had left him without an heir, his only other son (and two was pathetically few for a shogun) having already died. Immediately after Iemoto's demise, the divinities of the Nikkō mountains had shown their scorn for the succession by causing the ancient tree that grew beside the mansion of the hereditary keeper of Ieyasu's mausoleum to crash down on to the building, killing both the warden and his son.[95] Sadly, another of the shogunal titles was Great Tree (*taijū*). The Tokugawa line, their symbol and patronal space, as it were, keeled over together.

The next summer Ieharu attempted to compel Heaven into a more generous mood, if not by acts of virtue (apparently beyond him) then by ruse. He ordered performance of the New Year's rituals – in summer! To Genpaku, who put this fact in his *Essays*, it was 'laughable'.[96] Heaven remained silent for eighteen months, mulling its response then, on the sixth day of the ninth month, it spoke. Smoke billowed from a side peak at Ieyasu's original mausoleum on Mt Kunō (where the first shogun had been buried before translation to Nikkō) and continued to pour out for three days. The smoke then abruptly stopped, and locals attributed this to the leniency of Ieyasu's guiding spirit. But like the dead shogun's body, what had begun on Kunō transferred to Nikkō, and that same day a violent snow storm hit the latter mausoleum and submerged the precincts; a fire then broke out. Rescue work was impeded by the weather, and by night, most of the compound and the surrounding town (40 sacred buildings, 83 city blocks) had smouldered to nothing.[97]

Climatic irregularities often worked in tandem with political accidents and were understood as part of the same moral order. Some years later, a freezing January was coupled with a rumour that Ieharu had died. Titsingh penned a sublime juxtaposition in his official log on 19 January 1788: 'it had been rumoured that the emperor [shogun] has died. The barometer stands at 37½ degrees Fahrenheit [4 degrees C]'.[98] Frigid conditions sealed the earth until spring, when Heaven aboutturned and began to sweat noxious influence from its pores. The weather did not drop below 90 degrees (30 degrees C) all summer. Sugar (a major import until Sadanobu's ban) melted in the European holds.[99] The heat also took its analogy in the shogun's person: swellings broke out across Ieharu's body and he suffered his periodic 'eruptions on the face'.[100]

When Ieharu really did die, three years later, he had occupied – though not graced – his office for 26 of his 49 years. Genpaku summed up this period of rulership: 'when those in positions of reverence behave with folly, how much the more likely are the lower orders to come together and whisper complaint'. Avoidance of 'folly' (*kikai*) was ensured by observance of the rituals that oiled humanity's points of contact with each other and with Heaven. Ritual meant doing what had been established since times past. But Ieharu was arbitrary. To

Genpaku, 'the shogunal house has behaved in a manner that does not equate with precedent'. He concluded, 'the humiliation of recent affairs can only be deplored'. Heaven was reckoning similarly and gearing down.[101]

Time and the Hour

It is important to stress that what has been exposed above is a *rhetoric* of disaster. But this rhetoric is not one imposed by the modern historian. Different spheres of engagement could be (and have been) proposed for the age, which, as I have said, is more normally celebrated as the period of the 'rise of the merchant'. But many who lived through those times saw only agony and wanted to add ever more to the lists of misery. It was good news, not bad, that was the kill-joy at this feast of monsters. The proper response to decline, for those among the elite, was to promulgate laws, to re-establish 'rites', awaken virtue and regenerate mores. This was best accomplished by a consideration of ancient documents and pictures, and a realignment of such practices as had warped over time. This is what Sadanobu wanted to do. Accordingly, one of the first events recorded in the careful construction of Genpaku's *Essays* was a fire in 1760 which utterly devoured the archives.[102]

The shogunal city was fed and heated by open braziers and built of wood, so it was highly susceptible to fire. The virtuous Yoshimune, the eighth shogun and one of the best, 'in his ineffable clemency' (Genpaku's words) had decreed that every house must possess a fireproof store so that when conflagration hit the city, as it regularly did, artefacts and records could be saved, allowing the traditions to survive. It was not homes, we should note, but repositories that were given this particular attention. In 1760, as never before, the stores baked and cracked, and documents, pictures, personal effects, books, ledgers, ritual instructions, instruments and heirlooms tumbled out into the flames. 'Only in this disaster', wrote Genpaku, 'were people's treasured possessions not spared, such that our ancient documents, down to the last remaining scrap, were swept away'. This 'absolutely shattering occurrence' removed all chance of restoration. Heinously, this occurred within days of Ieharu's accession.

The inauspicious timing was not lost on the population. Someone of mordant humour composed a verse in intricate puns, weaving the fire into the accession celebrations. On its surface, the verse seemed to read:

37 Illustration from Su Koppei, *Myōmyō kidan*, 1815, monochrome woodblock prints. Shibano Ritsuzan, Sadanobu's ideologue, greets a student; a clock stands nearby.

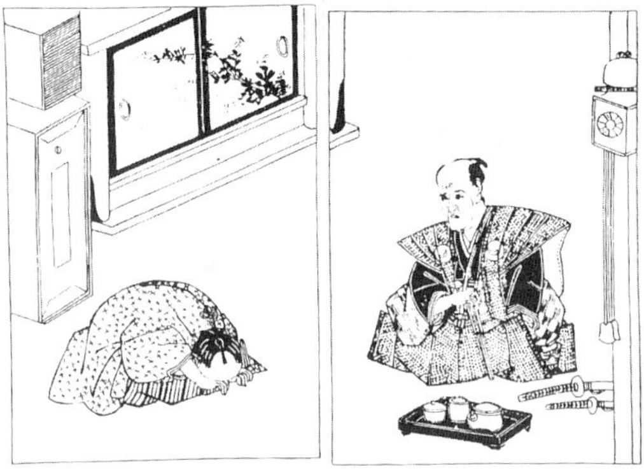

The sun is rising to right and left [in double happiness]
As today, the Great General of the Right [Ieharu]
Publicly inaugurates his august rule.

But the character for sun literally means 'fire', while 'publicly' (*oyake*) is nearly homophonous with 'greatly burned' (*ō-yake*); 'auspicious' (*medetaki*) slides out of 'dyed' (*somete*). Decoded, the verse goes,

Flames are rising to right and left
As today, the Great General of the Right
Begins his rule dyed in a vast conflagration.

The word-play cleverly orbits around Ieharu's official rank, which alone remains unchanged in both the readings. The shogun's persona is the hinge that swings the Edo cityscape from hope to abject misery. Ieharu might have offered some slim hope after his dribbling father, but in his beginning some already detected a final end.

Ieharu's period in office provided several interesting parallels with a past near enough to be recalled even without documentation. These were not edifying. One emerged in 1775, during the severest peasant revolt for a decade.[103] In the earlier case, a troop of hungry farmers had collected in Musashi and marched on Edo 'bellowing like whales', but they had been stopped 'by the virtue of Lord Ina'; convinced by his Coriolanian logic, they had dispersed. The next time, either the peasantry were of stiffer mettle or no lord had sufficient virtue, for when the farmers approached Edo, it was not an interlocutor that met them but a regiment. It opened fire and mowed them down, according to some testimonials leaving half a million dead. This marked a new and desperate contract between the populace and their rulers, for, as Genpaku wrote, 'since this august regime began, here was the first time we had heard of guns being used against the people'.

New and swingeing laws were passed. But hard on their heels came retraction. The shogunate lost its nerve. Tokugawa writ was not supposed to be so fleeting, but this was the period of the infamous 'three-day laws', so called by Edo wits because 'they are disregarded after that short period of time', as the diarist Buyō Inshi noted.[104] Yuasa Genzō also recorded the 'three-day laws' in his usual medical metaphors, stating 'what is commanded is not done, and what is condemned does not cease; this does untold harm to authority, and the sickness of the land cannot be healed by this treatment'.[105] Never mind three days, to Genpaku, 'in the morning they issue a law and in the evening they amend it'.[106] Legality became nebulous. Lower officials and magistrates 'are quickly disillusioned', wrote Inshi, for 'everyone knows the government merely issues writ whenever it feels the need of it'. That is, the obliteration of precedent had left vagary in its stead. 'There are those who ask themselves', wrote Genpaku, using understatement and unsourced quotation to accentuate his rebuke, 'what the government can be thinking of'. Non-samurai were more vulnerable to those in power, and Genpaku noted they 'simply gather together in groups and sigh'. Kōkan, a commoner, put it as openly as he could: 'the government does not seem to be helping itself with some of these new laws'.[107] The parameters of regulated life unhooked and fell away.

The most extraordinary example of shogunal vacillation occurred in the summer of 1787. Hordes of rioters burst through Edo's streets, bringing chaos right up to the castle walls in a rampage that lasted five days.[108] By the third afternoon, a thousand men were in detention. But there was no need for the mob to storm the bastille and liberate their comrades for, having filled up all its custodial units, the shogunate promptly let everyone out again, declaring no crime had been committed. The whole spate of mass violence was designated a 'squabble between individuals' (*kenka*), that is, outside shogunal jurisdiction. Soldiers were sent into the streets to distribute gifts of food in an ostentatious act of 'virtue' that must have rather lost its force for coming retroactively.

Unwittingly, the shogunate had announced that it was now operating *in time*, no longer in perpetuity. The once unthinkable thought – the end of the regime – cropped up in certain minds. What had begun would one day cease. The year 1766 saw the 150th anniversary of the death of Ieyasu, and, as that year came and went, it occurred to people that what he had begun would also have an end. Sadanobu accounted these times 'more dangerous even than outright civil war [*sengoku*]' and was so worried by 'the evidence we have that the [Tokugawa] dynasty is drawing to its close' that he counselled against celebrating the anniversary of Ieyasu, since the populace could not be trusted to treat it joyously and 'crowds milling around in disorder will only compromise the dignity of the shogunate'.[109] By the late 1780s, the youth of Edo were refusing to join in the regime's official state celebrations and boycotting the Tenka Festival (*tenka matsuri*) held at Asakusa. This left the decrepit to shoulder the heavy floats, 'which was painful to watch', wrote Mizuno Tamenaga, who was there; he also saw a middle-aged man unequal to the load severely injured as a portable shrine 'crashed down on his head'. The first law against juvenile delinquency in Japanese history was passed.[110] The old might cling nostalgically, but the young saw no future in what was around them.

From the mid-eighteenth century care can be seen to increase over the plotting of time. Writers and critics across the board engaged more conscientiously in the project of dating. Developments in time-keeping technology played their part. By the 1780s precision spring-escapement clockwork was diffused; standing clocks appeared in wealthy homes and established shops, and pocket watches became quite common among the merchant class.[111] Cities had known the ring of time-bells for decades, but the new clock told the time continuously; bells rang out suddenly from empty air, whereas a watch alerted its wearer to the arrival of up-coming moments. Time approached steadily and ineluctably. Moreover, if bells were faceless, watches were *watched*.

The symbolic force of the discovery of permanent, visible time cannot be over-stressed. Even if watches were not particularly reliable (as many were still not), they nevertheless revealed an absolute temporal progression, and the vector seemed less of progress than towards an abyss. The connection of time-telling to the mind-set of the later part of the eighteenth century was already recognized by those looking back from early in the following century. 'No one', wrote Ōta Nanpo in 1820 of the situation in the 1780s, 'was without his imported European clock slipped in at the breast'.[112] Clock-time too was an imported system of representation.

In 1812 the poet and scholar Okawara Kibun produced a lampoon on prominent figures from the close of the eighteenth century. He called it *Tales Curiouser and Curiouser (Myōmyō kidan)* and published it under the cheeky Chinese-sounding pen-name 'Su Koppei' (Su is a common surname, while *kokkei* means 'a joke' and *pei* 'a fart'). Kibun included many of those we would classify as from the Sadanobu stable, Tani Bunchō among them. Prominent was Shibano Ritsuzan, who functioned as Sadanobu's chief ideologue. Ritsuzan was Sadanobu's appointee as head of the shogunal Confucian academy in Edo. He was the towering intellectual presence that defined the period and, when Kibun depicted him, he showed him with a clock (illus. 37).[113] I can discern no reason for this inclusion other than that it somehow made Ritsuzan into a man visibly of that specific period: to those who lived soon afterwards, the polemic of this moment was most neatly encapsulated by the image of attention to time. Chronology has invaded a polity that was supposed to be immutable forever.

In all parts of north-east Asia, time was built into blocks that were confined to the regimes that declared them, that is, they were geospecific. These blocks were known as 'eras' (in Japanese *nenkan*). On the Continent, since the start of the Ming dynasty (1368), 'eras' had been coterminous with the reign of the *huangdi*, but in the Tenka they were more culturally cadenced and promulgated as required in response to great events about every decade or so. Names were culled from the classic texts to have a crisp, euphonic sound. Kansei, for example, which we have met as the era declared in 1789 (and lasting until 1800), came from an utterance of the sixth-century founder of the Chinese Sui kingdom: 'when conducting *government*, do so with *lenience*'.[114]

It was shocking how slapdash scholars had recently been in the assignment of names. Misnomers polluted temporality. Genpaku dilated on this, seeing error as having begun (of course) with Ieharu's first era, declared in 1764 and called Meiwa ('radiant harmony'): astonishingly, no one had noticed that a serious problem would arise in the ninth year of Meiwa, or *meiwa kunen*, which would be homophonous with *meiwaku nen*, 'year of tribulations'.[115] Realization did eventually dawn, but it was impossible to alter an era as advance prophylaxis, and as the eighth year closed people were on tenterhooks. They did not have to wait long. Only a few months into 1772, Edo was longer there; early summer saw the total erasure equivalent only to the incineration of 1657, and worse than that van Reede was to see a decade later. In Genpaku's florid phrases:

> Yesterday the jade turrets, golden halls and rooftops of the palaces of the daimyo and of lesser lords stood in rows. Shrines and temples pierced the city here and there, and the numberless dwellings of the merchants and artisans lined up together, vying with each other to exhaust definitions of beauty [. . .] [Now] all is thrown over. There remain just ashy hillocks, like unincidented moorland, stretching on for ever and ever.[116]

An area of 75 square km was lost, and tens of thousands of lives. There were not enough survivors to bury the dead. Coffins ran out. Those who survived simply expired in an excess of despair. 'After fires',

Genpaku told an audience who knew it perfectly well, 'it is the practice to visit and inquire how others have fared. But after this one there were none left to perform the courtesy'. The shogunal castle lost all its eight gates, as well as most of its interior: 'nothing is left but some stone ramparts jutting up disconsolately'. But it was the avoidability of the fire, which would not have happened but for the mishandling of symbols, that was particularly galling.

Nomenclature had been wrong before. In 1713, the appropriateness of the era Shōtoku ('correct virtue') had been debated. It was promulgated in 1711, and the following year the then shogun, Ienobu, died. Whether or not the character *shō* was inauspicious and had precipitated his decease became a famous contretemps between Muro Kyūsō (who said it had) and Arai Hakuseki (who leaned the opposite way). In fact, this was not the first time the character had been used in Japan, as they recognized, but on the other hand Ming diviners said it should be avoided – hence the room for disagreement.[117] At any rate, the run of errors that piled up at the end of the century was without compare. Meiwa was rapidly changed to An'ei ('peaceful and long'), but, as Ōta Nanpo bitterly remarked as he scoured for food in the ravaged city, horror was not so easily abated, and he punned 'peaceful' with its other meaning, 'cheap':

The era is changed to 'peaceful and long',
But does that mean things will be cheap for a long time to come?
Consumer prices are excessively high,
And we are still in a time of 'tribulation'.[118]

The year 1781 brought another change, this time to Tenmei ('heavenly radiance'). The experts in their ivory towers were unaware of it, but *tenmei* was a popular expression meaning 'difficulty'. Genpaku recorded that the people 'murmured that the resonances of the characters were not good'.[119] Sure enough, Tenmei saw the majority of the parlous developments that have been cited above; the description 'difficulty' was barely adequate.

Tenmei was terminated 21 days into its ninth year and Kansei declared. Ten days later, the populace awoke to find sweet dew unaccountably bathing the ground. It fell again on the last day of the twelfth month, as if closing a sweet parenthesis around the first year of 'lenient government'. One year later, on the anniversary of Kansei's beginning, the nectar fell a third time. And they had a bumper harvest to boot.[120] It was as if evil had receded, leaving behind nothing but limpid satisfaction. Sadanobu was in office.

Now the disasters become clear as literary events. Genpaku and others selected and filtered their accounts. The achievement of Kansei was to remove a lens of horror. Sadanobu ensured that his 'lenient government' was projected as such, even if this required intimidation. A wag punned on the word *ka*, meaning 'severity', and wittily renamed the era '*kasei*' ('severe government').[121] The comics got to work too, and Santō Kyōden, a best-selling writer from the Tsutaya orbit, produced a story in which the supposed wonders of the age were extolled with derisory excess, extending to thieves who gave to their victims and beggars who set up workshops in the Confucian classics.[122] The Sadanobu loyalist Yoshida Shigefusa, keeping to the official line, compiled a double-barrelled chronicle prolixly called *Record of Things Heard in Tenmei and Record of Things Heard in Kansei (Tenmei kibun kansei kibun)*, the lapidary title of which efficiently held the epochs apart, as if Genpaku had told only half the story. Shigefusa's first section begins with the adoption of Ienari to replace the horse-fallen Iemoto, accompanied by rice riots in the streets and the wanton murder of one of Edo's most venerable abbots; this is mixed with the first cosmic warning in the form of a mutant pheasant, huge and impervious to bullets, and curiously marked with characters reading *kantai kanki* – a message that clearly imported something but was impenetrable to latter-day Confucian experts. The section closes with Sadanobu's entry to power and the establishment of his school of Japanese studies. Part two begins with the decent burial of the dead from the previous era's disasters, promising much happier times. Although Shigefusa could not hide some continuing disasters, such as the fire that damaged the lovely Temple of the High Terraces (Kōdai-ji, on which see below), he was at pains to turn even these to advantage by noting that the temple's corroded bell had been dragged from the flames, refined to a brilliant gold.[123] Such was Kansei.

People of different ideological stances, or less afraid, did not necessarily observe this change from trauma to mellifluous happiness. Baron van Reede was clear that little had improved and that the government was still mistrusted. Sadanobu, he said, was 'hated and strict'. Caspar Romberg, who relieved van Reede, said he was 'feared and hated'. The populace changed its tune because it had to. Van Reede repeated a hushed rumour he had heard in 1790 that people 'have grave doubts whether this despotic government will last long, for since time immemorial life has never been so bad in Edo'.[124]

Genpaku, deprived of anything real to say under these terms, closed his *Essays* after just two pages on Kansei. But Sadanobu's many diaries take over, containing plenty of 'evidence' for the bounty. Nine was an unlucky number, so it was with pleasure that he noted in Kansei's ninth year (1797) that the stones themselves had turned precious, as certification of virtue in the regime. A farmer in Bizen found his blade running over luminous rock, two lumps of which were extracted, one 7 cm in diameter, the other 14 cm, and with an extraordinary sheen, as if to oppose the exhaustion of copper. Sadanobu's confidant, the geographer and scholar Furukawa Koshōken, was dispatched to investigate, and he was able to confirm the authenticity of the find, bringing the stones back to Edo with him. Sadanobu, then in retirement, called for them and jotted down satisfied memos of what he saw. An active member of the shogun's council acquired the rocks, using them thereafter as tactile proof of the worthiness of the administration.

The Loss of Keishi

The untrustworthiness of the ground on which Edo was built (quite apart from the ethical level of the rulers) gave certain peculiarities to the material culture of that city. Sadanobu admired the pared-down astringency, bred of the permanent requirement to be ready to flee, and observed that if Edo 'were not so prone to conflagration, its inhabitants might be more showy and flash'. As it was, 'the streets are subdued, even where the wealthy live', which, to him, was modest and good.[125] Edo was tenuous, tentative even, in its attitude to the accumulation of goods. On the other hand Keishi (later Kyoto) was the symbol of survival of the antique in concrete objects and of deferential behaviour towards the heritage. There were older cities than Keishi, but it alone stood symbolically for cultural weight – for *baggage*. Those who travelled there duly remarked on the venerable temples and storehouses bulging with classical wares. The incomparable completeness of Keishi and its traditions was the definition, to the point of cliché. A shogunal official, Kimuro Bōun, on a tour to Keishi in 1776 joked, as he walked along the banks of the River Kamo and looked at the nighttime lanterns, 'if this were Edo you'd take it for a fire!'[126] This was funny because such alarms were alien here. Bōun was also struck by the amount of building in stone, which gave a sense of permanence that contrasted with Edo's unresilient wood.[127]

The core function of Keishi, as concept, is evinced in its name: it was to be the 'metropolitan' (*kei*) 'master' (*shi*). It inculcated into other cities how they should be. Edo might be called '*kōtō*' (Edo of the east) or '*kōfu*' (government Edo). Keishi was central, and if it were called anything else, it was *kyō*, a character that could also be read '*miyako*' and is the same as *kei*. If Edo had executive power, Keishi had residual aura.

In the first month of 1788 Keishi burned down in its entirety. Shiba Kōkan made his first visit to Keishi (which he also called Kyō) in the ninth month of that year, but it cannot be called a visit since he could not bring himself to stay. Six months later he was back (having been to Nagasaki in the meantime to meet the Dutch and Chinese contingents) and spent just five days in the area, but only one in touring. He wrote tellingly, 'the shrines and temples nestling in the hills are lovely to behold'.[128] Keishi is not hilly; it is surrounded by hills.

It was mid-afternoon on the last day of the month when fire broke out. By 6 pm it had spread as far as Teramachi. By midnight it was at the Shimogamo Shrine. At 2 am the Dairi (the shujo's mansion) was threatened; shortly thereafter the main enceinte of the shogunal compound, Nijō Castle, was alight.[129] Edo had fire brigades, but Keishi, which had never before needed them, did not.[130] Rain fell, but it was not enough, and by morning 201 temples, 37 shrines, 36,797 common dwellings and a total of 1,424 city blocks in 20 separate locations were gone.[131] People in the surrounding regions swarmed to view the flames. One shogunal official later announced he had raced 20 km in just two hours to witness the metropolitan master taking its leave.[132] News spread quickly. At the farthest end of the land, van Reede recorded in his Nagasaki log for two days after the event the 'complete destruction of the great city of Miyako'.[133] The obliteration found its way into one of the first comprehensive books on the shogun's realm published in Europe, Titsingh's *Illustrations of Japan*.[134] Maps were sold showing the extent of the erasure so that all could assess the Tenka's loss.[135]

The physician Tachibana Nankei, who like Genpaku studied (and even practised) anatomy, went about talking to people and appraising the toll in medical terms, including psychological. 'Many', he said, 'were sent insane by the terror of their experiences'. In such a time odd things occurred, and Nankei also came across a man, previously affected by lunacy, who had been healed 'by the extraordinary confusion going on around him [. . .] which seemed peculiar to me'; but the freak cure only showed how logic was out of place and the doors of rationality were banging.[136]

The event spawned much sustained writing. Dozens of the literate put brush to paper in attempts to come to terms with the tear in their culture's fabric. A new genre of 'fire diaries' was invented. Those who experienced the eradication sought to salve themselves lexically, stemming the pain with the ointment of words.

Fujishima Munenobu, a middle-ranking courtier who attended at the Dairi, dashed out with a writing kit thrust in the folds of his clothes and spent the night tramping about, setting down when and where the flames were moving, and what, and how much, was gone.[137] He gripped the obscenity of the facts with the precision pincers of place and time. Munenobu did not stop when the fire was out, unable to effect closure, and kept on writing until he found some external force to relieve him of the need to continue. He ended on the first day of the fourth month, that is, the ritual day when winter clothes were swapped for spring ones and the earth burgeoned again. Revested and with the blossoms coming out, Munenobu could at last begin to think of his city reviving too. Others were less sanguine and Nankei, the physician, noted unbendingly that, after the fire, the cherries – those synecdoches of beauty – 'were never the same again'.[138]

Ban Kōkei was a furnishings dealer by trade but also an ardent chronicler of Keishi's unique traits. He tried to sort through his emotions after the blaze by compiling strings of verse, expressing his horror via a controlling rhetoric that hummed with the tone of balmier days. *Waka* were rarely used to describe anything more brutal than lost love or the sadness of aging, but Kōkei compelled this court genre to support his 'fire poetry'. Kōkei happened to be in the street when the flames struck, and he remained out of doors, seeing what he could, throughout the night. He returned exhausted and full of anxiety, to discover his own house was in the one unscathed part of the city (miraculously, this south-eastern area held two of Keishi's most splendid buildings, the Hall of Thirty-three Bays and the Great Buddha Hall – the former of which still stands).

I returned home
Thinking, let me learn the news.
All was so hard to comprehend.
'Would it have been the smoke that saved them?'
Sang the bush warbler.[139]

Smoke, in a perversion of the cloud that wafts through so much *waka* poetry, shrouded his home, but, paradoxically, its cover has preserved it – or has it? This riddle of chance survival is called out in the voice of the warbler (*uguisu*), a staple messenger in *waka*, as nature itself begs for explanations.

If Kōkei was spared, he nevertheless saw the night as one of visitation on all. He entitled the record he collated over the next weeks, in two bathetic phrases, *The Wildness of the God of Fire: first ten-day period in the second month, eighth year of Tenmei (Yagutsuchi no arabi: tenmei hachi-nen ni-gatsu shojun)*. The high-flown puissance of this seldom-invoked divinity crashes into time. Kōkei transcribed into his book some of the better examples of other poets' work. Many would be worth critiquing, but their shared trait is that they run fine language up against brutal fact. The appeal to the conventions of court writing only ironizes the mollifying power of verse. Two cases may be cited. One is an anonymous lament that juxtaposes destruction with the gentleness of plum petals, which fell in the first lunar month – i.e., early spring (when the fire had struck) – and were standard seasonal signifiers in *waka*:

Blow it back to its former colours,
You spring clouds!
It is the blossoming capital
That has now come fluttering down.[140]

The winds are asked to rewind and blow backwards so that the tumbled structures of Keishi can sweep back on to the tree of state. The other verse is by the celebrated poet Roan, Fujishima Munenobu's teacher. It became one of the most famous of the 'fire poems'; Nankei also commended its 'overwhelming pathos':

Look around this morning,
And you will see that all is a desecrated moor.
Is this burnt-out wasteland
Yesterday's jewel-spread precincts?[141]

The verse uses a standard range of language and is even conventional in its paralleling of the desert moorland and the stately city (viz. Genpaku's already quoted words on the destruction of Edo in 1771). Rōan uses the convention of the 'pivot-word' (*kakekotoba*), or phrase read twice, a technique we have seen in the verse on Ieharu's investiture overcome with fire. Since vernacular poetry is written phonetically without word-breaks and the Japanese language is small in range of sound, punning is endemic. This is hard to capture in English, but Rōan liaises the third and fourth lines, then flips *koko ya ki nō* between two possible meanings – 'is this yesterday?' and 'this burnt-out wasteland'. This has the effect of tilting the verse headlong into complete emotional collapse.

Another chronicler of the events was the court gentleman Machijiri Ryōgen. He was so unused to bustle or expedition that, having been awoken from an early bed by rude bells, he was unsure how to react.[142] He began his record in the aloof idiom proper to his rank, but more or less immediately broke down as the narrative addressed the ravaged outside. At the opening, the reader is made to mistake the ruddy sky for a fine dawn, as Ryōgen says he did: 'smoke and mist were of a soft red, feeling along the tops of mountains white with elongating cloud'. Ryōgen washed himself, combed his hair, performing his usual ablutions (no fire-drilled Edoite this) and composed his mind quietly at his desk. He then left the writing table and, with it, forsook his poetic vein. Inversion hit him, his metre and the city. 'Unsettled at heart', Ryōgen went into the street, where it looked as though stars were shooting upwards, 'careening from the surface of the earth' towards the sky and taking buildings and lives with them. Ryōgen found an apposite metaphor to capture the shattering of Keishi and the bankruptcy of any means to describe it: 'the clouds were so dark it was as if [my] ink had been splashed across the sky'. He could no longer write. There was so much to say, but no established way to say it.

Ueda Akinari responded in a similar way and, for one of the foremost authors of his age, who had made a name for himself as a specialist in stories of the supernatural, set in a style known for its richness, his tack is intriguing. To recount the fire, he stripped down to plain terms, as if such truth required no studied language, and he wrote with uncharacteristic surrender, 'the sound of screaming through tears, the sight of dashing about in confusion cannot be captured in any figure of speech'.[143]

For Ryōgen, the fire was *caused*. 'What can the gods mean by this?', he quizzed. Thinking back to the foundation of Keishi in the late eighth century (the Enryaku era), he drew conclusions:

> Remember, remember, and think how it was that the passing of generations have brought us to this point. The *tsuberagi* [shujo] of the Enryaku era moved the capital to this place, with mountains for its hems and a river for its girdle, erecting stout palace pillars – surely blessings enough to last a hundred million years! He laid out the city to conform to the geomantic diagram of the Four Beasts, to be a changeless abode for the *teitaku* [shujo]. How depraved times have become when a fire can break out even here![144]

Tomohito, the incumbent shujo, just seventeen, was not noticeably meritorious and, if not noticeably evil either, was implicated in the saga of decline. The preternatural quality of the fire was noted by all. Van Reede informed his Company superiors, 'fire which normally burns only wood and fuel, even consumed iron and stones and made them explode and it even looked as if the stones themselves were spouting fire'. Not unreasonably, he remarked, 'people are considering this to be a great and extraordinary heavenly portent'.[145] The culpability of the shogun and shujo was clarified in the heaven-wrought damage done to their residences, but the latter was specially singled out. As crowds looked on agog, a huge fireball, rolled up, it seemed, by some divine hand and not emanating from the blaze itself, came flying through the air and landed precisely on the shujo's mansion, which was the end of it. Matsura Seizan, daimyo of Hirado, pondered this. He mused, 'Where could it possibly have come from?', but he certainly knew where it went: it landed plumb on the *naishi-dokoro*, the shujo's ancestral spirit chamber.[146]

Tomohito and his court decamped to the Shimogamo Shrine, which was the prearranged muster point in case of need. But this established locus of retreat was denied, for that too began to burn.[147] They then hurried to the Temple of Sagely Protection (Shōgo-in), across the Kamo, well known to Tomohito since he had lived there as prince–abbot elect before an unexpected selection had made him shujo. Masses packed the streets, and the royal convoy was blocked. Rumour had it that Tomohito alighted from his vehicle in the *mêlée* and that his feet touched bare soil for the first time since he had left the Sagely Protection's precincts nine years before (shujo were always carried across ground).[148] Shocked guards moved forward to clear a path, which required hacking down people in the way until the dead numbered one thousand.[149] Tomohito was not chastened; he complained about his

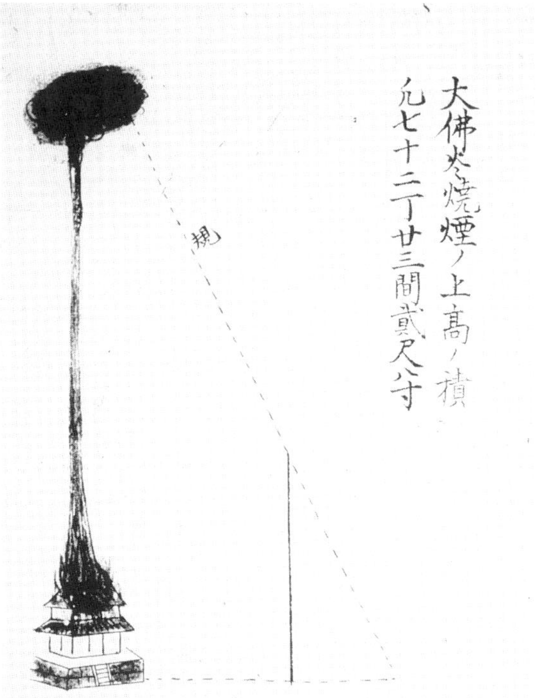

38 *Daibutsu-den raika enshō zuga*, 1798, monochrome manuscript. The anonymous author, seemingly an eye-witness, recorded his measurement of the smoke column.

大佛火燒煙ノ上高ノ積
凡七十二丁廿三間貳尺八寸

temporary post-fire accommodation and moved in with his father, Sukehito, who was nearby at the Temple of the Blue Lotus (Shōren-in). The ex-shujo, Tomohito's predecessor's still-living predecessor, was in the Temple of High Radiance (Shōkō-in) but moved in with the others some weeks later, although annoyingly for them that compound was beetlingly overlooked by the shogun's temple, the Chion-in.[150] Tomohito thought only of his rank and ordered improvements to his apartments before he would move back; elaborate alterations were made.[151] He broke out in a brief but nasty disease shortly afterwards, possibly from stress.[152]

Scales of Loss

Ban Kōkei almost exactly paralleled the conceit that Genpaku used. Both mapped destruction against previous nadirs in the past. For the Edo resident that meant the fire of 1657, but the Keishi comparison was much further back, to be found in the wasting of the city in 1175.[153] Kōkei quoted Kamo no Chōmei, whose experiences of that disaster were still widely read in his *Record of a Ten-foot Square Hut (Hōjō-ki)*. Chōmei had fled the city, living with brazen symbolism in a collapsible hovel. He invoked the ephemerality of life in his opening lines: 'Ceaselessly the river flows, and yet the water is never the same, while in the pools the shifting foam gathers and is gone, never staying for a moment. Even so is man and his habitation'.[154] According to Chōmei, in 1175, 'of the palaces of the great nobles, sixteen were entirely destroyed, and of the houses of the lesser people the number is unknown'. The eighteenth-century Kōkei belaboured the mathematics here: if, in that twelfth-century degradation, 'fire reduced the central part of Keishi to one third of its former self', which by Chōmei's tally it must have done, then this time it was much worse, for 'both within and without the city, more than nine-tenths have gone'.[155]

Only five major buildings survived: the Hall of Thirty-three Bays and Great Buddha Hall near Kōkei's house, the main hall of the Daihōon-ji (called the Senbon Shakadō), the main hall of the Shōkoku-ji and that of the Tōji, together with the Tōji's pagoda.[156] Outlying temples were saved, particularly fortunately the Temple of the High Terraces (Kōdai-ji), which contained Hideyoshi's sumptuously lacquered mortuary chapel. This was requisitioned for the residence and offices of the shogun's plenipotentiary in Keishi, the *shoshidai*. The shogun had not fared so badly in the fire, but was humiliated when the Terraces was lost to fire the following spring. 'Though it managed to survive last year's great conflagration', lamented Shiba Kōkan, who was there, the temple 'is now gone'; so Kōkan visited the Great Buddha, the Hall of Thirty-three Bays and the Daihōon-ji, completing the circuit of all worthwhile sites in a single day.[157] Romberg, also in Keishi at the time and living like everyone else in poor, temporary accommodation (the Company's long-standing hostel and stores had burned), stated that the additional loss of the Temple of the High Terraces had left emotions very sour.[158] Shigefusa, as we have seen, tried to make the best of the event, it being now the 'lenient' Kansei era, and claimed that at least the bell was refined by this second blaze, but the pretence rang hollow. On a single day a few weeks later, every bridge over the city's two rivers (the Kamo and Katsura) was swept away by floods.[159]

Keishi licked its wounds. There were shortages everywhere. There was no wood for rebuilding. Sadanobu took steps to guard against profiteering by lumber dealers, but this was little helped by Tomohito, who declared it illegal to purchase any wood until his own needs had been catered for.[160] There was talk of abandoning the city and letting Keishi die in peace. Laws were passed to keep the populace in place, and life faltered on.[161]

In 1798, almost ten years to the day after the fire and just seven days into Kansei's second decade, the Great Buddha Hall was hit by lightning. Despite formation of a chain of over 10,000 people to bring water from the Kamo, by morning the building was gone. This sequence of fires required mental ingenuity to come to terms with. The loss of the Great Buddha Hall (Japan's greatest temple) was a portent as blatant as any could be.[162] The Confucian scholar Ōta Kinjō concluded the gods had sent 'heaven-fires' (*tenbi*) to strike the building *because* it was the greatest achievement of the Tenka; annihilation of culture was thus the divine intent.[163] The hall was the largest wooden structure on earth, and the Buddha inside was fully 20 m high.[164] The burning was accompanied by other unhallowed events. Five hundred kilometres away in Edo, fireballs were seen flying through the sky, although there was no visible blaze, and one of these mysterious objects landed beside Sadanobu's garden as he sat in it, wrapped in thought.[165] An eccentric samurai painter, Nagasawa Rosetsu, sometime student of the celebrated Ōkyo, produced for the visual sphere what Kōkei, Ryōgen *et al.* had done for literature and bound this new disaster in a torque of well-figured artistry (see illus. 18). Rosetsu's painting is as unprecedented as those authors' writings, but like them it fitted into a standard artistic format, in this case, that of the hanging scroll. Rosetsu's *Burning of the Great Buddha Hall* could have hung in a normally proportioned room to goad and elicit explanations.

A series of pictures was made by an anonymous author who annotated them, listing on each the time and how much of the temple was left (illus. 38).[166] He also had recourse not to art but to the objectifying cushion of mathematics, calculating the height of the smoke by measuring its angle of elevation and arriving at 72 *chō*, 23 *ken*, 2 *shaku*, 8 *sun*, or rather over 7 km – as if that made any difference.

Rosetsu and this anonymous author could not expel visually by art or science the greater significance of the loss of Keishi's most important single building. The saving of the Great Buddha Hall in 1788 had seemed miraculous, but now it seemed only a tease. The loss recalled the burning of the Great Buddha Hall in Nara, the prototype of Keishi's hall and the archetype of all religious colossi, during the fighting that Chōmei had lived through. This event was apocalyptically described in the medieval *Tales of the Heike (Heike monogatari)*, when it was told how that statue was erected as the symbol of the faith of the Japanese peoples and

> . . . designed to serve as a representation of the eternal, indestructible, enlightened being whose physical body appears in the Land of Buddha-Reward in Reality, and the Land of Eternally Tranquil Light [. . .] [After the fire] those present who witnessed the sight averted their eyes; those afar who heard the story trembled with fear.[167]

Of this disaster the text concluded, 'it is impossible to imagine such a devastating blow to the Buddhist faith in India or on the Continent, to say nothing of in this country'. But disaster leapt from the pages of books into the actual present and hammered home the ignominy of the states, until the Tenka's modern glories and its inheritance from the past were removed from sight forever.

3 Image Management for Royal Power

'The King's a thing . . .'
'A thing my lord?'
'. . . of nothing.'
– Shakespeare, Hamlet, 1601

What a pity that the grand princes of these lands
should be a laughing stock for ants and fleas.
– Matsudaira Sadanobu, Seigo, 1788

The iconographic thinking of royal authorities in Japan, whether the shogun's or the shujo's, had much in common with that in other parts of north-east Asia. A Western visitor, though, might find it unexpected. The Swedish physician Carl Peter Thunberg, who arrived in Edo in 1776, set about trying to discover the ruler's name, his age or anything about him at all. In Europe, this would be a good start for learning about the politics and policies of a state. But Thunberg could discover nothing. 'Very few people', he recorded in surprise, 'in the whole empire know the emperor's [shogun's] name before he dies'.[1] By dint of hard questioning among the privileged few, Thunberg did learn a few facts, such as that the 'emperor's' personal name was 'Je Faru' (Ieharu), that he was of 'middle size' and 'hale constitution', and that his son and inheritor was called 'Je Moto' (Iemoto) and was then aged twelve (and more often called Prince of the Western Castle).[2] Exhumation of skeletons has allowed a firmer knowledge of the robustness or otherwise of some Tokugawa rulers' physiques (although, sadly, not those of any who figure in this book).[3] But to their subjects of the period the men had no tangible presence whatsoever as human entities. A silencing aura emanated from the shogunal family and expanded over the persons or personalities of other potentates too, whether daimyo or shujo. Virtually the only documents relating to their bodies come from European accounts, and even these are brief since, although the leading Dutch East India Company representatives were permitted extended encounters with a few daimyo, they spent just a few minutes annually with the shogun and never met the shujo. In any case, eyes and foreheads were supposed to be firmly directed towards the floor, and staring was taboo. In 1786, Baron van Reede met Ieharu and (Iemoto having fallen from his horse and died since

Thunberg's visit) the new adopted heir, later to become shogun, Ienari. Ienari was then aged thirteen. The following year van Reede met them again and remarked how the boy was 'still small standing'; in 1789, on his third encounter, he found Ienari 'considerably grown in two years'.[4] Such frank comments cannot be found in the writings of shogunal officialdom nor of other members of the Japanese elite.

When the shogun was on the move there was more possibility he might be seen and, although such trips were rare, every effort was made to ensure he was not looked at. Streets were emptied of traffic for several blocks around and people commanded down from upper storeys along the route.[5] If the shogun stayed out overnight, even senior retainers were warned not to take advantage of fire or other hazard to look at him if he made unscheduled moves. As regards the shujo, it took the massive fire of Keishi to put Tomohito on the street – the first time he had been out, it was said, for nine years. The Keishi fire also forced relocation of the shujo's ladies, and van Reede was able to probe ocularly into their less secure interim lodgings and indeed to write of this – an intrusion few locals would have attempted, much less recorded.[6]

This could seem an extraordinary abdication of the power of visual display. The pomp on which Western or Islamic kings relied to curry loyalty was simply not attempted. Yet shogun, daimyo and shujo all deployed images of rule that were unshakable, only they were not predicated on *revelation*. They were the opposite: elites occluded themselves with an iconography of *absence*.[7]

The Icongraphy of Absence

The shujo's mansion in Keishi was known by several terms. All were taken from designations used by the *huangdi* ('emperor' of China) in his capital. Most current was the label Dairi or 'Great Interior'; pronounced 'dali', this was the normal Ming-dynasty word for the palace. The equivalent of the best-known modern term, Forbidden City (*jincheng*), was used with the Japanese pronunciation 'kinjō'. There was also the 'Forbidden Interior' (*jinli/kinri*) and similar variants. All stressed prohibition, but this was understood to apply not just to entering but also to seeing. High walls blocked assault and invasion by the eye and prevented people from gleaning more than an outline of rooftops. No orchestrated sightlines guided people down vistas concentrating on a royal node of presence, as they did in Paris or Rome. This was in fact the period of Europe's grandest city planning. St Petersburg had been laid out to expose the glories of the Russian czars only shortly before. The

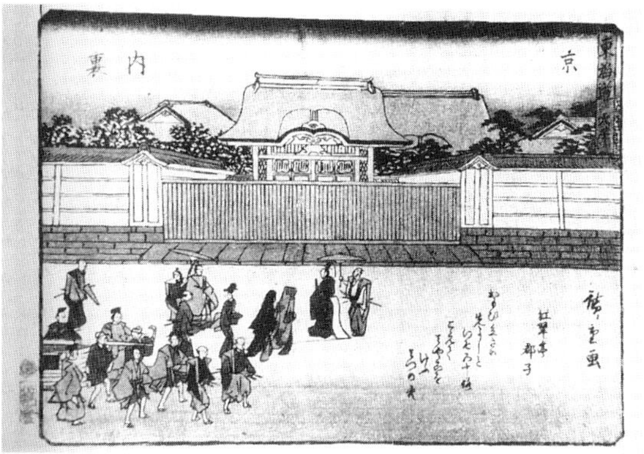

39 Utagawa Hiroshige, Print from the series *Kyōka iri tōkaidō gojūsan-tsugi*, c. 1840, multicoloured woodblock. The final station of the Tōkaidō highway was Keishi (Kyoto), represented here by the shujo's mansion, the Dairi.

concept of the palatial facade, like the vista, was utterly unexplored by Japanese architects, and the sole grandiloquent royal statement was the gate, which, though it might be finely ornamented, was invariably shut and sometimes double-blocked by wooden screens (illus. 39).[8]

The embassy district of Edo, where the daimyo mansions were, was called Kasumigaseki, 'barrier of mist'; true, the sea air hung there as it swept in from the bay, but this was conceived as nature offering its help in curtailing the collective gaze. The elements floated in to produce a miasma of imperceptibility that shielded authority from the rudeness of scrutiny. Rhetorically, absence was imagined as less a legal prohibition than the result of spontaneous precipitation. Technically speaking, castle walls were not therefore needed. Only tyrants live in castles (as 'Old Nick' Machiavelli also thought), but in the north-east Asian case nature stepped in to protect good rulers instead.

There were precedents and anecdotes aplenty to be referred to in support of these myths. The *locus classicus* was in the eighth-century *Chronicles of Japan (Nihon shoki)*. The semi-legendary shujo Osazaki (posthumously, Nintoku) is said to have climbed to his turrets and seen that no smoke was rising from people's homes, demonstrating that they were starving; he enforced brutal austerities on his household to alleviate their burden. The scantness of his residential splendour was an index of his virtue and the iconic collapse of his regime spoke, inversely, of its nobility:

> The Palace enclosure fell into ruin and was not rebuilt; the thatch decayed and was not repaired; wind and rain entered by the chinks and soaked the coverlets; starlight filtered through the decayed places and exposed the bed-mats.[9]

Osazaki's Dairi disappeared from view, returning to earth until it became one with the soil, after which it could be hoped nature would rally to succour him. In this dispensation, soaring castles looked dangerously defeatist.

The shoguns were legendarily rich, and their castles hovered above the city of Keishi, and more spectacularly Edo (where the keep topped out at 60 m).[10] This had been needed for military defence in the early seventeenth century when the Tokugawa were only shakily ensconced. As the likelihood of attack receded over time, the castles were left stranded, offending against an ingrained coyness. Sugita Genpaku's starting point for his *Essays in Hindsight (Nochimigusa)* was the great fire of 1657 that took away the main keep of Edo Castle. Possibly the shogunate would have dismantled it in due course, but flames happily pre-empted this. After the conflagration the skyline was suddenly denuded of its prime monument, but notice was posted that reconstruction would be foregone, 'because of damage throughout the city', inclining the good shogun to the benevolent act of minimizing his own constructions.[11] He became more unseeable, put his heretofore bellicose imagery behind him and entered the pantheon of the virtuous. The air above Edo was repaired of the puncture that recalled an age of war.

Early in the nineteenth century, the samurai and scholar Ōta Kinjō looked back at this event and set it within its proper philosophico-historical context:

> When the Great Castle was rebuilt in the wake of the disaster, it was done with all speed. But there was one interesting thing: perhaps because the official verdict was that sufficiency did not require a total rebuilding, the keep was not reconstructed. The main rationale for this was geomantic; the second was the belief that excessive edifices always succumb to fire – they must have known of the Palace of Adorned Buildings in the Han period, and the Palace of Luminescent Response to Pure Jade in the Song [which Heaven struck]. [. . .] Nowadays few people read books, but it is important for them not to lose touch with the significance of the magic of space.[12]

Heaven detested rulers who drove buildings into the unity of the skies, holing their integrity, and who arrogated gifts destined for the people. The shogunate pursued the same policy when the keep of their second stronghold, the Castle on Second Avenue (Nijō-jō) in Keishi, was razed by fire in 1750; it too was not rebuilt.[13]

There are those who have argued that the shogunate was too poor to reconstruct its castles or that the keeps had become militarily unnecessary. Both may be true. But I propose that the towers were *iconically* embarrassing and better done without. We may note that this norm continued even after the 'modernization' of Japan: when the new, Western-style Meiji emperor's palace burnt down in 1873, it was not rebuilt at all.[14]

Daimyo castles were managed similarly. All major repair work had to be sanctioned by the shogunate, and in general permission was declined. If lightning or fire obliterated visually intrusive buildings, all the better. By the mid-eighteenth century, not only the two shogunal bastions but also a good number of the daimyo ones lacked keep or donjon, or indeed much at all to look at. Towers were not wantonly dismantled, but if they persisted in manifesting themselves, trees and bushes were trained to cover their walls and lotuses to choke the moats, to emblematize the ruler's recognition that the love of his people had made protection otiose.

In 1791, in the midst of the greatest alarms over whether shogunal custodianship of the Japanese archipelago would continue, Sadanobu, then four years in office, took radical steps to heighten Ieharu's image. He did so by lowering the walls of Edo Castle. The most visible remaining ramparts comprised the double-redoubt entranceway (*masugata*), called the Fukiage Gate. Sadanobu determined, 'notwithstanding this is a castle, superfluous defences shall be taken down', and the gate was cleared away.[15] It is worth analysing this reform, and fortunately deliberations were recorded by the one-time bombardier Moriyama Takamori.

The double structure was to allow the pinning of intruders between the two-fold system of walls. But the gate was old and needed attention. The costs of integral restoration were huge, and economies were certainly desirable. Yet more critical was how the castle should look. Not all agreed to removal, but Sadanobu forced the matter through and the gate became single, with its arrowslits and gunslots sealed up. Takamori himself worried, 'Wherefore should the castle in which My Lord resides not have them? We should have points to shoot and fire through', although he conceded the slots undeniably made the place look 'untoward' (*iyō*) (in fact, they had always been disguised by flaps). A back-and-forth ensued which, perversely, saw the top echelon of government trying to persuade its underlings to allow it to scrap its hardware of preparedness. A compromise was reached and the single gate was given a platform behind its neighbours' walls, invisible from the front, but allowing shooting if ever 'the unwonted' (*hijō no koto*) should occur.

Restrictions multiplied at this time. Minor fire damage had been sustained by the shogun's principal residence, the Mansion in the Western Enceinte, spoiling its characteristic exterior tiling done in the cross-cross pattern exclusive to lordly institutions (known as the *namago*, or trepang, design). Sadanobu had the walls repaired, but in the form of plain boarding. Still no doubt unstintingly lavish on the interior, the outside, which gave onto the Gate of Cherries and Ricefields (the castle's principal southern entrance and thus widely seen), was rendered meek and like a commoner's home. Tiling was ornamentation, not a building need (its value as a fire-retardant was never much recognized),[16] so off it came. Sadanobu stripped his own mansion, beside the shogun's, and publicly refitted it 'using only seared planks'.[17]

Niggling over such apparently trivial issues of the visual grammar struck Thunberg as one of the chief differences between the shogunate and the monarchies with which he was familiar. He marvelled at what he termed the 'overstrained oeconomy' of elite Japanese life.[18] Yet this was part of a codified rhetoric of which he was insufficiently informed. Takamori's general summary of Sadanobu's alterations to the castle is worth quoting, for it makes clear which responses were being fished for:

> When ambassadors arrive from the Chosŏn, the Ryūkyūs or other countries [i.e. Europe], they can now see how the dismounting court at the Ōte is just turf, and that the castle cladding is of plain wood [. . .] They will return home with news that Japan is a lovely place, far beyond their expectations, and that it preserves a sense of restraint. Wandering through the shogun's Castle and city, they will look at the mansions of the daimyo, and realise how, contrary to all they might have expected, our lands are the acme of decency. Surely that is how we ought to be reported![19]

Sadanobu's period in office coincided with a general down-scaling of bluster and circumstance. This was part of a slashing back of the egregious symbolic inflation that had occurred during Tanuma Okitsugu's period in the chief councillorship. Privileged motifs were returned to the rightful users, who then were expected to duly deny their desire for such things.

Samurai had become accustomed to making unilateral visual upgrades on buildings, costumes and equipment, but they found themselves abruptly checked. Creeping luxuries were pulled off samurai housing since, according to Takamori, 'no one above has ever decreed that they should have them [. . .] and more likely someone just did it first off his own bat'.[20] Quite hilarious mismatches between official appellations and the things themselves were rife. The 'hempen up-and-over' (*asa-gamishimo*), the standard dress of a samurai on duty, was made of silk.[21] Disalignment advertised a modern cult of extravagance. The samurai and wit Ōta Nanpo (not the astringent type by choice) was amused at how Sadanobu's enforced reversion to the rudiments did away with brocade, figured cloth and gold braiding almost overnight: 'crisp white socks worn brand new each day in summer' were abandoned for buff, washable options, or even reckless socklessness, including in winter; for outer garments, 'a sombre coat good enough to ward off inclemencies became the order of the day', and 'how stern people looked as they went up to attend at the Castle!'[22] These changes had decisive economic effects. The Dutch East India Company was told to desist from bringing cloth-of-gold and silver, and prices halved. The cost of European finished accessories (such as vanity mirrors) dropped by 87 per cent.[23]

The prevailing economic theory was that elite extravagance tempted the lower orders into high expenditure, getting them into debt and so ruining the backbone of the states. Genpaku wrote, 'because the upper people crave more and more, the lower orders have fallen deeper into want'; over-spends among the elite made the poor embarrassed by what they had.[24] Merchants overstretched themselves with finery they had acquired legitimately enough but which, in former times, would have been seen only in samurai residences. Genpaku illustrated this with the case of 'someone or other called Horibe', who held a tea party at which all the accoutrements were overweeningly precious:

> The censer was in the form of a cock made of silver standing on a golden rice-bale; there was a silver vase, over 3 *shaku* [1 m] high, filled with seasonal blooms; a golden tea caddy intricately incised with irises was matched with a little brush of Chinese bird-feathers, and set on the shelf; in the hearth was a vastly outsized kettle in solid silver, and beside it a Nanking ware in *sometsuke* shape, of the finest sort, to be used for the water jar.[25]

Later a servant struggled in with 'a yellow Annam [central Vietnamese] terrapin-shaped incense box engraved in gold, and as if the tea caddy gracing the shelf hadn't been heavy enough, this box was simply too much to lift'. Under Sadanobu, non-samurai were forced to sell (or hide) such value-added items.

Actors, courtesans and those who purveyed fairy-tale and false existences, egged on by an avid populace, were rigorously forced to conform. The great female impersonator Segawa Kikunojō was arrested one night in 1789 for wearing an elaborate silk robe as he walked home from the theatre; it was what he had often worn, but now the diktat was different.[26] Prostitutes were banned from donning flamboyant dress, even though it had formerly been accepted as permissible in their trade. The rationale was presented that verbose brothel conventions were filtering out into bourgeois society. Takamori again: 'People took to placing floral pins in their daughters' hair, which, though pretty, made them look like trainee prostitutes from the pleasure districts'.[27] Samurai who befriended such people – like Kurahashi Itaru (alias Koikawa Harumachi) – were sacked or forced to desist.[28] In the secondary representation of pictures, publishers prudently demonstrated a new-found support for sobriety and in the 1790s printed images of actors, entertainers and even prostitutes (the bedrock of Floating World themes) show them with almost ostentatiously humble dress, depicted on the page in a wan palette (illus. 19, 40).

The European Example

Rolling back excess was a means of dealing with the chronic late eighteenth-century malaise that surrounded visual artefacts. Not only was there an anterior norm to return to, but commentators were aware that radically different solutions pertained elsewhere. The European case loomed. Pictures and samples were collected of European dress, and the many imported pictures showed the appearance of foreign objects. Kōkan discussed the imported prints he had seen of Western cities and cited the splendour of the architectural splash, with palaces and soaring towers.[29] The opposite of Edo or Keishi, these cities were loaded with royal icons. Visibility was the sea that kept European ruling houses afloat. It was accepted practice for lavish motifs of state to force rulers perpetually upon the public gaze. In 1809 Aōdō Denzen depicted a dense assembly of monuments in a city square in Germany, as he called it (actually ancient Rome) (illus. 41).[30] Where a city was conceived as the stage of a regime, a pitiful palace invited only scorn.

In 1783 a ship sank off the Pacific coast, leaving its captain, Daikoku-ya Kōdayū, and four survivors to float for months until they were at last rescued by a czarist vessel and taken to Moscow and St Petersburg. Kōdayū was treated well; he was shown major urban and rural sites, including churches, parks, galleries and mansions, as well as the opera, and he was given direct exposure to Russian potentates, including an audience with Catherine the Great. Two remaining sailors (three had died) returned to Japan in 1793, and they were brought before Ienari (screened from their view) and met by Sadanobu. They were then pumped for information, officially declared dead and

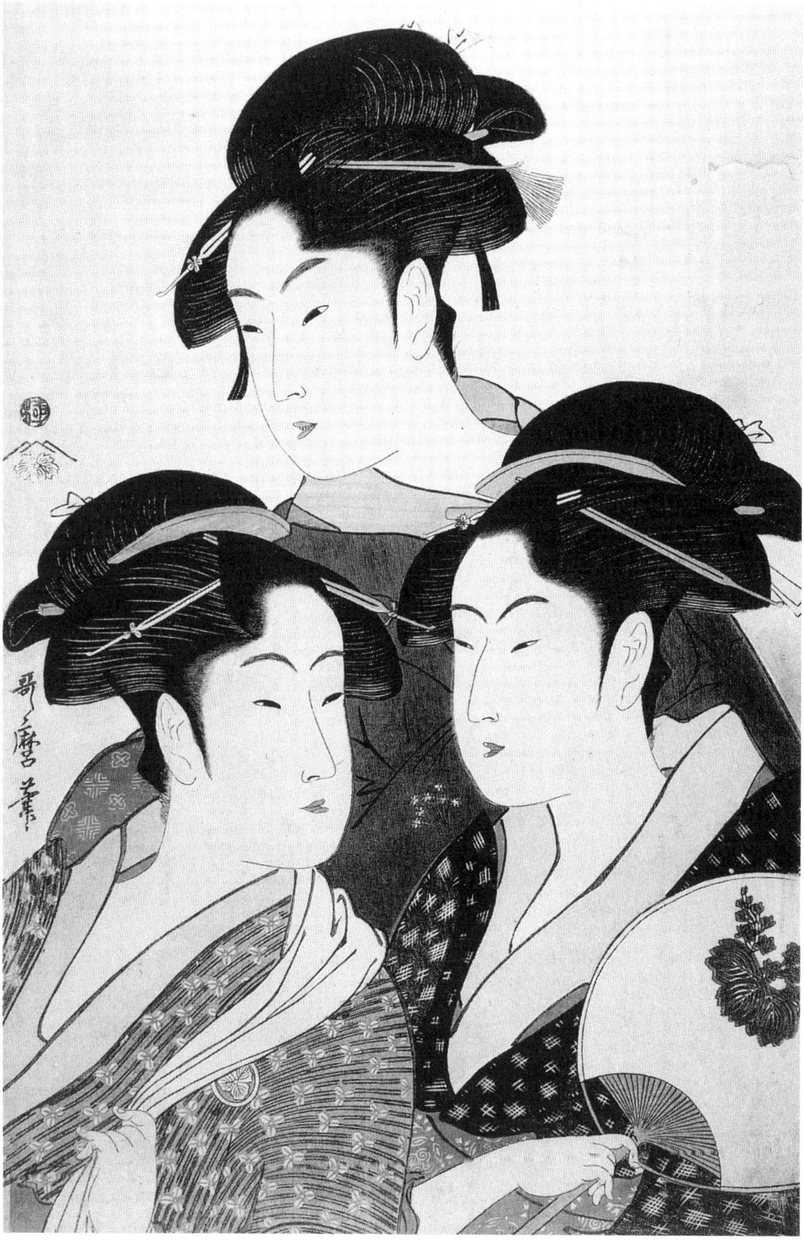

40 Kitagawa Utamaro, *Beauties of the Kansei Period*, c. 1790, multicoloured woodblock print. Published by Tsutaya, this image deliberately suggests a new sobriety in costume and style.

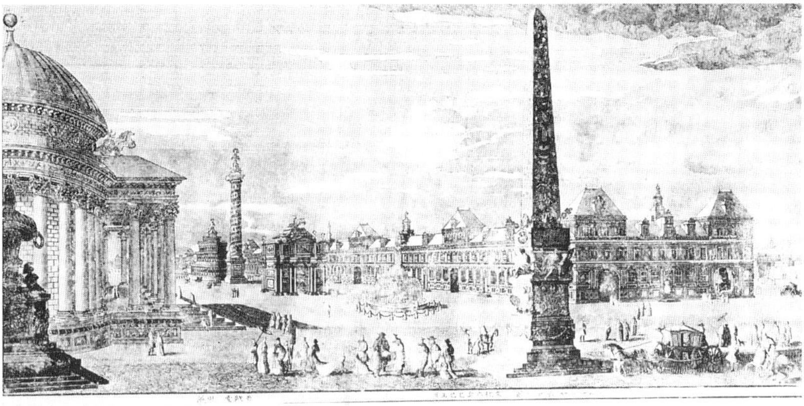

41 Aōdō Denzen, *City Square in Germany*, 1809, copperplate etching. What a typical European cityscape was thought to look like, replete with royal icons.

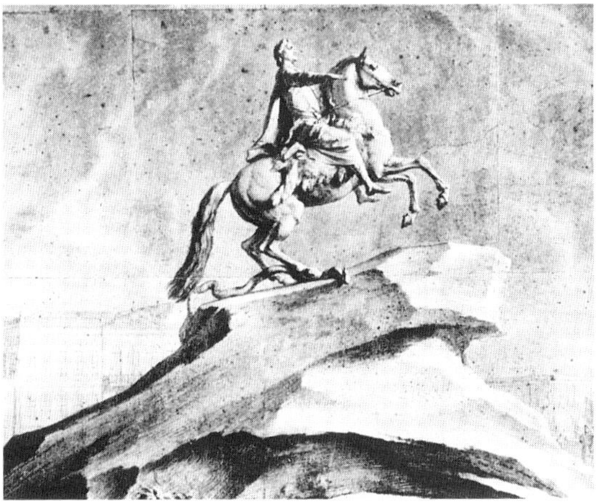

42 A. P. Losenko, *Etienne-Maurice Falconet's Statue of Peter the Great*, after 1782, ink on paper. One of the finest pieces of Baroque public statuary; note the realistic plinth.

locked away – in Kōdayū's case until his biological death, which came 35 years later. Their news was heady and dangerous, but, most stringently, it was the 'foreign symbolics of state' (*gaikoku no gi*) that they were never allowed to divulge again.[31]

Knowledge of the mechanics of European power was a state secret, for it constituted a challenge to the underpinnings of Tokugawa rule. But news filtered out, and Katsuragawa Hoshū, whose name was known in Russia through his friendship with Thunberg (Kōdayū heard of him while in St Petersburg), was present at Kōdayū's debriefing, and he finally obtained special leave to flesh out the castaway's clipped deposition into a lengthy narrative.[32] He never published this, but it circulated in manuscript form under the anodyne title *Brief Report on a Northern Raft (Hokusa bunryaku)*. The title belied the flabbergasting quality of the exposures.

To see St Petersburg was to be harangued by the glories of the House of Romanov. Kōdayū encountered for the first time the idea of the public facade: the palace was set 'on the south bank of the Neba, two *chō* [220 m] along the front [. . .] and rising to five storeys'; this open facade was surrounded by tall fencing, all see-through.[33] Near the city centre was the colossal statue of Peter the Great, one of the most celebrated works of baroque plastic art, twelve years in the making by that French giant of public scupture Etienne-Maurice Falconet, whose masterpiece it was taken to be (illus. 42). In Hoshū's account, Kōdayū informs the reader:

> Beneath the horse's hooves is a huge sculpted snake. At the foundation of Petersburg there was a poisonous serpent living in a place called Peter's Court and causing great harm, and not one person who went there ever returned. Peter heard of this, mounted his charger and rode to the site. The snake shrank back in fear. He trampled it to death with the horse's feet and made the place into a park.[34]

Kōdayū also noted that on the base was written 'Peter I, by Catherine II, inscribed this 18th day of June, 1782'. The aura of this 'virtuous ruler' was made to cling, life-sized, to the current Russian monarch. In a way, Ieyasu's aura clung to Ieharu and Ienari too, except that Peter was *visible*. It was the premise of the statue that was the antithesis of Tokugawa practice.[35] A decade later, another castaway, Doi Tsudayū, made a sketch of this equestrian image, slightly garbling it by including a plinth, the substitution of which with naturalistic rock was, in fact, Falconet's revolutionary innovation, but it was enough to shock Edo anyway. The picture was redrawn and included in the text of Tsudayū's deposition (illus. 43).

Every Russian citizen knew their ruler's name and face. Catherine was stamped on modern human habitation, as Peter was, toponymically, and Kōdayū was also taken to Ekatarinberg;[36] the czarina went about in a glass-windowed carriage and so was seen. Kōdayū brought back a print of Catherine, showing how monarchical imagery was accessible even to the lowest strata, and this image too was copied into the *Northern Raft*, complete with the curled-up edges of the cheap paper (illus. 44). Russians were expected to hang royal portraits up, each according to their budget, and these were placed 'among works on religious themes' and treated similarly, being 'venerated by means of glass candlesticks placed in front'.[37] Tsudayū, who was repatriated in

1804, brought back portraits of the new czar, Alexander, and of his wife. (Note that Alexander had 'accidentally' killed his father Paul, the previous czar, just months before Tsudayū's arrival in Russia, during the coup of 1799 that brought him to power.) A record of Tsudayū's travels was made in imitation of the *Northern Raft*, by Sugita Genpaku's student, Ōtsuki Gentaku and several images (including these and the statue) copied in (illus. 45).[38] The title of this account was *Strange Tales of a Circumnavigation (Kankai ibun)*, as Tsudayū had been brought home via the Americas, making him the first Japanese to go round the world.

The figure of the ruler was supposed to convey a sense of security and trust. All across Europe, royal names and faces were on the media of fiduciary exchange. Russia had a coin called an 'Imperial Catherine', and many states had 'crowns' and 'sovereigns'. Shiba Kōkan wrote that Western currency always carried 'the king's face on it'.[39] A Japanese–Dutch translator in the shogunal employ called Narabayashi Jūbei noted that, unlike in the Tenka, where specie was various and did not circulate beyond the issuing daimyo's jurisdiction, in Europe 'all coinage is said to belong to the Crown'.[40] Western money was amassed for curiosity's sake and was sold openly in Edo.[41] A merchant called

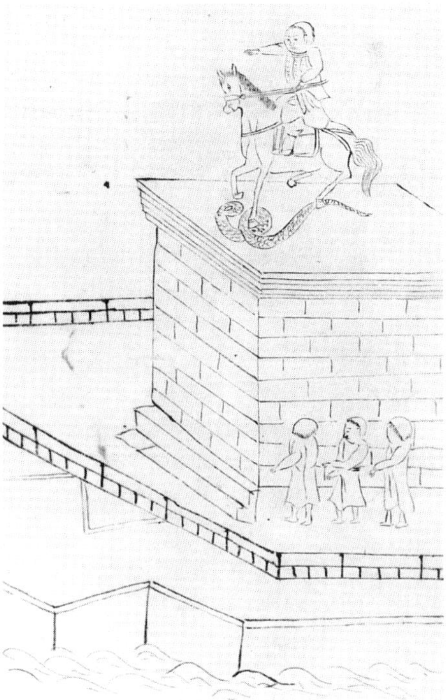

43 Copy of illustration from Otsuki Gentaku, *Kankai ibun* (1807), *c.* 1830, colour on paper. Falconet's statue, as misremembered by Doi Tsudayū, who saw it *c.* 1800.

44 Illustration from Katsurakawa Hoshū, *Hokusa bunryaku*, 1794, colour on paper. Copy of a cheap printed portrait of Catherine the Great bought in Russia by Daikoku-ya Kōdayū.

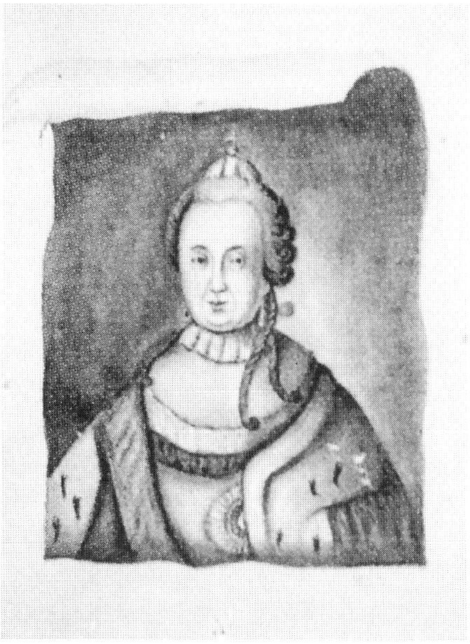

Suruga-ya Jūgorō, who was a close friend of Morishima Chūryō, showed off his significant collection to anyone interested, until he tragically died by fire and his sister sold off his coins.[42] Kutsuki Masatsuna, daimyo of Fukuchiyama, was Ōtsuki Gentaku's patron and one of the chief Westernists of his day. He was also an energetic numismatist and in 1787 published a large book called *Western Coinage (Seiyō senpu)* which displayed, in a series of plates ordered by country, examples of tender from most European states and their colonies (illus. 46).[43]

It was not that putting the king's head on coins had never been contemplated in the long history of north-east Asia. Rather, the idea had been explicitly rejected. As early as the Han period, expansionists had come across late Roman money that bore the monarch's head and had scoffed at this as inappropriate to their more advanced regime. Confucian classics dismissed displaying the portrait on money and these ancient injunctions were not forgotten for, as the Edo scholar Hattori Nankaku offered in 1720, 'minting coins with the king's head on' betokens 'primitiveness' (*ban*).[44]

An over-abundance of figures of a ruler might cause problems. In 1791 the despised Louis XVI was intercepted on his flight from Paris to Varennes by someone who recognized his face from a coin.[45]

Pictures locked a disembodied imperium into specific persons, who might be inept, foolish or hated, as Ieharu was, if Ienari less so. Images

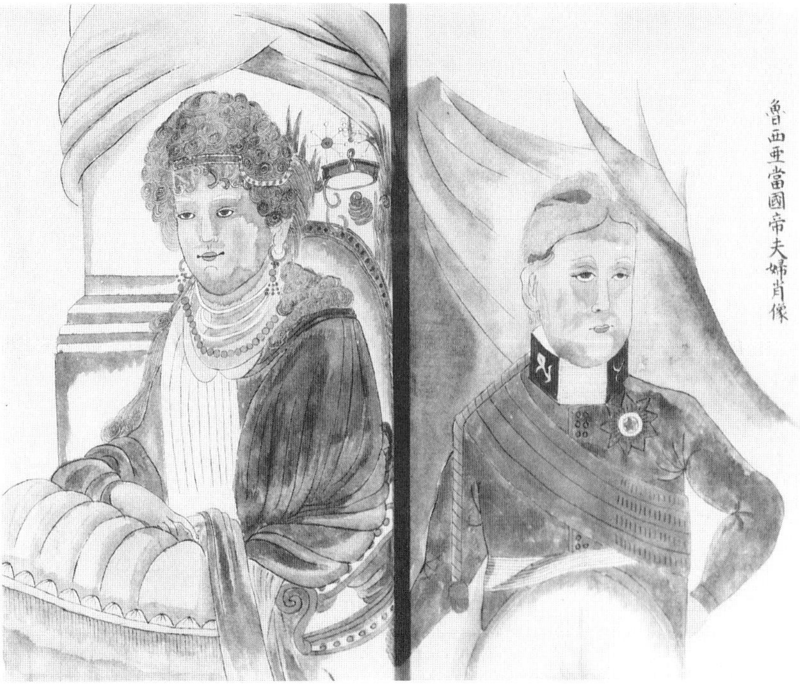

45 Copy of illustration from Ōtsuki Gentaku, *Kankai ibun* (1807), *c.* 1830, colour on paper. Czar Alexander and the czarina, whom Doi Tsudayū met *c.* 1800.

could also become foci of insurrection. News of the public desecration of George III's statue in New York may have been known, for this revolutionary event of 1776 was captured in an optical print of the kind much imported and enthusiastically viewed by, among others, the shujo Tomohito's father (illus. 47).[46]

Even beloved rulers died, and portraits might interfere with smooth succession. A taking down and a changing of icons introduced too visible a caesura for Tokugawa taste, where shogunal and shujo reigns slid into each other with few being aware of them. Ieharu's death, for example, was not proclaimed for two months after he breathed his last, and Ienari was not formally inducted to replace him for a further seven. Funerals were generally not announced, or only after the event, and public doles, though practised, were not linked to a named individual, so that the population often did not know who they were for. Moreover, information on obsequies and succession rituals were released on dates that mitigated the strain of transfer, with Ienari, for example, being installed two days before the anniversary of Ieyasu's

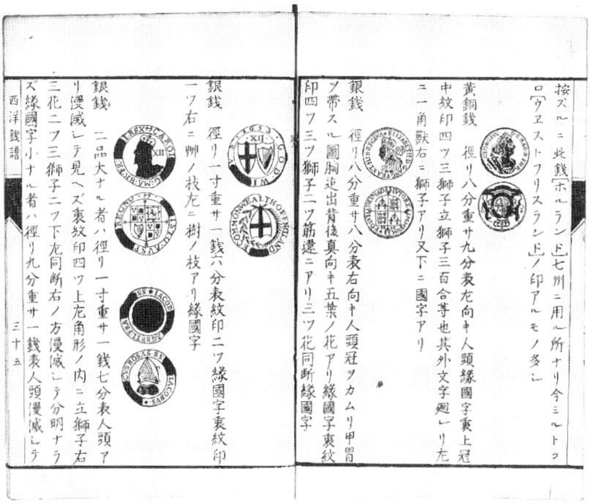

46 Pages from Kutsuki Masatsuna, *Seiyō senpu*, 1787, monochrome woodblock prints. Masatsuna, daimyo of Fukuchiyama, collected and sketched a large number of European coins and medals.

deification.[47] Often a shujo's accession rites were not performed at all, and the boy Sachihito was one of the first to enjoy a relatively swift ceremonial to make him the shujo Tomohito and that was for special reasons (as we shall see below).

The Iconographers of the Tenka

Discussion of official icons necessarily implicated more than simply the ruler's own image. It had a collective bearing on official motifs and subjects, and on those charged with providing them.

The Tenka's bipartite division of royalty had its counterpart in painting. Or rather, political dualism exerted a strong rhetorical force, inducing a dichotomous way of thinking that prevailed linguistically, even if it was hard to detect in academic stylistic facts. Government painting was divided into two major camps: the school of Kano (sometimes written Kanō) painted motifs of ethical rule, either in the form of narratives or of auspicious flora and fauna, for disposition by the shogunate; Kano work pertained to executive kingship and subjecthood. The school of Tosa painted literary and emotional themes for the shujo's court; these were consciously amoral since the shujo's position was based on blood, not on any (potentially losable) 'virtue'. Kano themes were largely derived from Continental icons of Chinese statecraft (sage kings, wizards, *hōō* birds, tigers and peacocks), since China was the place of dynastic rise and fall. The Tosa stemmed from the Tenka's own past, as known through vernacular literature, and they depicted the traits of an unbroken continuum, eternally there and just retrievable, if largely submerged by later political events. In practice,

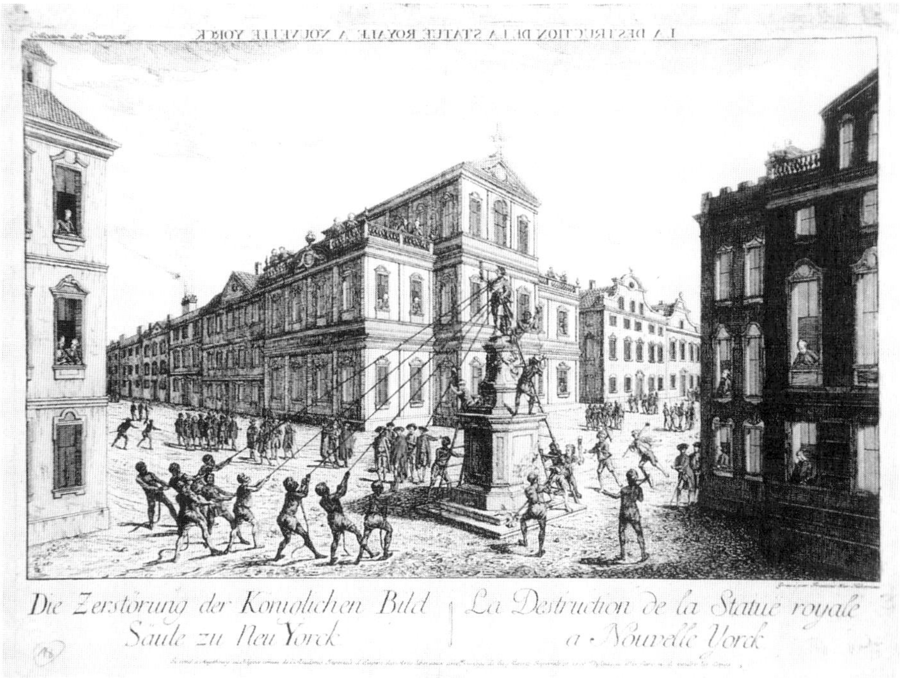

Die Zerstörung der Königlichen Bild Säule zu Neu Yorck
La Destruction de la Statue royale a Nouvelle Yorck

47 Austrian, *Destruction of the Statue of George III in New York*, after 1776, hand-coloured copperplate etching. Although this image was not necessarily imported, similar topographical views were, and in great quantity, Note the mirror-image title.

Kano and Tosa were umbrella terms, not styles, and it must be stressed that this division, though promoted by eighteenth-century art theorizers and their forebears, is utterly unconvincing to the art historian today.

Morishima Chūryō binarized, with a blitheness both rash and counter-empirical: 'The Tosa hand on the painting of this kingdom [*kyōkoku*], while the Kano teach that of the Continent; the Tosa do indigenous painting [*waga*], the Kano do Continental work [*tōga*]'.[48] This is unalloyed ideology. The Tosa was worth keeping alive as memory but useless for government, hence its allocation to the non-agent, ancestral shujo; by contrast, the shoguns needed the hortative strength of moral painting. By 'Continental', Chūryō meant pertaining to Chinese and Korean civilizations where the pre-lapsarian conditions enjoyed in the Japanese states until quite recent times (it was supposed) had never existed and which required morality to keep them placid. Chūryō wrote this in 1782. A decade earlier, the ripest polemicist for this brand of thought, Motoori Norinaga, had claimed:

> The [Continental] Way lies in goodwill and integrity, propriety and modesty, filial piety and respect for the elderly, loyalty to rulers and respect for one's fellows; these and others are euphemisms for indoctrination and control [. . .] In Japan nothing used to be argued over, which is why we never had rebellions.[49]

To Norinaga, the Continent had corrupted the indigene, necessitating disciplining morality, rule by shoguns and, with it, the Kano School.

The Kano were self-consciously an academy (*ha*), and they called their leader its 'director' (*shokutō*). The Tosa were a 'bureau of painting' (*edokoro*) headed by a 'junior minister' (*azukari*), titles taken from the defunct bureaucracy of the ancient Japanese court. The Tosa Bureau traced itself back to the mid-ninth-century artist Fujiwara no Toshimoto, who was made honorary marshal (*kami*) of Tosa, a state on the island of Shikoku. This was purely legendary, but accredited masters took the surname Tosa, and the head of the bureau was nominated to the sinecure marshalcy. In more concrete terms, the Tosa were reconstituted in 1657 when Tosa Mitsuoki received official recognition from the then shujo, Nakahito (posthumously, Gosai), in deference to which masters took the character *mitsu* as the first element of their studio name.[50] In the 1780s the junior minister and marshal was Tosa Mitsusada (illus. 48); waiting in the wings were his nephew Mitsutoki and son Mitsuzane. The Kano professed nothing so old and, as their role was to be master of the imagery of the later, ethicized world, they needed only to look as far as the beginnings of shogunal rule. Actually, they were older than the Tosa if legend is left aside, for almost two hundred years before Mitsuoki, in the 1470s, they had been founded by Kano Masanobu and his stupendously gifted son Motonobu (called Ko-Hōgen), who served the then shogunate of the Ashikaga family. Recognized Kano masters also used the name of the school as their surname. The Kano had entered Tokugawa service as 'painters in attendance' (*goyō eshi*) in 1617, when Kano Tan'yū moved his school to Edo from Keishi, one year after Ieyasu's death.

Both groupings were hereditary but also used adoption to ensure institutional continuity. Let us consider the Kano before returning to the Tosa.[51] Masters did not sell their work nor accept commissions, for as samurai they were under a hereditary obligation to one daimyo or to the shogunate itself, and they worked only as commanded by him in return for a fixed stipend. They were not 'artists' in any modern sense, but *eshi*, 'samurai in painting'. Their treatment was

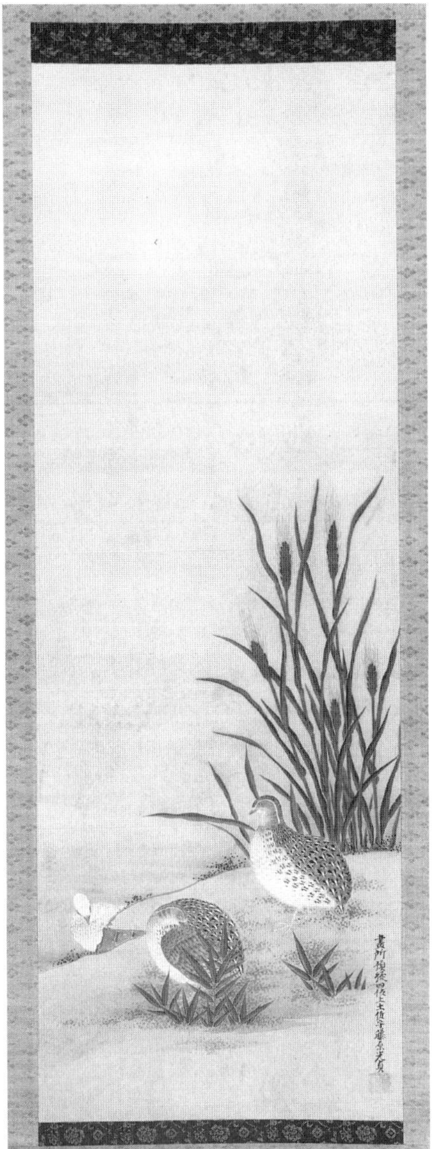

48 Tosa Mitsusada, *Quails and Wheat*, c. 1802, hanging scroll, colour on silk. Typical of the bright, emotive work of the Tosa School.

like that of any other specialist retainer of a low to middling level. Sadanobu had entered the school part-time in his early teens, and this was quite normal.[52] The Kano were open to a broad range of aspirants, and they functioned as a part-time training ground for many samurai boys. Non-samurai trainees could pass through the school but had to leave on graduation, becoming 'town Kano' (*machi-gano*), dealing in sub-standard, lower-genre work for commoner buyers; they did not go near castle interiors or produce government icons and were called *gakō*, 'picture artisans'.

After Tan'yū's death the Edo school divided into five main ateliers, ranked hierarchically and named after their location. Two came from Tan'yū's sons, two from sons of his elder brother, Naonobu, and one from a cousin, Sakon Sadanobu. The senior atelier was at Nakabashi (i.e. the Nakabashi Kano). In the 1780s its director was Kano Takanobu. Most daimyo had a Kano branch in their castle towns.

Keishi had retained a Kano branch after Tan'yū decamped, known as the Kyō–Kano. It traced itself to Kano Sanraku, Tan'yū's adoptive uncle, painter in attendance on Hideyoshi and his son Hideyori.[53] In deference to this, the Kyō–Kano took *san* as the first element in their names. In the 1780s, the head was Kano Eishun Sanboku. Unusually, the Kyō–Kano were not a blood-line (not even one supplemented by adoption) but handed on their title by nomination; in the Tokugawa context, this might be thought to reduce their authenticity.

The Kyō–Kano worked at Keishi's shogunal castle and daimyo residences, but from 1769 they began to work for the shujo too, a change initiated by Sanboku's teacher's teacher, Sansei.[54] A second Keishi atelier was already doing this, having come into existence in about 1700 at the request of the shujo, Asahito (posthumously, Higashiyama), who had desired the shogun to send him a master in the Tan'yū (as distinct from Sanraku) style. Tansen had come and, in deference to the Keishi tradition, had changed his name to Tanzan (the 's' mutates to a 'z'), fusing, as it were, his *Tan*'yū derivation with *San*raku's. Tanzan painted under his own surname, Tsuruzawa, not Kano, so that this line became known as the Tsuruzawa school. In the 1780s, the head was Tsuruzawa Tansō.[55]

This is intricate, but slightly more must be given. Just as the Kano ultimately provided pictures for the shujo, despite the claim, the Tosa had an arm working for the Tokugawa. It might in fact be argued that this Edo sub-group, called the Sumiyoshi, was the more vibrant. We have already met the late eighteenth-century head of the school, Sumiyoshi Hiroyuki, befriended by Sadanobu and teacher of Takamori's son (see illus. 4). The Sumiyoshi depicted their literary themes with a light brush, which commended itself well in Edo circles and was unlike the rich impasto of the pristine Tosa manner, which seemed recondite and burdensome to the newer shogunal elite.

It will be gathered that the clean division between 'indigenous' and 'Continental', between shujo and shogunal, insisted on by Chūryō and others, was in fact profoundly meaningless.

The full Kano training was a twenty-year process and was based on replication, in studio conditions, of the work of the respective branch-school's founder: in most cases this meant Tan'yū. Originals being rare (obviously, most had passed out of the school), copybook sketches or semi-finished studies were used. Pupils were expected to become adept at a range of manners. Innovation was not required. Kano ateliers were a match for any other samurai organization in their meticulous attention to code. In the rules that governed the Kano branch working for the daimyo of Chikuzen (one of the few extant), almost half relate to conduct: 'unruliness and impolite behaviour shall not occur in lessons', 'intercourse between master and pupil shall be on a proper ceremonial level' and so on.[56] Such a method of instruction was held to be the sole means of achieving flawless mastery of the corpus of style and subject relevant to the needs of rulers. The Kano identified what they did as 'real painting' (*honga*).[57] It was strict and firm, if gorgeously produced. Beyond this, there might be room for an art that was more limpid or inspirational, but that was not their point.

Theory and practice surely differed, and Kano masters probably undertook paid commissions, got things wrong and were late. There is evidence that they did experiment with the wider potentials of representation outside 'real painting'. Yet the central formulator of the school, Kano Yasunobu, head of the Nakabashi atelier for many years until his death in 1690, compiled a primer, *The Essentials of Painting (Gadō yōketsu)*, in which he emphasized the priority of 'real painting' over all others. He offered the division between 'learned' or school work (*gakuga*) and 'painting with personal qualities' (*shitsuga*), throwing his whole weight behind the former. 'Personal' painting, he readily admitted, might be 'marvellous' (*myō*), but its freedom of spirit meant it could not maintain 'precepts of utility for later times'.[58] Yasunobu enjoined Kano artists to work with a selfless collectivism that would allow them, as he put it, 'one brush, unchanged for a thousand generations'.[59]

Problems with the Kano

During the eighteenth century, Kano masters increasingly champed at the bit. One instance is found in a peculiar work by Kano Sōsen Kagenobu, head of the middling Surugachō Daichi atelier. Kagenobu's talents commended him to the overall leader, Kano Naganobu, head of the Nakabashi school (see illus. 20).[60] The painting shows a young woman in an unincidented background, bouncing a ball. Her unplucked eyebrows show she is unmarried; the modesty of her outer dress conflicts with her voluptuous red undergarment and it seems right to infer that she is a courtesan, although this cannot conclusively be affirmed. No client is present as she idly distracts herself. This casual piece is not 'real painting' and surely not a command-work; rather Kagenobu produced it for himself. The woman may be like the Kano master, momentarily unemployed and turning to unchecked, relaxing pleasures. The picture must constitute Kagenobu's contemplation, via the persona of the prostitute, on his own role. This association is made emphatic by her sash being inscribed 'painted by Kano Sosen'; the 'ball' she propels up and down with trivial abandon is an impression of the painter's seal, reading 'Kagenobu' within a circle. The marker by which he certified his oeuvre is just a prostitute's toy. Her sash makes her into him, so it is he himself, the kept man, who tosses his school identity about like a mere trifle. The piece of irony, both jocular and biting, implicates Kagenobu's career and, with it, all official painting. The work is undated, but in 1800, still in his early thirties, Kagenobu suddenly resigned from the Kano School, unable to endure any further the pressures of 'real painting'.

Others left too. Throughout this period the school shed many artists, including those today regarded as the best of their respective generations. Hanabusa Itchō, Yasunobu's pupil, walked out in the opening years of the century. Yanagisawa Kien left in the 1720s, with the romantic riposte that he would leap back and enter the tutelage of the ancients, who painted directly from heart and eye, without institutional strictures.[61] Itō Jakuchū extracted himself in the century's last decades, since, as the great abbot Daiten, his patron, recorded, 'he found copying [Tan'yū etc.] like pacing behind someone who was always running ahead [. . .] it created a barrier between himself and what he sought to depict, rather than which, he felt, he ought to use objects directly'.[62] Daiten went on that Jakuchū had 'mastered the Kano laws fully', but 'threw them away', thereafter devoting himself to pictures that, though still academically based, had little meaning within the canon of appointed themes. He rejected historical figures and symbolic Kano birds because (Daiten again), 'these were rarely to be seen', and instead he painted 'the cocks and hens that feed in the villages, and whose feathers are fine in colour too'. To make his orientation clear, Jakuchū kept a pen of poultry by his atelier window.

This appeal to empiricism was to emerge repeatedly, and a representative depiction by Jakuchū may be compared with a Kano one: Jakuchū's *Cock and Hen among Hydrangeas* and some anonymous late eighteenth-century Kano *Cranes* (illus. 21, 49). The difference is one of degree, but the degree is high. Jakuchū was a greengrocer by trade and, though too rich to do much of the weighing and sorting himself, was attentive to material texture and form. He knew how objects differ in luminosity, fluffiness and fall, and he wanted this captured in his picture. The Kano birds are spectacular and lavish but do not replicate avian truths. Nor do they seek to: the feathers are all of a kind and seem the same substance as the rocks and trees. If Jakuchū depicts birds, our Kano artist depicts *Kano* birds, going back to Tan'yū. Moreover, cocks are hardly 'real painting' subjects, whereas cranes are adulatory, long-living and auspicious signs. One refers to phenomena, the other to a tradition of renditions. When Jakuchū depicted cranes, as no painter could avoid doing, so routinely required was the theme, he still sought to make the imagery defer to the sense of a living fowl, creating beak, talons and feathers by means of different qualities of stroke. When prevailed upon to paint a tiger, he inscribed on it the somewhat churlish apology that he was painting something he had never seen and so knew he could capture none of its aspect of life.[63] The elite, of course, obtained Kano pictures precisely to have a Kano picture; they did not want their formal works to be mute about their ancestry, nor to bark of the farmyard. The opposition is between 'real pictures' and real birds.

Early in the nineteenth century the critic Tanomura Chikuden proclaimed that 'everyone has grown weary of the school of Kano'. He offers this as a truism not even necessary to prove. Chikuden attributed the collapse to 'the protracted peace reigning throughout the lands', that is, the polemics of virtuous kingship and loyal retainership

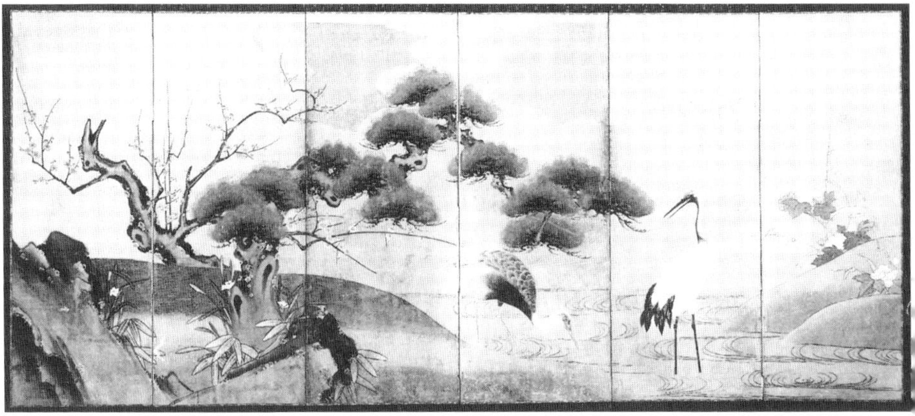

49 Kano School, *Plum, Pine and Cranes*, c. 1780, right-hand folding screen of a pair, gold and colour on paper. Exemplary of what was seen as the increasingly lumbering output of the Kano School.

had drifted out of mind – felicitous in itself, perhaps, but detrimental to the Kano project.[64] As a painter in the *nanga*, or 'literati' mode, anathema to academicians, Chikuden was hardly impartial, but Morishima Chūryō claimed the same, although he put it slightly differently. To Chūryō, the Kano had fossilized, with each generation attempting less, until 'since Tan'yū, the Kano style has undergone total transformation', that is, diminution, to the point that all masters now do is 'make fools out of those in authority', equipping them with facile shadows of yesterday's 'real pictures'.[65] Another commentator estimated that the early masters like Ko-Hōgen and Yasunobu had painted 'with great pregnancy' (*jūjoku*) and that Tan'yū had been good, but now 'the old Kano manner is defunct', particularly that of the masters of the end of the eighteenth century, whose good work was 'few and far between'.[66] The anonymous compiler of the *History of Popular Behaviour in the Kanpo and Enkyō Eras* (i.e. 1741–48) *(Kanpo enkyō fūzokushi)* looked back from the standpoint of 1792 and found the mid-century had been the time when the orthodox regime of art had stopped making sense. He concluded that, from then on, 'everyone agreed the Kano style was exhausted'.[67] Ueda Akinari, the Osaka fictionalist and fire-writer, thought it was 'the Kano posse being so disastrous' that accounted for the fracturing of representation, of which the emergence of Jakuchū and Chikuden were instances.[68] The diversity of later eighteenth-century painting manners is certainly unparalleled. In sum, if Tan'yū or Ko-Hōgen were accepted as summits in the painting world, the Kano line had succumbed.

The Kano were attacked on two fronts, both by those who sought in art a challenge and contestation of human experience and by those who wanted proper iconic order to be maintained. Conversely, their works were clamoured for by punters who saw in painting primarily a ladder for social mobility upwards. The appalling tea party that Gentaku had attended, with utensils of gold and silver, was, sure enough, decorated with paintings by Ko-Hōgen, flogged off by a daimyo house that was tired of them, and used as social cachet by the *nouveau riche* Horibe.[69] It needed serious money to acquire works of such grandeur. Original owners might sell for cash, or Kano moonlighters might secrete out bona fide work, while, if adequately rewarded, independent artists and Kano defectors might produce Kano-type work to support their more cherished endeavours. Yanagisawa Kien was approached by a buyer who wanted a 'Kano' piece, although Kien had cut his Kano ties. The person dismissed the sharp 'personality pictures' for which Kien was individually famous, showed him a printed book illustrating works by Kano Yōboku and

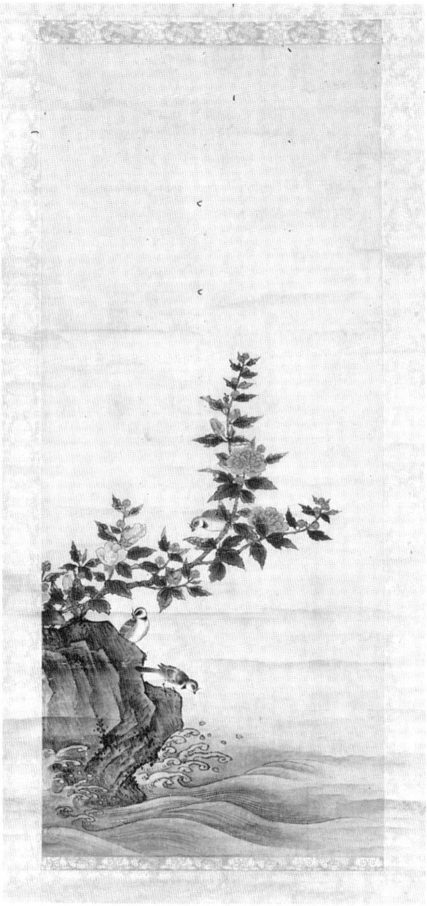
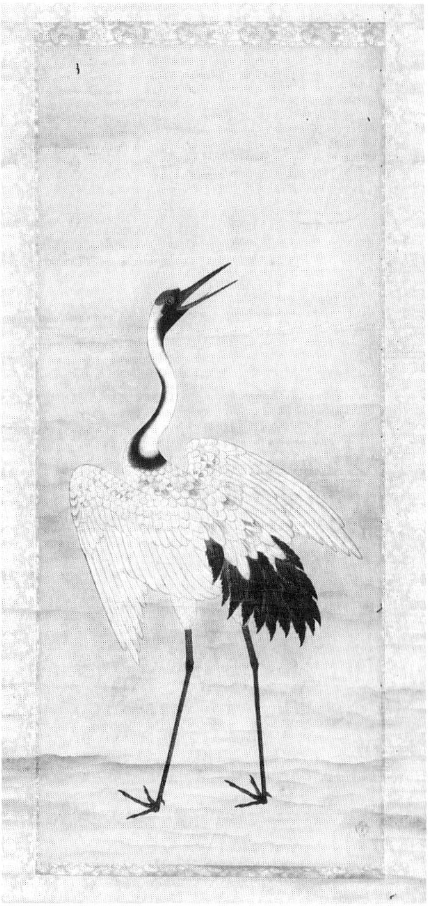

told Kien to replicate one.[70] Kien was livid but, for reasons of personal obligation, could not refuse.

Vast effort was expended on obtaining Kano pictures through underhand routes from those prepared to loan or sell their holdings, through genuine need, or to release money for more congenial alternatives. A certain townsman named Horikawa from Shimo-dachiuri in Keishi blued his entire business fortune and acquired the truly incredible debt of one million *ryō* by buying 21 Kano paintings and other appurtenances that he thought would raise his station.[71] Satirical comments on such pretentiousness were not few. Tan'yūs, being the most in demand, were the most often fraudulently produced and, given that copying was the regular mode of learning, *soi-disant* Tan'yūs could easily filter from the ateliers. A *senryā* verse (a short comic genre that specializes in contemporary fads, highly popular from the mid-eight-

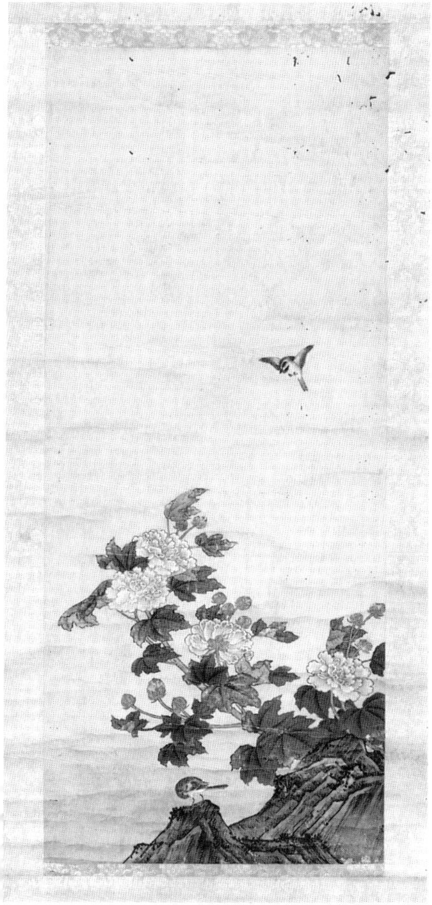

50 Pastiche after Kano Motonobu (Ko-Hōgen), *Crane with Sparrows on Rocks by a Stream*, c. 1780s, triptych of hanging scrolls, colour on silk. The work is hopelessly anachronistic: triptychs barely existed in Motonobu's day, and the practice of setting motifs against empty space had not been invented. The silk was deliberately distressed to simulate age.

eenth century) suggests that 'Tan'yūs' were now the flagship possessions of all and sundry, including even the higher grade of prostitute:

The woman with a private boudoir
Hangs up
A fake Tan'yū.[72]

(Controlling their own private room was the privilege of top courtesans.) Better even than Tan'yū was Ko-Hōgen, although he was so historic that credence might be stretched. *Hōgen*, literally 'dharmic eye', was a title granted to senior academy artists and other skilled professionals; *ko* meant 'old' or 'antique'. This sobriquet (the artist's real name, remember, was Motonobu) was not understood by some would-be purchasers, as was stated in another *senryū*: a social climber mistakes the *ko-* for a homophone meaning 'son' and tries to get one up on his friends:

Smugly
He says he's got one
By Hōgen *père*![73]

This is the level to which Kano ownership had sunk. Vast numbers of pseudo-Ko-Hōgen, Tan'yū and other paintings from the late eighteenth century, some exceedingly elaborate and often done on deliberately distressed paper or silk, continue to lurk in collections (illus. 50).[74]

If terminal decline was conceded to have set in during the 1740s, this corresponded with the directorship of Kano Terunobu (see illus. 67). His highest commission had come in 1748 when he headed the team producing screens to be given to the Chosŏn *wang* – the first such diplomatic gift for nearly 30 years.[75] The period of aesthetic sclerosis does not coincide with a diminishing institutional profile, more like the opposite. Also working on that royal commission for Korea was Kano Eisen-in (also called Michinobu), an interesting figure who inherited the directorship of the Takegawa Kano at the age of two. His father, also called Eisen-in (but written with different characters), died in 1732 aged 36, and his adoptive father, Jusen-in, shortly afterwards, aged 17.[76] The Takegawa was one of the minor Kano ateliers, but owing to his great ambition the young Eisen-in was able to assume control of the entire Kano world. He was raised with a sense of the precariousness of the school's future hold and developed a strong sense of himself as one who (in the words of the official *Tokugawa Chronicle (Tokugawa jikki)*), was 'the last member of a great house' and so was required 'to labour without stint'.[77] Virtually every collection of Japanese art around the world contains work by Eisen-in (illus. 51). He changed the Kano world. But his prolific labour seems to have been geared to *institutional* fortification. Akinari assessed, 'my lords delight in the painting of Eisen-in, claiming men like him are seldom found and that he is the greatest success since Tan'yū; I may not know anything about art, but I can't detect much to admire in him'.[78] As one commentator nicely put it, using the established musical metaphor, Eisen-in was so aggressive in forcing through the Kano prerogatives that 'he will not shift his bridge or adjust his drumskin': in other words, he scorned those who actually wanted modulated artistic stimulation.[79] He was playing a game that had little to do with the excitement of artistic expression. Eisen-in was problematic, too cleverly manipulative for some, but he skilfully restarted a machine that ran on

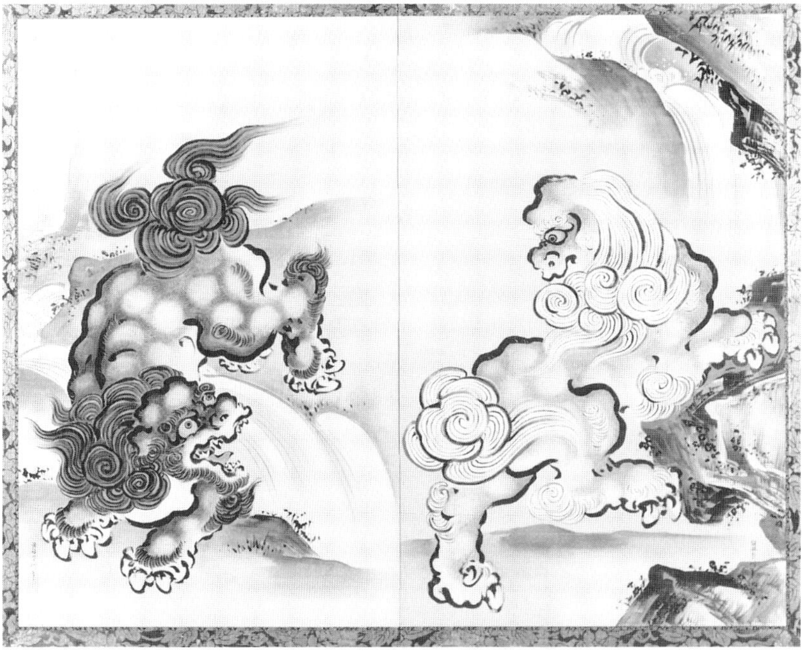

51 Kano Eisen-in, *Chinese Lions*, c. 1780, single-fold screen, gold and colour on paper. A classic example of the hortative and symbolic work of the Kano School, of which Eisen-in was director.

until his death in 1790, after which his son, Korenobu, took over.

The Kano had always been open to the objection that they neglected virtually everything that came before Tan'yū. The critic and painter Nakayama Kōyō complained in 1775, 'they only take him [Tan'yū] as their guide of what to do, and learn by copying his manners' and 'drilling themselves in the rules of this one lineage it is hardly surprising they have become sick'.[80] The broadest went back only to Ko-Hōgen. Eisen-in's young diligence was said to have manifested itself in an even more constricted view, and his singular achievement was said to be the gathering of 'all the directives of the masters since Yōboku and assembling them into a teaching treatise'.[81] In other words, he went back precisely as far as the second head of his own Kano branch, or the 1650s.

The cramped state of Kano painting did not entirely rule it out of favour with the elite. Ieharu met Eisen-in and liked him. The chronology is unclear, but it seems Ieharu deliberately intervened to secure a restructuring of the Kano apparatus that resulted in Eisen-in's overall leadership. The artist was removed from the Takegawa atelier, which was closed down, and re-established in grandiose premises in the Kobikichō district of central Edo; Eisen-in received a large mansion abutting this site. The new 'Kobikichō' Kano branch was given precedence over all the other lines, including the previously top Nakabashi.[82] Eisen-in successively absorbed more rights, took more students than any other master (they numbered in scores[83]) and flooded the Tenka with his work. He was always at the shogun's side, and Ieharu showered on Eisen-in 'special favours not bestowed upon others' and 'daily love and kindness'.[84]

The Ieharu/Eisen-in axis was a powerful one, and for the leery Tokugawa it made political sense to use this aggressive and slick young man. In 1763, just three years after taking shogunal office, Ieharu invented a title for his friend, 'inner painter' (*oku goyō-eshi*), that is, responsible for the shogun's private quarters. Previously, the Kano peak had been simply 'painter in attendance' (*goyō-eshi*), as established for Tan'yū. The new title was complemented by the creation of inferior 'outer painters' (*omote-eshi*), responsible for work in the public parts of the castle. In 1774 the inner paintership was linked to the rank of 'inner physicians' (*oku-ishi*), or doctors who treated the Tokugawa family (one of whom was to be Hoshū); this conferred the privilege of free range in all shogunal chambers, as well as access to the shogun's person.[85] Shortly afterwards (the date is uncertain) Eisen-in was himself made *hōgen*.

When Ieharu died in 1786, Eisen-in was 56. Power shifted. Sadanobu, poised to take headship of the new shogun's council, was not greatly pleased with the Kano handling of government icons. In later life he was to destroy all his own juvenile attempts in their manner, distancing his brush from theirs.[86] Sadanobu preferred to rely on peripheral artists who had academic mentalities but no rigid affiliations, like Tani Bunchō, Aōdō Denzen and Sumiyoshi Hiroyuki; these men all owed him, not their birth, nor even their teacher, primary allegiance. Sadanobu ambiguously defined Eisen-in as 'an adept painter and remarkably proficient at securing the patronage of important persons'.[87] As so often, Sadanobu's feelings were more openly expressed for him by Moriyama Takamori, who pointed out how unscrupulously Eisen-in had garnered power; he characterized him as 'compromised'. Although Takamori conceded Eisen-in was 'a good painter', he also found him to be a self-advertiser. After the *hōgen* honour was bestowed, Takamori wrote, 'one hears of very few artists becoming topics of general conversation, but recently when Kano Eisen[-in] received the accolade *hōgen*, we were certainly made aware of it'.[88] Eisen-in trumpeted himself as much as the Tokugawa. As for his ability to hold painting in true, despite the number of pupils, the evidence is that Eisen-in could not stop the bleeding from the school. Those who remained took a leaf from his own book and increasingly undercut collegiality by cults of personality, evinced in lifestyle if not in painting styles, corrosive to original corporate ideals. The pupils speak for themselves: Chōbunsai Eishi became close to Ieharu through Eisen-in, which benefited him mightily, but he abandoned 'real painting' to produce pictures of the Floating World, steeping the shogunal space in low-life revelry and eroticism (see illus. 19); Suzuki Rinshō, 'the toast of prominent figures', was invited to every banquet in the 1780s but trivialized the historic Sesshū manner he adopted and squandered his talents by 'hawking his pictures anywhere'.[89] Kano masters had once been bureaucratic stalwarts, but now they were celebrities. The genuinely popular Utamaro may have intended a dig at the populist Eisen-in in 1788 when he produced a series of parodies of various artistic styles old and new, culminating in one signed 'Hōin Eisen'; *hōin* ('dharmic seal') was the grade higher than *hōgen*, which few since Tan'yū had gained and Eisen-in was never to achieve.[90]

The location of Eisen-in's school and mansion was problematic. The reasons for selecting the Kobikichō site are uncertain, but Kobikichō was associated with kabuki for there were many theatres there; large numbers of actors roamed the streets, with attendant drinking and eating establishments, and this did not make for dignity. Kabuki was viewed askance by the regime and, although tolerated, was subject to intermittent legislation.[91] It was taken as an agent for the spread of vulgar manners into the city and even into the upper classes.[92] Kabuki produced fictionalized depictions of urban life to appease the masses, at odds with the official representation. More particularly, kabuki was the hub of male prostitution. Attractive actors supplemented their earnings by accepting paid engagements with fans. Full-time rent-boys took the title 'stagehands' (*kagema*) to excuse their hanging about at night: the word literally meant 'in the shadow' (i.e. off-stage), but the pun was obvious.[93] Kabuki had a ring not concordant with Kano aims. Takamori noted with distaste the location of Eisen-in's atelier and home, which smacked to him of an artistic inversion that spilled into the political, not least because the Kano compound was next door to a residence reeking of misaligned values – Tanuma Okitsugu's mansion. Okitsugu was Takamori's byword for upset and discord. He was not the only one to see pre-Sadanobu error as centring on Okitsugu's home; Sugita Genpaku did too, calling it a magnet for graft and simony.[94] The daimyo of Hirado was amazed at the grotesqueness of the building, and his horror was matched only by his fury at being kept waiting while those of lower rank, but bringing larger gifts, trooped in ahead.[95] In distinction to Sadanobu, whose glass windows in his turret of One Thousand Autumns gave a feeling of cool objectivity, Okitsugu had glass *ceilings* fitted, and goldfish could be seen swimming above the heads of astounded guests.[96] It was a perfect symbol of the inversion of order. When Okitsugu was finally ousted, destruction of his mansion was one of the in-coming administration's first acts.[97] Of Eisen-in, Takamori concluded: 'if he was good enough to be given a mansion next to this one of Tanuma's, of all places, he cannot but have been tainted to the core'.[98]

Eisen-in was regarded by many as so woven into the Tanuma regime as to lose the ability to act independently or to work for the shogun with due poise. Some took him as Okitsugu's spy and his home as both the literal and figurative door to the venal chief councillor's parlours of intrigue. People were seen after dark entering Eisen-in's mansion and then passing on surreptitiously into Okitsugu's.[99] It was wittily said with reference to the male prostitutes that at Kobikichō 'the selling point is that what should be done up at the front is done around at the back'; 'front' and 'back' (*omote-ura*) were code terms for lies and truth, and so we might paraphrase that Kobikichō was a place where correct norms did a volte-face – or even, to capture the humour, *volte-fesse*.[100] Ieharu was frittering away his time, Okitsugu's administration was rank, and the Kano were conniving with circumstance instead of representing unchanging good. Takamori would not have been alone in shuddering to think of so much going in and out of Eisen-in's rear entrance by night.

Subjects and Themes

About this time, the physician and scholar Tachibana Nankei recorded seeing a late sixteenth-century depiction of the medieval Genpei Wars (in which the Great Buddha of Nara had been destroyed) – a routine Kano theme. The work was by Kaihō Yūshō, a student of Kano Eitoku, a master regarded as third equal with Ko-Hōgen and Tan'yū and indeed whose reincarnation Tan'yū was hyperbolically said to be. Nankei approvingly noted that, although by Yūshō's day wars were fought with spears, the artist had not been misled by this, and in his painting 'none of the samurai holds a spear, but all have long swords'.[101] Anachronism was avoided. This was Nankei's advice for those who wished to reauthenticate Kano painting. He felt, 'anyone who attempts to depict events recounted in old narratives must pay attention to close details'. Casualness with historical accuracy, along with inattention to the real forms of nature, were the charges laid at the Kano door.

Ignorance frustrated imagery and vitiated the moral purpose that was the sole justification for the commissioning of 'real pictures'. The Genpei Wars were emblematic, for they provided the store of legend that continued to spur on the Tokugawa military elite and without which valour dwindled into the twilight. Nankei feared precisely this, and he moved from his discussion of the decline of painting to a consideration of the demise of what he called the 'Japanese warrior' (*Nihon no bushi*):

His mind is fixed on the thought that in desperate times he must go down before his lord's horse, fervently believing his life is at his lord's disposal. He concentrates on defeating the enemy to ensure the survival of his state, and seeks to conduct his lord into the ways of virtue. He brooks no flinching in the business of honour due to his lord.

That was how it used to be, but nowadays 'our modern Confucianists would have a good old laugh at this. To them, the Japanese warrior is a fool who rejoices in a dog's death, and fails to understand the real meaning of loyalty'.[102]

Sophistry was interfering with moral absolutes, and Kano painting was charged to keep it away. Nankei cited a concrete case to substantiate his argument. A painting of the medieval general Onen Yoshiie had been done by Sumiyoshi Hiroyuki's father, Hiromori.[103] Someone praised the work but also offered the criticism that 'the complexion was not appropriate to someone like Yoshiie' because it was not rugged enough, being done in a powdery white. Hiromori countered that, although modern samurai might imagine uncouth sunburned brutes in opposition to their own blanched chamberers' aspects (thereby imagining themselves superior to the past), actually ancient warriors had been able to conjoin refinement and toughness, and so 'the painter laughed', said Nankei, reporting Hiromori as 'asking, "Are you so entirely ignorant of the uses of military make-up?" And, Nankei went on, bringing things up to date, 'my friend, the scholar Gakutan, heard this story and commended the artist for his knowledge of the specifics of history' – and of course for his inclusion of them in a picture, to inform and inspire the modern viewer in the range of true military accomplishment.

Such anxieties found wide agreement. *Pace* Nankei, many Confucian scholars were behind moves to renovate painting through a study of historical and literary texts. One was Tachihara Suiken, appointed rector of the important Confucian academy in Mito in 1786 and a dominating force in historical studies, even after his forced retirement in a common-room coup of 1803.[104] It was probably after his removal that Suiken began writing on art, and he attributed the loss of relevance in Kano painting to masters no longer reading the books from which their imagery derived. He cited many cases of contemporary error which, though pedantic, were to him cumulatively enough to vitiate the whole 'real painting' endeavour and so were in urgent need of addressing. Suiken objected to anachronistic crowns worn on portraits of the ancient shujo, to characters in the *Tale of Genji (Genji monogatari)* depicted as dressed in leather, which was not worn at that time, and suchlike minutiae.[105] Scholarship would purge these mistakes and roll back the concatenated blunders, making the past shine clear again. The paragon of filial piety Guo Chen, for example, was routinely shown beside a golden pot, but Suiken pointed out this was a grammatical howler: it should be a pot *of* gold, 'pot' (*fu*) being a

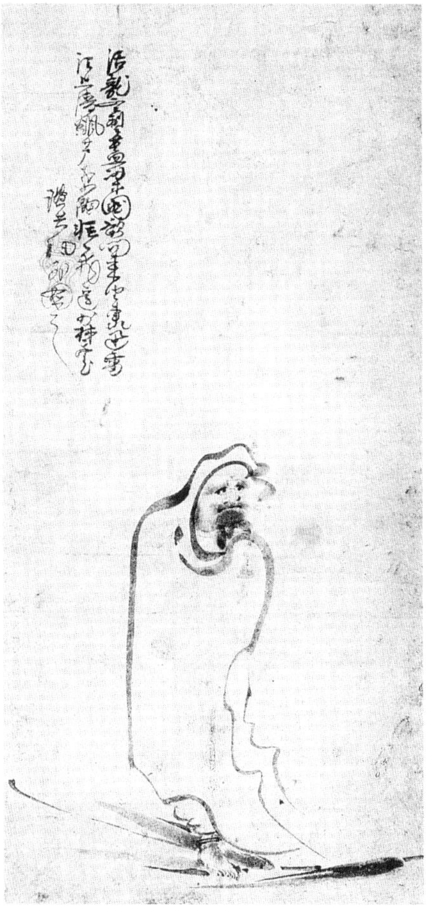

52 Fūgai Keikun, *Bodhidharma Crossing the Yangzi on a Reed*, c. 1630, hanging scroll, ink on paper. The typical way of representing the patriarch's passage from North to South China.

unit of measurement (equivalent to 12 litres), not a type of receptacle. The sea god Ebisu was shown carrying a bream, pronounced 'tai', but properly the *tai* intended meant a kind of sword. The founder of Zen Buddhism, Bodhidharma, was shown crossing the River Yangzi 'on a reed' (illus. 52) – a miracle perhaps. But no: Suiken deplored the sight of the bulky patriarch on his impossibly tiny stalk and reported that 'reed' (*zhan*) properly meant a type of boat.[106] On such abstruse points rested the coherence of representation. Interestingly Suiken's son, Kyōsho, born the year Suiken took over the Mito school, became an artist wedded to representational accuracy, although he specialized in topographical, not historical, work.[107]

Tempers could run high in such debates, as is seen in an exchange between the Kano master Katsuyama Takushū and Soga Shōhaku.[108] Shōhaku was an eccentric and famed for the 'personal qualities' of his art, but he still demanded that 'real pictures' get things right, for all the differences of their style from his. At some undetermined time this Takushū, who died in 1778, painted *The Floating Bridge at Sano*, a common academic subject illustrating a verse by the great classical poet Fujiwara Teika:

To pull up my horse
And shake out my sleeves
There is no shelter;
The crossing at Sano
This snowy twilight.[109]

The limpid verse was often read and mused upon, as one visualized the old courtier on horseback, weighed down with snow. Not much is specified about the nature of the crossing, but anyone who read around in the tradition would know that Sano had a pontoon bridge (*funabashi*). It had to be depicted as such. Takushū showed a fixed bridge and even put railings on it. Shōhaku condemned this as 'a disgrace to the artists of Keishi' and rudely demanded that Takushū (his social superior) 'repaint it as it should be, straight away!' Takushū's reply is instructive; his rendition needed no emendation, he said, because 'it is based on a sketch by the hand of Kano Tan'yū himself'. Precedence is given to school-based traditions over cultural lore, never mind over nature. Motoori Norinaga was to deplore this as the dominance of 'in-house rules' (*ie no hō*) over truths.[110]

Calls to make painting more accurate were not unique to this period, but in the late eighteenth century the complaints became a din of voices. No one put it more succinctly than Norinaga, whose *On*

Pictures (E no koto) of 1799 was an attack on the whittling of the power of art by inaccuracy, and the counter-productiveness of half-baked modern academic painting. He openly stated his rationale: painting must be correct, 'for foreigners and also for those of this royal land too'.[111] To know the appearance of the past we all rely on pictures.

The artists around Sadanobu provide examples of those who thought along similar lines, eradicating error without rescinding their commitment to classical themes. Sadanobu applauded his retainer Takegawa Yōkei, a quondam student of Eisen-in, who went on to produce a set of seventeen scrolls on the Genpei Wars. He 'researched deeply into the facts of antiquity [*kojitsu*]', reworking the ancient tradition and ridding it of mistakes, but also supplementing it with a real emotional charge readable in the present. People needed some help to feel the authority of history, and adaptation was acceptable as long as it elucidated, rather than obscured, how things really felt. For unstated reasons (incapacity or death?) Yōkei downed brush with the job unfinished. But his son Ishū took over, demonstrating both filiality and industriousness, and Sadanobu summarized, 'they brought out all that was good in [Genpei] imagery, while reworking it'.[112] The crux was to make a subject relevant without compromise.

History and nature were two sources of moral inspiration. The present might also provide models, and when auspicious events occurred it was the job of artists to capture them for circulation and for the edification of future times. Painting supported government record-keeping or, to Sadanobu, could even supplant it:

Information passed on either orally or textually cannot ensure complete transmission. For example, you can refer to a thing as red or white, but neither spoken nor written words properly capture what redness means in the context, or how whiteness is white. This is why we collect data in picture albums, to supplement our libraries of written records.[113]

Sadanobu took it as a government duty to stop painting degenerating any further along the path of 'the laughing stock so much of it is today'. He appealed to international norms, as did Norinaga, only with a different emphasis: 'In most countries they make albums of pictures and in our states too it is vitally important to do so'. But where these were being made, they were not being made well. Sadanobu wondered why it was that, whereas

. . . you can use the Tang-period depiction of the Eighteen Scholars to understand the clothing of that period, or use the 'Annual Rites' segments of the famous Origins of Kasuga and Origins of Ishiyama to tell the appear ance of the dress, palace architecture, forms of weaponry and other fittings and furnishings of that age,

contemporary painting offered no such pegs.[114] Sadanobu set himself the task of fostering an accurate style of 'painting of the present' (*imaga*), literally 'pictures of now'. Present-day themes were the stomping ground of Floating World artists such as Utamaro, Shigemasa, Masayoshi and Eishi, but their brief was to prettify and to eroticize society. Theirs was the most flamboyantly successful school of the later eighteenth century, but as a group they could not gainsay the objection that they falsified the present, making it wanton, loose, over-dressed and glib. Sadanobu called them a 'debased school' (*iyashiki ryū*).[115] Floating World artists shunned high events in favour of the worlds of pleasure, the definition of 'floating' being that which was unregulated, undisciplined, not 'fixed'. The school was without the intellectual wherewithal or stylistic urge to depict auspicious things; indeed, as Sadanobu did not adequately acknowledge, since this was a townsperson's school, Floating World artists would have risked punishment had they attempted ambitious political themes. Nevertheless, to him, even when 'mounted and displayed as hanging scrolls', such pictures were not serious or trustworthy, and 'in future times what will people have to turn to when they seek to investigate our social mores?' The chief councillor hated the thought that his period of custodianship of the states would be adjudged on the evidence of representations in pictures of the Floating World.

Sadanobu took elite flirtation with the pleasure districts as yet more evidence of the 'trickle-up' of proletarian manners that had occurred during Okitsugu's inverted administration under the spineless Ieharu. The shogun had not only tolerated Eishi's switch from the Kano School to the Floating World manner but had celebrated it, although Eishi was a senior samurai: his father, grandfather and great-grandfather had all been chancellors of the shogunal exchequer (*kanjō bugyō*), and he might have been so in his turn.[116] Ieharu let Eishi keep his lodgings in Edo Castle even after he began producing eroticized painting and relieved him of all official duties so he could concentrate on it more, making him a shogunal 'companion' (*yoriai*) – usually awarded to venerable men obliged to discontinue service for medical reasons. Pictures of the Floating World brought in their wake actualizations of low life, such as brothel singing, flashy dressing or partying with members of other social classes, and they propelled even once-staid personages into flightiness, until the economy was wrecked by libidinous extravagance. The prince–abbot of the Temple of the Wondrous

Dharma (Myōhō-in-no-miya), for example, Tomohito's older brother and no flibbertigibbet, when in Edo on ecclesiastical business in 1800, saw an Eishi painting; he loved it and took it back to Keishi with him, where he showed it to no less a person than the retired shujo, his adoptive grandparent.[117] This work is lost, but it is known to have depicted the River Sumida, a theme in which Eishi excelled, but to judge from extant examples would have taken viewers on an imaginary trip up Edo's arterial waterway and deposited them not in invigorating countryside but in the Yoshiwara brothel district some three miles upstream.[118] Did the ex-shujo really need to see a thing like this? We are talking, after all, about an elderly lady (she had been one of the few female shujos), now 60 and something of a blue-stocking. But far from recoiling, she let it be known she had viewed the work with pleasure, permitting Eishi to use the title *tenran* ('viewed by the court').[119]

Sadanobu, when in power, could not stop Eishi painting, but he could take institutional counter-measures against him. Eishi was made to remove himself from Edo Castle and resign his hereditary position; although over 40, he had failed to produce an heir (evidence enough of social irresponsibility), so he was required to hand on to an adopted son, Tokitoyo. As he was a senior samurai, Eishi's lapse was glaring. But it was not isolated. There was Kurahashi Itaru, whom we have already met as the ambassador in Edo of the daimyo of Suruga-Ojima, writer of the parody on Sadanobu's kite-flying metaphor, who used the pen-name Koikawa Harumachi; in 1789 Sadanobu summoned him to the castle to answer for that and other Floating World writings and japes.[120]

Sadanobu also intervened directly to reorientate the popular Floating World print-maker Kitao Masayoshi who, although not nearly so elite as Eishi or Itaru, was originally of samurai stock and so ought to set an example. In a reverse of the trajectory taken by Eishi, Masayoshi was persuaded to give up his 'debased' idiom and enter the Kano School and so, from 1794, he began studying with Eisen-in's son, Korenobu, who now ran the Kobikichō atelier.[121] Masayoshi excelled in his new persona, perhaps accepting the career advantages this change of circumstance brought him. His lapsed samurai status and surname, Kuwagata, were restored to him (these had been on his mother's side and so had gone into remission), and three years after moving into the Kano orbit he took the formal atelier name Keisai. As Kuwagata Keisai he became painter in attendance to the daimyo of Tsuyama who (no coincidence) was Sadanobu's cousin. Thus recycled the ex-Eishi painted for Sadanobu too, producing for him a scroll on the impeccably 'real' theme of pious legends associated with Ieyasu's mausoleum at Nikkō.[122]

Outside an age of battle, routine painting on up-to-date themes focused on labour, humble relaxation and the look of towns and cities more than on infrequent processions, inductions or miraculous occurrences. 'Painting of the present' needed to be accurate but was not necessarily lofty in subject, only in purpose. Genre painting had long been used politically. By it, daimyo assessed the appearance of their states and the pacificity of their people. Even if beautified, genre painting at least erred on the side of ethical idealization, suggestive of model polities, but the Floating World pictures that had swallowed genre painting erred the other way. Often cheaply printed, they could be consumed by the lowest classes and, from being a means for rulers to view the commonality under their sway, genre painting became a means of self-valorization by commoners themselves. They tempted viewers who could least afford it into profligacy in pursuit of the excessive delights shown. Artists were culpable of enticement. They never showed workers (unless actors, prostitutes or wrestlers). Sadanobu deplored that there was now no way to make 'paintings of the present' except in the idiom of the Floating World.[123]

Takamori expanded this fear, offering the very modern-sounding concern that pictures of the Floating World were damaging children by showing them the wrong templates:

In the past we used books for children to learn from, and ensured the pictures inculcated the difference between right and wrong; there were the lives of Kusunoki and of Yoshitsune. Even when stories were fictional, they never omitted to instil virtue and chastise vice.

But this sensible pedagogy had made an inglorious exit:

Now these books have fallen by the wayside, and we let children see things they cannot be expected to understand, and which ought to be kept for adult amusement only. In this category I would put illustrated stories of the Floating World.[124]

Feckless mothers, inflamed by such imagery, even fancied becoming courtesans themselves; they dressed their daughters up like young trainee prostitutes they saw in pictures and had their sons wear crests of actors-cum-callboys.[125] Genpaku maintained fathers had come to think it normal for their daughters to be indistinguishable from whores, and some had hit on the idea of renting them out from brothels rigged up in their gardens, 'and next thing you know, they'll be doing as much with their wives'.[126] The cause was attributable to the circulation of evil 'pictures of the present'. Pictures of the Floating World were also known as 'Edo pictures' (*Edo-e*), and they were much exported throughout the Tenka; for people to take these as the real likeness of life in the shogunal capital was, to Sadanobu, mortifying.

A nadir was reached in 1804 when two Edo publishers, the Kagaya and the Moriya, printed sets of depictions of Hideyoshi ('the Taikō') by Utamaro; they were probably taking advantage of a Hideyoshi boom stemming from publication that year of his fictionalized biography, *The Illustrated Life of the Taikō (Ehon taikō-ki)*.[127] Hideyoshi was the great potentate of the immediately pre-Tokugawa period. The publishers fused all that was wrong with history painting with all that was wrong of pictures of the present.[128] Full details are not known, but one image issued showed Hideyoshi viewing cherry blossoms with his 'five wives'; this was an event that had really occurred, in the spring of 1598, when the group had gone to the Temple of Clarified Butter (or ghee, the Daigo-ji). It might have been better to show the gentleman in a more heroic moment, but, fair enough, like everyone else he relaxed sometimes. However Utamaro had shown the wives as modern women, and as typical denizens of the Floating World to boot: that is, looking like prostitutes. Another print showed Hideyoshi fondling a boy lover; true again, he had indulged in them, but the child was not depicted as the kind of hero-in-waiting that Hideyoshi had (surely!) actually associated with but as a vacuous and sappy modern. One of the earliest accounts of the stir that the publication caused was left by the Edo fictionalist Takizawa Bakin:

> . . . [they] put out the figures from the *Illustrated Life of the Taikō* in the format of multi-coloured prints, making everyone look like modern-day prostitutes such as you find in [Floating World] picture books [. . .] in the autumn the *Illustrated Life of the Taikō*, from Osaka, was withdrawn from circulation.[129]

Although Sadanobu was now formally in retirement, punishment was triggered. Utamaro was manacled, by some accounts imprisoned, and two years later he was dead.

Rebuilding Keishi, Making Kyoto

The destruction of Keishi in the Great Fire of 1788 provided an opportunity for rethinking how the regime might better represent itself. As we have seen, a standard response came to the fore when the lost central enceinte of the shogunal castle was bombastically not rebuilt, but the case of the shujo's manion, the Dairi, is more complex and merits examination.

Shogunal and shujo lines had intermarried and achieved a sort of balance, although this was never satisfactory and often acrimonious. For the first half of Ieharu's period in office the shujo had been a woman, Toshiko (posthumously, Go-Sakuramachi), the blue-stocking. The precedent for a regnant female had been set in 1629 when the then shujo, Kotohito (posthumously, Go-Mizunoo), attempted to seize power from the still new shogunate and, failing, resigned in favour of his last-but-one daughter Okiko (posthumously, Meishō).[130] Kotohito's sons were dead, but this nicely illustrated how the shujo's office was no longer serious enough to warrant a male holder. Okiko herself was just six and the first female ruler for some eight hundred years (in high antiquity there had been several). Toshiko, on her ascent, was an adult aged 22 but was still only the second woman in nigh on a millennium. Something of the depleted sense of a woman shujo can be surmised from the fact that she and Okiko were omitted from the official dynastic portraits.[131]

The posthumous names that shujos were given (or sometimes chose) were the placenames of the part of Keishi with which they were most associated, selected also for euphony and poise. In this period the designations form a list whose self-referentiality bespeaks an uncommon introversion, like a constricting circle. The four incumbents from the second quarter of the eighteenth century are Sakuramachi, Momozono, Go-Sakuramachi and Go-Momozono (*go* meaning 'the later'). Perhaps not unlike the James I, Charles I, Charles II, James II that bracket the monarchical slump of the English Civil War. But whereas serial replications were routine for European monarchs, they are unique to this time in the shujo court. Physiologically too, the line was weak, the four incumbents dying aged 31, 22, 74 and 22 respectively; 22 was the youngest any shujo had died during the Tokugawa shogunate. Only one achieved a natural span, and that was the woman.[132]

Many a shujo felt greater prominence would become him. One such was Tomohito. The despondency of the shujo house was well articulated by Ichijō Teruyoshi, scion of one of the most ancient families and Tomohito's Great Minister of the Left, or chief advisor. The shogun was taking more and more away; if one pole rose, the other naturally fell. Teruyoshi objected, 'the sense that the military has of its own dignity is rising to greater and greater heights' and added, seething, 'I cannot bring myself to discuss the subject'.[133]

The immediate cause of Teruyoshi's anger was Ieharu, or more correctly, his corpse. The shogun had died a fortnight before and, although many saw benefits in this, the obsequies required protracted mourning, including month-long ceremonies and a ten-day silence. These stood out starkly against the mere three days' mourning for a shujo's death. But here the timing fell badly for Teruyoshi personally: 'Today', he wrote on the sixteenth of the ninth month of 1786, 'I was due to celebrate my birthday, but a moratorium has been placed on hunting and fishing owing to the dolorous occurrence in the Kantō [Edo]'. Buddhist prohibitions on killing were being strictly observed. Teruyoshi did not see why he should go without his party:

Our cupboards are quite bare, and although there was one market selling vegetables, the military disapproved and closed it down. We thought we might at least be allowed not to suffer for lack of greens, and crowded the stalls, but they shut it on the grounds of their 'August Peace' [*onpen*].[134]

That year, Tomohito was sixteen. Invested young, he remained in place for almost half a century, longer than any shujo until Hirohito (posthumously, Shōwa). Like Ieharu's successor, Ienari (who had been too rapidly adopted), Tomohito had a rather questionable legitimacy. Ienari was a distant cousin, but at least the shogunate had no absolute assumption of father-to-son descent, and indeed the 'virtuous' eighth shogun, Yoshimune, was tenuously linked, being the previous shogun's great-great-grandfather's brother's grandson. For Tomohito it was more awkward. He had been elevated when the old shujo died without issue, and his father was royal but had not been shujo, which constituted the first break in filogeniture since 1212.[135] Problems in coping with Tomohito appear in the wavering over finding a suitable name for him; he was instituted as 'Morohito' but a few weeks later made 'Tomohito' – an irregularity that is not adequately accounted for.[136] Uneasiness was felt by Tomohito himself, and his repeated signing of documents '120th generation since Jinmu' (Jinmu was the legendary first human shujo after the god-kings) is one indication of neurosis, for signing with lineage number was not normal.[137] Tomohito had been properly adopted (albeit with unseemly speed and rancour) and there was no question on that score, but adoption itself was problematic.[138] The *Conversations Transcribed on a Short Night (Sayo no kikigaki)*, compiled in 1801 by an author who wisely left his name off the manuscript, periphrastically recorded:

The present shujo is really the youngest son of Kannin-no-Miya Sukehito, and was only adopted by the previous ruler, Go-Momozono-in; the situation did not suit the precedents [*furei no toki*], but the latter was already on the point of passing away. Their blood was distant. It is not that people could actually be said to scorn him on this score, but still, it is not like having a real descendant [*jisshi*].[139]

The author then admits: 'there are some bold fellows who do treat him with contempt'.

Most famous is Tomohito's prickly regard for his father, Sukehito; until the latter's death in 1794 he petulantly insisted on him being addressed as 'retired shujo', a masquerade that it was quite impossible for the shogunate (who ratified such things) to stomach. As a conciliatory gesture Sadanobu doubled Sukehito's salary, but he forced him to remain with his prescribed title.[140] What followed was a cantankerous exchange during which at one point the shujo's ministers came to Edo to remonstrate, only to be unceremoniously locked up by Sadanobu; Tomohito played at being ill in an attempt to force the shogun to come and visit him in person, and when that did not work he pretended to be dead.[141] Titsingh recorded grim fears that such 'manifest proof of his [Tomohito's] displeasure might furnish a pretext for enterprises, that would occasion the greatest commotions'.[142] Gijsbert Hemmij, the incumbent Dutch leader, noted bluntly of shujo and shogun, 'these two rulers are in discord'.[143]

Troubles were brewing when the fire hit Keishi. A questionable shogun and even more questionable shujo, as well as their ministers, embarked on a vitriolic struggle to control the imagistic fabric of the Tenka's core city which they both shared. The policy Sadanobu devised aimed at delegitimating the shujo relative to the shogun, precisely by making his icons too impressive. Sadanobu debased Tomohito by over-inflating him, while heightening the Tokugawa by dutiful reduction. Tomohito fell headlong into the trap. The struggle focused on the Dairi.

One word occurs incessantly with reference to the rebuilding of the Dairi: *fukkō*. Sadanobu had it constantly on his tongue, Tomohito forever on his lips. Dictionary translations cover 'revival' and 'restoration'. It carries here a nuance of 'fabrication'. The new Dairi was a mock-up of that supposed to have existed in ancient times, but, although architectural evidence was studiously gathered, it was too scant for the project to be viable.[144] The move to 'restore' carried with it invention. The idea to fabricate came from the shujo's entourage and was initially refused by Sadanobu, who first felt Tomohito could have a mansion like anyone else's or even (he baldly suggested) no mansion at all, since he could put up with friends.[145] He mustered 'forceful arguments' against Tomohito's escalating demands and reminded him that a nice palace for him meant 'blood and sweat for the little people'.[146]

But Sadanobu changed his mind once it occurred to him this might be a way to silence Tomohito by calling his bluff. The point is, a 'restored' Dairi had to be much bigger.

Sadanobu revealed how he came to accept the proposed structure. He visited Keishi after the fire and, on his return to Edo, stopped to pray at Ieyasu's burial site on Mt Kunō; it was raining hard and the sky was black. Sadanobu vowed that if the weather had cleared by the time he left, he would 'revive' the Dairi. While he was within, the downpour transformed itself to sunlight.[147] This no doubt embroidered tale proposes 'revival' as Ieyasu's direct wish. It made shujo and his court beholden, so that, Sadanobu thought, 'one and all they will be filled with gratitude for the bounty of the Kantō', and it pushed Tomohito to the limits of the iconography of tyranny.[148] The shogunate paid for the resulting building, rather than soliciting funds from daimyo as was usual with construction projects. The cost was an astronomical 160,000 *kanmon* plus 465 *koku* in rice. At 25,041 *tsubo* (nearly 1 hectare) the compound was almost a third as large again as what it replaced.[149]

Few among the populace who shivered through the winter cold would have quite understood what a 'revived' Dairi was, but all realized how fulsome the edifice was compared with the last one. For over a year Tomohito absorbed all the available wood in Keishi, and none could be sold to anyone else until he was done. Again, this may be malign rumour, but it is what the Keishi citizenry believed and, if true, was surely shogunal strategy, for Sadanobu was sensitive to how lack of building materials might cause anger, as well as the danger of profiteering.[150] When it came to points of symbolic importance, Sadanobu too could hold his ground, as when Tomohito demanded eighteen stairs leading up to his daïs, which he insisted was the antique way; Sadanobu made him do with just nine.[151] Matters became so fraught that the shogunal plenipotentiary in Keishi, into whose remit shujo buildings fell, was relieved of this responsibility and Sadanobu took over personally.[152]

These manifestations of splendour at the Dairi may be compared with notions adumbrated by Sadanobu in his *Words on Government (Seigo)*, an important treatise that plots his thinking on kingship. One chapter is entitled 'Virtue in a Ruler is Manifested by Modesty', and it cites the case of the legendary sage-kings:

It is recorded that in ancient times Yao and Shun said not to trim their roofs, so the palaces were left with uneven thatch. They said not to use a plane, so their beams were left with the roughness unsmoothed.[153]

Yao and Shun used earthenware vessels, not gold or silver, adorned themselves with neither jewels or jade, and wore no silk or clothes with ornamental linings, patterning or designs; their garden walls were not whitened. 'This', Sadanobu concluded, 'is why they have served as mirrors for rulers for over 100 generations'. Walls and roofs were all that chance passers-by would see of the Dairi, and Tomohito's brilliant white wall was matched by gleaming tiles which replaced the unpolished cedar shingles he had indeed had on his former palace.[154]

The Dairi wall brought the visitor to an ornate gate, double-shut, looking due south (see illus. 39). Beyond this was a cloistered courtyard permitting a prospect of the main building, the Hall of the Screened Mansion (Shishiiden or Shishinden), and to its left the Pure and Fresh Hall (Seiryōden) (illus. 53, 54). By definition, pictures of the Dairi are hard to come by. The two-volume court circular, published annually in Keishi and Edo from 1758 as the *Bright Mirror of 'Above the Clouds' (Unjō meikan)*, opened with an overview of the precinct (the book's only illustration). The work was highly deferential, as is suggested by the euphemistic title, and the editors' *politesse* extended to avoiding mention of Tomohito's adopted status (although all other adoptees were noted as such), but the picture is useful. The Dairi illustration that appeared in the 1758 edition was reprinted for each issuing, unaltered. The edition of 1788, though radically cropped, even showed the buildings that were no longer there.[155] There were no editions in the period 1789–91. But the next issuing, 1792, had a recut illustration, and it grandly offered a prospect of the new compound, with the wall and double gates, and cloisters giving on to the Hall of the Screened Mansion (illus. 55).[156] The picture only matches other evidence generalistically, but that it was produced at all is an indication of how the cultural status of the city was being renegotiated. It was not quite Catherine's palace in St Petersburg, but the new Dairi became part of the townscape in a way no Dairi had previously been. Such display amounted to a major rethinking of political iconography.

In the eleventh month of 1790 Tomohito moved back from across the river to take up residence. His retinue spent eight hours processing with great pageantry along the road of just a few kilometres.[157] A pair of screens was commissioned in celebration from Yoshimura Shūkei, showing the shujo's *hōō*-topped palanquin passing over Sanjō Bridge and entering the city proper (see illus. 22–4). The circumstances of production are unknown, but Shūkei was a senior member of the recently established Yoshimura school of Osaka (a Kano offshoot derived from Tanzan) and held the rank of *hōgen*. This was surely 'painting of the present' at its mellifluous best. However, the paintings were soon

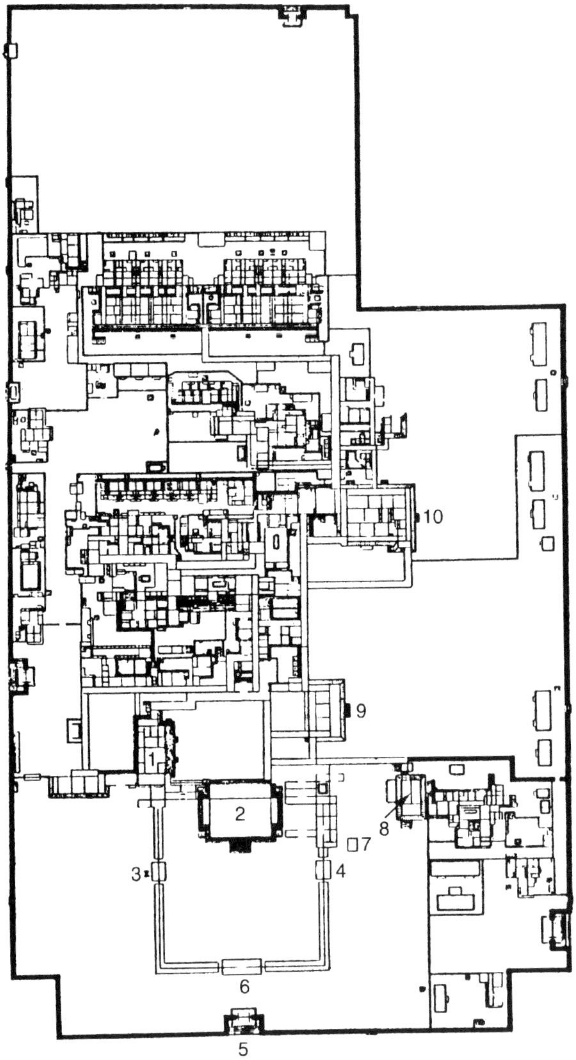

53 Plan of the Dairi in 1790, based on Fujioka Michio, *Kyōto gosho* (Chūō Kōronsha, 1987). The Dairi was larger and more imposing than before, and notably had a new cloistered forecourt. *Key*: *1* Pure and Fresh Hall; *2* Hall of the Screened Mansion; *3* Moon and Flower Gate; *4* Sun and Flower Gate; *5* Noble South Gate; *6* Gate of Bright Informing; *7* Palanquin Garage; *8* Ancestral Spirit Chamber; *9* Lesser Chambers; *10* Daily Chambers.

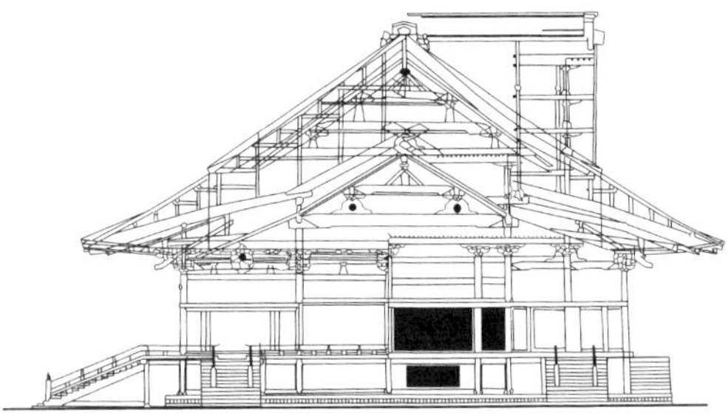

54 Cross-section of the Shishiiden in 1790, based on Fujioka Michio, *Kyōto gosho*. Known as the Hall of the Screened Mansion, this was the main ceremonial space, containing the crucial *Sage Screens*.

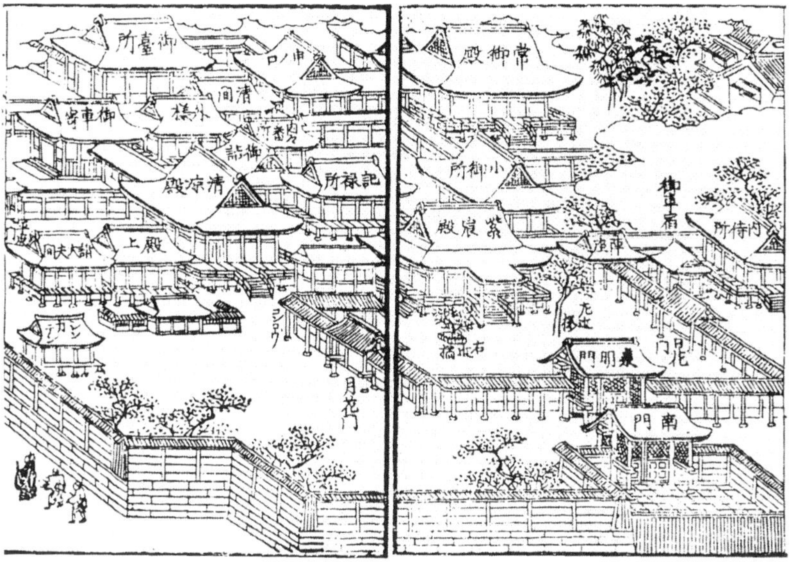

55 Illustration from *Unjō meikan*, 1792, monochrome woodblock prints. This often-published court circular did not alter its illustration of the Dairi until this edition, when the new buildings were shown.

forgotten and, within a century, were sold off, their subject misidentified, overseas.

While the Dairi was nearing completion, Kurahashi Itaru, using the name 'Koikawa Harumachi', had included in the same satirical story that mocked the kite-flying fiasco, a dig at the shujo's buildings. A shujo who is ostensibly the tenth-century Atsugimi (posthumously, Daigo), known as a stand-in for hyper-punctiliousness in matters of ritual, appears in a pose that mimics the virtuous Osazaki who had let his turrets collapse and his coverlets become soaked (illus. 56; see illus. 2).[158] 'Harumachi' twists Osazaki's lines at seeing no smoke rise from cooking hearths and makes sordid innuendos: 'looking into the distance, I see something like [the brothel district of] Yanagiwara, where you can rent a woman for 24 *mon*'. Illustrations to the story were supplied by Kitao Masayoshi, whom we have already encountered as the man soon to be 'recycled' as Kuwagata Keisai. It may also have been at this time that this *senryū* appeared:

Toribe Moor
Smoke unmentioned in that August statement
Rises up.[159]

Toribe Moor was Keishi's cremation ground where the fire-dead were sent.

The Dairi rebuilding was part of a restructuring of all Keishi, also undertaken under the rubric of 'revival'. Other historicized entities rose up. The garden Murasaki Shikibu was said to have owned when she wrote the romance of civilized antique life, *The Tale of Genji*, was restored.[160] Revivalism necessitated artificial manipulation, so irksome that many shopkeepers and artisans sought to decamp to neighbouring Osaka and Fushimi until this was banned.[161] Keishi was denuded of much of its life as Sadanobu silenced the clamour and reinvented the streets as places of refinement and charm. From this time, the infrequently encountered name 'Kyoto' re-emerged, with Sadanobu seeming one of its more consistent advocates.[162] 'Kyoto' became 'culture', leaving Edo to remain executive. Sadanobu drove entertainers to the perimeter of the city (perversely, this was where the only original buildings survived) and herded drinkers and pleasure-seekers into a red-light district, the Shimabara, sequestered beyond fields. In just 48 hours, to his great pride, he had removed over a thousand undesirables, observing, 'the many people who come here do so to see the famous sites, and yet they veer off into the brothels, and in just one or two days all the money they brought from their home countries ends up there'.[163] The irony was that the majority of the 'famous sites' had to be recreated.

The Screens

Central to shujo rituals were the wall paintings in the Hall of the Screened Mansion. These depicted 32 ministers of Chinese kingdoms up to the Tang dynasty; their biographies were written above them. The disposition of these *Sage Screens (kenjō no sōji)*[164] derived from mainland royal practice and marked the shujo out as a ruler in the international constellation. The Tenka's first set was said to have been made in the ninth century by the matchless Kose no Kanaoka with calligraphy by Ono no Dōfū.[165] (These were legendary artists: nothing by either has survived.) In the Edo period, the Kano School was responsible for periodic replacements. A set by Kano Takanobu survived a burning of the Dairi in 1641, was transferred to the Temple of Ninna-ji and provides the best extant examples (illus. 57).[166] Tan'yū had produced an earlier series, which was known from his preparatory sketches and these were copied by all Kano adepts as the culminating step in their training.[167]

In 1788 the *Sages* commission fell to the most senior Kano painter, who was Eisen-in. This was a huge honour, not least because (characteristically) this time the screens were to be larger than any previous ones.[168] Eisen-in travelled to Keishi to begin work the following year but died suddenly four months later, aged sixty.[169] Korenobu would have expected to take over, but he was not invited, either because he had not yet been invested as Kobikichō head or for another, unstated reason. Sadanobu stepped in and awarded the task of completion to Sumiyoshi Hiroyuki. This was a departure from protocol, and as Hiroyuki was Sadanobu's close associate it suggests a deliberate intrusion into the central icons of the shujo's visual array.

The half-finished *Sages* were not reassigned immediately, and complicated jockeying was surely underway. The shujo had the distinct impression that Sadanobu was procrastinating, and Hiroyuki

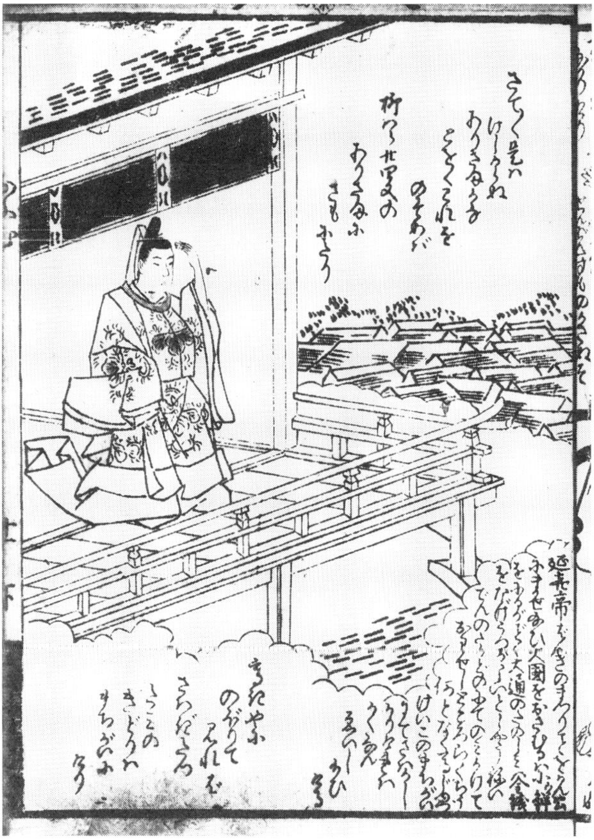

56 Kitao Masayoshi, Illustration from Koikawa Harumachi, *Ōmu-gaeshi bunbu no futamichi*, 1789, monochrome woodblock prints. From the same book as illus. 2, this image parodies the shujo's building projects.

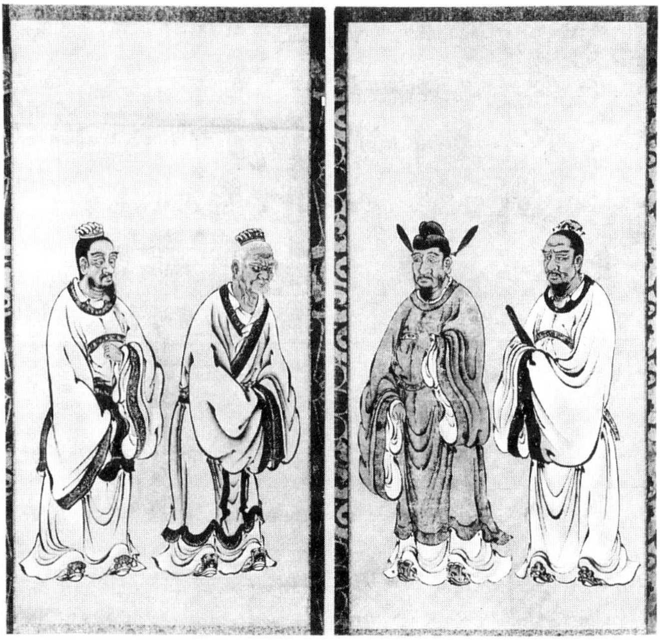

57 Kano Takanobu, *Sage Screens* from the *Kenjō no sōji*, *c.* 1614. These were painted for the Dairi, saved when it burned down in 1641, and transferred to the Ninna-ji in 1647; the figures are (right to left) Zhong Guan, Liu Yu, Tai Gongwang and Fu Shanzhong.

eventually went to the new Dairi in only 1792. The atmosphere was tense, and fear of a furore is seen in Hiroyuki's quitting Edo quietly, followed soon after by Sadanobu's ideologue, Shibano Ritsuzan, and another confidant, Yashiro Hirokata, who left under cover of darkness 'on orders from above, issued in secret [*nainai no on-sata*]'.[170] On arrival, the party reconvened but continued to behave covertly, retiring at night to separate temples. They held meetings with the enigmatic monk Kairyō, whose carefree wanderings in the classic 'untrammelled' manner of the literatus are thought to have concealed his role as a Sadanobu spy.[171] Kairyō vetted the *Sages* just prior to their installation.[172] A hush hung in the air and, although it was only the ninth month, the city lay under a blanket of snow (Hiroyuki caught a cold and worked through sneezes).[173] The results of the collaboration only survive in rough sketches (illus. 58, 59). But the screens were much acclaimed, including by Ienari himself (a formality, since he had not seen them), and Hiroyuki was awarded 50 sheets of silver and 4,000 *koku* of rice, while Ritsuzan, whose activities were as historical adviser, earned two sheets of gold.[174]

Before any work on the *Sages* or other paintings had begun, a court circular was put out stating Tomohito's pre-emptive wish that everything 'must be done, above all, in the Yamato manner' and that 'while patterns are being made available, no ill-considered work is to commence'.[175] Yamato pictures pertained to the Tosa school and its leader, Tosa Mitsusada, was ordered to prepare the patterns. But the meaning of 'the Yamato manner' was open to some interpretation. It seems to have been intended to imply an indigenous, non-Continental style, 'Yamato' being the area around the shujo's ancient base in Nara; Keishi/Kyoto was not in Yamato. Possibly the Tosa association meant the pictures were to be literary and thematically amoral. Tomohito seemingly meant his paintings to evoke the old heartland of shujo sovereignty, pre-dating shogunal times, and that they should not refer to Edo or the Kano School. Tomohito's injunction states his ideological as much as stylistic preference. Hiroyuki may have been chosen for the *Sages* to appease Tomohito, as the Sumiyoshi were quasi-Tosa in orientation, but they did smack of Edo and, as a member of the shogunal circle, Hiroyuki cannot have been the type of artist Tomohito intended.

Beyond Eisen-in, six artists bearing the Kano name are recorded among the Dairi decorators, and they even worked in the 'daily mansion' (*tsunegosho*), or living quarters, over which Tomohito probably exercised direct control. These, though, were all from the Kyō–Kano School (also recently deprived of their head, Kano Eijō, and directed by his eighteen-year-old son, Eishun). Kano-trained artists bearing non-Kano surnames are also found, although here too confined to men from the Kyoto–Osaka region; best represented is the Tsuruzawa school, with Tansō, his pupil Ishida Yūtei, his pupil Maruyama Ōkyo, and his pupil Nagasawa Rosetsu; Hara Zaichū, Kaihō Yūtoku and others feature too. It seems Tomohito wanted artists from 'his' geographical space and was less concerned with issues of style than of the nearest affiliation of artists to himself that he could get away with. 'Yamato' here denotes the geopolitical orbit of the shujo.

The Hall of the Screened Palace had few paintings other than the *Sages* and, despite Hiroyuki's engagement, was an inalienable Kano preserve; on the contrary, the Pure and Fresh Hall was assigned (though not in its entirety) to the Tosa school. The screens in the second hall were less codified and so better illuminate the direction in which Tomohito saw his formal iconography developing. Themes that had decked successive Dairi for centuries were brusquely chopped in favour of 'revived' ones, with paintings mostly produced by Mitsusada), his nephew Mitsutoki and his son Mitsuzane (who at eleven could not have been much practical use). Kano Tansō contributed elements (although as we shall see rather special ones), but the Kano-associated range of moral themes which had adorned the Pure and Fresh Hall since medieval times was expelled. Out went shogunal-type admonitory pictures – the *Mirror of Rulers (Teikanzu)*, the *Four Accomplishments (Shigei)* – and violent ones such as *Tigers*. The standard *Tartars on Horseback*, which was painted in Chinese palaces too, was substituted with a nostalgic *Japanese Courtier on Horseback*.[176] The bulk of the replacement paintings represented views of famous sites (*meisho*) throughout the Tenka. In a sense these were 'revivals', but the specific references are more significant. Tomohito

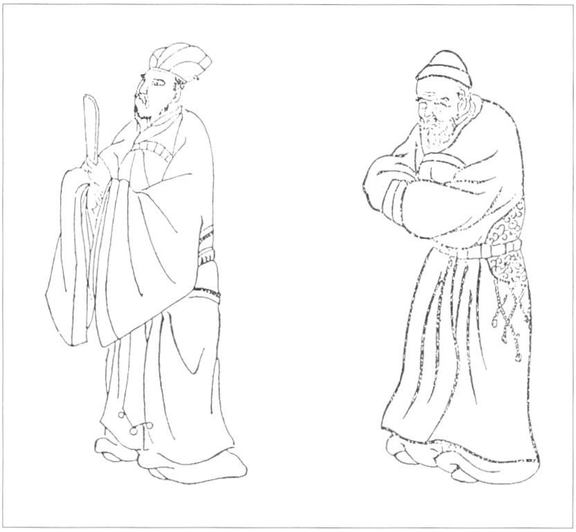

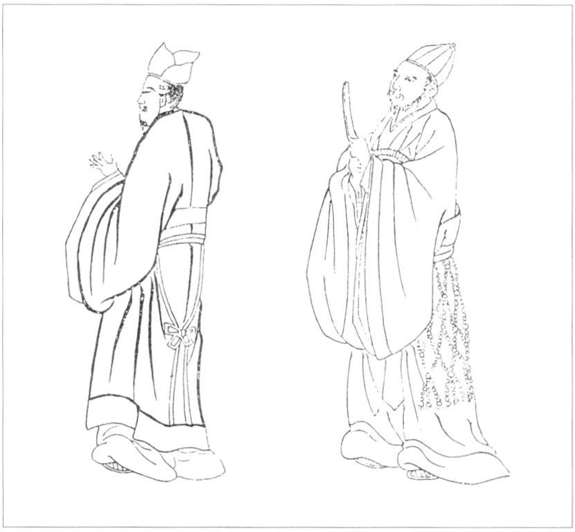

58, 59 Illustrations from Minamoto Shūryū, *Hōketsu kenbun zusetsu*, c. 1800, from edition of Imaizumi Sadasuke (Yoshikawa Kōbunkan, 1927). These sketches are all that remain of Eisen-in's and Hiroyuki's *Sage Screens* of 1789–92; the figures are the same as in illus. 57.

was reinventing himself as custodian of the lands and their heritage. He removed the shujo from the international rhetoric of rule by 'virtue' – which could become disfigured by vice leading to expulsion from office (as sequential shogunates and countless Chinese dynasties attested) – and repositioned himself in the amoral order of rule by inalienable blood, whose iconography was the Japanese soil.

The Pure and Fresh Hall contained the shujo's 'campaign seat' (*jin-no-mashi*), somewhat equivalent to a throne; the other designation, 'daytime seat' (*hiru-no-omashi*), was now preferred. Around this were brushed excerpts from Chinese poetry (*honmon*), as tradition demanded, but abutting these along the north, west and part of the east sides like a wrapper were eight smaller rooms where the *Famous Sites* were put (illus. 60).[177] Depiction of beauty spots was anodyne, but in this location they constituted a huge claim, and probably alluded to a similar series painted for Takahira (posthumously, Go-Toba), whose period as shujo coincided with establishment of the first shogunate. That set, commissioned in 1207, advertised Takahira's refusal to accept the loss of his entitlement to what he had just been stripped of and were intended as a curse on the shogunate.[178] Although it had all happened long ago, this was intensely relevant. For Takahira's successors, his sons Tamahito and Morinari (posthumously, Tsuchimikado and Juntoku), had been shujo, until both were exiled by the shogunate, which opened up the succession to their cousin Yutahito (posthumously, Go-Horikawa), whose father had not been a shujo and whose anomalous elevation therefore formed the only precedent for Tomohito's. The *Famous Sites* in the new Dairi, then, functioned multivalently, proclaiming the rightfulness of shujo possession of the lands, while also rationalizing deprivation of control over it and recalling the legitimating antecedent of Tomohito's peculiar succession. They also set the whole in a language suggestive of heinous shogunal interference, not of the shujo's drastic inability to breed.

Tomohito's arrangement of the *Famous Sites* was also radical. Unlike most renditions of this much-painted genre, the series was made to follow an empirical, seasonal logic. In *Famous Sites* sets it was usual to follow one year's cycle per room, thus one season per wall; this would be repeated for as many times as there were rooms to be decorated. Moreover, the 'Famous Sites' genre was really the depiction of *poems on* famous sites, so that the season would be derived from the poetic associations of the place, which might or might not be when the actual site was at its most lovely. Sano must be shown in winter because the poet spoke of snow and, even if Teika's verse was not the sole reason for admiring Sano, it would be gauche to depict it out of

60 Plan of Seiryōden in 1790, based on Chino Kaori, 'Kenchiku no naibu kūkan to shōhekiga' (Kōdansha, 1991). The shujo's seats are central; the daytime seat is in a room open to the east and in front of the nighttime seat; eight lesser chambers block the north-eastern, northern and western aspects.

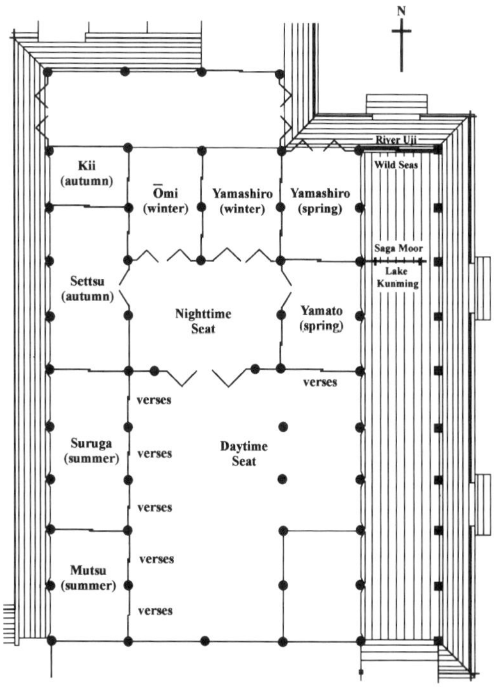

kilter with its most valued celebratory verse. The arrangement of sites would be determined by this criterion, augmented by the flow of linguistic or imagistic links. Geography was rarely a concept. Tomohito had each of the eight rooms devoted to the scenery of one province in one season. This instantly valorized actual political space over literary space. In total seven provinces were shown, as Yamashiro (where Keishi/Kyoto was) had a double allocation – perhaps the dignity of Tomohito's presence there defied its containment within the prescribed ambit. Since the Japanese archipelago had far more than seven provinces, selection was needed, and again politics was the key. For example, Musashi, the Edo region, was omitted altogether; this was less to indicate acceptance of the shogun's arrogation of it than to excise all indication of Tokugawa rule from Tomohito's purview in his painted jurisdictional zone. More contestable was Suruga, where the shogunate also had significant holdings, and where Ieyasu had hailed from and Mt Kuno was. This was placed near the end of the series, out of Tomohito's sight. Furthermore, the shogunal features of Suruga were not represented, with sites shown referring to shujo activities in the area, notably to sites where court poets had lamented the uncouthness of the region; the only element of the whole sequence with which the shogunate might identify was Suruga's hallowed *Mt Fuji*.[179]

The southerly section of the eastern corridor had no abutting rooms, but two free-standing screens were placed there, not technically part of the *Famous Places*, but painted front and back with landscapes. These stated Tomohito's sense of his alignment with foreign powers.[180] Both were set on an east–west axis, and on the northern sides were a *River Uji* and a *Saga Moor*, particularized in fishers and hawkers: the ingenious environment is lauded for its sustenance and yield. On the southerly aspects were *Lake Kunming*, a much praised Chinese place, and *Wild Seas*, which showed those humanoid barbarians from beyond the ocean, the long-arms and long-legs (illus. 61). As the shujo always sat looking south, he saw the northern sides only (notionally, since in practice both were beyond eyeshot), such that foreignness is construed as that which is removed from the sight of his face, while indigenousness is what is illumined by it. High and low foreignness was shown, the latter being that further from the shujo's seat. To clarify this bold thought, the 'local' sides were done in the 'Yamato' manner by Tosa Mitsusada and the 'foreign' ones by Tansō in the Kano way.

The *Famous Sites* sequence itself moved anti-clockwise from Yamato in the east, through Yamashiro, leading round to Suruga and finally Mutsu. The two rooms on the eastern side were occupied by the

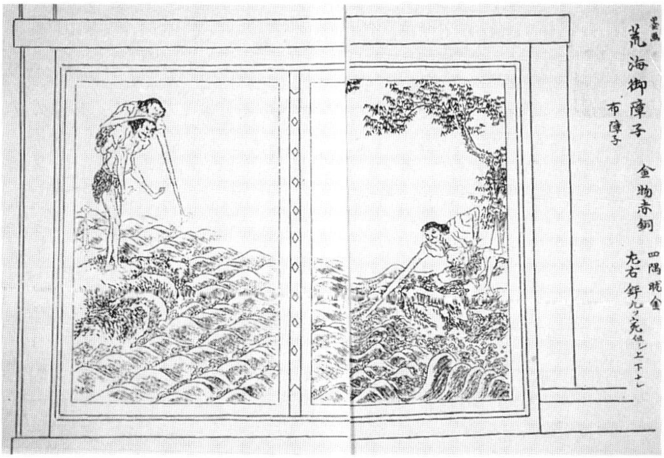

61 Illustration from Minamoto Shūryū, *Hōketsu kenbun zusetsu*, c. 1800, from edition of Imaizumi Sadasuke (Yoshikawa Kōbunkan, 1927). The 'long-arms and long-legs' screen, *Wild Seas*, was a standard fixture, but is here positioned in the north-east looking south.

provinces most associated with the shujo line (Yamato and Yamashiro), and these occupied the best locations since they received the morning sun; these were also in the unlucky north-eastern direction, and so guarded the shujo's seat. The two provinces most associated with the shogunate (Suruga and Mutsu) were on the longer western side, far from the shujo's seat, and lit only by dying light. In point of fact, Suruga and Mutsu are to the east of Yamato and Yamashiro, and the sun greets them several minutes earlier, but in this symbolic construction they had to defer.

The whole hall represented one year with two rooms per season. Tomohito sat in the centre as the cosmic motor for this, his face taken as the sun, completely overriding actual solar motion. Spring began to his left (the most honoured side), but next came winter; winter was often depicted on north walls, but here it is frigid because it is behind Tomohito's seat. Autumn was third, a pleasant time of year, being neither too hot nor too cold and poetic for its traditional associations with depth of feeling. This conveniently left summer for Suruga and Mutsu (in reality the Tenka's coldest provinces), as they languished in a never-ending burn. This, then, was Tomohito's world-view.

Over the ensuing decades Tomohito did not lose the taste for bravado in the personal icons that he acquired at this time. Towards the end of his period in office he (or those around him) was to invent a new pictorial theme, taken from the classic *Book of Odes (Shijing)*, extolling the ruler's prowess. This was called *Nine Similes of Heavenly Protection* – 'heaven', of course, meaning Tomohito himself. One scroll each showed the ruler protecting like mountains, hills, ridges, ranges, ever-flowing streams, waxing moon, rising sun, like the perpetuity of the mountains in the south, and the eternity of green of the pine and cypress (illus. 62). A set was commissioned in 1824 the 45th anniversary of Tomohito's installation as shujo. In 1837, not coincidentally the year of Ienari's death, another set was made. Both were ordered from the now dead Sadanobu's personal artist, Tani Bunchō.[181] Three years later, in 1840, Tomohito himself died. He was buried with unprecedented honours, including, to the amazement of all and sundry, 'restoration' of a title abandoned in 887, *tennō*, 'heavenly ruler' (the Japanese monarchy has continued to use this). Tomohito also ensured he was not given a posthumous name restricted to one quarter

62 Tani Bunchō, *Protecting like the Waxing Moon*, from the series *Nine Similes of Heavenly Protection*, 1824, hanging scroll, colour on silk. This series proposed nine ways in which the shujo guarded the states.

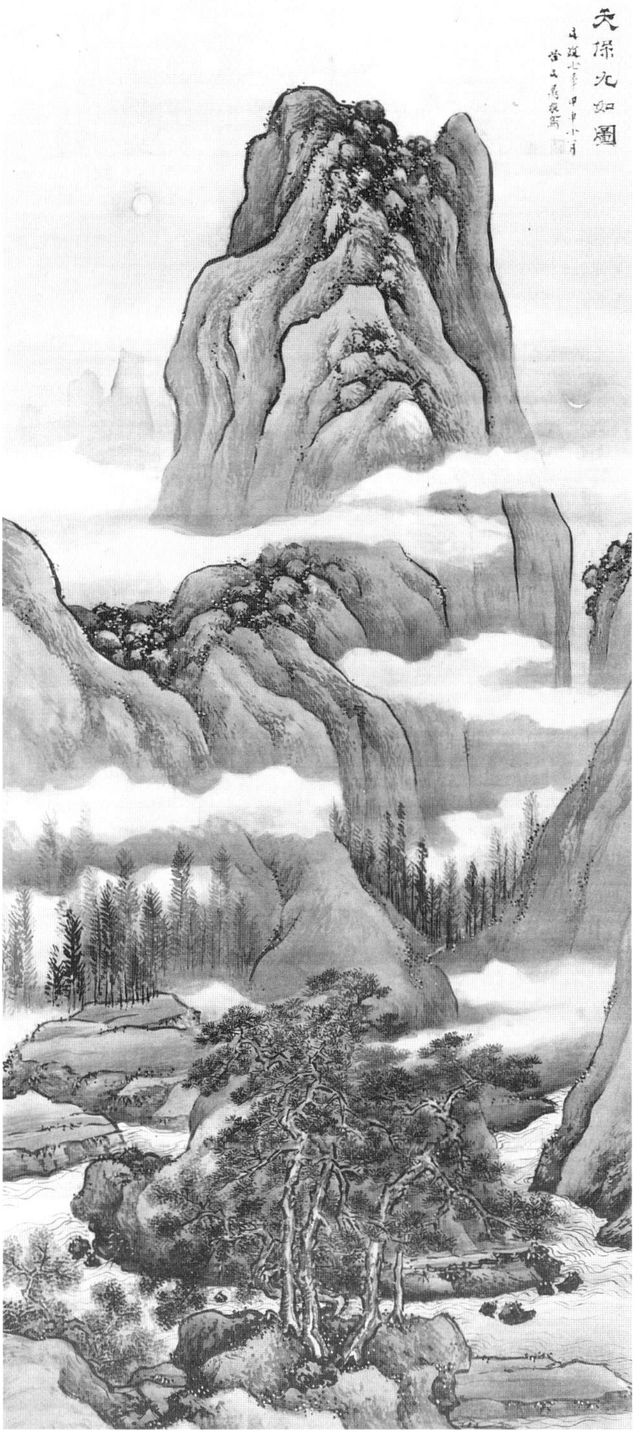
天保九如圖

of Kyoto, but a 'revived' majestic one, *kōkaku*, 'Radiant Qualities'.[182] A painting of the funeral cortege was commissioned and entrusted to Reizei Tamechika, the man destined to become pioneer of the manner called 'revived Yamato pictures' (*fukkō yamato-e*).[183]

Tomohito thus had the last laugh, but this was not quite the end. In 1854, with Ienari's son, Ieyoshi, invested as shogun and Tomohito's grandson, Osahito (posthumously, Kōmei), installed as shujo, the Dairi burned down again.

4 Ōkyo's 'New Concept'

One must somehow enjoy a swindle to
apply one's mind to the study of pictures.
– Samuel de Sorbière, *Lettre* IX *à M. Boucheat*, 1660

Today people think they achieve understanding
on their own, and someone might even look at a painting of
hell and say, 'Seems quite nice!'
– Izumi Kyōka, *Shunchū*, 1906

The problems encountered during decoration work at the Dairi exposed inadequacies in the painting worlds of Edo and Keishi. Their institutions were unsound, and a yawning gap between pictorial practice and representational authority had emerged. In the language of the time, painting had lost touch with 'authenticity' (*makoto*). The eighteenth century had its supporters of the effusive, heterodox styles, and the dilemma in painting was felt to incriminate mostly the formal schools. The users of the copybook – rather than the external environment or the imagination – for their didactic tool found their art worlds unwinding and losing tension. Their pictures carried insufficient weight to convey the messages they contained. Many critics will be cited in the pages below, and some have been above.

The work of Maruyama Ōkyo, on whom this chapter centres, was pivotal to resolving this crisis. He stepped with extraordinary acumen into the breach left by the academies and fashioned for himself a style and identity, and with it, clawed home a substantial market share. Ōkyo secured his place in the crowded arena of government art but, in offering a scintillating solution to a concern generally felt, he achieved wide acclaim and aspects of his work were avowedly populist. Ōkyo's proposition was simple: he said he had rid art of its calcifying shell to allow the play of 'depicting life' (*shasei*), also called 'capturing reality' (*shashin*). This blithe assertion was the platform on which he stood up to scourge inauthenticity. But, importantly, Ōkyo did not tinker with the established range of themes. He reinjected blood into the ghostly imagery of Kano and Tosa, which was well-known but had been draining away for generations, and through observation he became official without being formulaic. Ōkyo's practice was built upon the rejection of the copybook and the prioritizing of *looking*.

Tachibana Nankei, the physician who admired Kaihō Yūshō's avoidance of inaccuracy in history painting, saw some Ōkyo works in the 1780s and wrote: 'Kano, Tosa and other indigenous manners had greatly declined. There was not a soul who enjoyed looking at them. Then Ōkyo appeared and everything underwent change'.[1] Nankei entirely approved of this. An early biographer of Ōkyo, Oku Bunmei, made the master above all into the destroyer of formulaicism. Bunmei was Ōkyo's student and so perhaps not impartial, but he had undeniably been exposed to Ōkyo's studio behaviour. Bunmei quoted Ōkyo's opinion of 'the schools we now have with us', namely that:

> . . . they train their pupils by making them replicate old works, which are then appropriated as their own. This is thought to be enough. Students put their name to these [derivative] pieces, and stamp their seals on them with not a whiff of shame. Teachers even forbid innovation [*shin'i*]. This behaviour is simply foolery with brush and ink.[2]

Ōkyo told his own group to use just their eyes, for that, he assured them, was 'the true method of production' and would be 'sufficient to secure fame'.[3] He never had his students replicate his own work nor anyone else's – or at least, that is what he said. And yet he became a veritable academy in his own right, an academy of self, as solid as Kano or Tosa, or even more so, and supporting a vast capacity for production.

Pictorial Logic

Some preliminaries must be considered. We have already seen how lack of attention to nature and failure to match ink-stroke patterns to real depicted form was widely condemned. But there was a more precise criticism that Ōkyo neutralized. In 1799, the nativist critic Motoori Norinaga wrote his condemnation of painting, summing up recent errors and outlining the first steps for reform. Ōkyo had died in 1795 and Norinaga did not mention him by name but, as we have seen, he cited 'house styles' (*ie no hō*) as the greatest annihilator of 'authenticity' (a term he repeatedly used).[4] Ōkyo, having no publicized institutional freight, was not susceptible to this charge. 'Authenticity' was not inhibited by his mode of working. 'Authentic' was, indeed, a label routinely pinned to him. The poet and intellectual Minagawa Kien, a close friend of Ōkyo, wrote a verse on him outlining his attainments. He disconnected Ōkyo from Kano-type practice and centred him within this new language of representation:

Some, following usual painting ideas,
Hold that rote copying is the proper thing to do.
But he only looks at things,
And copies their forms with authenticity.[5]

Norinaga had defined 'authenticity' as not just observation of natural forms in isolation but as a supple treatment of their conjointedness and interconnection. He appealed to the value of 'cohesion' (*torishimari*).[6] This was 'authenticity' at its full pictorial best. Norinaga's strongest criticisms were reserved for those who failed to configure a painting as a unity and fractured space so that, however adeptly it might be done in its parts, the composition was illogical overall. For example, he cited fowls landing on trees whose branches were too spindly to support them, or birds with wings too stunted to bear them aloft.[7] Parts had to relate to wholes.

Ōkyo was critical of the Nagasaki School of artists, charging them with exactly the same errors. They undermined the impeccable accuracy of their brushwork by lunatic anomalies, as gross as any schoolman's. The charge struck at the core. Shen Nanpin was an avowed realist and had left his native China to spend some months in Nagasaki (hence the name of the school) in 1731, passing on his style. It had seemed to offer the promise of rectification, and many Japanese artists followed him, notably Kumashiro Yūhi, who in turn taught Sō Shiseki, who brought the manner to Edo in mid-century in the hope of ameliorating painting there. In Shen Nanpin's *Nightingale on a Flowering Plum*, Ōkyo witnessed a bird some dozen centimetres tall on a tree no more than ten times that size: 'How', he wondered, 'can this make sense?'[8] The painting is not extant, but Nanpin's output includes many similar instances of misalignment (see illus. 25). Ōkyo criticized Shiseki by name. But Su Koppei used the pages of his *Tales Curiouser and Curiouser (Myōmyō kidan)* to hang continued non-cohesion on the Nanpinists, for, he claimed, 'they paint waterfowl whose lengths of neck and legs do not match up' and seemed ignorant of 'how the beak of every species differs', for all the precision of the brushwork.[9] 'Cohesion' became a battle-cry. Many who moved into the European style – including both Satake Yoshiatsu, daimyo of Akita, and Shiba Kōkan – had tried the Nagasaki manner but abandoned it as insufficiently radical in its attention to a totalized pictorial truth.[10]

A *Crane in Snow* by Kishi Ganku, possibly of about 1790, provides an example of good 'cohesion' (see illus. 26, 27). It joins a long line of depictions of these auspicious birds, but Ganku considered his subjects not just as symbols but as *life*. He gauged how much a crane would weigh, how much pressure this would exert on its talons, and how far this would sink them into soft snow. The picture is strikingly novel but comes to the aid of tradition, enlivening the motif through consistent application of 'authenticity'. Ganku's picture comes midway between the anonymous Kano mannerist *Cranes* and Itō Jakuchū's lively but imagistically redundant *Cock and Hen*: the birds are for real but are also pictorial staples (see illus. 21, 49). Ganku was from Kanazawa, but he finally settled in new Kyoto and became close to Tomohito's circle. He had also travelled widely, including to Nagasaki, where he associated with post-Nanpin Chinese expatriates such as Yu Shuwen and Tang Jihui. Rather chauvinistically, he presented them with a *Mt Fuji* done 'authentically' to take back home to the Continent.[11] It was, for him, explicitly the power imagery of the Tenka that had to be redeemed, and the impressions this had on foreign people was a matter over which he took care. The move towards authenticity had its own momentum, but for Ōkyo, Ganku and others it did not at all entail the rejection of classic themes. Authenticity, for them, was the means to re-implant vitality into once-valued but now withered themes whose hortative power it was folly to let slip away.

The breakdown in rudimentary logic was noticed by late eighteenth-century commentators across the board. Satake Yoshiatsu decried artists who left blanks and vacancies in their work so that, however admirable the details, the pictorial space did not lock together. He took the example of renditions of boats with a few token waves drawn around them, but no sea integrally filled in, and of plants 'just hanging in mid-air', as the Nanpinists did them.[12] Yoshiatsu wrote the first Japanese treatises on Western art (one in the vernacular, one in Chinese) and in them noted that European art ordered space more scrupulously and avoided such pitfalls.[13] It may have been under the guidance of his retainer Odano Naotake (provider of the illustrations to the *New Anatomical Atlas*) that Yoshiatsu began to experiment as a Western-style artist (see illus. 28) under the Dutch seal-name Segoter vol Beminnen ('sea-god full of love' – or 'of *lenience*').

One over-arching law of unification used in European art was mathematical perspective. This was well known in Japan and vanishing-point perspective had been practised since early in the eighteenth century. Scenes so rendered were designated 'floating pictures' (*uki-e*). Yoshiatsu castigated the traditional perspectival expedient of placing further off objects higher up and closer ones lower down, as too *ad hoc*. He went so far as to claim that 'it is the core obligation of painting to establish a standard of scale for objects within the field of vision'.[1] Ōkyo spent a period working on perspective views and was proficient

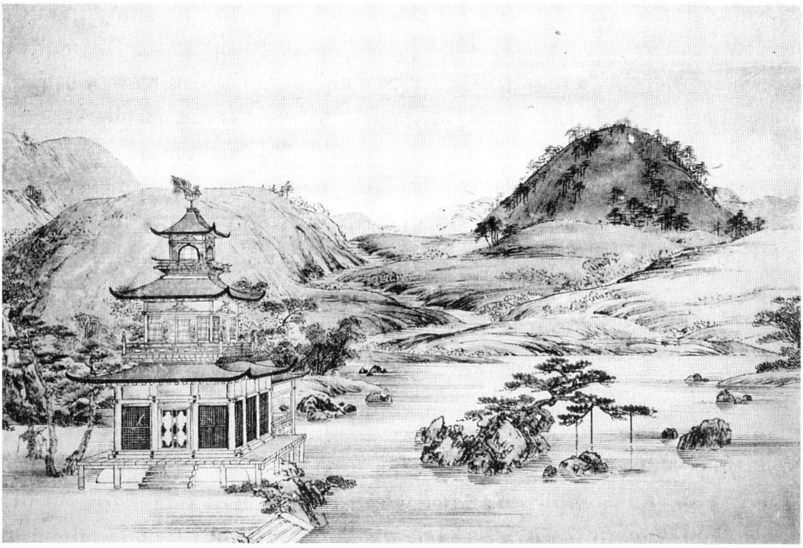

63 Maruyama Ōkyo, *Golden Turret*, c. 1780, colour on paper. This work imitates European topographical etchings; it was painted in reverse to be viewed through an optique, or 'Dutch glasses'.

in their regimented draftsmanship (illus. 63, 68, 100). Long before Kōkan cracked the riddle of copperplate printing or Denzen was employed by Sadanobu to make etchings, Ōkyo was producing adaptations of European topographical prints done in paint.

'Cohesion' was, however, a more subtle matter than just perspective, and few critics seriously proposed a general adoption of the vanishing-point. Indeed, over-reliance on that one Western idea as a general heal-all could have adverse effects, as informed Westernists themselves warned. Shiba Kōkan advised in his *Talks on European Pictures (Seiyō gadan)*, completed in the same year as Norinaga's *On Pictures*, that 'most people believe Western pictures are no more than perspectives, but this is a risible opinion'.[15] 'Floating pictures' had a bad reputation, for they were all but monopolized by popularizing themes and carried the aura of the fair ground, where they were often exposed in peep-boxes called 'Dutch glasses' (*oranda-megane*), for hilarity's sake.[16] If a transfusion of Western art were to be injected into the representations of shogunal power, it had to offer more than perspective, and those who took European postulates seriously, as Sadanobu did, knew more was to be found.

Pictorial consistency was advocated long before the eighteenth century and had been articulated in quite ancient treatises; indeed, there was something of a tradition of complaining about its lack.[17]

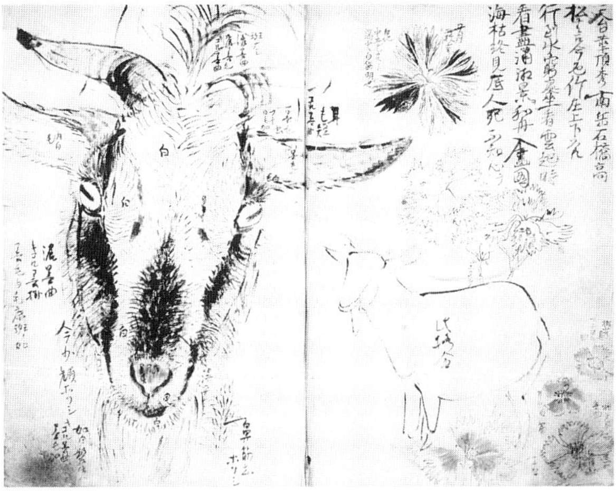

64 Maruyama Ōkyo, Section of *Shasei zatsuroku-chō*, 1771–2, ink and light colour on paper. Empirical studies taken from nature.

Ōkyo estimated that he was the first to erase the error *entirely*. With some gall, he explained 'mistakes crop up all the time in the work of the ancients', but never, by dint of careful execution, in his own.[18]

Ōkyo's achievement was to place taut and vibrant living forms inside thematically conservative compositions and make images meaningful on both levels. The problem of European art was that it seldom provided themes that appeared relevant to the Tenka's authorities. Ōkyo shunned them, and he contributed nothing to the realm of subject matter burgeoning all round him in the work not only of Westernists but also of heterodox masters. One example of his mode of subject selection will do. Ōkyo sketched a goat's head (illus. 64). Jakuchū sketched cocks, and Westernists knew empiricism was a root value in European art and made studies of diverse animal forms. Ōkyo's goat may well have been done on one of the trips he said he frequently took to the hills around Keishi to observe nature. But Ōkyo stopped at the sketched animal: goats were not part of the thematic canon, and the draft never became a finished picture. Ōkyo's goat, though, became a section of a finished picture, for he imported it into the one official theme in which it had meaning, namely a rendition of the sage Huang Chuping, whose iconographical marker the animal was (illus. 65). It cannot be said whether a scroll of the sage was commissioned, prompting Ōkyo to study the goat, or whether seeing the animal determined him to paint the image, but the forms in the picture (not just the goat, but the men and tree) are startlingly done. The iconography is utterly standard.

Ōkyo's command to students to go out into nature and depict what they saw was thus circumscribed by the grip of established subjects. He was also disingenuous insofar as, even in the eighteenth century, it was acknowledged that no reality could be so simply transferred onto the page. No painting can replicate the three dimensions of life unproblematically, and choice, filtering and man-handling of objects is the very business of the artist. Images were verisimilitudinous in the measure that they were repositionings of elements seen, in construc-

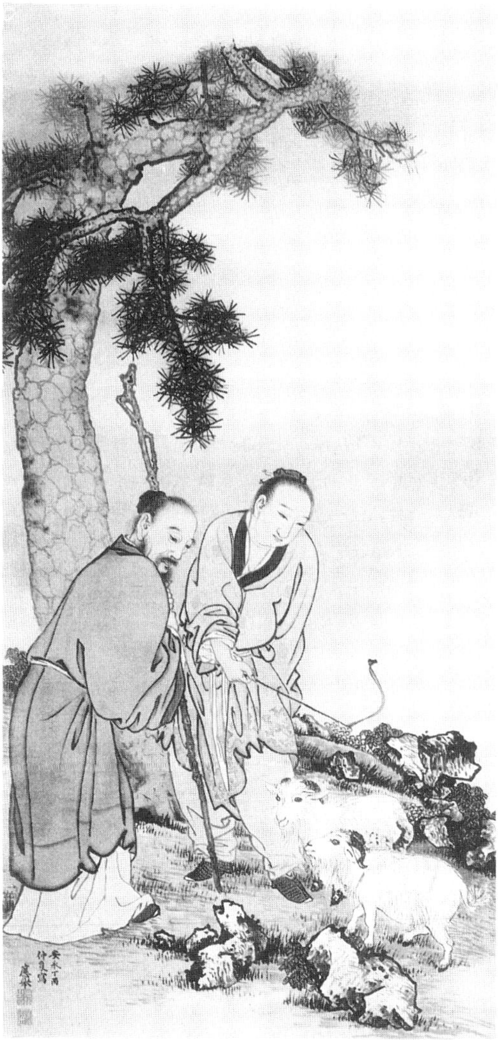

65 Maruyama Ōkyo, *Huang Chuping*, 1777, hanging scroll, colour on silk. The sketch of a goat's head, made five years earlier, was incorporated into the image of the Chinese sage.

tions that gave the flavour of truth. Norinaga was to argue this with the case of boats: they list with the wind when gusts hit them abeam. This was what they did in fact, but if rendered so in paint the result looked odd. To him, 'such would be an instance where following too closely the actuality of things, results in failure'.[19] Hence, 'if you depict exactly according to how things really look, this will not make a viable picture'. The fissure that this implied was precisely the area that was policed by the codes of art, being policed differently in different schools, allowing their several types of painting to exist. Sadanobu called this 'the inherent pictoriality of pictures' (*ga no ga-taru hon'i*).[20]

Ōkyo used ruses in the attainment of his goals, which contemporaries duly commented on without censure. The cleverness of his adaptation of nature so as to create coherent pictures was praised in succeeding generations. Anzai Un'en, writing in the second quarter of the nineteenth century, analysed Ōkyo's *Carp Ascending Falls*, completed in 1783, which is useful since the work is extant (illus. 66). This was a hackneyed theme and it needed help if it were to speak out again and fulfil the purpose for which the painting had been commissioned – here enjoining undaunted striving against the odds. Kien had already praised this painting nearer to its time of completion, but Un'en latched on to how it was the very counter-empiricality of the rendition, if logic were pushed to the limit, that ensured Ōkyo the final accolade.[21] The typical arrangement was to have the fish half-in, half-out of the fall, or even leaping above it. A leading painter of the Kano School in the mid-eighteenth century, Kano Terunobu (also pronounced Hidenobu), depicted the subject like that (illus. 67).[22] Fish cannot flip like this, but in a way it makes sense, for that is how a fish would have to move if it were to prevent the force of the water driving it back down. To Ōkyo and Un'en, though, this would be like Norinaga's tilting boat, an oversight of the 'pictoriality of pictures'. Carp do not ascend waterfalls anyway, so over-ratiocination was also misplaced. Ōkyo's solution was radical. He showed a fish submerged in streaking water. It looks impressively real but depicts a physical impossibility. Un'en wrote, 'If a carp really were in the midst of the fall, it could never go up', and so 'there will be those who argue the depiction runs counter to the proper conception [*hon'i*] of a carp ascending'. Yet, more sensibly considered, Ōkyo shows 'exactly how you would think a carp should look when going up'. Not despite, but because of the trickery, 'in this realm, no one at any time has equalled Ōkyo in the wondrous accomplishment of the depiction of life [*shasei*]'.

By serving up meaty iconic fare, Ōkyo pre-empted the attack

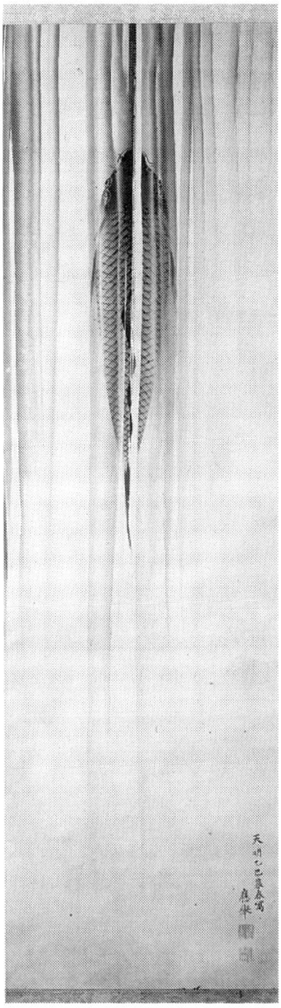

66 Maruyama Ōkyo, *Carp Ascending Falls*, 1783, hanging scroll, light colour and ink on silk. A hackneyed theme is subjected to 'new concept' treatment. Three versions of the image are known; this is the earliest.

Sadanobu was to make on the Nanpinists, namely that their realism was merely decorative, devoid of moral message, and so 'the next nearest thing to superficiality'.[23] Sadanobu tolerated such artists when they were depicting 'things relating to the Continent' (i.e. those divorced from the orbit of the Tenka's political concerns), just as Westernists might be momentarily enjoyed when they showed the quirky aspects of Europe, but few found either group able to contribute to the edification of the home space. Synecdochically, Sadanobu wrote, 'they have no interest in doing a *Fuji* or *Cherry Blossoms*'. (It would be interesting to know what Sadanobu might have thought of Ganku's *Mt Fuji* sent to China.) To Su Koppei too, Nanpin and his followers only thought of devising a style that would sell, that is, by co-opting realism for commercial gain they had disconnected it from high meaning.[24]

Ōkyo: Life and Career

Ōkyo's life is not well documented. He is known to have been born in penurious circumstances in 1733 in the village of Anō in Tanba, not far from Keishi. By 1749, he was studying under Ishida Yūtei, himself trained by Tsuruzawa Tangei, head of the Tsuruzawa Kano school. But Ōkyo was never an accredited Tsuruzawa affiliate and thus never a Kano master. He did work on some high-level projects with Yūtei's successor Tansaku, including at the Dairi, and Ōkyo's prestige is evident in the fact of Yūtei's son (also called Yūtei, but written with different characters) being sent to study with him.[25] But during the next decade Ōkyo distanced himself from the Tsuruzawa, objecting, it

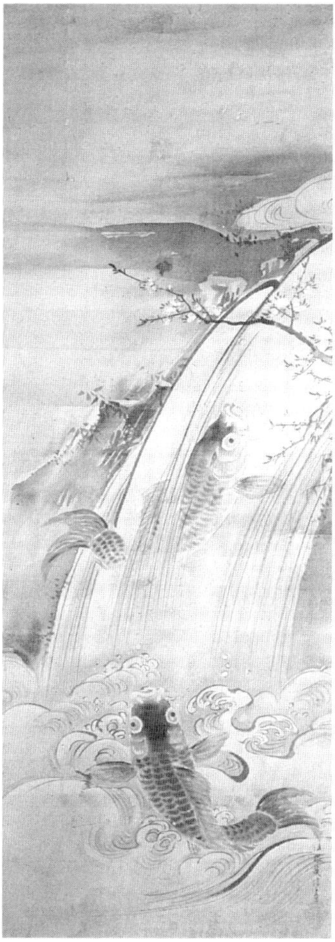

67 Kano Terunobu, *Carp Ascending Falls*, 1746–62, colour on silk. A classic rendition of the theme.

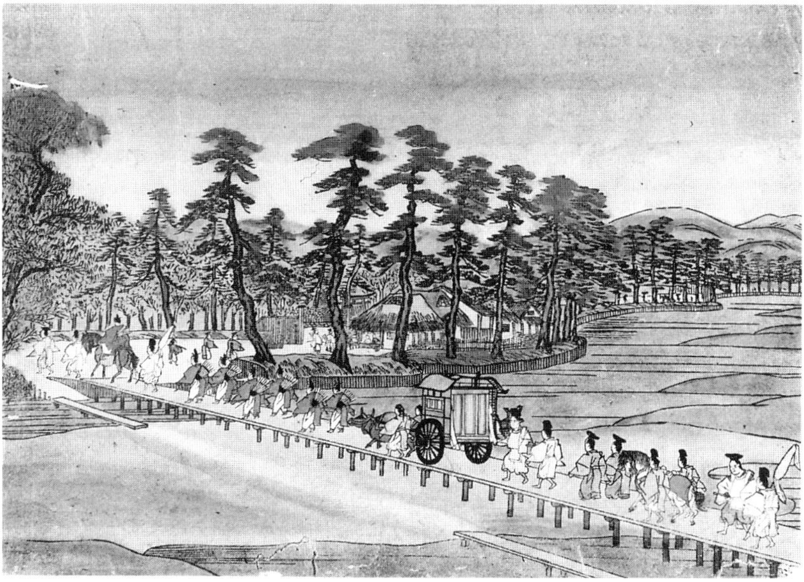

68 Maruyama Ōkyo, *Hollyhock Festival*, *c.* 1780, colour on paper. One of Kyoto's main festivals depicted in the manner of a European topographical etching.

is believed, precisely to the Kano-derived logic of space.[26]

A concern for cohesion seems to have arisen early in Ōkyo's mind. It was immediately on leaving Yūtei that he began making his perspective pictures, probably in the 1770s (see illus. 63, 68, 100).[27] Ōkyo shunned not only the Floating World themes most often attempted in that idiom but even the exotic topographies typical of Kōkan, and he depicted only sites pertinent to the culture of the Tenka or, at the furthest, of the Continent. Kōkan's views had included an English stately home and a Dutch hospital; Utagawa Toyoharu – held as the 'floating picture' maistro – had copied an imported copperplate version of Canaletto's *Grand Canal*.[28] But these lacked resonance when put on the art market in Edo or Keishi. For his part, Ōkyo showed the Hall of Thirty-three Bays, Uji Bridge and the Golden Turret (Kinkaku). Whatever the shock of the style, the views he purveyed were normalized by tradition. One of Ōkyo's works was of the Kamo Shrine rites, which were among the three sacred events of the antique monarchy. The rites had lapsed for centuries but had recently been revived by the shogunate under the name of the Hollyhock Festival. Surely this picture was a fine demonstration of the potentials of the innovative 'pictures of the present' (*imaga*) and of the union of the shogunal and imperial courts (illus. 68).[29]

Ōkyo had as little interest in the technology of Western art as he had in its themes, and although his painted perspectives replicate the effect of the copperplates (note the hatchlines), he never experimented with etching. To erase the brush by printing might appeal on a popular level, but it removed the scope for 'brush-dharma' (*hippō*), or that sublime amalgam of ink and the lofty human spirit that alone brought representatation to its apex. Different styles made the brushwork more or less visible, but to relegate it as such expelled imagery from the purview of art. Ōkyo avoided silencing this loudest voice in the painterly chorus.

His policy of minimal Western borrowing as a method for redeeming the old stands in contrast to the more common reaction, which was to write antiquity off. A *senryū* captures the words of a Nagasakiite familiar with imported trends and commensurately dismissive of classical representation:

'Tan'yū –
I don't think much of him',
Says the Maruyama woman.[30]

The Maruyama was Nagasaki's red-light district, and so this woman is also a denizen of the Floating World. Formal depiction has become irrelevant, and she has given up on it.

Ōkyo soon moved out of perspective views, which probably carried with them a sense of Westernness that proved inalienable, whatever the theme. His style does owe much to his Kano training and to study of other and earlier styles, and indeed he was a plunderer of the past. Empirical observation was but one piece in Ōkyo's stylistic armoury, but, more to the point, it was his subterfuge. He mustered a welter of styles, crunching their disparate elements, adding a leaven of imported manners compacted into classical themes. He identified this as his 'new concept' (*shin'i*). The 'new concept' posed as a kind of styleless style, or depiction without oscillations, hiding its debts to the past and to abroad, and announcing it was the pure conflation of iconography with observation. Everything was swallowed and then claimed as Ōkyo's own. A major detractor was Ganku's son, Gantai, who objected to how Ōkyo 'thrust forward his own innovations' and obscured his pedigree until the pictures looked 'unlike what is to be found in history'.[31] They did, though, work remarkably well for those who needed work for the here and now. Gantai disliked this 'affiliation of himself with the present', but Ōkyo's success, though not immediate, was sensational. As a concept this might be new, but all Ōkyo's pictorial elements were standard, only here they were homogenized. Uniquely, Ōkyo told his pupils not to treat the manners of old masters as separate entities but to be synthetic. Whereas it was normal to make statements of artists that they took figure painting from X, landscapes from Y and religious works from Z, Ōkyo's work was composite. Nankei astutely noticed that Ōkyo's trail-blazing lay in synthesis: 'combining modes as if that were the natural thing to do'.[32] Nankei particularly noted that the ideological divide between indigenous and Continental styles (*waga/kanga*) was overcome, and he might have added that European art was fused in too.

The 'new concept' produced compositions that were widely adaptable and widely usable. Nankei went on that 'every artist' now 'mixed manners as if it was the obvious way'. According to Un'en, 'there were few in Keishi who did not adopt his way', which rendered Ōkyo 'uncontestably the greatest hand of our age'.[33] Passing through Keishi in 1788, Kōkan saw Ōkyo's work:

> It is not Continental, nor yet indigenous. It is done in a system that is of his own fabrication. Ōkyo produced his New Concept and won praise throughout the capital, and everyone has begun to copy him. His sort of painting has become extraordinarily prevalent.[34]

The Ōkyo manner, then, was a kind of public property. This was the judgement universally repeated. Akinari wrote that 'when Ōkyo appeared, his style called "copying life" became all the rage, until it was as if all painting in Kyō were done by his hand alone'.[35] The rhetoric of obviousness and openness is present, and not all this bandwagon of artists had studied with the master: all aspirants had to do, it seemed, was look. But the actuality of Ōkyo's proprietorship was also furiously maintained. It remains *Ōkyo*'s new concept. He offered a direct assault on the official schools, yet not in an avant-garde way, to destroy the intellectual base of what they were doing, but conservatively, to displace them in the execution of establishment commissions. Emphasis on observation was a safe house from which to launch raids on others.

I have deliberately not yet introduced a work in the mature Ōkyo manner for discussion. There is a reason for this: the 'new concept' was a rhetoric, an ideological position, and not, in the end, a style. Un'en, Gantai, Akinari, Kōkan and others dilate on Ōkyo as a phenomenon but appear to have found in the 'new concept' few hooks for sustained debate in terms of style. It seems that Ōkyo's paintings left the viewer in no mood for protracted analysis. But this was just the point: viewers did not expound on the handling of ink and line (as they did of literati and heterodox work), nor were they tickled into patter on the painting's surface charms (as with the Nagasaki school) or on the exotic draftsmanship or subject matter (as with Westernist painting). The lull that descended over this 'new concept' (which everyone mentioned in four or five words and then dropped) was the corollary of the loud cry Ōkyo gave to the subject matter. His paintings were loud in theme. They scattered throughout Japan, being found in mansions and temples, but also in teahouses, restaurants and homes of those of small fortune and, again, in the Dairi. For the first time in history, all were bound together across class and geographical division by a single imagistic entity, and it was called 'Ōkyo'. The number of practitioners of the Ōkyo mode was nothing compared to its consumers. Bunmei gushed, 'from the kings in their courts down to the common people', all 'esteemed Ōkyo's paintings precious'.[36] Hardly a soul protested as Ōkyo commandeered the whole world of depiction. Among kings, he painted a *Peacock and Peony* for the boy Sachimiya when he was installed as Tomohito and worked on several palaces and royal temples. At the other end of the social spectrum, Kōkan saw an Ōkyo hanging in an Osaka brothel. Tomohito awarded him the court clan-name 'Minamoto', the shogun raised him to samurai rank, and commoners said his brush could actually sing.[37]

Unusually, Ōkyo used just one name throughout virtually his entire professional life. Artists generally had several *noms de plume*; Hokusai (admittedly an extreme case) had over thirty.[38] Masters of official ateliers signed their works with a bevy of characters indicating rank, status and studio name, so that Eisen-in, for example, might sign himself 'Kano Eisen Fujiwara Michinobu Dharmic Eye [*hōgen*] in the Ministry of Central Affairs' or some similar sequence;[39] Mitsusada signed 'Junior Minister of the Painting Bureau, Associate Fourth Rank, Upper, Marshal of Tosa, Fujiwara Mitsusada' (see illus. 48). This was a stock habit in the official ateliers. It was mocked by some who sought to cast pictures as effervescent objects, not products of famous houses, and Shōhaku (whom we have encountered as twitter of the Kano master Takushū) invented a tongue-in-cheek inheritance for himself in the Soga school. This illustrious group, founded by Soga Dasoku in the early sixteenth century, was long since defunct by the 1770s, but Shōhaku was prone to sign with deliberate absurdities such as 'Associate Member of the Junior Fourth Rank, the Governor of Hyōgo, the Lord Terusuke' and 'Descendant in the Tenth Generation of Dasoku', to stress the way in which artistry was ensnared by social hierarchies.[40] Ōkyo signed with no more than 'Maruyama Ōkyo'. The Ōkyo brand was unconfused. He never coveted the Tsuruzawa, Ishida,

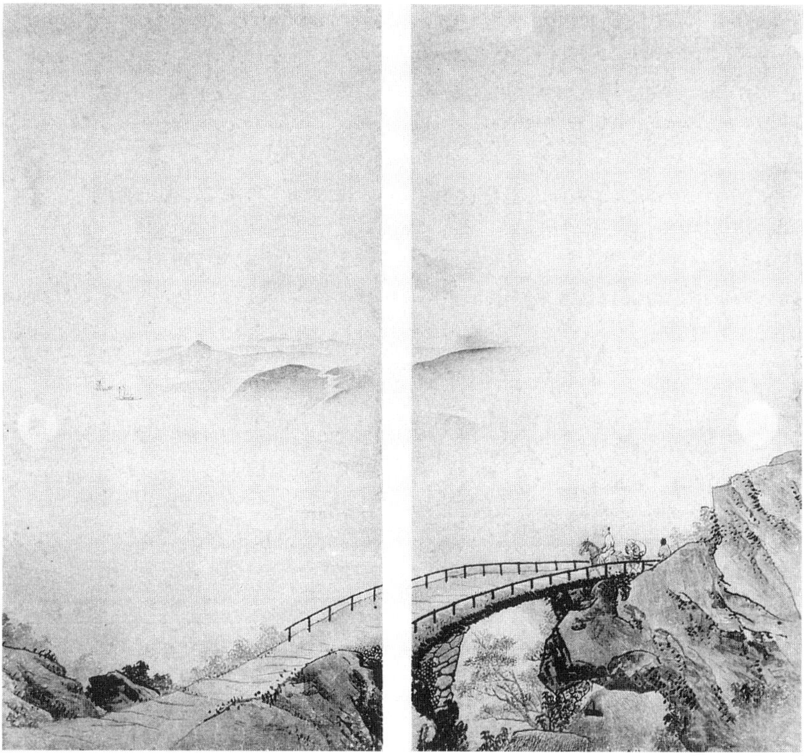

69, 70 Two sections of Maruyama Ōkyo, *Landscape*, 1788, sliding doors remounted as hanging scrolls, ink and light colour on paper. Even the evocative vagueness of ink-wash landscape has been given an abnormal amount of spatial cohesion.

or much less Kano, names. Ōkyo also added the date. Here was another anomaly, for official art was rarely dated. The Kano, being 'one brush' (as Yasunobu put it) 'unchanged for one thousand generations', conceived of themselves as exterior to time.[41] Ōkyo construed himself as within it. He was a person ripe for the moment. The only other handle he added to his signature was 'of Heian', that is, the first name of Keishi, non-existent except in the most historicized and poetic of contexts since the twelfth century. Ōkyo's radical revival was directed towards the most receded of traditions.

Ōkyo's prodigious output necessitated a full reliance on academy practices. Work was apportioned between master and pupils, and sometimes few, sometimes no, lines on an 'Ōkyo' were put there by the man himself, although the finished work bore his signature. His power was to seize a commission and fulfil it; people ordered by theme, and it was subjects that carried the day.

Time treated Ōkyo kindly. During the Great Fire he was burned out of his studio and relocated to the nearby Temple of Joyous Clouds (Kiun-in).[42] He then moved to the Temple of the Golden Vajra (Kongō-ji) in the village of his birth, where he began a programme of some 60 screens for installation in the abbacy (illus. 69, 70). During this project he evolved a system of spatial integrity appropriate to large interior spaces, executed in this instance in ink and the lightest of colours, but capable of appropriation for other treatments. This stood him in good stead when he returned to new Kyoto. During his absence his paintings had become media of exchange. Those who had lost works to the flames received gifts from those who had not, and transfer was generally up from a low to a superior owner (one rarely gave 'down'). There was a ratcheting-up of ownership in which Ōkyo, as already the most famous artist in the city, figured large. A secondary consequence was that little-seen works came to light, as stores were emptied and unburned suites of pictures were put in locations where there was an immediate need. Ōkyo's landscape series made for Kyōrei-mon-in, the cloistered widow of the former shujo Tōhito (posthumously, Momozono), was moved to the Sanji Chion-ji Temple, where it would have enjoyed greater visibility.[43] Ōkyo had several more active years, and soon, back in Keishi, he took up his brush again. Much of his best work was done after the Great Fire. Being presented with an urban *tabula rasa* was beneficial and a fillip for ruthless stylistic takeover. 'Ōkyo of Heian' could, and would, re-equip Keishi with a corpus of imagery, done 'his' way, right for the time and available to all askers.

The period of Ōkyo's later flourishing coincided with Sadanobu's term in office. Direct connections between the two are difficult to determine. Given that Sadanobu spent so little time in Keishi and Ōkyo never went to Edo, they cannot have been close, and there are no records of them having met during Sadanobu's visit of 1788 to inspect the fire damage.[44] The team he sent to oversee the *Sage Screens* (Hiroyuki, Ritsuzan and Hirohata) held discussions with Sumino Tōshirō, an Ōkyo pupil, although perhaps not a senior one; Ritsuzan certainly knew Ōkyo well enough to receive a painting from him as a farewell gift when he left Keishi to run the shogunal Confucian college on Sadanobu's invitation (symbolically, it was a *Nightingale Leaving a Springtime Valley*), and Tani Bunchō sought out Ōkyo's son Ōzui after Ōkyo's death.[45] When Sadanobu retired, he had Bunchō make a scroll of portraits of the people he felt had most defined his age, including artists, scholars and other influential figures. Ōkyo was in it, together with Ritsuzan, Kairyō, Daiten, Ganku, Koshōken and Minagawa Kien, and Ōkyo's pupil Goshun

71 Tani Bunchō (attrib.), *Maruyama Ōkyo*, from his *Kinsei meika shozō zakan*, c. 1831, handscroll, colour on silk. Sadanobu had a series of portraits of men he viewed as significant to the age – the first (and largest) is of Okyo.

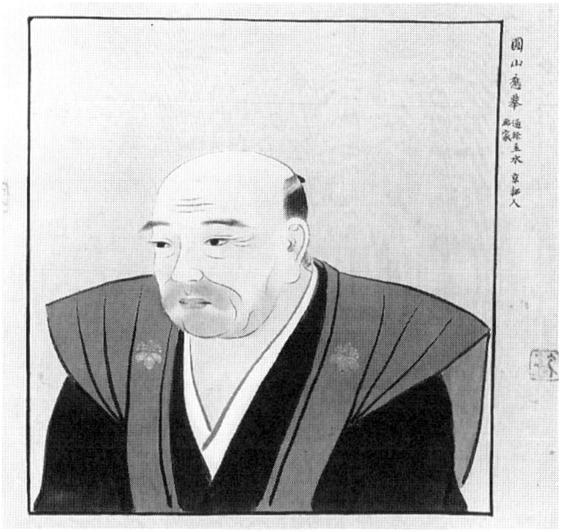

(on whom more below) is also shown. In fact Ōkyo comes first, and his image is nearly twice as big as any of the others (illus. 71).[46]

The circle of Ōkyo's personal acquaintance is hard to retrieve. This is relevant, for the prevalence of artists in the small, literate city of Keishi made for a sense of friendship and *communitas*. Many figures remain accessible today in the diary comments of their cultivated friends; comportment, *bons mots* delivered at parties, or views of life and culture were often appreciatively preserved. Ōkyo seems hardly to have known anybody or left any imprint. His sole appearance is in the form of a painterly phenomenon. He said and did nothing else. In the 1770s Ōkyo lived less than ten minutes' walk from Keishi's other artist of renown, Sha Shunsei (also called Buson), yet there is not a shred of evidence they consorted, although Buson was sociable enough.[47] The Mito Confucianist Tachihara Suiken nearly met Ōkyo in 1795, but Ōkyo cancelled.[48] Akinari managed a meeting with the painter more than once but was quite unexcited by the encounters; to him, Ōkyo lacked social aplomb, *joie de vivre*, or fashion sense, with no grip on that core desideratum 'elegant poise' (*fūryū*).[49] Few, after spending time with Ōkyo, emerged with much to jot into their note-books, unless talk turned to pigment and practice. One of his few festive attendances was at an annual plum-blossom viewing in the outskirts, where drinking and partying were the order of the day. On one occasion this included a certain Kōzan Tekien, who wrote the trip up in a verse. But he failed to mention Ōkyo's presence, Ōkyo evidently having contributed nothing to the day's pleasures.[50]

Despite its rags-to-riches glamour, Ōkyo's private life was exception-ally colourless. Some references allow us to piece together a few associates, but the only culturally significant figure with whom he consorted frequently was Minagawa Kien. Through him Ōkyo must have met others, perhaps including Kien's friend the abbot Rikunyo, as the distinguished prelate composed nine verses on him. Notably, Rikunyo's poems indicate love of Ōkyo's paintings but say nothing about the man: perhaps they had not met, or perhaps Rikunyo could not remember.[51] Kien claimed he and Ōkyo were 'brotherly', but this was written in the context of a funerary elegy where human fondness was necessarily played up. Anyway, one friend does not constitute much company.

Okyo's worked defined him. He had no discernible diversion outside its production. His interest in human communication seems restricted to those who used (and bought) his paintings. No less a person than Tomohito's older brother invited the artist for a chat, which was a huge honour. But Ōkyo sent word he was 'too busy painting' to attend. Two months later he did call by, but he could only spare the hours after nightfall when it was too dark to work.[52] Ōkyo would readily have painted for the prince, but meeting him seems to have been non-essential. In another encomium, Kien stated of Ōkyo that 'the space before his gateway was never empty of carriages'; if so, these must have been those of people coming to order or collect the paintings. Discussions were in short supply.[53]

The above must be read with care: Ōkyo's lack of social skills was his *atelier construction*. He could also be smooth in dealing with persons of consequence. He was aware that he was taking commissions that might once have gone to other schools. Ōkyo was alert to the fact that any painter needed an aura, or 'image', which was a marked feature of Keishi's emerging picture market. The deliberate erection of a public persona was standard practice, with affirmational mythologies generally coming from the master himself, to be circulated by students, who would ultimately write them down for later generations. Jakuchū ran away and hid until they thought he was dead; Shōhaku rode backwards on his horse; Taiga forgot the money due on his pictures.[54] These stories were generated to express something about the respective painter's mentality. The samurai collectivities of the academies were different, for they were overtly corporate, but independent artists needed legends to cultivate their clients. Some characterization was also necessary for Ōkyo. He stuck to the middle ground and cultivated the appearance of boredom. This shielded him, just as his 'new concept' did, from those aggrieved at how he thrust himself forwards. The dull persona furthered the ends of the homogenized style, for it removed the possibility of the all-too-common distraction where owners or admirers missed talking about a picture's content because they were so enthralled by the artist's odd-ball life. As today, most eighteenth-century viewers were uneasy talking about art and found it more comfortable to move to anecdotal remarks about lifestyle. The Ōkyo viewer could not make that shift, and the paintings occupied the sole discursive space.

Ōkyo specifically forbade his followers from spreading legends about him. 'Before he died', wrote Bunmei, 'Ōkyo was adamant that though it might be the modern practice to tell stories of people and erect memorials, it was a custom that fed on lies and nonsense, and he wished no such thing to be done for him'.[55] And it was not. Not until some five years after the artist's demise, when loss of memory was about to consign Ōkyo the man to oblivion, did Kien and Bunmei countermand his instructions, feeling a few comments had to be set down.[56] They constructed a record that is so brief as to read more as testimony to having nothing particular to say than the celebration of a unique human life. All the pair could come up with was that Ōkyo intervened to stop evil, promoted virtue, cared for his relations, was generous towards his servants and gave of his own to alleviate the urgencies of others – admirable characteristics, but pure cliché, pinnable to almost anyone's breast.[57]

Against this can be put the many tales about Ōkyo's patterns of labour. 'He worked throughout the day until twilight', wrote Bunmei, 'and then on into the dark – how would he not have been successful?'[58] Although nothing snide was intended, the relevance to Ōkyo of 'success' is not to be missed. Such words would not have been applied to Jakuchū, Shōhaku or Taiga, for whom conventional plaudits were inimical (or were constructed as being so) and whose lives were said to be 'untrammelled' (*ipin*) by ordinary concerns. Studying to achieve fame was not the carrot held out to artistic hopefuls in most schools, who would rather be tempted by attainment of 'elegance' (*ga*) or 'beauty' (*bi*). Ōkyo's assurance to his pupils, quoted above, that by committing themselves to him they would 'secure fame' highlights this orientation.

Ōkyo and Goshun

When Akinari met Ōkyo, he found him 'calculating', too clever (*kashikoi*).[59] Akinari retailed an exchange between Ōkyo and his pupil Matsumura Goshun (called Gō Gekkei) (illus. 72). Ōkyo was conspicuously abstemious (or again, constructed as being so) to counterpose his toiling in paint. Goshun was independently wealthy (his father was

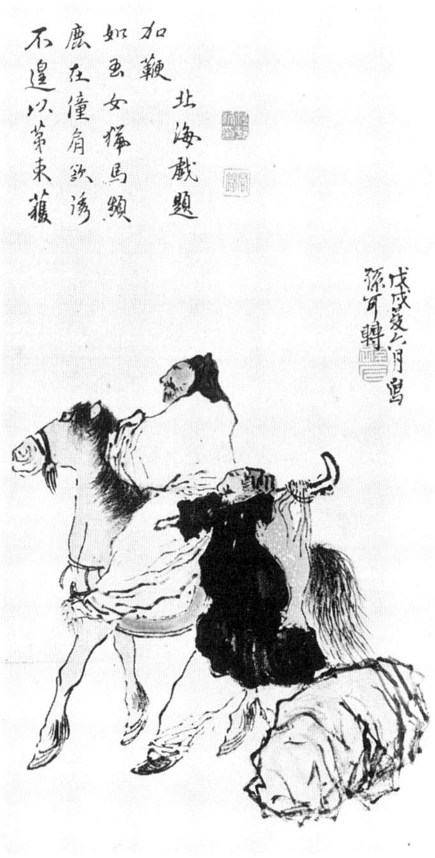

72 Gō Gekkei, *Huntsmen*, 1778, hanging scroll, light colour on paper. Gekkei (Goshun) working in his early Buson manner.

head of the Keishi mint), and he claimed painting was just part of his many refinements; he even announced, 'being a gourmet is a prerequisite for artistic accomplishment'. Akinari knew Goshun to enjoy 'a plentiful and a varied trencher, and to be cultivated in all manner of respects'. Eventually this sybaritic lifestyle and gourmandizing aetiolated Goshun and made him ill, which seems not to have displeased Ōkyo, who made him into an object lesson. Ōkyo told Akinari that when he had last met Goshun, he looked like 'an unholy, weather-exposed corpse'. Uni-directionalism was a policy to reassure the market that its needs would be professionally met on time, and to incapacitate objectors. So many of the tales that pepper the biographies of literati and heterodox artists entail acceptance that they were unable to get orders completed as scheduled or turn out what was expected; this was all very 'untrammelled', but not very workable. Kano and Tosa were never late. Astringency was Ōkyo's tenet, and it

73 Gō Gekkei, *Thoughts of Rain in a Ravine* and *Snowy Landscape by a Pond*, c. 1800, diptych of hanging scrolls, ink and light colour on silk. Gekkei (Goshun) working in his later adaptation of Ōkyo's 'new concept'.

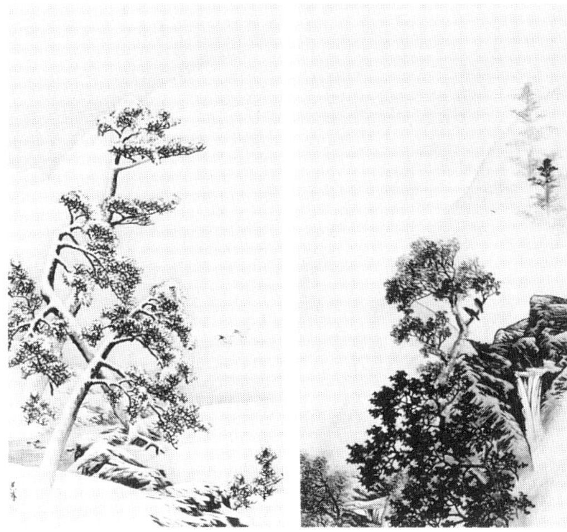

also increased health and prolonged life, giving a commensurately extended duration for his creativity. The only known portrait of Ōkyo, existing in several copies (including Sadanobu's), shows him as a rugged workhorse, square and virile and so dismissive of polish that he has not even shaved (see illus. 71). This image originated with Ōkyo's pupil Yamaato Kakuryō and would have presented the master as he specified he should be seen. Ōkyo won through his capacity to provide muscle for a troubled aristocracy, not because he aped them. In the end, Ōkyo lived to 62 and Goshun to 60, so the latter's career was not much clipped; blindness also deprived Ōkyo of his powers some years before his death in 1795.

The more serious connection between these two artists is important. They seem to have met when both were burned out of their studios in the fire and subsequently moved (apparently coincidentally) into the same temple.[60] Goshun was converted and, a few months later, abandoned his previous manner, which he had learned from Buson and was redolent with sinicized aspirations, and absorbed Ōkyo's 'new concept' (illus. 73). This was immensely hurtful to Buson's memory (he had died in 1783), for he had always treated Goshun more as a confidant than a student, and shortly before his death had made his daughter Goshun's ward. Goshun's first art name (Gekkei) had been created by fusing that of his first teacher, Suigetsu, with a diminutive of Buson's family name, Taniguchi (*tani* 'valley' goes to *kei* 'crevice').[61] He publicly disaffiliated himself.[62] Ōkyo's all-compelling torque now reeled the artist in. Many never forgave Goshun for this betrayal. Tanomura Chikuden warned Buson's other student of real stature, Ki

Baitei, that he was now holding the precious light all alone; he also said of Taiga's non-'new-concept' and Buson-like successor that 'because he transmitted the proper sort of painting when Ōkyo and Goshun were "offering hawks and viewing tigers" [carrying all before them], he was genuinely admirable', nicely expressed given that the man, Aoki Shukuya (called 'Taiga II'), was not regarded as a very able painter.[63] Chikuden's editor interpolated the comment that this commendation was worth over ten thousand in gold and that Shukuya 'cannot doubt he did the right thing'.[64]

Goshun was of larger consequence than the anonymous hordes who emulated Ōkyo and was sought after in his own right. Having entered the Ōkyo arena, Goshun worked on it from the inside and eventually changed the school, wresting it away from Ōkyo's son and official successor, Ōzui. To Ōkyo's family name (Maruyama) which Ōzui took over, he added the location of the atelier he had personally inherited from Ōkyo in Fourth Avenue (Shijō) so that, to later generations, the 'new concept' post-Ōkyo became 'Maruyama–Shijō' painting. Perhaps in premonition, Ōkyo had said 'there are no other masters around here to worry me, but I am afraid of that fellow Gekkei'.[65] It was Ōkyo's pride and also his anguish to have stolen the best pupil of his only serious rival. But the power of Goshun, well-dressed in its recognizable, if vestigial, cloak of effete all-roundedness, could not be assimilated into Ōkyo. 'Ōkyo' had to be twisted. That Ōkyo persisted in calling Goshun 'Gekkei' is relevant, for this was the name he had used in his early career under Buson. Goshun had stopped using it himself, but Ōkyo continued to wave it as publicity for his takeover. The name 'Gekkei' also allowed Ōkyo to pause momentarily the genesis of the full 'Goshun' who would undo him.

Some annoyance at Ōkyo's careful constructions are apparent. Two are attributable to Buson. These appear as inscriptions on lost Ōkyo paintings, whether beknown to Ōkyo or not is unsure. On a *Terrapin*, Buson wrote: 'I thought to myself how much better it was to be like this, dragging one's tail in the mud, than to be always straining for public acclaim'.[66] In seeming to praise the work, Buson actually chides *arrivisme*, and he went on to link the reptile to the 'money terrapin' (*zeni-game*), surely not the type that Ōkyo had in mind when he did the painting. Buson continued with a verse:

This money-terrapin
Has no inkling of the muddy depths,
In its clear mountain stream.[67]

Mud is the source of valuable nutrients (it should not here be taken to indicate dirt or slime), and so it is better to drag along the bottom of a fecund pond than to swim in the chill aridity of translucent water. Ōkyo's clear stream lacks life. Exactly this image was also used against Sadanobu, whose state was Shirakawa, which literally meant 'white' (that is, clear) river. Ota Nanpo had composed a curt verse on instigation of the Kansei Reforms:

In Shirakawa/In the clear stream
With its pure flow
Nothing remains alive.[68]

Buson's critique is inaccurate in that, I think, financial rewards were not Ōkyo's goal. He wanted representational monopoly, not wealth. But the linking of Ōkyo's pictures to the brittle brilliance of glassy water was apt. On a *Black Dog* by Ōkyo, Buson wrote:

From its own body's darkness
It cries out,
This autumn midnight.[69]

The black dog has disappeared into the dark, but its real occlusion does not proceed from external conditions but from the crepuscularity of its inner self. Autumn was proverbially the season of bright moons, but this dog's heart of darkness comprehends even that radiance. The dog yelps, nevertheless, on and on, for attention. This interpretation can be combined with another. Buson used the poetry name Yahan ('Midnight') which he had inherited from his *haikai* master, Hayano Hajin; he was often called Yahan-tei ('Master Midnight'). Thus, it is also *Buson* who is in gloom. This allows the last two lines to be read, 'I, Yahan, cry out', as Ōkyo eclipses Buson's star.

There were those who thought the 'new concept' a piece of massive charlatanism that had paid off. Rai San'yō, a prominent literati artist, felt Ōkyo had been right to detect a problem in the prevailing dispensation but had smothered, rather than solved, it with the coarseness of his idiom:

. . . [Ōkyo] replaced old putrifaction with something new, and devoted himself exclusively to 'copying from life' [*shasei*]. But he had no truck with what was historical. You may well call it 'copying from life', but you can hardly call it good painting.[70]

Famously, Shōhaku once told a potential buyer that if it was 'art' (*ga*) in all its nuanced limpidity that was wanted, then he, Shōhaku, was the man, but if banausic work (*zu*) would do, then Ōkyo was the one to turn to.[71] In 1801 the painter and formulator Nakabayashi Chikutō called Ōkyo 'worse than awful' (*ge-gehin*) and, more tellingly, when constructing a typology of artists, he dropped Ōkyo into a category he called the 'cloying' or 'sickly sweet' type (*amattarui*), or, as we might paraphrase it, 'unsavoury'.[72] He said it ought to be made illegal for beginners to look at Ōkyo's work – and that went for Goshun's too – as it was 'bad' and 'meritriciously bewitching' painting.[73] Ōkyo was 'crude enough to amuse women and children, but insufficient to impress the eyes of the educated'.[74] The trouble was, this polemic was factually untrue.

The Ōkyo Process

Ōkyo had much to say about how he wished his paintings to be viewed. In contrast to the pretence that depiction was just a matter of looking and copying 'authentically', viewing, he allowed, presented a cognitive challenge. This in itself was not unusual, for literati artists positioned their painting the same way. Chikuden was to write:

> Looking at paintings is harder than making them, for you must have principles both ancient and modern in your mind, and the brilliant rays issuing from the divine inside your eyes. Only then will good, bad, beautiful and ugly appear, all else sinking out of sight, so that nothing is left hidden in shadow. Compared with this, the problem of mixing and applying paint is trivial.[75]

Ōkyo's stress was different. To Chikuden, viewing was taxing because beholders had to empathize with the tenor of the work and cause to well up within them a mindset that stretched across chasms of time, linking the present and the past via the ink that the artist had deployed. Ōkyo was novel in taking viewing as the *painter*'s duty. The artist was maker and first viewer, and if he properly considered this, he pre-empted the role of beholders, easing their access into the work and forcing their understanding of meaning to conform to his own. Ōkyo's sketchbooks are full of jottings made for his own benefit, not the kind artists often included as *aides memoire*, but those associated with a second-party adjudicator: 'too much black here', or 'this sketch is unreliable', or – on the goat made for inclusion in the *Huang Chuping* (see illus. 64) – 'the face is done a little too narrow' and 'the tail's too flat and thin'.[76]

More than teaching painting, Ōkyo took the view that he taught 'the inspection of paintings' (*kanteihō*): the student's own.[77] The picture is just 'made' (no problematization of this process is offered) but is then hypercritically viewed. This opinion was recorded by the prince–abbot of a sumptuous temple, the Enman-in, on Lake Biwa, who was the adopted son of the shujo's regent (*kanpaku*) and was properly referred to as Prince Dankai of the Temple of the Garden Citadel, although his clerical name was Yūjō. Ōkyo was befriended by the prelate but, in the way that all his associations gravitated towards the studio or else were severed, Ōkyo preferred to see Yūjō as buyer or pupil. Yūjō wrote down all that he heard from the still young Ōkyo, although none of it relates to anything but studio practice, on which subject, however, he is quite complete.[78] Ōkyo recommended Yūjō not to envisage a sequence whereby a work was made by the artist and then criticized by a buyer, possibly leading to alterations to the product, but where the artist assumed both roles. Yūjō was told:

> Look at your own work as if you were inspecting a classical piece. Hang it up in a formal display area where the light conditions are good, and peer at it through a magnifying glass. Consider what the differences are between what you have made and your original intent. Leave the picture hanging for a time, and come back repeatedly to it to look.[79]

Mistakes would be noted for future reference, then a title (*gadai*) assigned, and the work sent out as a completed picture. The owner's critical role was obviated, and all he or she had to do was learn from the implications of the subject.

Experimentation with several viewing postures (the coming and going Ōkyo enjoins) was critical for artists working on large-scale compositions. Ōkyo's remarks to Yūjō imply a hanging scroll, but the elite formats were more often the sliding or folding screen, or wall; these were produced in quantity by Ōkyo. Screens put pressure on any artist who sought to contrive a unified space, for they are to be seen from a number of stances, some nearer, some further away, some higher, some lower (by status); ample cohesion for one meant anamorphosis for another. Folding screens also had a concertina surface, the angles of which were not predetermined, with users manipulating them to fit the requirements of the room or event. Those who most often provided such elite objects (i.e. the Kano) never attempted more than a modicum of spatial unity and sensibly used vagueness as a method to permit multiple-viewing situations in a big space. This was not appealing to Norinaga, who wanted more coherence and who questioned 'modern artists' who 'ruined' aristocratic décor by 'belabouring the detail' at the cost of tying the picture together.[80] But as a policy it

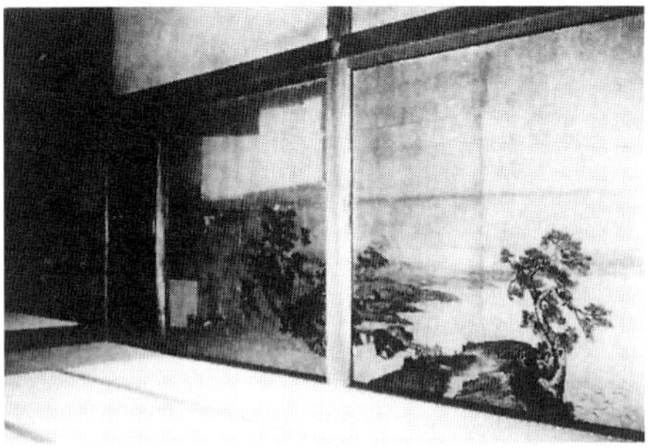

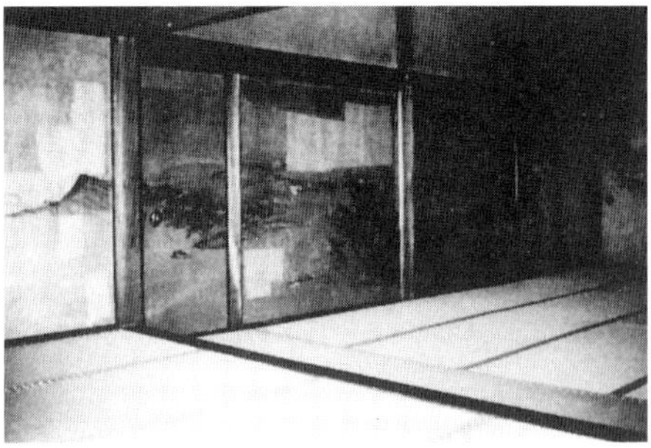

74 Ōkyo's landscape in the Temple of the Great Vehicle. The angle is from the lower seat to the upper one.

75 Here the angle is from the upper seat to the lower one; the scenery coheres in both directions.

made some sense.

Ōkyo was aware of the distinction between 'pictures for close viewing', where a certain kind of unity was possible, and 'pictures for looking at from afar', where the viewing angle was not shared. His solutions are best seen in several of the rooms in the abbacy of the Temple of the Great Vehicle (Daijō-ji), near Kinosaki on the Korean side of Honshū, where he and his pupils worked extensively the year before the Keishi fire. Several experiments are seen. In the second room was a moral theme, *Guo Ziyi and his Grandchildren*, that is, the eighth-century 'pacifier' of Tibet, who through longevity and progenitivity had so many successors he could not remember their names (see illus. 29). The figures lack all background, which is painted out in gold. The life-sized bodies occupy a zone that shimmers slightly when viewed by oil lamp (as it would normally have been) and in which the metal pigment recedes relative to the coloured paint. The substantiality of the people is affirmed, while the absence of background retains their logic from whatever position they are seen. This substantiality extends to pointing of feet, sensations of body beneath the robes, and a layering of hair. All are aspects of Westernist depiction, and yet the painting had no apparent exoticism. Those who visit the temple also affirm that (like Mona Lisa's eyes) Guo Ziyi's face appears to turn as viewers move, and that he looks at them wherever they look at him from.

A flat gold background was required in such a senior chamber of the abbacy. In the next, Ōkyo produced a landscape, as was proper to that room. A different tactic had to be applied here. The landscape was so contrived that its depths looked plausible, if different, whether viewed from the visitor's seat at one end of the room, the host's at the other, or any of the 180 degrees separating them; none is privileged (illus. 74, 75).[81]

Mechanics of Seeing

Oku Bunmei warned against accepting any of his teacher's rhetoric at face value: Ōkyo's methods of picture-making were far more sophisticated than he led people to think, and those who did not delve beneath the blandishments would be as deluded as the fool who 'saw a leopard through a tube' and thought he knew it, or as we would say, a giraffe passing by a window.[82] There was no doubt that Ōkyo encouraged a kind of *pleine-aire* drawing that the other schools did not, but there was more to the 'new concept' than empiricism. There were rules (*shūhō*) to be learned, and some of these dealt with manipulating and restructuring things seen.[83] Ōkyo maintained he was never without a sketchbook:

For my part, I always have a small diary with me for use in daily drawing. When I see mountains, rivers, grass, trees, birds, animals, insects, fish, people and anything else in its living state [*ikimi*], I believe I should copy it down.[84]

This was easy to say. The first objection might be that most of nature was irrelevant to standard painting themes. The range of flora and fauna appearing in Ōkyo's or any other artist's work is limited. Conversely, many of the animals encountered in art are timorous, nocturnal or rare. Empiricism has at once to be supplemented. There were many ways to do this, offering differing degrees of compromise. Ōkyo used machines of viewing and liked to be seen with lensed equipment as part of his rhetorical stance; when he went to view the plums with Kōzan Tekien, he took a telescope. He advised Yūjō: 'If you go too close to birds or animals they will take fright, tense up, and become difficult to sketch; it is best to draw them as seen through a telescope'.[85] One can only conjecture on the degree of help a telescope of this period would give. Even though this was a sort of supplemented empiricism, it was not sufficient in practice, since the living forms that appeared in official painting either did not come before the eye at all (dragons and tigers) or else were too fleeting to train a lens on. Ōkyo advised Yūjō to cannibalize from what could be see unhurriedly. A restless monkey, he said, could be convincingly rendered if one started out from the shape of a dog and made the rest up; he stressed a dog was

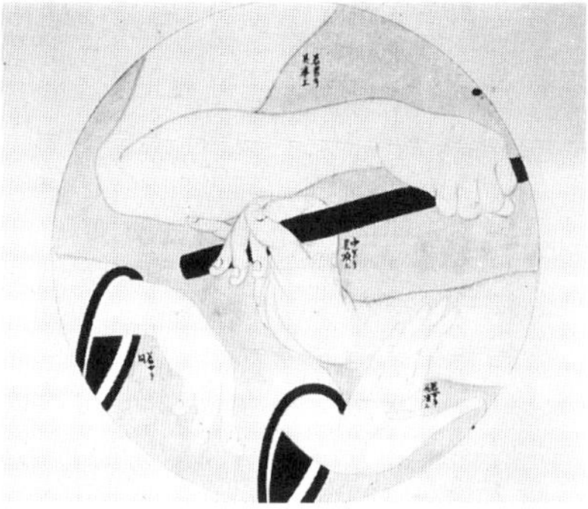

76 Maruyama Ōkyo, Section from *Jinbutsu seisha sōhon*, 1770, handscroll, ink and light colour on paper. The round frames suggest copying from reflections in a telescope or mirror.

a better model than a human, contrary to what might be supposed, for if done after a human 'the ear and the neck will come out looking too close'.[86] Many tips were dispensed. Do not assimilate the form of a deer into that of a sheep, 'which will not be successful; deer ought to be modelled on horses'. The eyes of a sparrow resemble those of a puppy, not a fish. When Yūjō complained he could not get the beaks of birds right, Ōkyo suggested 'the beak of a sparrow looks as if it were made out of earth'.[87] Eventually, mnemonics worked out on paper ousted naked viewing. The living forms must look right, but this need not be achieved by actually viewing them, so long as the tricks of plausible rendition are acquired.

In figure painting there was no dilemma of fugitive subjects, and there Ōkyo expended more time on first-hand observation. Many sketches attest to an intrusive, even unsanctionable gaze – an old woman entering a bath, a boy masturbating ('do the semen in powdered or crystalline white', he noted in the margin).[88] Ōkyo has several scrolls of depictions of bodies inspected in many positions, and he made a collection of sketched body parts, some appearing in roundels as if viewed through a telescope (illus. 76). He certainly made these sketches, but they were done very early in his career (mostly in the 1760s), and he does not seem to have maintained the custom once he had a series ready to show prospective commissioners. And precious few of the sketches can be matched with known paintings. Even if a pictorial lexicon might be built up, some aspects of humanity were resistant, such as the looks of members of foreign races (like Guo Ziyi). Ōkyo advised Yūjō that this was not consequential, for he could draw a local person first, 'adding the overseas flavour afterwards' in clothing or hairstyle, as taken from reference books or other pictures.[89] Ōkyo also worked from physiognomic traits, not actual faces, so that his figures matched the moral worth of the person according to scholarly tables.[90]

The connections between Ōkyo and the academic discourse of the body can be taken further. He was surely aware that the practices he was claiming as his mode of production were the basis of depiction in the West. Morishima Chūryō had written in 1787 in his *Miscellany on Europe (Kōmō zatsuwa)* that, in Europe, 'those who wish to make pictures first study the details of bones and joints in the male and female bodies; after that, they learn how to depict naked humans. Only then do they put clothes on them and make the finished work'.[91] This sequence appears in some Ōkyo sketches (illus. 77). Ōkyo was using the language of the sort of painting commonly accepted as empirical, for even those who mistrusted European pictures profoundly accepted they had uncanny approximations to the real.[92]

Ōkyo also kept anatomical books available.[93] While studying with Ishida Yūtei he may have met Yoshimura Ranshū, a pupil of Yoshimura Shūzan who founded the line to which Shūkei belonged (see illus. 22–4). Ranshū left Shūzan to pursue anatomical illustration and, in 1783, produced pictures for the *Illustrations of the Organs of Heijirō (Heijirō zōzu)*, fruit of an autopsy conducted by Tachibana

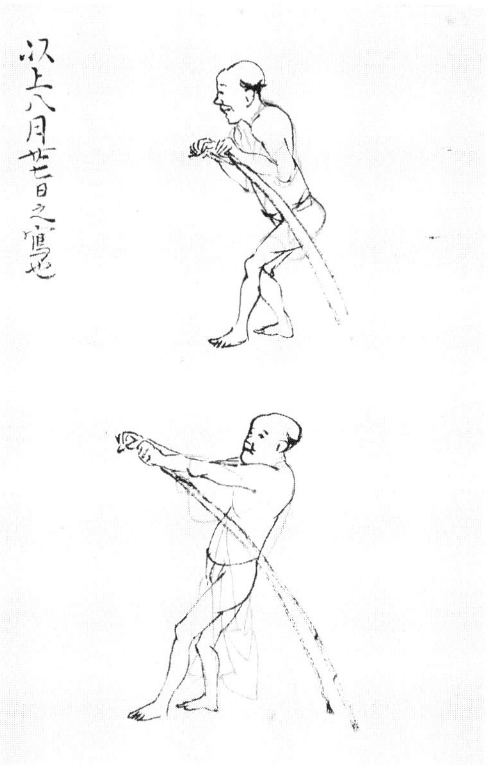

77 Maruyama Ōkyo, Section from *Biwako ujigawa shasei-zu*, 1770, black and red ink on paper. Inscribed 'drawn on 27th of 8th month of same year [1770]'. Clothing was added in red ink over the black-ink bodies.

Nankei (see illus. 30).[94] Ranshū's son Ranryō, who did not attend the Yoshimura school, studied with Ōkyo and was later numbered among his 'ten greatest followers' (*jūtetsu*). After Ōkyo's death, he too turned to anatomical illustration, aiding his now elderly father and Ōkyo's third son, Ōju, with the celebrated *Seyaku-in's Illustrated Male Anatomy (Seyaku-in kai dantai zu)*, a fine book completed in 1799, by Mikumo Kanzen (i.e. Seyaku-in) and labelled bilingually in Japanese and Dutch (illus. 78).[95]

Ōkyo himself was involved in neither project, but more critically, for all that autopsies were in a sense exemplary of an empirical investigation of the body, the pictures do not suggest any practical link between dissection and completed paintings as Ōkyo would have defined them. It is not evident how the dismemberment of corpses, without formaldehyde or suction, could have been of much service. There is, however, an immediate rhetorical link. Even amongst doctors, autopsies were seldom performed, and bodily structures were experienced more through the pages of imported books than through dissection. The appeal to empiricism was a trope that the 'new concept' borrowed from medicine and bedded snugly to advance its claims.

The Power of Ōkyo's Images

There is little biographical anecdote about Ōkyo and not many concrete reports on the specifics of his style, but there are massive depositions concerning the emotional charge of his work. He was the solution to the failure of imagery to convince, and the brio with which his work caught viewers up was often recounted. Yūjō had keenly felt the increasingly supercilious treatment which the ethical lessons of painting were winning for themselves and, being an abbot, he particularly regretted the scant attention religious icons commanded. The eighth-century Wu Daozi, by contrast, regarded as the single most accomplished painter in the entire north-east Asian tradition (although his work was lost), was proverbially said to have made Buddhist imagery upon seeing which 'viewers abandoned poulterer's and butcher's and fishmonger's'.[96] In vegetarian Buddhist terms, this meant his oeuvre had made people moral, earning for him the laurels. Latter-day folk were more likely to laugh sacred pictures aside: depiction no longer engaged.

From the early 1760s Yūjō began to think of making a set of illustrations of the rewards of good and bad karma. It was a basic tenet of Buddhism, analogous to its creed, that actions brought with them reactions which affected the perpetrator through present and future

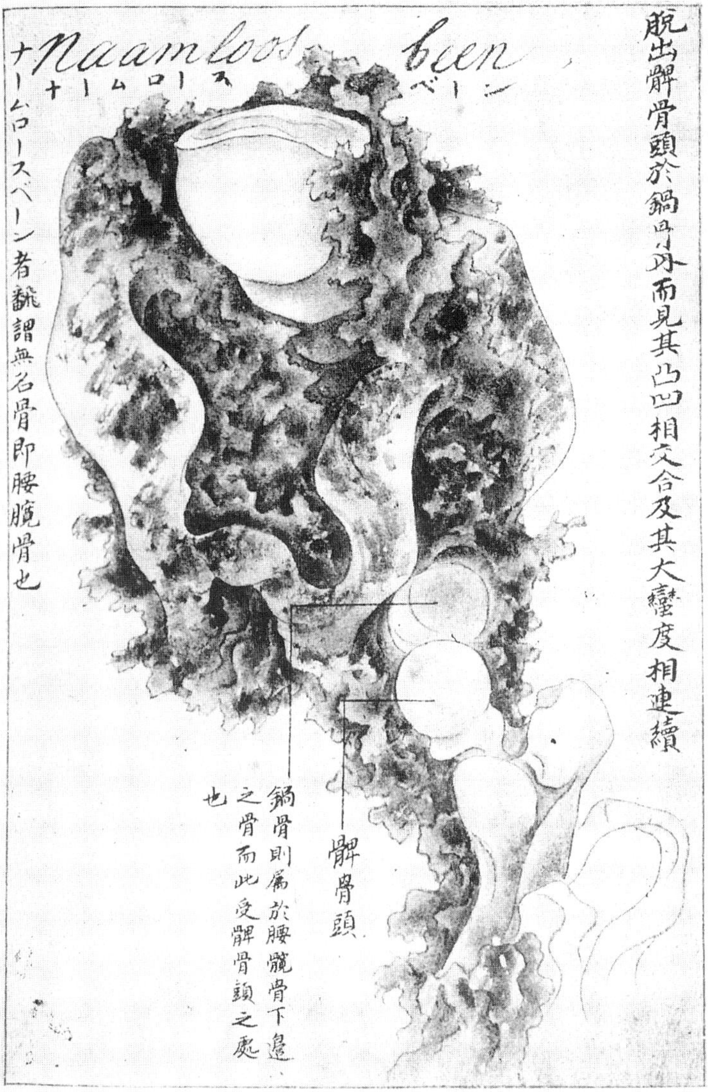

78 Yoshimura Ranshū *et al.*, Page from Mikumo Kanzen, *Seyaku-in kai dantai zu*, 1799, colour on paper. This bilingual book captures the facts of a dissection rather than offering objectified knowledge.

lives. Yūjō wanted works that would revive the fear of retribution and the yearning for bliss. The set was to be called *Seven Tribulations and Seven Blessings (Shichinan shikufuku)* and consist of a sequence of episodes exposed over three handscrolls, one showing tribulation by natural causes (flood, tempest etc.), one the hardships wreaked by human wickedness (war, rape etc.), and a third rewards (wealth, offspring etc.).[97] Yūjō tried to do the painting himself but found he was not skilled enough to elicit the desired effect. He looked vainly for someone to entrust the project too, which, given the artistic climate, was a bleak prospect. In 1765 he met Ōkyo and engaged him at once, stipulating only two requirements: that the set must be firmly grounded in the canonical texts (as detailed in the *Sūtra of the Benevolent Kings – Niō-kyō*) and should be painted 'in a way that seems near to the eye and ear'. That is, Ōkyo was to make a set that was uncompromising in Buddhistic terms but at the same time was appropriate to the needs of the modern viewer. In three years the scrolls were done (illus. 79, 80).

The *Seven Tribulations and Seven Blessings* became Ōkyo's most famous early composition and was extensively copied. To Bunmei, it offered first and lasting proof of his master's skill:

It picked up the teachings that our Lord Buddha gave – about the Forest of Swords and the Boiling Cauldrons, and also about the many bounties we are to receive – and transposed them into the reality of the present [. . .] How could this not be without effect in turning people [from vice] and directing them [towards virtue]?[98]

It was Wu Daozi all over again, as if Ōkyo had restored to painting what had languished for 1,000 years. Bunmei went on:

Those who see the pictures break into sweats, their hair stands on end, and even though they are not cold, they start to shake. From such work is born a determination to incline towards goodness and to avoid crimes deserving of punishment. It is a truism that painting is in decline, but who would deny it can still serve to further social instruction.

The invocation of sensory and even physical response in front of Ōkyo's paintings, rather than aesthetic admiration, is important. The 'new concept' broke the caesura between viewers and object, so that unwittingly they accepted the painted world as real and reacted to it accordingly. Ōkyo tugged this power back from the highest reaches of antiquity.

The death of Ōkyo sank painting back into despond. When the writer Takizawa Bakin visited Keishi about a decade afterwards, he stated the situation had yet to recover and that there were only two good artists in the city, one Goshun, the other Utanosuke (whom we have met as Kishi Ganku), but they could not equal Ōkyo. Painting had died with him, such that 'it is not possible to say the extent to which he is

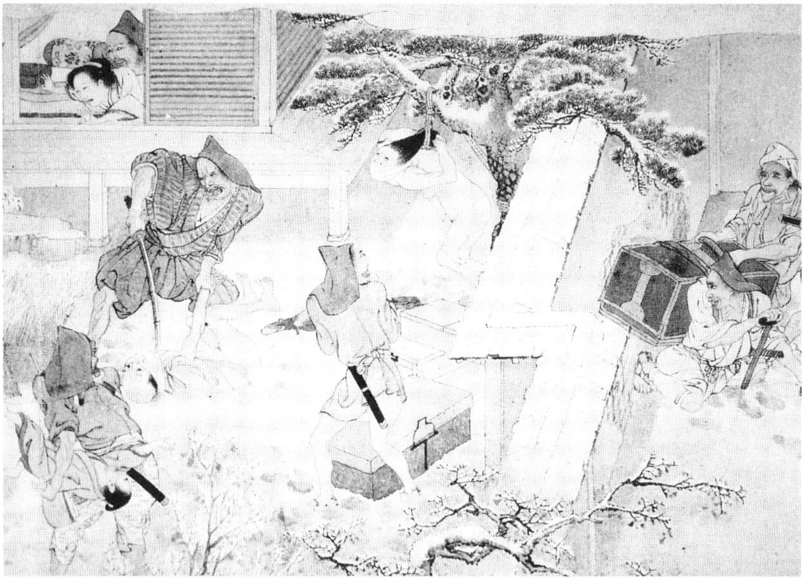

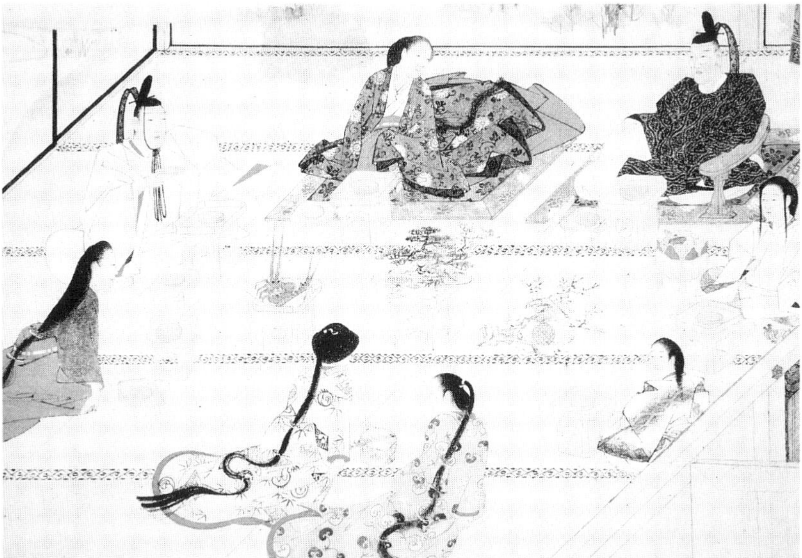

79 Maruyama Ōkyo, Section from *Seven Tribulations and Seven Blessings* (*Shichinan shikufuku zukan*), 1768, set of three handscrolls, colour on paper. Bad karma brings its reward in depravity wreaked by human hands.

80 Another section from *Seven Tribulations and Seven Blessings* (*Shichinan shikufuku zukan*). Good karma brings wealth and happiness.

missed'.[99] Ōkyo's conservativeness in theme ensured this power was entirely at the disposal of those maintaining the status quo. He was on the side of rulers and, with him gone, a regime had lost its most compelling proponent.

Hidden Colours

It may seem perverse to terminate our inspection of the highly rhetorical achievement of Ōkyo with something so rudimentary as a discussion of pigment. Yet his fame was based at least partly on his ability to handle colour astutely, in defiance of those who followed the traditional preference of assessing painterly worth by the calligraphic handling of ink. Even the Kano and Tosa, who made great play with colour, paid lip-service to the superior importance of calligraphic line.[100] Compositions in recognized brush modes are not absent from Ōkyo's oeuvre, and he often worked in evocative ink monochrome. But these are virtually absent from his contemporaries' discussions of him. Gantai regretted 'there is nothing to debate with him in terms of brush and ink'.[101] Yet all those who talked to Ōkyo noticed how frequently he discussed paint itself. One of Rikunyō's verses on Ōkyo identified him as 'a hand without peer in the Tenka for application of red and blue'.[102] This was formulaic, but the formula Rikunyō selected was not arbitrary, and it pointed to Ōkyo's forte as being in colour, not line. Literati painters like Taiga, Chikuden or Shukuya used few shades – usually only three – so as to be able to produce work spontaneously as they wandered, extemporizing in the open, as the mood took them; or, at least, they deliberately made their paintings appear to have been produced so. Ōkyo told Yūjō to take just two colours with him when he went outside – red and black – but for a quite different purpose: one was to draw and the other to correct the drawing.[103] Ōkyo never attempted full pictures outdoors or recommended others to do so, for his polished imagery looked, as it was, only producible at home.

Rai San'yō wrote of Ōkyo, 'When I look at what he does, I feel that it is basically European painting, only minus the shadows'.[104] To say something looked 'European' was to impale it on a two-pronged fork: the comment both deprecated the lack of attention to calligraphic quality and applauded its handling of colour. This conception of European pictures is clear from many commentaries, most amusingly in a teasing verse offered to Satake Yoshiatsu by his retainer, Hirazawa Heikaku, after the latter viewed one of the daimyo's efforts in the Western manner (see illus. 28):

In our fair realm too
Such pictures
Can be seen.
Talk about shading!
Talk about colour![105]

Ōkyo's removal of shadows was a policy decision to keep his pictures within the known regime of the art of the 'fair realm' (*fusō*) and to allow pictures to be viewed from any angle and in variable conditions of light, while retaining the conviction that a realistic handling of colour could impart.

Ōkyo was careful not to tip viewers over into the callow thrill of exoticism, and his work did not appear to most people as startlingly foreign as San'yō professed. To most, painted things and the spaces they inhabited exactly fitted their equivalents in the outside world, blending the work into a harmonious 'authenticity'.

The pigments available to Ōkyo's generation were unlike those known even shortly before. The potentials of colour were changing. Artists had once ground ink rhythmically while acquiring the meditative state that prefigured their brushing of paper or silk. The mystical triad of brush, inkstick and hand had been extolled for centuries, even by schoolmen who in practice consigned the tedium of liquefying inkcakes to pupils. As oil paint and mineral novelties were introduced, this assumption was challenged, for all that imports came in small quantities and were expensive. Oils were banally produced by boiling with gum arabic, in a process more scientific than spiritual.[106] The new-style colourist was *ipso facto* a non-philosophical painter – or, otherwise put, his philosophy abided within the subject of depiction, not in the method of its rendition. Annoyance at the prejudice against colour paint was articulated by Satake Yoshiatsu, who rounded on those who said working with minerals 'severed from the user a right to the name of artist', since these had none of the hallowed qualities of sticks of ink. He objected to the criticism that Western pigment was in itself vulgar, observing that highly prized lacquer was only the gum of a tree and that 'doctors make medicine out of whatever is efficacious'. In pictures, he wrote, 'we should make use of anything that will be effective'.[107]

Sadanobu also wrote about pigments and their manufacture with a frequency unusual for the journals of a senior statesman. He saw careful disposal of the latest battery of hues as essential for reinvigorating icons. Brush modes, for him, intruded and he was pretty much of Ōkyo's view:

. . . ink flowing like cloud or smoke among wispy distant mountains terminates in nothingness; dense areas of black may be more or less recognizable as woods and forests, but the landscape is purely of the painter's own devising, deriving from nowhere. This can be a rare thing to behold, and I would not dismiss all as shoddy, but it was because everyone has gone unthinkingly down this stylistic path that painting has become the piece of nonsense it is today.[108]

That is, ink styles were not able to depict genuine sights and so were not iconically useful. Norinaga seconded the censure, castigating artists who turned meaningful subjects into smears, depriving them of sense, 'and then excuse the result as a manifestation of their personal affinity with ink'. Yoshiatsu bluntly warned of the same danger in figure painting, 'we make pictures of rulers tilling the soil to encourage agriculture, and of field marshals in the thick of the fray to concentrate the mind on victory; if these fail to look like the real things, how can they fulfil their objectives?'[109]

Several pigments were imported, although there was also much inaccurate reportage circulated by those who had never seen them used. Westernists spread disinformation to inspire would-be purchasers, stressing durability and imperviousness to rain such that oil paintings were said to be virtually permanent, even if hung outside. Kōkan claimed that, when dusty, they could be simply wiped clean with a damp cloth; Satō Narihiro (a samurai botanist working not far from Nagasaki) added that, when an oil picture grew begrimed, 'you just wash it in boiling water which will clean off any soot', after which 'the colours appear again as new'.[110] Only two Western oil paintings were on open display in Edo, both by the Dutch artist Willem van Royen, sometime artist in residence to the Elector of Brandenburg. These were part of a set of five brought as gifts for the shogun Yoshimune in 1724 and deposited by him in a temple on the city's fringe. The works were a *View of the Rhine* and a *Still Life with Peacock*, and they continued to elicit gasps well into the nineteenth century at how even after hanging for two centuries the pigments had not dulled at all. (The pair were much copied, including by Tani Bunchō and Ishikawa Tairō.)[111] But this was scarcely enough evidence on which to build a theory of Western art.

Narihiro wrote a few pages on Westernist painting in his journal. He liked the imported style but found fault with the practice of rendering it in local pigments – a hybrid which he states was popular in Edo, although it has left no vestige visible today. This type of work was 'a mockery of European painting'.[112] To Narihiro, these efforts inverted the priorities: to him it was pigments that ought to take pride of place, and if they were unavailable the style ought not to be attempted. It was the colours that he valued, not the style itself, nor (presumably) the replications of foreign themes.

In the absence of a sufficient flow of imports, artists sought to create surrogate oil paints by any available means. Success was varied. Kōkan devised what were called 'mud paintings' (*doro-e*) using a fish glue; this looked good for a while, but peeled when the image was rolled for storage, and even when kept rigid flaked badly and had to be intermittently repaired.[113] Sadanobu suggested painting with a concoction of 1 *shō* of perilla oil (*egoma*) to 5 *senme* of amberoid (*gunroku*), 'mixed until half-suspended'; alternatively, he wrote, 'you can stir in cayenne or suchlike', but 'this does not have a very felicitous result'.[114] Tachibana Meisai composed a text in 1802 explaining how to apply turpentine (*chan*) to regular Japanese paintings to give them a European-looking finish. Meisai is unknown apart from his signature on this text, although he may be the same Meisai who took the Western-inspired name 'Rantoku' (*ran* from 'oranda', Holland), and was known to Aōdō Denzen. Turpentine seems to have been a preferred solution, and references to '*chan* pictures' appear in several Edo contexts.[115]

In his writing on Western pictures Narihiro stated that, to be done properly, they required a spectrum of seven colours. Yoshiatsu said ideally there should be more, and he listed fifteen desirable pigments in an appendix to his treatise on art; five of these (including gum arabic – not technically a pigment but a binding agent) were near unobtainable.[116] There is neither space nor need to investigate all of Narihiro's seven or Yoshiatsu's fifteen here, although two colours merit individual attention. Both also appear in several other contexts but were probably first mentioned by Hiraga Gennai, the polymath and mining expert who introduced Odano Naotake to Westernism and through him first stimulated Yoshiatsu's interest. Gennai had studied in Nagasaki, where he communicated with many Europeans, winning the particular respect of the East India Company leader Jan Crans. Gennai was known as 'a great friend of the Europeans'; in 1779 he died in peculiar circumstances while in prison on a charge of murder, secretly poisoned by the shogunate who, it seems, feared riots if his execution were publicly announced (the matter has never been resolved).[117] In an important mineralogical and botanical study published sixteen years before his death, Gennai mentioned these two pigments. One he called '*berein buraau*', that is, Berlin (or Prussian) blue, a bright, deep shade invented in 1704.[118] Berlin blue excited attention all across Europe in the next decades, the *Encyclopaedia Britannica* of 1771 defining it as 'next to ultramarine for beauty'.[119] Tachihara Suiken, quoting Gennai, affirmed the tint was 'quite remarkable'.[120]

Blue was vital for any range of tonality, especially if artists wished to paint the sky and water – which, of course, they did not do in north-east Asian art, where such areas were left blank, gilded or lightly washed. It can be no coincidence that blue skies appear in Japanese painting at precisely this time, the first instance generally being said to be Taiga's *True View of Mt Asama* of 1760.[121] The dating of the arrival of Berlin blue is problematic, and the direction of influence may be either way: did Berlin blue provoke the painting in of skies, or did a separate desire to depict them prompt a search for a deeper blue than the then current indigo and azurite (Taiga did not use Berlin blue)? At least one other imported blue appeared, for Yoshiatsu enthused about a certain 'blue indic' (*burai inteku*), said to be 'brought by the Dutch, but extremely difficult to get your hands on, rather like our "composite blue" [*henshō*] in shade, but deeper and fresher-looking'.[122] Yet Berlin blue was celebrated as peerless, becoming known by the indigenized name of '*bero*' or variants of this (such as Narihiro's '*pero*').

Though widely discussed, *bero* was hardly used, and even in Europe it was rare. Still, quantities increased and, although it was not readily available in Japan until well into the nineteenth century, Chinese intermediaries had certainly imported some by 1782, earning it another name – *tōai*, 'Continental indigo'. Already in 1778, the East India Company leader Arend Feith had been asked for Berlin blue by the Nagasaki governor, and although Feith said he would be 'very happy' to import it, none was then in store, and it seems none was officially ordered. In August 1785 Romberg was asked by the new and much-hated governor for the pigment, by which time it was kept in the Company godowns, and he sent him over 600 g. The Dutch began modest formal imports from 1789, and the repeated solicitations made to European traders demonstrate improving expectations of procurement, although obtainability was still haphazard. In 1790, the pigment was still issued mostly on the level of a gift, not as a regular trading good.[123] In 1800, Jacob de Chalmot's 16-volume dictionary of 1778 was imported, with its 4 pages of illustration and 22-page description of distillation of Berlin blue, although it would not have been possible to act on this knowledge without the ingredients.[124]

Perhaps more intriguing even than Berlin blue was another pigment, the search for which took on grail-like proportions. Unlike Berlin blue, it has been entirely ignored by modern scholarship. The material was variously called *gōrudo* or *gorudo*, or something similar; Ōta Nanpo called it *korarudo*.[125] The words sound like the Dutch *goud* (or English 'gold') and must be related, but the substance was said to come from

'Shamuro', or Siam. Another name for *gōrudo* was a garbling of this, '*shamudei*'. The vernacular *shōdo*, 'baked earth', is also attested. Although widely mentioned in the eighteenth century, quite what this was is lost. I would hazard a guess at carmine (from the Arabic for crimson), a pigment much used in the Qing empire for ceramic firing which, when heated, produces the red colour known in porcelain as *famille rose*. *Gōrudo* may however have been red iron crystals.[126]

Gennai's initial statement about *gōrudo* formed the basis for many other comments. Gennai stated that the material was 'not a naturally occurring substance' (carmine is from cochineal) and 'has to be ground and mixed'. On arrival in Nagasaki, it had failed to find a buyer and in pique was flung into the harbour. This is said to have been in the second quarter of the eighteenth century, although the dating may be insecure.[127] A Kano School record of 1690 mentions a 'silver vermilion' (*ginshū*) brought by the Dutch East India Company, and although this is not linked to Siam it may be the same pigment; notably, at that time the Siamese prime minister was married to a Japanese woman, and the Ayudhyan kingdom sent occasional (though less and less frequent) vessels to Japan right up to its destruction by Burma in 1767; the Dutch station in Siam was closed in 1743.[128] Seemingly *gōrudo* was ignored until Gennai picked up the tale as part of the general rethink that pictorial production was undergoing. Rumours of its extraordinary properties surfaced and spread. Ōkyo seems to have been unaware of *bero* but discussed *gōrudo* and, whether or not he used it, he told Yūjō it was European. By the late eighteenth century, this seems to be how its origins were taken.[129]

The precise colour of *gōrudo* is unclear. Ōkyo called it 'the shade of giant snakes [*orochi*], that is, matt yellow', although other sources imply something red. Gennai called it 'breath-taking in depiction of autumn scenery', which could cover either. A pigment able to capture the red or amber of autumn, though, would be paradigmatically desirable, for the turned foliage of maples was the most conspicuous marker of autumnal beauty and was paired with cherry blossoms in spring as the high point of the natural cycle. While white cherries were easy to paint, the red of leaves was always said to defy capture. A *senryū* versifier wrote in the 1780s, with comic reference to Kose no Kanaoka, who had thrown away his brush in despair at the loveliness of Mt Sekihō:

There was that discarding of the brush,
But in autumn,
It's the paint pot you throw away![130]

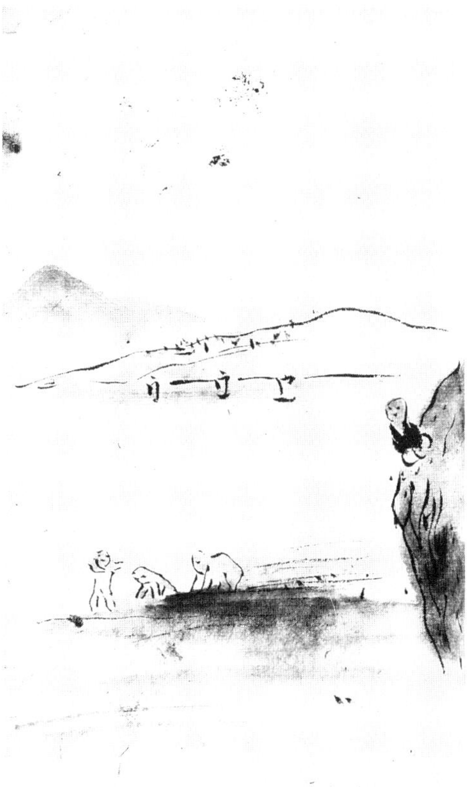

81 Yokoi Kinkoku, Illustration from his *Kinkoku shōnin on-ichidai ki*, 1790s, manuscript with sketches in light colour. The author and some boys hunt for *gōrudo* while Kairyō watches from a rock.

Kanaoka had been defeated by a sublime outline, but red leaves beggared the power of colouration. Could a modern pigment retrieve the last unpaintable thing?

The *gōrudo* had been cast into the harbour, but Gennai claimed it was fished up by entrepreneurial Nagasakiites and sold. Presumably the jars in which it was imported had kept their seals. Ōkyo said it was to be found at 'dealers in artists' materials'. It was none other than Sadanobu, however, who ordered a full salvaging of all *gōrudo* still languishing on the harbour floor. His agents went to Nagasaki and hauled up 'six or seven horseloads', which they commandeered and removed.[131] After this, wrote the monk–artist Yokoi Kinkoku when in Nagasaki in 1793, it was 'only to be found in the storehouses of the rich'. Kinkoku was overstating, for by his own account Sadanobu's agents had done an incomplete task, and *gōrudo* was still being found by diving children, who would 'take it to temples and other institutions for use in the decoration of their walls'.[132] Kinkoku himself decided to get some and, in his illustrated autobiography completed several years after this trip, he included a picture of the proceedings, himself and some skinny lads wading into the water (illus. 81). Perched on a rock nearby sits another figure in monastic garb. This bulb-headed form is Kairyō, 60 years old and too venerable to strip and plunge; Kinkoku had carried him piggy-back all the way to the waterfront. Kairyō lodged with Kinkoku in his rented accommodation in Nagasaki and, as both men were in holy orders and by strange chance came from the same little village of Shimokasa, their cohabitation was not exceptional – geographical solidarity counting for much in the federalized Tenka.[133] Kinkoku is thought to have used the itinerant Kairyō as something of a role model for his own wanderings, although we have already met Kairyō as a Sadanobu spy. Perhaps Kinkoku did not know the older monk's full story. Kairyō's life is hard to reconstruct, unsurprisingly given his metier, but he suddenly becomes impossible to track after arrival at the only international port. He remained there a full year, supposedly studying spoken Chinese and Dutch (themselves covert activities), and, after leaving in 1794, he returned on several subsequent visits.[134] It is improbable that checking on the seizure of *gōrudo* was his official brief, but it may have been part of why he was in Nagasaki, for the search for better and more lasting pigments was occupying many senior figures in the administration. The state of the shogun's and shujo's icons was a source of real alarm, and the use of government operatives in seeking a solution was a reasonable use of their time.

It would require mineralogical analysis to determine the extent to which *bero* and *gōrudo* were applied to paper or silk in this period. It would aid my argument if one or both could be found in Ōkyo's oeuvre or in that of artists directly associated with Sadanobu, although this cannot yet be done. But it seems odd indeed that Ōkyo, whose life was colourless, should have been celebrated as so formidable and innovative a user of colours. The mismatch of his powerful and compelling paintings and his washed-out personality was in fact made the subject of a *senryū* verse which also referred to Ōkyo's phenomenal success in depicting the most taxing of themes – the supernatural:

All go pale
At sight of
Ōkyo's palette.[135]

5 Boundaries for a Centre

The tears of the subjects could also provide a substantial waterfall
– Friedrich von Rebmann, on Prince Karl Hesse-Kassel's garden, 1795

You govern the Tenka and all the family of states;
the mountains, hills, seas and deeps of the ocean are your
garden — do not be satisfied with an ornamental tray!
– Matsudaira Nobuaki, to Tokugawa Ienari, *c*. 1795

When Sadanobu laid out the Garden of Bathing in Obligation (Yoku'on-en) in Tsukiji, he planted a clump of trees in the south-east corner (illus. 82; see also illus. 14). This was a copse of unprecedented significance.[1] Sadanobu's trees (species not recorded) had each been gathered as saplings from famous sites, and in this they were like the 'famous places' section of his Six Gardens on the other side of Edo. But drawn together in the 'famous places' of the Tsukiji bosk were ancient boundary posts, not generic sites but allusions to the frontiers of the Tenka in the distant past and the strongholds that had divided it from a barbarous beyond. Sadanobu wished to call this perpetually to mind. Successive polities had pressed further, so that the final line of the Tenka had shifted. Every edge was contingent. The spacing of progressive barriers marked the exhilaration of expansion, but these barriers also acknowledged limits. All the boundary-post buildings had long since fallen down, so Sadanobu referred to them by using trees. Enunciated in this was the half-metaphorical, half-geographical truth of the wavering reality of a delineated 'Japan'. Sadanobu's laying out of

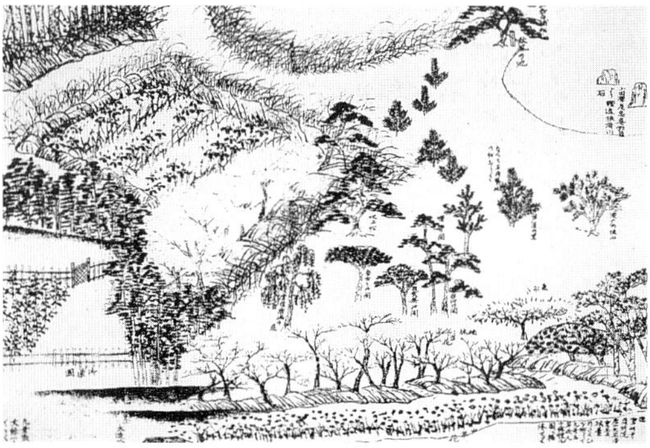

82 Detail of illus. 14. The Boundary Grove is towards the front; the Ship Hill is above to the left.

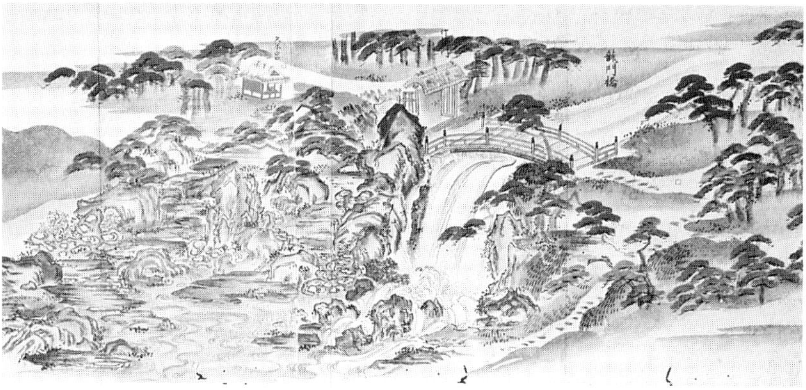

83 Section from *Toyama Garden*, *c.* 1790, handscroll, colour on paper. The daimyo of Owari's famous trick waterfall.

his garden is deeply illustrative of his notion of in and out, or regulation, and of the co-opting of outsides by insides.

One of the most relished of 'famous' sites was the Barrier at Shirakawa. In high classical times it had been the furthest outpost of rule in the north-east (geomantically, the unlucky direction). Shirakawa was quintessentially where home space brushed against the uncouthness of a difference that lay beyond. This Shirakawa that was the icon of termination had become, over time, a city and was the capital of Sadanobu's eponymous state – he was the prince of Shirakawa.

In the garden, the ancient barriers reconstituted as living trees brought the liminality of frontier stations right into the shogunal city of Edo. Tsukiji was a waterfront site, so that this park was not only awash with 'obligation' but also with the tides. These rolled in from foreign coasts and were, as discussed in Chapter One above, newly associated with alarm. Sadanobu and his guests would wander through the leafy shade rustling with pastness, hear the heaving seas and think, predominantly, of the contingency of culture.

Literature was full of writing on the barriers. Chinese poetry had a genre of verses written in the guise of missives sent home from desolate border garrisons, and these were echoed in early compositions in Japanese.[2] Vernacular Japanese verse (*waka*) also used barriers as loci for the expression of sentiments of alienation, trepidation and loss. In literary accounts, passing through the barriers, especially – though not only – that at Shirakawa, brought to the traveller a sense of collective and personal challenge. In 1689 the great *haikai* (haiku) poet Bashō had taken off on his famous trip to the end of *terra cognita*, spending some 30 months on the road. The Tenka's polity by then extended well beyond Shirakawa, but, according to the journal he wrote subsequently, Bashō's initial impetus for travel was to 'go to the Barrier of Shirakawa' and then push beyond it to what he called the 'deep' interior (*oku*). Bashō was plentifully imitated, and this conceit of Shirakawa as the magnet of self-challenge became mixed with its older status as representative barrier, in which dual mode it found its way into much Edo writing, even as Shirakawa became a thriving and civilized city.[3]

The 'Garden Arts of Japan'

Many daimyo gardens contained constructions giving the illusion of travel. Members of daimyo houses might engage in real journeying infrequently and so gardens provided them with pleasing figments. There were paths that wound among trees and rocks, designed to lead the user into spaces of mental remoteness, and there were falls, beaches by lakes, and cliffs. The Edo garden of the daimyos of Mito, one of the Three Noble Houses and a Tokugawa collateral family (in whose castle town Tachihara Suiken ran the official academy), included a stretch of path flagged to look like the roadways of the Continent (the Tenka's highways were unpaved). Parts of this garden were laid out by the Qing-period émigré Shu Shunsui to present visitors with the sensation of passing through Chinese lands. Some gardens incorporated so lively a feeling of the danger, as well as the excitement, of journeys that they were genuinely perilous to walk in without good care, and records tell of users too afraid to take certain pathways or of slopes they could not envisage climbing without breaking limbs.[4] Women, and those educated into excessive timorousness, were recommended not to go into some parts, since the scenery surpassed leisurely amusement. In the early years of the century, the mother of the then shogun came to reside in the Mito estate, and it had to be fully remodelled lest she injure herself as she wandered through.[5] The daimyo of Owari had an artificial waterfall in his park at Toyama, on the outskirts of Edo, which was controlled by hidden sluices that would be suddenly opened as his guests crossed stepping-stones artfully placed in the lower pool; the flash flood dropped six metres and foamed and thundered terrifyingly but was cunningly contrived so that the water did not quite moisten the feet (illus. 83). The daimyos of Owari were also of the Three Noble Houses, such families having the biggest estates. In 1793, Ienari was exposed to their artful waterfall; Mikami Kikan, who accompanied him, wrote of the event and, as none of the party had been forewarned, of the horror they felt at momentarily confronting death.[6] Ienari loved it and came back three more times. In 1798 Tani Bunchō painted an album of pictures of the garden, on commission from the Mito daimyo, who wanted to show the place off; Ritsuzan composed verses to accompany the scenes.[7]

Sadanobu's grove was like this, except that it was a garden-perilous to the mind. He brought specific topography to generic wildernesses and particularized the fear of wandering in fastnesses in a historical line between acculturated and rude space. Plenty of gardens recreated famous literary sites as a way of reaffirming the resilience of the classical tradition over time. No other garden bumped poetry into desolation in Sadanobu's way. At the Barrier Grove, in a small sequence of steps, one recalled the history of concerns over the end of the Tenka's sanctioned world; one felt psychological fear and realized a new edge still pulsated mercilessly in the present.[8]

The trees were planted to abut the side of an hour-glass pond called the Lake of Autumn Winds. This left-hand side, when viewed from the mansion, was mostly planted with Continental flora. It opposed the Lake of Spring Winds on the other side, which was stocked with plants and trees from the Tenka. Hour-glass lakes were common, but Sadanobu's was unusual in deploying (although not entirely consistently) a geocultural division. To the right, as he looked from the Turret of a Thousand Autumns, was the indigenous garden, which terminated in what was reputed to be Edo's finest view of Fuji. The Continental side ended in the masts of ships in Edo Bay. The use of 'borrowed scenery' (*shakkei*) from outside the confines of a garden was also a well established convention, but, again, Sadanobu's use of this was special. The two sight-lines counterposed two views, one the symbol of domestic enlightenment (Fuji), the other the icons of roaming to distant places (ships). The division was calculated to be ideological, for while Fuji is stable, ships are not, and (given the maritime technology of the time) they were desperately insecure. The Continent is uncertain of access. The indigenous aspect was edged with a stand of flowering cherries and so looked best in the effulgence of spring; the Continental side had maples and so came into its own in the autumn. The vistas sorted a burgeoning, solid Tenka from a tumbling, porous Continent.

The two halves of this diode were made to penetrate each other, and the postulate was not that the Continent could be kept, literally, at bay. On the nearer side of the spring lake was a gantry encircled by cherry trees. Visitors would climb to this to be lost in the blossoms, as if floating, with only Fuji visible above. But at the base of this was a bed of bamboo, brought from India, and so referring to the lands of the Buddha. The indigenous was secured after mounting through

Continental space. Secondly, dropped into the middle of this spring side of the pond was an island called Hōrai, the Japanese pronunciation of the Chinese Penglai, the mythic Isle of Immortality. Pine-trees grew on it and, in Okamoto Jishō's picture, cranes circle; this was precisely the iconography of Penglai, as known from much official painting.[9] The location of this Isle of Immortality in the Tenka axis set the promise of eternal life within the indigenous grasp and suggested the mutuality of Continental legends of eternal blessedness and the enlightenment of Japan; Fuji is homophonous with 'no-death' (*fu ji*).

This interplay was matched in the other half of the pond. The autumn side also had an island, and on it stood a building called the Hall of Heaven housing a statue of Hitomaro, the sixth-century poet said to have perfected vernacular verse. If Penglai formed the button to secure the upholstery of the Tenka's garden, Hitomaro formed the support for the Continental one. Penglai islands were not unknown in gardens (the Mito garden had one, planted with pines and built in the shape of a terrapin with a crane on its back). Sanctuaries to Hitomaro were rarer, although not unknown, and the Owari garden had one, containing a painting of the poet that was much admired by Eisen-in during a trip there. This would seem to have been intended to parallel a similar hall famously gracing the Mito garden and housing a statue of Wen *wang*, the 'literary monarch' of the Chinese state of Zhou in the twelfth century BC.[10] Continental erudition is transferred to the local. The statue of Wen had been given by the 'virtuous' shogun Iemitsu to the future daimyo of Mito, Tokugawa Mitsukuni, when at seven years old he had been offered anything he desired; although at that age most boys would have chosen something fatuous, Mitsukuni had asked for the statue.[11] The event was taken to be prescient and survived as a famous anecdote, for as an adult Mitsukuni had gone on to collate the monumental *History of Japan (Dai-nihon shi)* and be a 'virtuous ruler' in his own right. Wen's sanctuary was set firmly in the centre of the Mito park, but Hitomaro's was isolated and only just reachable across a bridge in Sadanobu's: the culture Hitomaro represents is hard to find and keep and, although more secure than the immortality of Penglai, whose island is inaccessible, it is not to be taken for granted.

The most quoted verse in Hitomaro's oeuvre was on Fuji, and the standard depiction of him was seated by a lake with the mountain soaring above (illus. 84). When Sadanobu sat on his banks, composing his own verses, he sat like a reformulated Hitomaro. Mostly he composed in his turret, so he saw the mountain through his glass windows, cut off and more remote. Neither did he see Fuji alone, for if he turned his head the opposing Continent came into view.

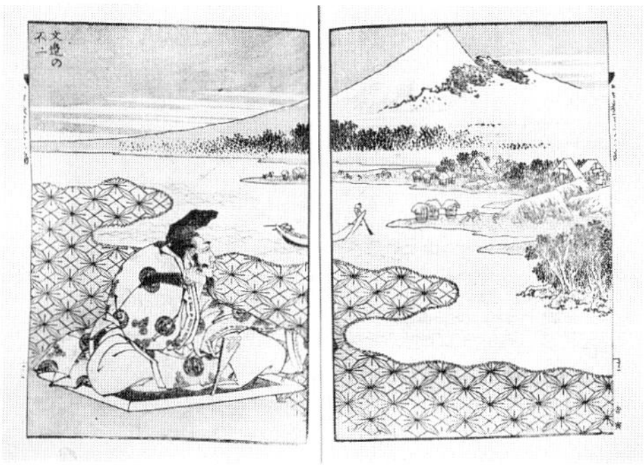

84 Katsushika Hokusai, 'Literary Fuji', pages from his *Fugaku hyakkei*, 1830s, monochome woodblock prints. Hitomaro views the mountain that inspired him.

One further structure in Sadanobu's garden may be considered, and it returns us to the question of barriers. This was a teahouse built right on the shoreline, all but lapped by the waters of the bay. Sadanobu's twin pond was connected to the sea tidally, with this hut at the conduit. The water-level of the lake rose and fell, governed by a process that was controllable, but only moderately so, by the lock-gate. The hut offered a place to put ebb and flow before the gaze. Edo had only three such tidal gardens, the other two being at the shogunal Beach Palace (Hama goten) and at the Ōkubo family compound on the other side of the bay. These other two were constructed in the mid-seventeenth century and offered viewers the unusual chance to inspect brine ponds.[12] Sadanobu's alone was of recent make, and the only one that was so studied in the symbolism of its parts. His teahouse broke with standard nomenclature by not being named a 'pavilion' (*-tei*) or 'hermitage' (*-an*), as was normal, but rather a 'barrier' (*-seki*). The hut was called Fuwa-no-Seki, or 'unbroken barrier'. The nub of irresistible ingress and egress of the sea was presented as a structure of resolute closure: a fast and doughty barrier. This was also a reference to a real antique barrier that bore the name and which, like Shirakawa, had been copiously used in the literary tradition because of its obvious evocativeness. The Fuwa Barrier had in fact collapsed in early times, so that later writers invoked it *not* to signify robustness, for its belying of its name. A widely memorized classical expression of the oxymoron of Fuwa was a verse composed in 1201 by the courtier Ryōkyō:

Abandoned by people,
Fuwa Barrier House,
Its planking is all in pieces.
Nothing is left there but
Autumn wind.[13]

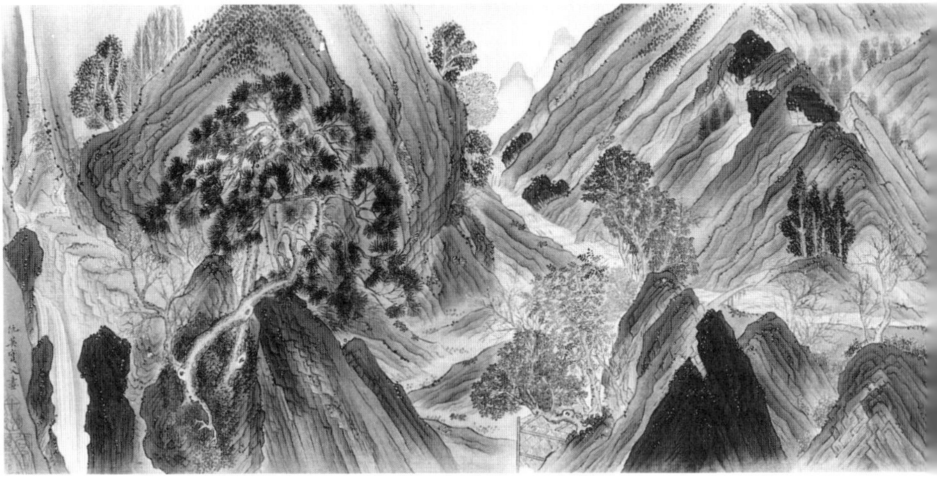

85 Tani Bunchō, Section from a copy of Chou Ying's *Peach Blossom Spring*, *c.* 1800, handscroll, colour on paper. The original early 17th-century work was the most famous Chinese version in Japan.

Again, we see autumn as the time of chilly sear, but more, it buffets a barrier that has come undone. Sadanobu deliberately invoked Fuwa at the only place where the constructed space of his garden met the outside world. The seawater that joined an entire globe together flooded his garden, willy-nilly.

The Garden of Bathing in Obligation had a sustained symbolism of boats, stemming from its proximity to, and synergism with, the sea. All daimyo gardens were equipped with punts and skiffs, and Sadanobu's was no different. But he also constructed a large earthen bank along the left-hand side of his pond to form the shape of a large boat (see illus. 82). This suggested further travel than the coastal shipping that habitually docked in Edo Bay. This Ship Hill (Funayama) was planted with snowflowers (*unohana*) at its base, and they blew in the breeze to give the sense of foam cut by a wooden hull.[14] Any flower might have done, but snowflowers were densely meaningful because they were the symbol of Shirakawa. This vessel rides on Sadanobu's own domain. The prow looked towards the bay and made the ship seem ready to slide off on a voyage to the far beyond.

Sadanobu mused on travel by water and the bracing freshness it would give. He conjured up this image for others too. He gave the third Noble House of Tokugawa collaterals, the daimyos of Kii, a plaque to hang on the teahut in their Edo garden, inscribed in his own hand 'pavilion to wash the heart' (*shinsen-tei*) and written on a salvaged

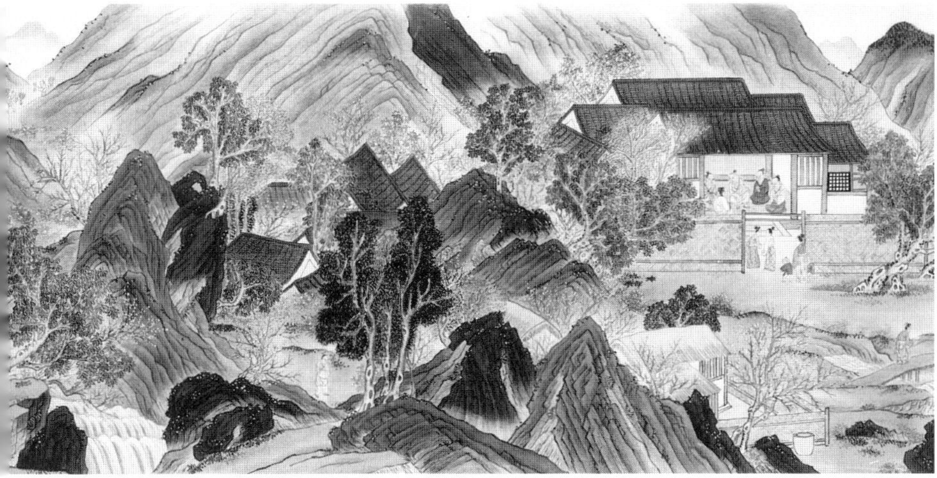

shipboard.[15] But this hill ship was not generic, for along its spine was a line of peach trees, and these fixed it into a specific legend, namely that of the Peach-blossom Spring. The standard source for this exceedingly well known story was the early fifth-century Tang poet Tao Yuanming.[16] Tao Yuanming told how a fisherman called Wuling went adrift and came to an island with a spring gushing in the shade of peaches by which lived a community of sages who knew no evil. Wuling peeped through a rock crevice at their sublime condition, before rushing home to inform his friends and bring them to see for themselves. But once gone, he could never find the place a second time, though he spent his whole life looking.

The Peach-blossom Spring was in the pictorial canon and was painted by many schools. Sadanobu researched the matter. He commissioned Bunchō to reproduce one of the most famous Continental versions then in a collection in the Tenka, Chou Ying's early seventeenth-century handscroll (illus. 85). The foremost painting theorist of the previous generation was Dong Qichang, who, when he came across a painting of the Peach-blossom Spring by the fourteenth-century Wang Meng, which set the story in an actual landscape, had tried to purchase the property shown. (Dong was infamously rapacious as a landlord, so perhaps it is as well he was unable to secure the sale of such evocative real estate.)[17] Sadanobu's quite different reaction – to replicate and paperize – was typical of him too.

The legend was alluded to in parks, although Sadanobu may have been the first to do so. When Ienari was shown around the daimyo of Owari's Toyama park on his first trip there (which coincided with the year of Sadanobu's resignation), he was led in by a rear gate so that he saw the park through a crevice, rather than as laid out before the residence. All agreed this made them think of Wuling.[18] But Sadanobu's garden did not offer assuasive ruses suggestive of the ocular proof of sagehood. His ship was still on the waters, searching.

Edo had spectacular gardens, but, as in all of north-east Asia, there was also a tradition of condemnation of private parks as places of waste. The corpus of park-appreciation literature is interlarded with pre-emptive assurances that, in regard to the particular garden under discussion, this was not the case, that the people were not battened on for it and that rebellion would never be provoked by its extravagance.[19] Naming furthered disclaiming. Sadanobu's garden name (Bathing in Obligation) suggested he would use the space to meditate on his dues to the Heavens, the state and the people. The Mito estate was called the Garden of Pleasure Taken Afterwards (Kōraku-en), as if the owners took their rest there only after ensuring that all others were at leisure too. The park of the daimyo of Mito in his own city was the Garden of Pleasures Borrowed (Shakuraku-en), as if all delights were snatched and would be returned to the weal soon enough. Indeed, Tokugawa Mitsukuni did open his gates for the commonality to enter his gardens. In the late eighteenth century the Mito gardens, and many others, were shut to popular access for the first time, which caused great offence and set the late eighteenth-century revival of garden arts in a new language of meanness and tyranny. The Confucian expert Ōta Kinjō was able to gain a rare permit to see the Garden of Pleasure Taken Afterwards, and he condemned its general closure as a usurpation.[20] Kinjō also noted how modern selfishness had actually de-ethicized the space, with many of Mitsukuni's moralizing garden features (including the sanctuary to Wen *wang*) having been cleared away. Name and garden, Kinjō thought, had gone askew, and such was now regularly the case. Late eighteenth-century daimyo took their pleasures *first*, and in conditions of tight security. Sadanobu was no different, although he also used his garden to goad and unsettle his pleasures.

The shift in the perception of garden rights from loci of education to exclusive playgrounds was paralleled by a change of name. The old labels began to seem pedantic and heavy: they were always quotations from classical texts. It seems to have been at this time that the daimyo of Hikone renamed the park by his castle (which absorbed a good tranche of the best land in town) the Garden of Pleasure Taken Upon Pleasure (Rakuraku-en), which can hardly have seemed other than a spoof on Mitsukuni *et al.*'s high-mindedness.[21] Sadanobu was against such moves, and he specifically praised the ethical stance of 'Pleasure

Taken Afterwards'; he had a plaque made inscribed 'pleasure' (*raku*) to hang in his own garden, but put it at the *rear* gate to indicate that his pleasure came afterwards too, with disportment last in his list of gardening priorities.[22] Sadanobu strove to keep the philosophical orientation of gardens alive and encouraged others to do so too. When the wealthiest of all daimyo, the ruler of Kaga, Maeda Narinaga, had his garden remodelled at the turn of the eighteenth century, he deliberately included only half of the six criteria of landscape excellence stipulated by the Song-dynasty poet Li Gefei. Narinaga asked Sadanobu to contribute a name, and he chose the Garden of Six Excellences (Kenroku-en) to highlight and applaud Narinaga's restraint.[23]

Ienari himself used public horticulture to bolster his reputation as a 'virtuous ruler'. Yoshimune had done this before, sponsoring the cultivation of medicinal plants and turning over his hunting grounds at Asuka-yama to city use. This latter act had been much appreciated, and a stele detailing the largesse had been erected at the site.[24] Cherry trees were planted where once shogunal horses had galloped. Ienari grubbed up Yoshimune's trees (which would have had only some 40 years' growth) and reforested Asuka-yama under his own name.[25]

But it is clear that the eighteenth-century revival of gardens and of park-appreciation literature coincided with a period of worried withdrawal by the elite from larger open spaces. Ienari gardened his way into obliviousness of the real conditions of the Tenka. When he visited Asuka-yama to see his new trees, the populace had to be cleared out for three days in advance, as their joyous reaction to his presence could not be depended on.[26]

Toyama had a mock-up street where *Marie-Celeste*-like reproductions of normal town life were used to educate the daimyo of Mito's family in the workings of a happy community. Items were strewn about in the Potembkins to suggest recent occupation, and sometimes servants dressed up to play the parts. At the entrance was a signboard like those erected in real towns, listing laws and regulations, but this one had comic injunctions and a meaningless date, all made up of wordplay, the intention being to suggest that this ideal neighbourhood had gone beyond the need for legislation.[27] The construction was a century old when Ienari visited the garden, and in a different moral environment it was now viewed differently. The sign attracted opprobrium. It made a stark contrast with the actual world and its hated 'three-day laws'. Ienari's advisors contested whether the sign should have been removed before the shogun saw it.[28]

On another occasion Ienari was confronted by a brave young retainer called Matsudaira Nobuaki and scolded. As the shogun fiddled with platter bonsai, the Tenka was running to seed. In the words appearing as an epigram to this chapter, Nobuaki remonstrated that the Tenka and all the family of states (*kokka*), the mountains, hills, seas and deeps of the oceans were the shogun's garden – he must not be satisfied with an ornamental tray![29] Those present broke into sweats at this rashness. Ienari was honest enough to ponder the injunction and, realizing the discrepancy between the aspirations and the realities of his rule, he momentarily donned the cloak of the 'virtuous ruler' and accepted the criticism in good part. A major indicator of virtue was the readiness to listen to justified admonitions. Ienari promoted Nobuaki – and then had his just deed written up in the chronicle of his reign.

Rebuilding Shirawaka

Gardens might be contested spaces where arguments were made or demolished. But in the end, however sprawling, they remained reduced sites. Sadanobu's garden-building was part of his larger project of spatial reconstruction of the entire Tenka. He conceived of parks as distillations of, not escapes from, the wider realm. Where open landscape was susceptible to the same value enhancement as enclosures, he was willing to accord it attention and funds. Open landscape was more generally available, and it appealed to him that the common person might move among the kind of artefacts that were the furniture of elite gardens. Sadanobu also strove to reify culture *sur place*. This is apparent in his treatment of his own state of Shirakawa. Sadanobu created gardens for himself there, but he also dotted the open landscape with markers stating where great things had happened or beauties were celebrated, which he had planted at the real sites. One instance was his erection of the Stele of the Well-buffed Life (*magaihi*). This pillar was dedicated to the memory of the fourteenth-century hero Yūki Munehiro, who had held Karame Castle (forebear to Shirakawa) against all odds. On the site of Munehiro's old outworks was set the record of his inspirational deeds. Sadanobu himself brushed the text. It became a popular place to go and was nicknamed 'the stele inscribed for recollection of loyalty' (*kanchū meihi*).[30]

A clearer example still is Sadanobu's work at the site of the Shirakawa Barrier itself.[31] This barrier was more often written about and poeticized on than can be adequately recapitulated here. The *locus classicus* was a verse by the wandering twelfth-century monk Saigyō, whose verses had secured many a locale the designation of 'famous place'. Even then the barrier was in decay, and it was Saigyō who had most poignantly twisted the meaning of Shirakawa from a bastion of civil defence against barbarity beyond to a site of mental trauma; like Fuwa, Shirakawa was broken. The shogunal polity had been extended further, obviating the need for an actual barrier, but this only meant that Shirakawa scored a sharper line in the mind than it did on the ground. Saigyō wrote:

Shirakawa
Its barrier hut has moonlight
To guard it.
Here a person's heart,
Is stopped and searched.[32]

Apparently he fixed the written verse to a surviving pillar. Saigyō also referred to a willow growing at the site, which may have given Sadanobu the idea of replicating all the Tenka's great barriers in an arboretum.

Any educated visitor was obliged to contribute a personal stitch to the thickening blanket of culture at the officially sanctioned beauty spots.[33] Sites were rather more prompts to recall the history of the verses written about them; plain empirical admiration was too coarse. Bashō followed this practice in his wanderings. When he came to Shirakawa, however, in contrast to his easy flow of verses at other sites, he felt paralysed. At Shirakawa, and there almost uniquely, Bashō's brush would not move.[34] He was stopped, searched and stripped, or rather, taking his lead from Saigyō, he took Shirakawa as the icon of ambivalence. He told a friend:

There was the arduousness of the road, the weariness in my body, but I also had a sense of being disempowered by the site. I seemed to be torn apart internally by the associations of the place.[35]

This is myth. Bashō's travelling companion, Sora, makes it clear that Bashō came out with a verse promptly enough.[36] Bashō's inability to write at Shirakawa is a narrative figure contrived for the public pages of his journal. Other sites provoked ever more writing, but Shirakawa was a place of problem and muting. Lest the reader conclude this compromised his genius, Bashō made it clear his mind soon unstuck again, and after a lag of a few short days he completed three entire books on the barrier. Not to have left his mark would have been, Bashō himself disarmingly said, 'idiotic'. Shirakawa is where the possibility or otherwise of continuity in the cultural tradition was the only real theme.

Some relics of the barrier may have been visible to arrest Saigyō's heart (the pillar), but by the eighteenth century there were none. Bashō claimed he was held apprehensively at the collapsed timbers, but this is poetic licence – as Sora reveals too.[37] Even the location of the barrier was forgotten. Sadanobu ordered the geographer Furukawa Koshōken to make an inspection, and in 1788 he reported that books giving its whereabouts were 'grossly erroneous [. . .] written on pure hunch'.[38] Sadanobu set about finding the precise place. By dint of careful research, he managed to do so and recorded this with another pillar, inscribed on the front 'Site of the Ancient Barrier' and on the side:

> The exact whereabouts of the Shirakawa Barrier had been lost in the mists of time. To the west of the village of Hatayado is a shrine at a place where the ground rises slightly. The white river of Shirakawa flows below. I have investigated ancient documentation and poetry, and inquired of elderly people in the vicinity, and have determined that without doubt the barrier was here. I erect this pillar to be a sign.[39]

Sadanobu's steles were many, but at the centre of his jurisdictional zone he searched for the concrete presence of the icon of cultural tremulousness and resurrected its memory. A person could now journey to the core site of consternation and feel in their body, not just in their minds, the exact location of fear. As with so many of his projects, anxiety is the woof that matches the weave of 'revival'.

The New Outside

As Kyoto rose from the ashes to become the wellhead of 'Japanese culture', the ancient barriers assumed a new appeal – Kyoto had been the Tenka's centre when the barriers had been built in antiquity. A revived inside needed its revived outer demarcation: the embarrieredness of golden-age antiquity implicated what 'Kyoto' was 'reviving'. The real political fringes of the Tenka, however, now lay elsewhere. In the modern world these were less Fuwa or Shirakawa, which had become fairly central cities, than Matsumae on the nearer side of the north-east straits, Hakodate beyond on the tip of Ezo, Nagasaki in the extreme west or the Isle of Tsu, mid-way to the Chosŏn state. At Hakodate and Matsumae there were the indigenous Ainu and occasional infiltrations of Russians, while in Nagasaki Europeans, Chinese, Koreans and Ryūkyūans, with the occasional Thai, Philippino or North American, were to be seen; on Tsu the division between 'Japanese' and 'Korean' had lost most ethnic meaning.

In about 1800 the then daimyo of Mito, Tokugawa Harumori, who had inherited his state in 1797, produced a verse to highlight contemporary military facts:

Hakodate Barrier
Guardsmen,
Be alert!
This is not a time
When only waves come to shore.[40]

Nagasaki had been established as the sole international port in the early stages of Tokugawa rule. The Europeans and Chinese leased artificial islands in the bay, the former one fan-shaped, the latter square. The Chinese island was used as a store, but the Europeans' was also residential. Occasional mention is heard of a Korean island. The Russians briefly established a compound in Nagasaki too.[41] The European, or 'Dutch', island was called Dejima ('advanced island', i.e. lying just off the coast – the same name, incidentally, was given to Ireland). Dejima was testy, and the only bridge from it led directly to the Nagasaki magistracy and a part of town symbolically called Edo Ward. A large cannonball was fixed into its shoreside as a warning of the firmness of shogunal purpose, should foreign incursion be contemplated, this object having been salvaged from the great Tokugawa trial of strength in 1638 against a Christian (thus, foreign-inspired) uprising.[42] Similarly, a Korean canon seized by Hideyoshi's army in the late sixteenth century was fixed to the waterfront at Matsumae.[43] The shogunate also conducted the annual Dutch East India Company embassy to the notorious Ear Mound (*mimizuka*) in Kyoto, in which were the severed body parts of Koreans taken in Hideyoshi's campaign (illus. 86). The authorities kept their sense of international clout alive by these means. The arrangements were not always convincing to others. Korean emissaries were not taken to the mound after the middle of the century to avoid counter-productive overloading on Japanese 'militarism' (*bui*), and in a deliberate insult (for which their own government upbraided them) the Russians nonchalantly sailed up to Matsumae and stole the Korean cannon.[44]

Sadanobu declined to enthuse about international contacts and, when trade slowed for the reasons outlined in Chapter Two, he presented this in a positive light, quoting Ieyasu that Europeans were like 'poisonous snakes kept in the breast pocket'; he also likened them to cruel hawks massing against innocent Japanese cranes.[45] During the latter part of the eighteenth century, most European seafaring nations began to intrude into Japanese waters. In 1771 a German ship 'flying a

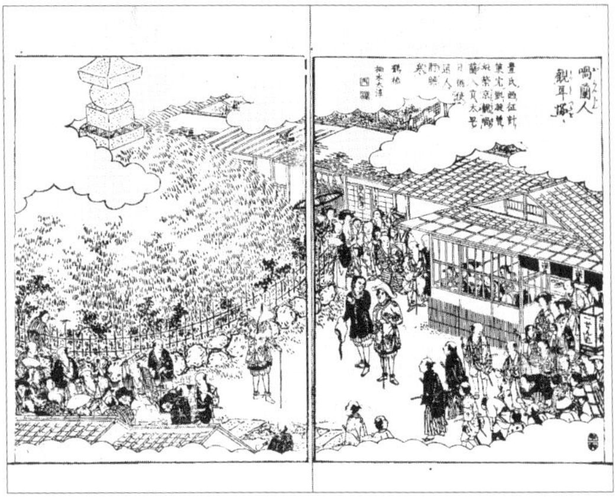

86 Tachihara Shunchōsai, Illustration from Akizato Ritō, *Miyako meisho zue*, 1780, monochrome woodblock prints. The Dutch contingent are shown Ear Mound in Kyoto.

double princely flag' hove to off Edo, captained by Moritz Aladar, commander of the fleet in Fredrick the Great's navy. Although it did nothing indecorous (Aladar even presented Ieharu with six pepper pots and a painting of a German landscape), its arrival was shocking.[46] Louis XVI's Pacific fleet toured the Japanese coasts in 1786 and encountered a shogunal vessel, sailing close enough to call out to it, laughing mightily at what they saw as the absurdity of its construction (had the French Revolution not interposed, more might have come of this; the shogunal ship did in fact sink some days later, through wrighting errors).[47] A Russian ship arrived in 1791 and, although it was fobbed off, the officers on board inferred an invitation to return, and in 1805 Czar Alexander's first chamberlain, Nicolai Rezanov, in the company of Count Tolstoi and sundry dignitaries, came back and sailed right into Nagasaki Bay.[48] 1808 saw the arrival of the bristling British *HMS Phaeton*. A hefty and on-going ledger called the *Overview of Shipping (Tsūkō ichiran)* in 350 volumes with 23 supplements was compiled to log uninvited vessels.[49] Sadanobu wrote of this new leakage of foreignness, working out a train of thought that was uniquely his:

> A Dutch ship that docked at Nagasaki related the news that France, England, Russia, Turkey and various Asian lands are at war. I thought such things no longer happened. It is a gripping story, but it makes me consider how fortunate we are to live under our august and placid regime. Old pictures demonstrate how military men once wore armour and moved about in block formation, even at funerals. But our present dispensation is so bountiful that this is quite unthinkable.[50]

The past and its images serve as buttresses to the present, but Sadanobu's assessment is far from accurate. Bounty was in scant evidence. In his attempt to make the present seem fair, Sadanobu took to browsing among documents of the worst days of historic warfare. He found an old compendium of framed inscriptions, one of which read 'confound all enemy countries' (*tekikoku kōfuku*), said to have been brushed by the tenth-century shujō Atsugimi (posthumously, Daigo). He summarized:

> I do not know if the attribution is trustworthy, but it is certainly a very old piece and quotes a royal command. 'Enemy countries' must refer to foreign states, but I cannot conceive a ruler today talking about 'enemies', or soliciting their downfall. This is because auspicious and bountiful reigns successively bathed in blessing have caused such commands as are given in the four massive characters written on this plaque to pass out of memory.[51]

Sadanobu, of course, was restoring them to memory. His interpretation of history does not convince even himself for, after making these remarks, he went on immediately to discuss the effectiveness of Dutch mortars and cannon, citing another piece of his recent reading, *On European Military Manuals (Ensai gunsho kō)*.[52] Sadanobu protests too much. When he wrote a public pamphlet on how more effectively to deal with foreign menace, he entitled it *My Excess of Leisure (Kan naru amari)*. Only among his close circle did he circulate his crystalline opinion paper, *Thoughts on Government Defences of the Coast (Umibe gobi gui)*.

Nagasaki was horribly permeable, but it was at least under direct Edo control and disciplined by established codes of engagement. Matsumae was looser, had its own independent daimyo and was not choreographed to deal with foreigners. Matsumae Michihiro was the incumbent daimyo in the 1780s and he boasted a high level of autonomy, as is suggested by the unusual feature of his surname being one with his state. He was not a 'virtuous ruler', at least in Sadanobu's book, but rather a reckless roué. After gaining control of the shogunal council, Sadanobu took the difficult and unusual step of removing Michihiro from office and, from 1792, installing his pliant teenage son, Akihiro.[53]

Matsumae, at the extreme end of the main Japanese island, was oddly placed, not quite in or out of the Tenka, both integrated and ungovernably wild. It gradually replaced Nagasaki in the popular mind as the site of greatest porousness – hence Tokugawa Harumori's poem quoted above.[54] Indicative of the ambiguity was Michihiro's brother and the new daimyo Akihiro's uncle, Hirotoshi. He had been adopted out into a collateral family, the Kakizaki, and taken to Edo, where he had resided in the Matsumae embassy, continuing with some government work. He had also begun to study painting. He chose the Nagasaki style and worked under its best Edo master, Sō Shiseki.[55] This choice seems appropriate for a Matsumae man. The style was popular, but it pertained to the alterity and difference of the Tenka's other open end, Nagasaki. Hirotoshi is known to art historians by his studio name, Kakizaki Hakyō.

After one of the periodic Ainu uprisings, Hakyō produced a series of twelve portraits of the chiefs whose quisling efforts had assured the Matsumae victory (see illus. 31). He took the set to Keishi while the city still lay wasted by fire, and they were widely viewed and admired. Ōkyo's friend Minagawa Kien applauded the realism of the rendering, as he would do of Bunchō's views of the Edo coastline some years later (see illus. 15). Hakyō's and Bunchō's pictures are only two years apart, and they form a notional pair of attempts to grapple with the idea of geographical and human frontiers.[56]

As did Europe, the Ainu lands, or Ezo, evinced both splendid and heinous features. If Europe displayed technical advances with which the Tanka could not keep pace, it was also brutal; the Ainu on the other hand revealed a noble simplicity that the Tenka had moved beyond. Tachibana Nankei wrote:

> The Isle of Ezo has not yet been opened to culture, so that they do everything in a natural way [*shizuboku nomi ni shite*], just as people did in Japan and on the Continent in high antiquity. They have no gold, silver, rice or other media of exchange, and no fine or figured clothes.[57]

But, he went on, 'they have their ancient treasured objects, handed on from the past'. Ancestral norms still prevailed, not tainted or lost by time. Nankei noted, 'in a land without writing, you can never know how old heirlooms are [. . .] and even their agricultural instruments may date from the time of the Gods'. The Ainu knew no fracture, or rather, fracture was being brought to them by insecure shogunal actions, invasions and bribery in gold and silver.

The shujo, Tomohito, struggling for a visual vocabulary of power as he camped in his temporary hostel, inquired into the ancestral regalia (*kuwasaki*) of the Ainu. He pored over Hakyō's portraits (which earned the latter the title of *tenran*).[58] Tellingly, Hakyō sought out Ōkyo, who was providing Kyoto with robust imagery, and they spent some months together, after which Hakyō was revealingly nicknamed 'Matsumae Okyo'.[59]

Matsumae gave on to the channel beyond which was the last 'Japanese' enclave and the only one on the Ainu island, Hakodate. It had been founded as a bridgehead but might also be construed as a puncture. Once the Straits of Matsumae were crossed, there was no obvious natural frontier until one island-hopped all the way to Siberia. In the measure that the Tenka's culture was used to suborn Ainu chiefs, their things filtered inwards too. Ezo brocade was prized (actually this came from northern China, but this was not realized), and Ezo seaweed (*konbu*) was part of festive fare on account of a pun with *yorokobu* ('rejoicing').

The status of Ezo was imprecise and so was its landscape, which had never been mapped. Small-scale cartographic efforts began under Tanuma Okitsugu, and Sadanobu continued to sponsor studies, but the Russians were moving in too. Intense alarm was registered when the Russian ship that arrived in 1791 was found to contain spectacularly accurate maps of Ezo, not even manuscripts, but printed; these were the famous naval charts of Jean-Baptiste d'Après de Mannevillette, published in 1787 in St Petersburg (illus. 87). The shogunate had already asked for a copy of Mannevillette's book, *Neptune orientale*, but had been refused. In 1796 the British navy began a complete survey

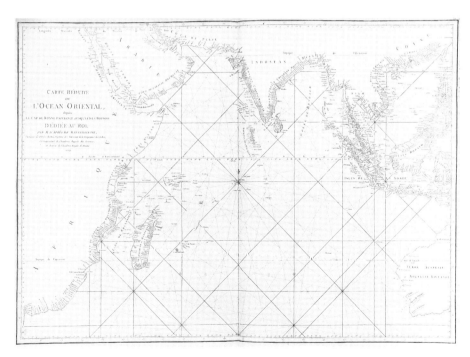

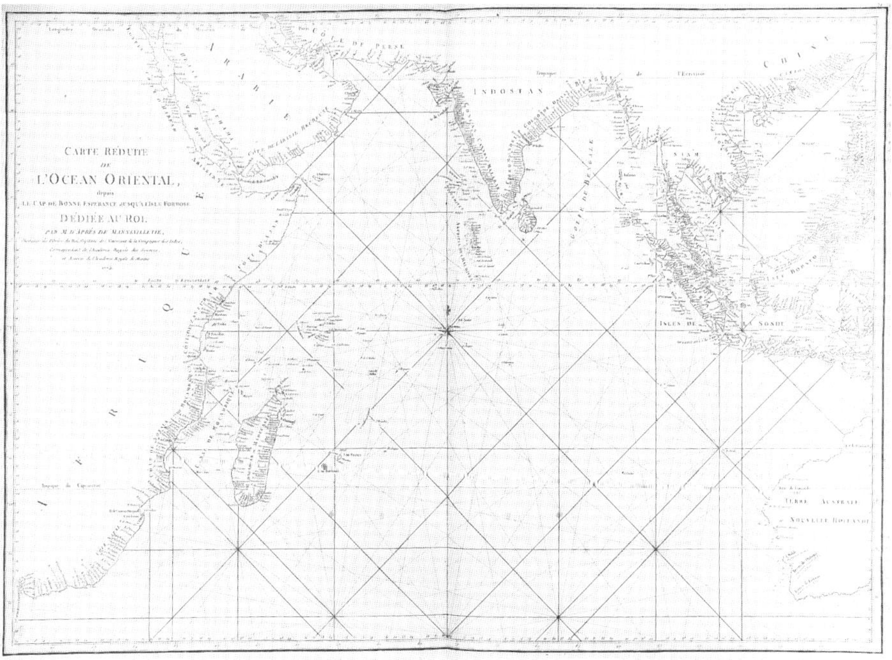

87 Jean-Baptiste d'Après de Mannevillette, Page from *Neptune orientale*, 1787, copperplate etching. An extremely famous collection of charts; Japan as such was not yet mapped.

of Ezo's coasts with *HMS Providence*.[60]

Sadanobu's Ezo surveys had the ambivalence of many of his other projects. The Ainu were to the north-east, geomantically an unlucky direction, and lying to the Tenka as Manchuria did to the Chinese kingdoms. Pushing there contaminated, as the Ming had discovered to their cost in the cataclysmic Manchu invasion and founding of the Qing (Manchu) dynasty in 1644: if the Ming had only sealed the border and not picked at it, this might have been averted. Sadanobu observed in discussions with a legate of the Ryūkyūan king, who had diplomatic relations with the Qing (the Tenka did not), that over the period since Manchu seizure, what had once been postulated as 'Chinese culture' had been modified out of recognition; 'in their court, old Chinese [*han*] and Manchu usages have grown inextricably mixed', Sadanobu wrote, 'and it makes me alarmed to think how close the different parts of the world have now come'.[61]

Even the uninformed public experienced an Ezo that had pulled very close. In 1777, an anonymous author wrote a comic best-seller *Happy Seaweed: Don't Expect Me to Wait for You Matsumae (Yorokonbu kimi o matsu-mae)*, the flippant title collided 'rejoicing' with *konbu* seaweed, as was trite, but 'Matsumae' is also brought together with the negative suggestive form of the verb *matsu* ('to wait'). And how long might it wait before the border was overrun?

A more consistently probing story followed in 1788, by Kurahashi Itaru (pen-name: Koikawa Harumachi), whom we have met as the pillorier, the following year, of Sadanobu's parrot cry of 'martial and literary arts'. Kitao Masayoshi illustrated this Ezo lampoon, as he was to illustrate that one. The title is again totally based on puns, meaning overtly *Rejoicing: A Picture Book You'll Love*, but offering a latent sub-reading, *Seaweed and The Advantages of a Push into Ezo (Yorokonbu hiiki no Ezo oshi)*.[62] Itaru made Ezo so close that in the story it is accessed via a kabuki stage trapdoor (illus. 88). A shogunal army is sent there, and they bring down the happily feeble Ainu stronghold by spraying ricewater at its *konbu* walls (illus. 89).

These stories reflect a popular realization that the authorities were not entirely in control. In 1802 Akihiro was ousted for his own inefficiency as daimyo of Matsumae and the shogunate took direct control. For no apparent reason, five years later they gave up, restored Akihiro and even let the still-living Michihiro oversee the state.[63]

The Sea and the Seal

The high seas which had previously served the Tenka's long and mean-

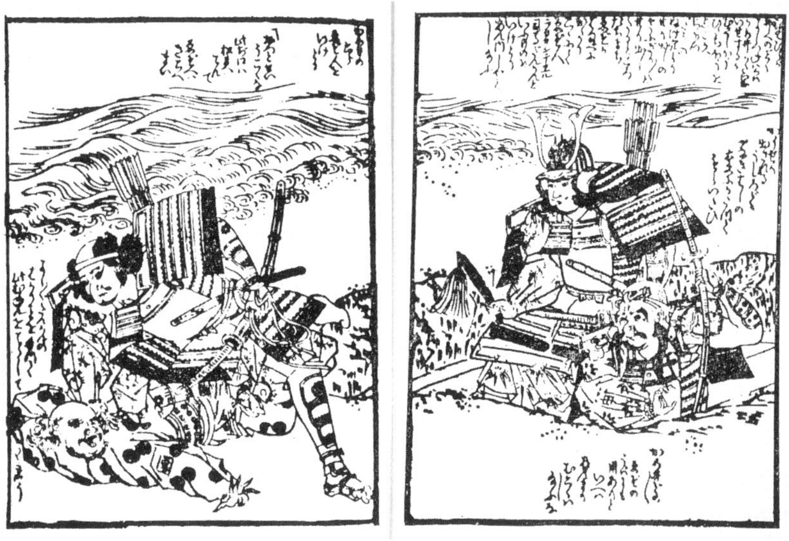

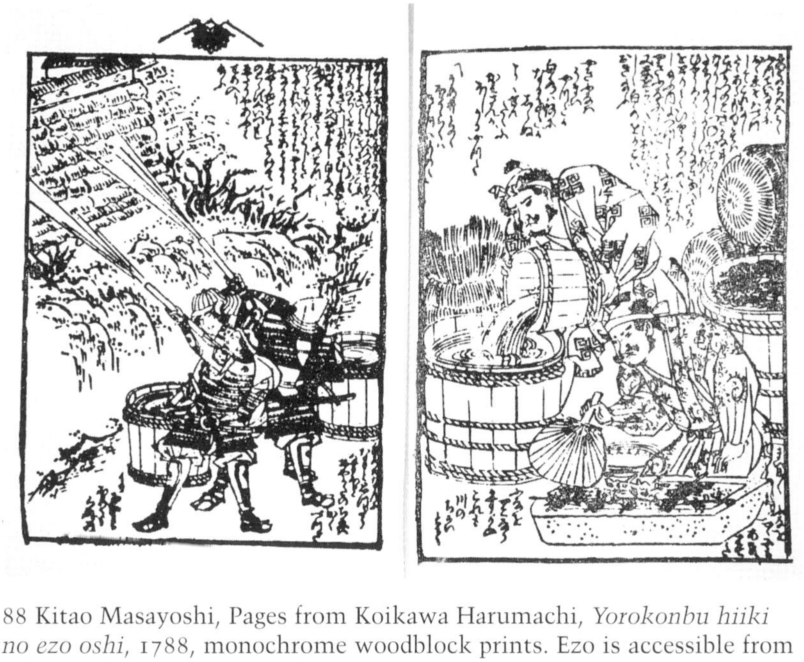

88 Kitao Masayoshi, Pages from Koikawa Harumachi, *Yorokonbu hiiki no ezo oshi*, 1788, monochrome woodblock prints. Ezo is accessible from Edo via a kabuki stage trapdoor.

89 Kitao Masayoshi, Pages from Koikawa Harumachi, *Yorokonbu hiiki no ezo oshi*. Shogunal forces spray ricewater at the castle's seaweed walls.

dering coastline in the office of a wall came to seem a liability. In 1804, in a ten-point challenge to the government Aoki Okikatsu, a samurai in the direct shogunal employ, pointed out how what had once been the Tenka's strength was now its weakness. Okikatsu warned:

> . . . the primitive [i.e. European] people pass their time in roaming the countries of the world in ships, assessing the condition of each place, and planning their naval assaults; where attempts to land are frustrated and booty cannot be seized, they just reduce everything to dust and ashes – this is what they consider the rightful function of their navies to be.[64]

The shogunate had no defences. Nagasaki alone was equipped with military installations, although not good ones. Engelbert Kaempfer had remarked at the end of the seventeenth century that the bay 'had a number of water-gates to allow for the mounting of cannon (which do not exist)' and that the guard-stations were 'open and unfortified'; these were augmented after the Russian arrival of 1791 but could never have seen off a concerted assault.[65]

Warnings had been issued long before Okikatsu's. The Mito scholar Hayashi Shihei had spoken out in 1785 in an important book, *An Illustrated Account of the Three Countries (Sankoku tsūran zusetsu)* – i.e. Chosŏn Korea, the Ryūkyūs and Ezo – which Tomohito had read (earning Shihei too the *tenran* title).[66] Shihei outlined the political structures of the Tenka's neighbours. Thus emboldened, the following year he produced *Military Talks for Maritime States (Kaikoku heidan)*, which was far more devastating in its assessment of shogunal preparedness and contained the graphic and much-quoted phrase, 'if you think about it closely, you will realize the sea is an open road running without obstacle from Nihon-bashi [the centre of Edo], right to the Continent, and even to Holland'. Shihei mulled the advisability of publishing, but five years later, in 1791, he finally let it circulate. Sadanobu rewarded him with house arrest.[67]

To Moriyama Takamori, mapping had to be accomplished before the Tenka was defined (prior to erasure?) by forces from without. A turn in military treatises towards coastal defences is to be detected at this time. Their illustrations show ships, and sometimes the round-eyed men of Europe gazing avariciously at cityscapes (illus. 90, 91). Such books were often adaptations of imported originals, so the Western eyes can be accounted for in that way, but it would have been possible to redraw the unnerving ethnic traits had that been wished. Foreign aggression did not only take the form of looking. The headlands and bays of the Japanese archipelago were being given foreign names in the

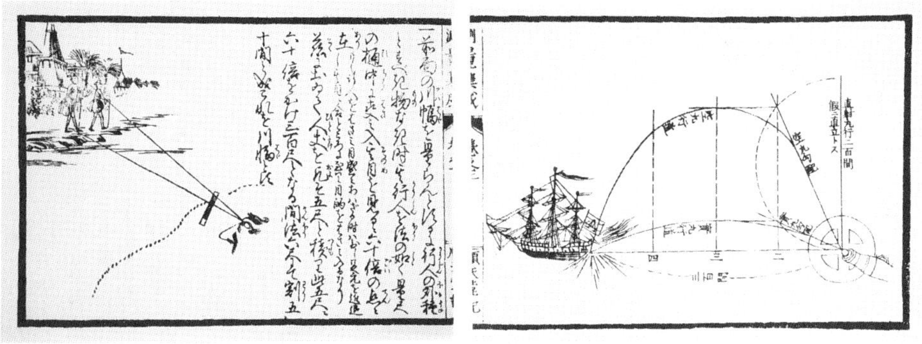

90, 91 Pages from Fukuda Riken, *Sokuryō shūsei*, 1856, monochrome woodblock prints. This was a reissue of older works on surveying belonging to the Fukuda house.

manner of colonized spaces. Takuboku-jima, off Nagasaki, has long been known in Europe as the Papenberg (Pope's Hill), from a massacre of Christians there, but examples multiplied: Ōsumi-kaikyō became the Straits of van Diemen and the southern protrusion of Kyushu became Cape Chirikov.[68] What Sadanobu must have thought of this arrogation of the right to classify the Tenka may be seen in his suppression of Edo's only prominent toponym with a foreign ring, Christian Slope (Kirishitan-zaka), which in 1792 was denuded of the venerable old Christian mansion that had graced it for nearly a century (it was a prison for Christians); the site was turned into a gunnery training ground, thenceforth to be called Tange Slope, after a local landlord.[69] Conversely, Sadanobu enjoyed the sense of power outreach he derived from commissioning maps of Europe made with the local names translated into Japanese.[70]

A new metaphor of closing and sealing became available at this time, and Sadanobu displayed an interest in it. This came from a device he called a '*riukuto ponpu*', that is, a *luchtpomp* or air pump. It was held in Europe to be a triumph of Western science and it fundamentally altered conceptions of the integrity of space.[71] The pump was a demonstration instrument whereby a living object was placed in a glass cell and the air evacuated, causing death by suffocation. By extension, it elucidated the need for nutritional environments and how the loss of basic requirements (air) caused death. The air pump was invented a century before, but perfected and popularized as a piece of philosophic equipment in the late eighteenth century. These pumps entered the homes of studious people and crossed the seas. When Arend Feith died unexpectedly in Java in 1783, after a spell as Company head in

Nagasaki, his possessions left on Dejima were inventorized and were found to include an air pump (as well as a static-electricity generator – broken – and a planetarium).[72]

The shogunal authorities wanted information on this breakthrough in existential thinking. In 1793 Gijsbert Hemmij was approached by an official armed with one of F. van Bleyswick's illustrations to Petrus van Musschenbroek's study of 1736, *Beginselen der natuurkunde*, and asked for explanations (illus. 92, 93).[73] An interest was manifested on popular levels too, and the air pump was mentioned in a vernacular work of 1800 aimed at a commoner audience and compiled by Arima Genchō from the opinions of his teacher, Ōtsuki Gentaku. The book took the form of a dialogue:

My question is this: There is an object generally referred to as a 'life and death glass', or a 'life killing carriage', into which you put an animal, such as a rat or weasel, and make it live or die. What kind of a thing is this?

My answer is: The device is called a *ryukuto pomupu*. All living things exist in atmospheres of the earth or sky, and the device demonstrates as much by allowing them to breath or not, and hence to live or die. It has been constructed by inventors in those [European] countries and is to be found illustrated in their scientific books.[74]

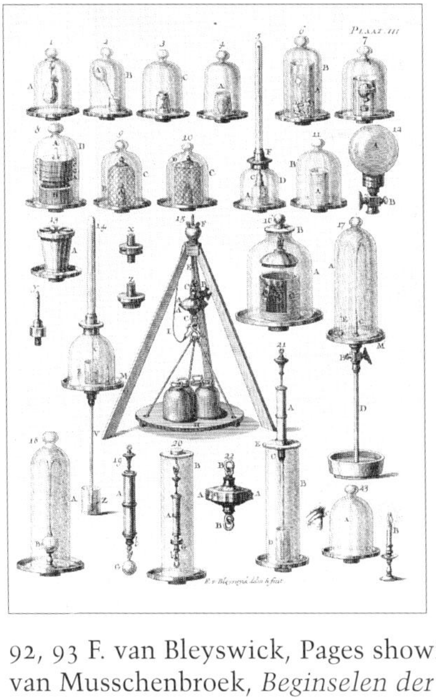

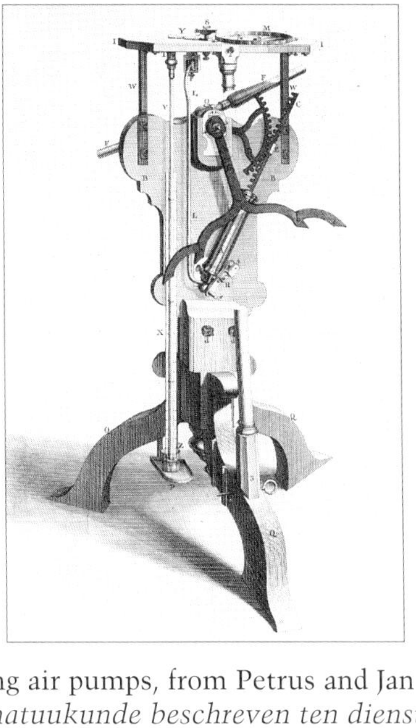

92, 93 F. van Bleyswick, Pages showing air pumps, from Petrus and Jan van Musschenbroek, *Beginselen der natuukunde beschreven ten dienste der landgenooten*, 1736, copperplate etchings.

Among the commonality, a forbidding name takes the place of the (variously rendered) transliteration. Genchō and Gentaku may be referring to Musschenbroek's study, which had four plates on the air pump, or more probably to Egbert Buys's *Nieuw en volkommen woordenboek*, completed in 1778 and well known in Japan, including to Sadanobu. Buys illustrated a terrified rat struggling for life in the emptying glass (illus. 94).

Air pumps relied on a perfect seal, the difficulty of fabricating which accounts for the long period of gestation in scholarly laboratories before pumps were able to provide inspiration and metaphors to the wider world. The bung on an air pump was only an improved variant of that sealing any bottle, but even some of the most rudimentary of these were startling in Japan, where cloth or wooden stoppers always leaked. Bottle caps were repeatedly requested by Nagasaki or Edo worthies. The absoluteness of the Western seal came from new materials. One was ground glass. Glass secured the separation of windows, but it also allowed the total and frictionless closure of receptacles. Morishima Chūryō's brother, Katsurakawa Hoshū, was among those to

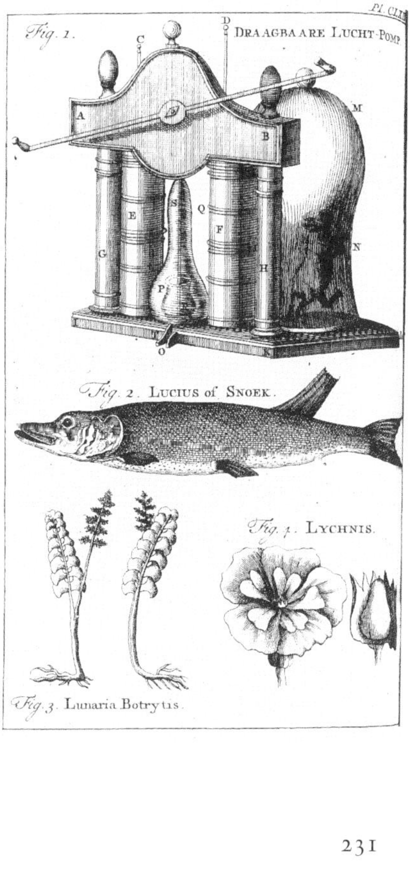

94 Illustration showing an air pump and other objects beginning with 'l', from Egbert Buys, *Nieuw en volkommen woordenboek*, 1769–78, copperplate etching.

admire how glass seals allowed the pristine quality of whatever was bottled to be secured forever.[75] Cork was also introduced, and Chūryō's teacher Hiraga Gennai first described it to Edo's reading public in 1763.[76] The obscenity of the pump was that its seal was not to preserve but to despoil the interior. In eighteenth-century English, emptying the bottle was called, in a pregnant term, 'dispiriting'. Sadanobu was intrigued by the air pump:

> The *ryokuto ponpu* is a device which kills animals. I wished I could have one made. All things live by breathing, and if you put a small animal in a glass jar and draw out the air, it will at once die.[77]

He added, over-optimistically, 'If you restore the air, it will equally immediately revive'. And again:

> There is a thing called a *ryokuto ponpu* which I have heard of, though never seen. Occasionally it is illustrated in primitive [European] books, but its manufacture has always been unclear. Some people here thought to make one, but so long as the principles were not understood and the workings not grasped, this proved impossible.

Then, in 1797, the riddle was cracked: 'this year, the project of making one has come to fruition'.[78] Although Sadanobu maintained the discovery of death caused by an absence of air was unremarkable ('children who put a hand over their mouth and nose understand this'), yet he could not keep from discussing the device. I consider Sadanobu's interest in boundaries to have inclined him to the air pump. His desire for a whole and *inspired* Tenka led him to a macabre attraction. His delight in the enclosed unit, which teasingly showed how entry and exit could deeply affect life in and outside, was akin to his delight in gardens. He could consider the animal in the flask as like a person in an atmosphere that was culturally encoded. It was crucial to retain control of the sluices.

Passing Through the Tenka

Sealing off the outside gave a unity to what lay within. Inside space, once secure and breathing freely, could be looked at and assessed again. A revealing shift of this sort can be seen in painting. Bunchō's depictions of the coasts, like Hakyō's chieftains, were billed as 'copying authenticity' (*shashin*): in modern Japanese the term means a photograph. The word was a historic one but had been reappropriated shortly before Bunchō by overt Europeanists such as Shiba Kōkan. Bunchō was later to decry Western art as 'meaningless' (*imi nashi*) for the very authenticity of its unacculturated scenes, but he was happy to use the blankness of the style to replicate views where the imposition of style was not desired, as in pictures made for military defence.[79] The nullity of the subject of coastal scenery, vacant of 'famous places', made 'copying authenticity' the right mode for it.

A belief that this manner was appropriate for delineating precisely the points where meaning stopped is also notable in the work of Bunchō's brother, Tani Gantan, who took up the style and became a specialist in it (Bunchō was more polyvalent). Gantan produced illustrations of the unincidented landscape of Ezo for his employer, the daimyo of Tottori (illus. 95). This was a style for extremities. Bunchō's pictures suggested (fallaciously) that the coast had been viewed, mastered and could be defended, as Hakyō's suggested Ainu warriors could be encompassed and deactivated.

This pleasant notion permitted 'copying authenticity' to be used for interior landscapes too. Once doors to the outside were secured, it seems, 'authenticity' could be brought to bear on the actuality of literary

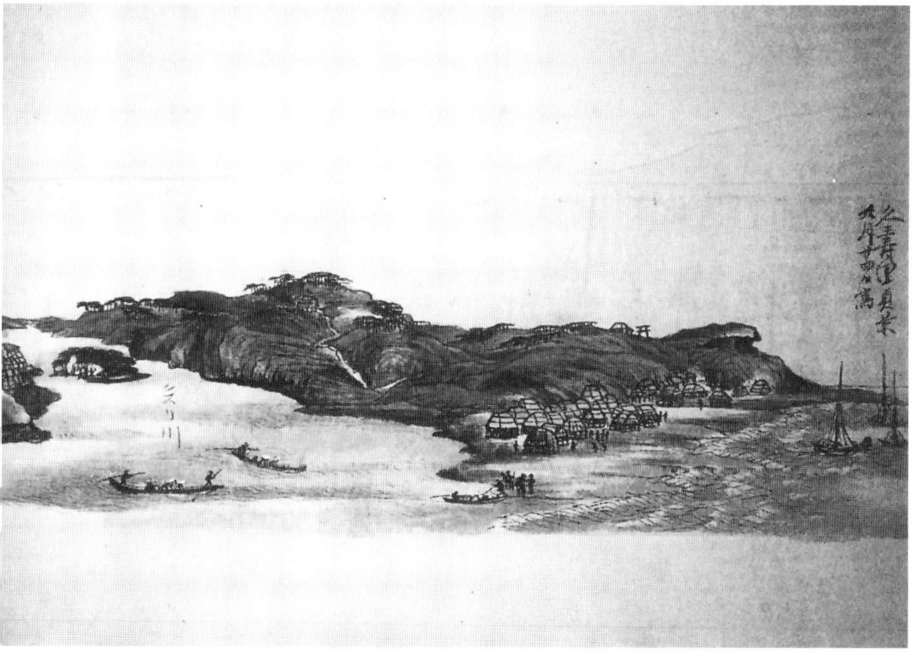

95 Tani Gantan, Section from *Ezo shinkei zukan*, c. 1800, handscroll, colour on paper. The 'styleless style' used to depict unacculturated foreign space.

sites and relics. It even engulfed poetic places.[80] Aōdō Denzen produced a view of Ōtsumi Falls in Sugagawa, including the famous memorial to Bashō there (see illus. 7). One of the most consistent users of this style of no style was Shiba Kōkan, who may even have been aided by a camera obscura. Kōkan took on that most hallowed of all sights, Mt Fuji (illus. 96). Writing of this in 1813, he stated:

. . . the people of Kyō have never seen Fuji so I give out a good number of pictures of it [. . .] My *Mt Fujis* represent the finest scene in all Japan, done entirely according to the rules of 'copying authenticity' which derives from Holland.[81]

To him, Fuji could be shown without artistic flourish, for it was good enough not to disappoint even when unenhanced. He concluded:

. . . the school painters we now have – Kano and Tosa and more recently the Continental [*nanga* and Nagasaki] way – cannot capture this; even Kano Tan'yū, in all his images of Fuji did not produce one that really reveals its form, for he was over-preoccupied with the energy and artistry of the brush.[82]

The mountain was equal to rendition in a 'meaningless' style. A stripping of otiose aura in favour of open revelation is also seen in the decision of 1800 to allow females access to Fuji for the first time.[83]

In 1797 Sadanobu launched an expedition to study Fuji, giving his team a similar brief to that which had been given for work along the coast, although now what was to be secured was 'culture'. The survey lasted a month and was recorded visually by a monk from Shirakawa, Hakuun, who had studied with Bunchō and was in Sadanobu's personal employ (see illus. 32). Under Hakuun's sharp lines, Fuji loses its exhilarating conical shape and, in the sequence of pictures that becomes increasingly harsh as it focuses down on the rugged portions of the face, the mountain becomes fully de-aestheticized. Sadanobu was confident that rock and soil alone could convey Fuji's awesome presence.

When the power of a place was incontestable, this treatment worked. But many sites did require pictorial up-grades to flourish in their lead roles. To depict the Shirakawa Barrier 'authentically', for example, would have been unrewarding, even after the site was located, as neither barrier nor willow was there. As traffic moved with increasing volume through the Tenka, and the danger and discomfort of the road (much harped on by Bashō) faded, attitudes to the landscape changed. There were no longer no-go or impassable areas, and from the hazily placed 'famous places', understood in armchair ways from reading or

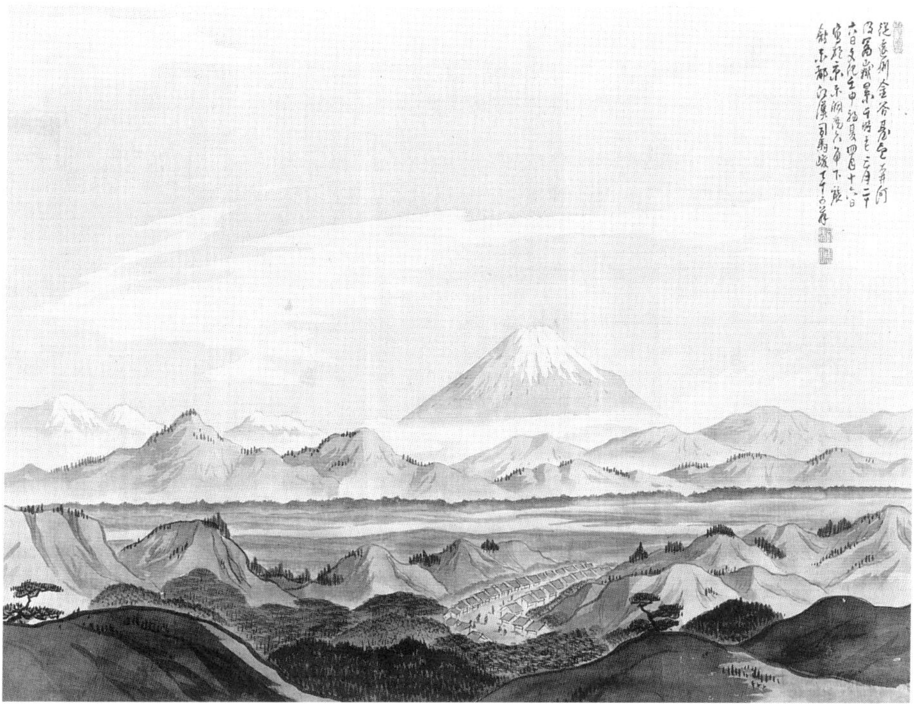

96 Shiba Kōkan, *Mt Fuji Seen across the Ōi from Kanayadai*, after 1812, hanging scroll. Kōkan shows Fuji as he had personally seen it, working in the 'Dutch' way.

picture-viewing more often than from visits, grew the tourist spot.

An urge to discover the true state of the countryside is to be seen in the rise of official investigative travel, a practice dear to the Qing court, where the *huangdi* would tour the empire to see with his own eyes how it looked; the latest such trip had taken place in 1784. Sadanobu studied these progresses and their pictorial representations, appealing for opinions from an unnamed Qing emigré.[84] Royal progresses were difficult to orchestrate and highly artificial in terms of what was actually seen. Disguise might be attempted, and it was conventional for the *huangdi* to dress down (a fact that attracted Sadanobu) so that he could view without too much fawning by those he met (or was it to avoid assassination, mused Sadanobu). This was taken further in Japan. Shimazu Shigehide, daimyo of Satsuma and Ienari's father-in-law, actually wandered the streets of Edo incognito; Caspar Romberg bumped into him 'wearing the costume of a servant' and, so as not to blow his cover, Shigehide revealed what he was up to, speaking in Dutch.[85]

The tradition of assessing the conditions of the land and people by overheard snippets or popular songs was ingrained. In China this had prompted the genre of critiques of government written in the idiom of the folksong but composed by disgruntled members of the elite, and sometimes planted by them among the local data culled.[86] When in 1785 the governor of Nagasaki was told of a song sung in criticism of the hardness of his rule, he might have reacted like a 'virtuous ruler' and amended his policies, but instead he had the song banned and sent anyone heard singing it to jail for nine years.[87] This was of no avail since the lyrics had already spread to Keishi and Edo, but it showed a callous lack of attention to the conditions of the states among those of the highest rank.

Would-be good rulers were enjoined to send emissaries to quietly acquaint themselves with town and village life, and act to ameliorate the situation. Sadanobu built up a dedicated inspectorate (*junkenshi*). In 1789, he dispatched six men, three each to work inwards from either end of the Tenka. The men were few in number and, as localities were tipped off, the validity of the information gathered was questionable, but the data were scrupulously sent back for processing. Romberg was interviewed, noting that Sadanobu's project was to 'traverse the Empire to take notes on everything'.[88] Sadanobu's use of informants contrasted diametrically with that attributed to Tanuma Okitsugu, who, it was said, punished those who returned with unwelcome news, positively forcing them to lie. The term used for Okitsugu's spies was *inmitsu*.[89] Sadanobu also employed a larger group to move in real silence through the states, and these were punningly known as the 'official secrets' (*on-mitsu*). Kairyō was probably of this band. By definition the organization is hard to analyse. Shiba Kōkan was in Nagasaki some time after Sadanobu's installation as chief councillor and was taken (mistakenly, he insisted) for one of 'the Prince of Shirakawa's official secrets', which however allowed him unparalleled hospitality, including access to the normally off-limits Dejima.[90] Romberg noted how the Dutch compound was now 'teeming with informers'.[91]

These spies passed invisibly and noiselessly. Sadanobu did not allow them even the minimum that bureaucrats expected, like having the flooring replaced where they stayed and the latrines redug.[92] Some were not happy with the loss of perquisites, and Koshōken, the government geographer, objected that he ought at least to have been allowed to take precedence over other travellers when he moved between postings.[93] When the daimyo of Sendai rode past him without ceding place, Koshōken hoisted a flag with the vermilion seal indicating shogunal business, provided for emergency use, and, when this was ignored, the daimyo seemingly knowing the new codes, Koshōken fulminated against the 'outrageous rudeness' of this 'sleight to protocol'. But Sadanobu was happy: he wanted local information, as it were, copied 'authentically'.

Koshōken's reports were models of their kind and have survived. Sadanobu ultimately rewarded him with a place in the scroll of portraits he commissioned from Bunchō to keep with him in retirement (see illus. 71). In the preface to data submitted in mid-1788, Koshōken alluded to his new manner of journeying. While he used as a private individual to travel joyously to famous sites and savour them poetically, he now went softly up to the edges of shogunal space, to look at the line where there was nothing more. Of his most recent trip he wrote:

> I went as far as the strange and untold frontier, to identify with my own eyes which peaks are awesome as they rise range upon range. I pushed to the limits of remarkable but outlying places, bivouacking my thoughts where the blue seas heave fold upon fold, and taking my ease at the flames of unknown brushwood fires.[94]

As a preface to a longer piece of writing, the language is necessarily ornate, but these sites are true and personally observed. By such means he was able to cover much ground and find out a good deal. He corrected existing gazetteers and compendia, many of which were outdated or in error, he delineated where dialects began and ended, where architectural norms came and diverged, what goods were available and where: in short, he learned how the cultural pieces of the Tenka came together and where, potentially, they might break asunder.

Koshōken was sent to spy on daimyo castles, for these were centres from which alternative gravities pulled. He was issued with the *Collected Master Plans (Shūzu gōketsu)*, a sensitive work which came into his hands, as he guardedly put it, 'owing to circumstances'. It contained 'transcriptions of all fortified places in the various states'.[95] Koshōken was also extraordinarily adept at prising out information orally. At Takeda Castle in Kyushu he heard of a secret escape tunnel and made the garrulous locals divulge everything. While admitting 'it was forbidden to tell outsiders of its existence'.[96] At Saga-no-Seki, although he was not able to get close to the castle, he concluded:

> Although I am no expert in military engineering, I would think from the lie of the land some leagues around, that there must be an access gully to

the east; uneven slopes come in from the west; the South Gate allows a direct means of approach, and although in the north the road is circuitous, there is a short-cut.[97]

Efforts to constrict regional autonomy ensured a 'Japanese culture' safeguarded against its intrinsic friability. The discipline of *chiri* was born. The term now means geography and I have used that term above, but in the eighteenth century it signified something additional like local ethnography, that is, it estimated both the land and its human superstructural mesh. Among those who worked in *chiri* was Tachibana Nankei, although Koshōken was supreme. In Nankei's case, both new-style traveller and practising anatomist came together, and he cut through clichéd lore and flesh to find the core of fact. One of Nankei's travel chronicles was illustrated by a team of Ōkyo's followers (his sons Ōzui and Ōju, and students Goshun and Nagasawa Rosetsu), with Yoshimura Ranshū and Kōkei assisting.[98]

Shiba Kōkan deplored what he strangely saw as Sadanobu's lack of interest in *chiri* and said he was 'in the next nearest position to not having studied it'.[99] This was surely not true and is more like a Sadanobu smoke-screen – the image he preferred to circulate. Concomitantly, Sadanobu played up the role of himself as an old-style muser on the landscape for whom going to its sites was meaningless without the miasma of poetry. It was politic not to reveal the vice he was attaching to the Tenka's disparate landscapes. Sadanobu had a close relationship with the shogunal official and antiquarian Nakamura Butsuan, and they bonded precisely over their shared travel myth. Neither could travel much. Butsuan had a collection of walking sticks by which he alluded to classical poetic wanderings to places whose value accrued from literary traditions. Each stick was taken from a bit of a 'famous place'; this is not unlike the wealthier Sadanobu's storehouses of 'famous place' gleanings in his Six Gardens.[100] Butsuan had guests write verses on these sticks, and Sadanobu provided one. This, though, is a reinterpretation, temperamentally unlike real classical travelling. Sadanobu and Butsuan may not have realized it, but they were already in a quite different ideology of land. For Saigyō and Bashō the idea of a physical souvenir was anathema, and the prompt for a verse was a site as seen through a billow of earlier verse, not a piece of woodwork torn off it.

Rebuilding History

Sadanobu's time in office, as well as his extended period of influence in retirement, was a notable epoch in the rebuilding and improvement of ancient monuments. Fuji needed no extenuation, but much did. The shogunal mausolea at Nikkō were refurbished, and several major temples, including Edo's biggest, the Asakusa Kannon, were restored to original finishes.[101] This was not extravagance, because it was heritage that was being burnished, not just the residences of the rich. People began to discuss the state of historical furniture as travellers read each other's accounts and cross-referred. Real travel had an impact on the ground. Nankei noted how Kōkan had described an old stone pagoda in Ōmi as in a state of sad collapse, whereas when he saw it a dozen years later it was fully restored.[102] As more attention was paid, equivalently more vocal calls came for the propping up, or realignment, of tilts and warps. Sadanobu took an interest and offered sponsorship. As any conscientious restorer must, he also investigated the history of alterations to assess the authenticity of what remained. In a high-profile move, Bunchō and the head of the shogunal Confucian academy, Shibano Ritsuzan, were sent to the Tenka's single most important ancient institution, the Great Eastern Temple (Tōdai-ji) in Nara, to investigate the main image hall and its contents. Yashiro Hirokata worked as team scribe, filing a report on the original state and past interventions to it:

> We inspected restoration work carried out after the last fire. Few are aware how on each petal of the [Great Buddha's] lotus throne a Buddha image is engraved, with a pagoda representing Mt Sumeru. We estimate these elements to date from the original foundation of the temple [752]; during subsequent repair work they were welded back into their proper places [. . .] A board is affixed to the top of one of the pillars detailing other proposed work, bearing notification by the daimyo of Satsuma.[103]

What was real and what had been done later was clarified so that travellers would not be misled. The old parts were brought back to prominence and later accretions warned against. These issues had been of no moment to olden-style poetic travellers, much less to those who composed verses on places they had never seen, relying only on the verse tradition to guide them. Bashō actually exaggerated the desuetude of some places, so as to heighten poetic nostalgia, and would never have advocated restoration. At the Temple of the Central Deity (Chūson-ji), for example, a splendid complex in Hiraizumi, a former military city dating to 1124, he doubled the antiquity of the place, the better to put its relics against a deep flow of time. To Bashō, the halls 'will shortly be celebrating their thousandth anniversary' (actually their 565th). In an accompanying verse, he wrote as if the totality had sunken into weeds, which it certainly had not:

Summer grasses
Warrior after warrior –
Just relics in dreams.[104]

By the end of the century an inverse reaction is seen. When in 1788 Kōkan came to another gilded building, the Golden Turret of 1397, he sought to stress how the structure was alive and well, still decked with its old plaques and with the fine ceiling painting by Ko-Hōgen intact (the building had just ceased to be used as a residence for some of Tomohito's displaced ladies).[105] Although little gold was left, Kōkan expressed pleasure that 'around the corners of the pillars' it was still visible, rather than disappointment that there was not more. This was the new way of viewing. A *senryū* verse composed after new looking modes had evolved advertised Kyoto's sights to prospective visitors similarly; it twins the Golden Turret with the century-later Silver Turret on the other side of town, again offering the best possible interpretation:

They may be duller now,
But the temples' names shine brilliant
In gold and silver.[106]

The gold was certainly scant (the Silver Turret never had been leaved), but pictorial reproduction allowed more freedom. When Ōkyo produced a perspective view of the Golden Turret, he unilaterally remetalled the upper part of it (see illus. 63).

Bashō's nostalgic poetic mood at Hiraizumi may be contrasted with Tachibana Nankei's comments at the same place a century later in the 1790s. Yes, much had gone, but this was now a call to action: 'When you try to visualize what once was here', he wrote, 'on the basis of what is present now, it all seems very regrettable'. He does not minimize change, but he does not revel in it either. Regret is the first step on the road to repair. Nankei, indeed, went on to consider concrete issues relating to costs for the creation and hence maintenance of such structures:

In its first glory, Hiraizumi was endowed with only the equivalent of 600 *ryō* of gold, plus some donations in kind. [. . .] Today, even many urban commoners are able to make donations of 1,000 or 10,000 in gold without difficulty. This means we are actually better off for precious metals, and it seems there never was a time so copiously provided for.[107]

So the mature response was to refurbish. It was shogunal business to do this. Edification also took the form of 'Edofication'. It is possible to see this sense in another *senryū* on the Golden and Silver Turrets:

Those temples in Kyō
Under currency conversion,
Are rebuilt in Edo.[108]

The joke is that if Kyoto's richest monuments were the Gold and Silver Turrets, Edo's first temple shared its name with a unit of coinage (Kan'ei-ji and *kan'ei tsūhō*). Precious ancestral metal is minted into the shogun's calibrated specie. Kyoto's heritage comes under Edo's charge, which entails a carting off of its prestige.

When Edo's new urban commoners travelled, it was likely to be for commercial purposes. They bought things up and took them home. Even the self-consciously poetic Butsuan pulled a strip off the Golden Turret to make one of his walking sticks. Most, though, wanted the attractions to look complete. Ritual sites had always demanded 'worship fees' (*haikenryō*) or 'mountain coin' (*yamazeni*). Ike Taiga, an inveterate hiker, ran up costs of well in excess of 2 *kan* (about ten nights' lodgings) in 1760 on his trip to the sacred peaks of Fuji, Hakusan and Tateyama.[109] But the full-scale admission fee seems to be an invention of the close of the century, with the Golden and Silver Turrets charging 2 *monme* (about a week's sustenance) for parties of up to ten; the fee was dolled up as a voluntary donation, but without it the monks would not open the gates leading in.[110] The cash kept the compound spick and span.

Empirical travellers on business took in tourist sites rapidly, with little prior psychological preparation, and much less reading. Bashō had claimed he had left Edo in 1689 because he was 'summoned by the gods of the roadside'.[111] The eighteenth-century traveller would have felt hopelessly pretentious claiming this. Tourists' broadsheets were published for those with scant time to invest. Outlying people came to view Edo. There was 'Edo Sightseeing Covered in Four Days' (*Edo kenbutsu yokka-meguri*), arranged in blocks, one per day, for maximum viewing with minimum wastage of time (illus. 97). The famous story of Ko-Hōgen's casting away his brush in despair at the great beauty spot was amusingly coupled with the ideology of the new travel guide. A *senryū* of 1775 had it:

The mountain he threw his brush down at
Is picked up
By the guidebook.[112]

This was the era of the comprehensive guide aimed at those who had neither the time nor the inclination to internalize literary traditions. The causal root of the shift was both the increase in the numbers on the move and a disengagement from the poetic tradition. Books could run to several volumes and aimed to be exhaustive. They were assigned the name 'complete illustrated famous places' (*meisho zue*). They gave facts in full, uncluttered form, arranged for ready reference, with pictures. The new tourist had no need to mix with locals to learn the oral lore nor to ferret out scholars or poets as Bashō did; the tradition of the 'guests in ink' (*bokkyaku*), whereby wanderers repaid hospitality by sharing discourse, poetry or painting with eminent people along the way, was degraded into 'who's who' publications, put out so travellers could gawp in front of mansion gates. 1788 saw publication of the ex-fire diarist Ban Kōkei's *Biographies of Remarkable Modern*

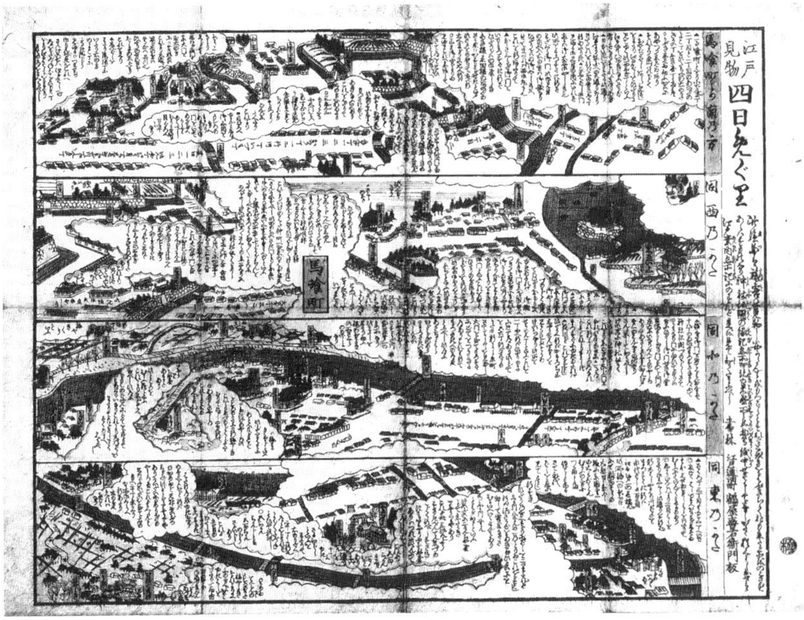

97 *Edo kenbutsu yokka meguri*, *c.* 1780, monochrome woodblock print. Each of the four registers suggests a single day's sightseeing in Edo.

People (Kinsei kijin-den), which provided thumbnail life histories of Kyoto's live wires (Taiga and his wife Gyokuran figure in the section on 'elegant and aloof' people, *fūryū hyōetsu*) so that those who could never have met them, much less held their own with such idiosyncratic prodigies conversationally, could nevertheless pick up scattered cultural quidnuncs.[113] Ritsujō-tei Kiran's *Famous People along the Tōkaidō (Tōkaidō jinbutsu-shi)* of 1803 listed the names worth dropping at each portion of the Edo–Kyoto route.[114]

Tourists wanted correct information, and oral lore might in turn be construed as error. When Kairyō was accidentally blown ashore at Zentsūji in Shikoku, he was saddened by how residents were muddled about the role their city had played in history, saying all the wrong things and confusing data. He laid on a series of lectures to correct them.[115] Not many had access to Kairyō's depth of reading and so they turned to guides.

Since early in the previous century, guidebooks telling what and where to eat, relax or accumulate local products had been known, but these were mostly unhelpful in terms of historical detail. They gave the general know-how to a city, but their arrangement was seldom for practical movement or comprehensive visiting. Often novelistic (a tourist is the protagonist), these books were known to pirate whole sections from each other, even where the source was about a quite different city.[116] The redefinition of the guidebook owed much to the mind of Akizato Ritō, who made his debut in 1780 with the *Complete Illustrated Famous Places of the Capital (Miyako meisho zue* – i.e. Kyoto*)*, the success of which led to an *Epitome* of the original (*Shūi miyako meisho zue*), issued seven years later. Ritō told his readers his illustrations showed the sites but also included 'pictures of travellers enquiring the way when they get lost, passing across open land and meeting a squall which blows their hats off, and things like that', in other words, self-validating imagery for those who were intruding into, and fundamentally changing, places where they did not really belong.[117] One picture in the *Epitome* shows a man and servant in the company of a professional guide, reading a book just like Ritō's; the group stands before a breathtaking view of Seta, their heads buried in the text (illus. 98). A verse by one Sōseki is inscribed above:

Famous sites
Are known to the
Capital tour guide
Or via the illustrated book.
We depict them here
As you would like to see them.[118]

The novelty of such travel laid it open to scorn. Reliance on guidebooks was derided in the best-selling road tale of the Edo period, Jippensha Ikku's *Down the Tōkaidō on Shank's Pony (Tōkaidōchū hizakurige)*. This had made a hero of its previously unknown author immediately on the appearance of its first instalment in 1802. The two protagonist travellers, Yaji and Kita, lack all education and persist in merry ignorance throughout the entire trip – but at least they are having fun. Without either the old poetic store of knowledge or the application to read guidebooks, they ridicule the new-style tourist. One man they meet holds forth about the sites they pass until his winking palanquin-bearers let on, 'he should know a bit considering he just sits in his litter looking at the guidebook!'[119] Those who do not already know, the reader concludes, should not try to fake it via a book. But Yaji and Kita were fighting a losing battle. Ritō produced guidebooks at an extraordinary rate. After the two Kyoto books, areas covered were Yamato (1791), Sumiyoshi (1794), Izumo (1796), Settsu (i.e. Osaka, 1796–8), the Tōkaidō, Ise and Ōmi (all 1797), Kyoto gardens (1799), Kawachi (1801) and Kisoro (1805).[120]

Ritō's illustrations were at first undertaken by the able Takehara

98 Illustration from Akizato Ritō, *Shūi miyako meisho zue*, 1787. The guidebook takes precedence over the scenery.

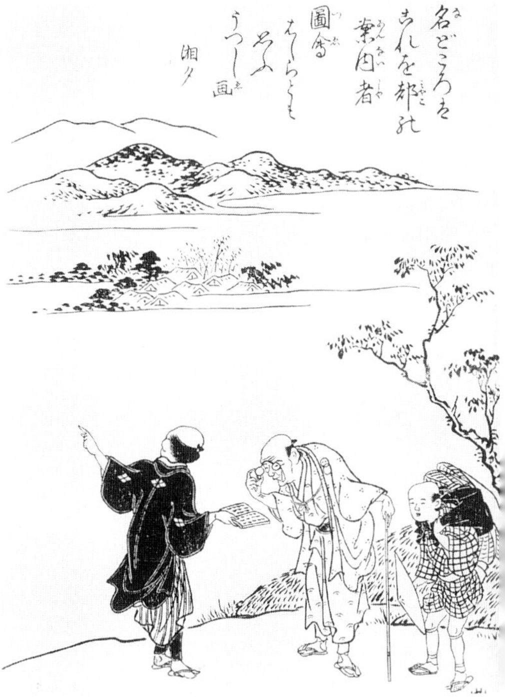

Shunchōsai, who was awarded the honour 'dharmic bridge' (*hokkyō*, one below *hōgen*), but he fell ill in the 1780s and was replaced by a team, one of whom was Ōkyo's pupil and biographer, Oku Bunmei. It seems to have been Bunmei who introduced a new idea for illustrations (one destined to become, and remain, an essential visual aid for any tourist): the city panorama.[121] Bunmei's first essay of this kind appears in Ritō's *Complete Illustrated Gardens of the Capital (Miyako rinsen meisho zue)*. Note that the idea had not occurred when making his two earlier books in 1780 and 1787. All is laid out for inspection in a view that users are encouraged not only to savour but also to recreate for themselves if they go to Kyoto; they are told how to find it, at the eastern edge of the city, at the Temple of the Pristine Dharma (Shōhō-ji) above Yasaka (where, they are helpfully informed, there is also a restaurant serving pleasant meals) (illus. 99). The notion of the 'panorama' was a creation of this period. In Europe, the word is attested from 1792.[122] Although there was yet no term in Japanese, experiments were under way. The recycled Floating World artist Kitao Masayoshi produced many under his new name Kuwagata Keisai, raising himself from the vagaries of Edo's pleasure districts to obtain a clean gaze at Kyoto.[123] Bunmei's inclusion of the picture in a guidebook was an innovation and relates to the tourist's new wish to possess and master the whole visited area. Technically and stylistically, though, this image was borrowed from one of Ōkyo's perspectives, which was reversed as it was made for viewing in a mirrored peep-box (illus. 100).[124] Bunmei has turned it back for bare-eye viewing. He also made subtle alterations, especially to the figures. Ōkyo's people of the 1770s are surely locals who have climbed to escape the city with its noise and humidity to enjoy a cooling breeze; their dress shows it is summer. They do not look out or notice the existence of the 'panorama'. Bunmei's people display the unhabituated enthusiasm of tourists, and one's ocular reach is enhanced by a telescope. About twenty-five years, and the fire of 1788, come between the two pictures.[125] Keishi was replaced by Kyoto. Note that what Bunmei has not done is concretize the buildings in Ōkyo's hazily indistinct vista.

Rebuilding Bridges

Almost immediately after coming to power, Sadanobu was presented with an opportunity to adjudicate the status that the materiality of the past should have. This pertained to Uji Bridge, one of the most famous of all historic sites, with a deep cultural incrustation. It featured in the *Tale of Genji (Genji monogatari)*, was the site of conspicuous fighting

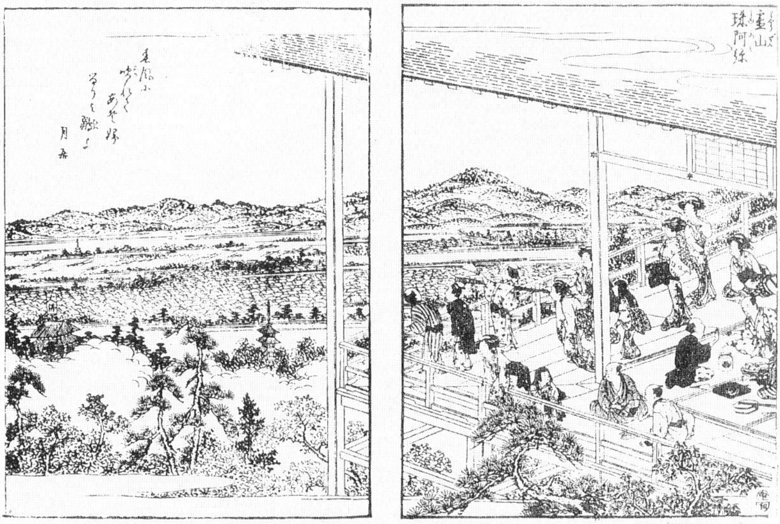

99 Oku Bunmei (attrib.), Illustration from Akizato Ritō, *Miyako rinsen meisho zue*, 1799. A panorama of Kyoto gained from the Shūami Hall of the Shōhō-ji.

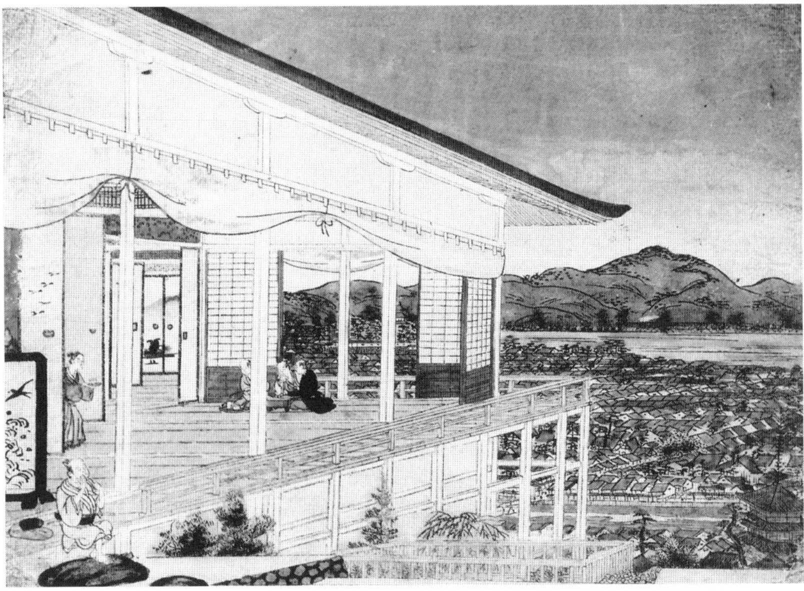

100 Maruyama Ōkyo, *Shōhō-ji*, *c.* 1780, colour on paper. Reverse-painted for viewing in an optique, this image is clearly the model for that in Ritō's book.

recorded in medieval battle romances and the setting for several nō plays and innumerable poems. To one end of the span was the shrine to the legendary Bridge Princess (Hashigime), said to have vainly awaited her lover there, and to the other the Sumiyoshi Shrine.[126] Uji was a veritable log-jam of memory and allusion. More baldly, the River Uji that flowed beneath was prone to flooding, and destruction of the bridge's 150 m arch was periodic. First erected in 646 (as Ritō informed the reader in his *Famous Places of the Capital*[127]), the bridge was not the same entity in the eighteenth as it had been in the seventh century, nor was it quite on the same spot, having shifted to the east over the ages. Time had changed the site.

It is worth considering Uji's visual image before returning to Sadanobu's actions. Over the millennium, Uji had been copiously depicted. We may take a pair of anonymous screens of the early Edo period as representative of what was still the eighteenth-century norm (illus. 101). These pack the whole aura of Uji into their sixteen hinged panels. Poets had alluded to the swiftness of the current, so baskets of rocks are seen placed at the banks to prevent erosion. Weeping willows were metaphors for the tangle of tragic loves, so they are shown; waterwheels were said to circle like the karmas of those associated with the place, and they were conventionally included too. Other such screens have barques in the stream laden with charcoal, and grazing horses on hills above, both included in many verses as special to Uji. None of these poetry-derived features was necessarily evident to a visitor on site. The painter does not care. In all probability he had never been to Uji himself. The wooden bridge is golden and crosses the plain in a vault that is grand, but architectonically imprecise. It scoops beholders up at the right (the beginning of a picture in the north-east Asian manner of reading) and deposits them in cloud; the bridge leads to a bank of emotions, not an opposite shore. The silvery trees, now oxidized to black, offer a ghostly repoussoir through which to penetrate the mysteriousness of past thought. Such a rendition's profound eloquence had persisted over centuries but then came to seem inadequate. To reveal what occurred, a comparison may be made with the illustration in Ritō's guide (illus. 102).

Sadanobu had his opinions about the former, emotive kind of 'famous place' painting. He referred not to Uji, but to Yoshino, a range of hills known for its cherries, one of the peerless and often-poeticized sites of the Kyoto region. Sadanobu wanted Yoshino rendered in empirical 'authentic' views. Artists, he regretted, 'will not defer to the true formation of the land, and allow themselves to paint a waterfall where there is not one in fact, or put pine trees on a hill that does not have

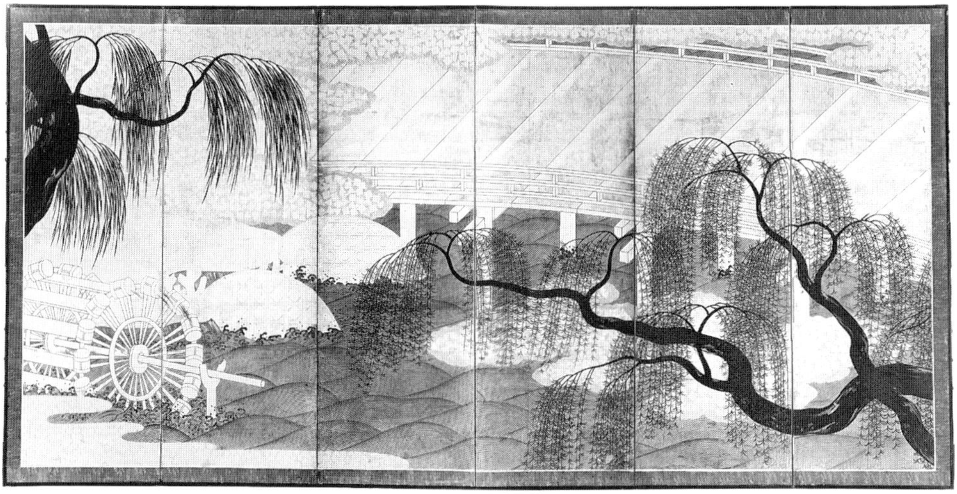

101 *The Willow Bridge with Waterwheel*, c. 1620, pair of six-fold screens, gold, silver and colour on paper. Although known conventionally by the title given here, this is certainly Uji Bridge.

them', and he concluded this had made landscape painting into 'mere diversion' and 'pure licence'.[128] Sadanobu had ingested the requisite body of verses, but he worried for those who had not, and he feared older-style depictions failed to meet the need of the contemporary viewer for concrete conviction. Ritō's illustrators offered sights complete in terms of poetical reference but also in terms of geography. Viewers could orientate themselves on arrival at Uji or Yoshino thanks to the pictures. They could also know the truth of being there, even if they could not actually go. And then they could learn from the texts.

The injunction to defer to the realities of a site had its corollary in a requirement to manage the ground so that it properly replicated the literary claims. The cherries must not be allowed to die off at Yoshino nor the bridge to collapse at Uji. Natural scenery needed only moderate tending to be kept in true, but the historical fabric of buildings and other structures needed constant attention. This brings us back to Sadanobu and Uji. In 1756 the bridge had been washed away and replaced with a scaled-down structure with a beaten-earth surface; the princess's sanctuary had been amalgamated with the Sumiyoshi Shrine. Although supposedly temporary, this expedient was still unamended over a generation later; when Kōkan was there in the winter of 1789 the bridge had become so rickety he was advised to use a ferry.[129] Sadanobu interposed and commanded 'restoration'. Although

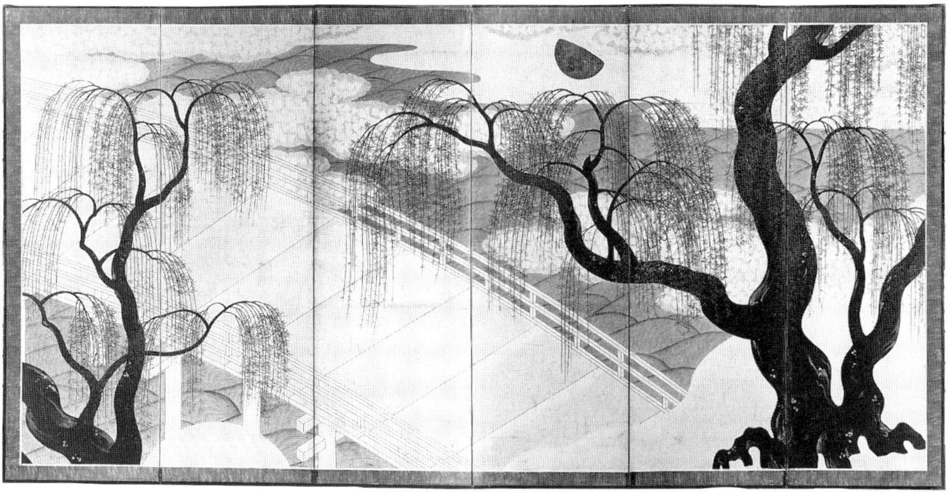

the temporary bridge 'reduced expenses all round', economy was a lesser imperative. He delved into old descriptions and pictures, some exceedingly historic:

I asked if this could possibly be right, for I considered it thus: in old pictures, the River Uji [crossing] is made of wood, and there are literary descriptions saying things like 'He pulled up the bridge planks'. Surely from antiquity the bridge has always been wooden. As for the Bridge Princess's shrine, you can read about it in the old poetry anthologies.[130]

The ripping up of the bridge planks was a dramatic moment in *The Rise and Fall of the Taira and Minamoto (Genpei seisuiki)*, and the old anthologies contained many verses on Uji, notably by Hitomaro in the eighth century and Fuijiwara no Teika in the late twelfth.[131] Sadanobu concluded: 'I commanded integral reconstruction, and it was rebuilt to original specifications'. He ignored later technological developments and improvements that might have eased traffic flow (the bridge was heavily used), preferring antiquarianism; the princess's shrine had originally been built into the span itself and pilgrims milling about collided with those trying to cross, and it had seemed reasonable in mid-century to do away with this annoyance. No longer. In the spring of 1791, a man working on the princess's shrine turned up the 1100-year-old stone stele inscribed with the original order to erect the bridge. The wording exactly matched that preserved in ancient documents, proving the authority of the archives and their suitability as

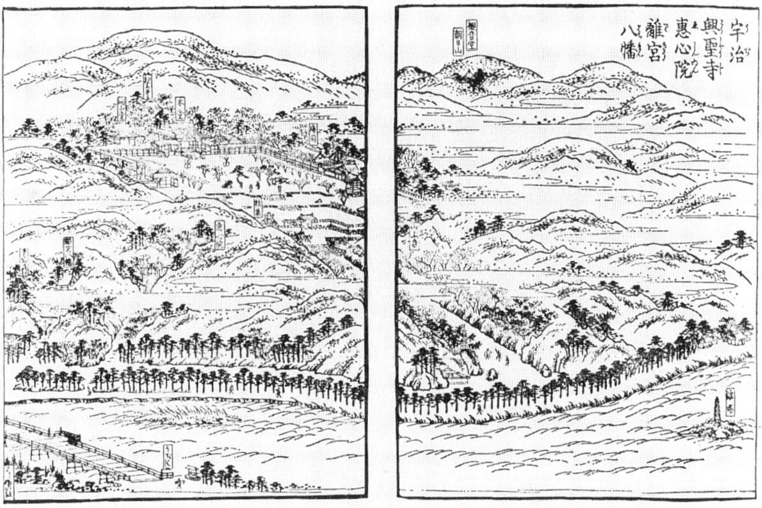

102 Illustration from Akizato Ritō, *Miyako meisho zue*, 1780. The bridge and landscape of Uji.

models for restoration and the bridge's true age.[132] The inscription stated that, since countless lives had been lost fording the swift river, a bridge would be put up out of empathy for their plight, signed Dōto, monk of Yamashiro. History was not only provable and true, it was also full of 'virtue'.

This restored bridge was ripped away again in a flood of 1802, along with the new princess's shrine.[133]

The resurrection of Uji as a place of both on-the-ground and poetic appeal was achieved by manipulation of its space and by submersion of its real history. The glorious and poignant events probably had happened there, but from the beginning of Tokugawa rule the intermittent rebuildings had been enforced on criminals as a punishment. In the early seventeenth century, a sighted man had usurped the blind persons' guild and was forced to atone by paying for repairs; in 1700 the Nabeya family of Keishi, convicted of usury, had been compelled to fund a rebuilding.[134] It is unclear why no convict had been assigned in 1756, but an air of felony hung about the place. To Sadanobu, Uji could not bear a criminal badge. He leap-frogged over several intervening centuries to reach 'antiquity'.

Restoration on Paper

Among visual cultural vestiges that enlightened the present, none were more vital than paintings. They occupied a midway point between formless literature and environmental structures. Time and again Sadanobu ordered repairs to old pictures, or copies of them, with Bunchō's circle being regularly asked. Perhaps most impressive was Bunchō's 80-day stint in camera at the Temple of the Stone Mountain (Ishiyama-dera), which owned an ancient set of pictures of its history called *The Illustrated Handscrolls of the Origins of the Temple of the Stone Mountain (Ishiyama-dera engi emaki)*.[135] Sadanobu had seen five scrolls in the temple on his way to burned-out Keishi in 1788 and had made rough sketches. He was not happy to learn, though, that two of the scrolls were missing. He determined to investigate. Sadanobu was stunned to come across the lost duo in his own collection in Shirakawa, and he determined to have the set united. Restitution took the form of reproduction, for neither owner would surrender their portion. So in the winter of 1804–5, Abbot Sonken hosted Bunchō and his pupils Tani Bun'ichi and Hoshino Bunrō to copy his scrolls. Also present was Okamoto Jishō, a samurai amateur in Sadanobu's entourage who took an intensive painting course with Sumiyoshi Hiroyuki in preparation for the trip; Jishō would later depict Sadanobu's Garden of Bathing in Obligation (see illus. 3, 14, 82). Jishō also kept a record of the proceedings, noting that Sadanobu forbade Bunchō and the rest 'to do even a blade of grass, even a tree, as their own idea, and to keep minutely to the ancient scrolls'[136] (see illus. 33). Bunchō took the copies to Edo, where it was Jishō's task to find an artist to copy the two Shirakawa scrolls to send to the temple. He suggested the head of the Tosa Bureau, Mitsusada, or failing him, Hiroyuki. Sadanobu overruled this: his own artist, Bunchō, would do these too. The set was preserved and multiplied and brought under Sadanobu's control. But something else had happened too, for, in truth, the original scrolls were the work of at least four people and were executed over some 500 years; they were not a single work, and there was no consensus on which old master had done which bit (Hiroyuki offered a reattribution of them all). What occurred, then, was a reification and consolidation of disparate vestiges into an official masterpiece. This was then inserted into the canon of government-sponsored 'Japanese culture' as a public monument rather than a temple treasure. Sadanobu paid off the temple with an additional gift of 'a modest quantity of silver'.[137]

Bunchō's utility to Sadanobu lay in his ability to silence the personality of his mind and brush, and to paint without the intrusion of self.

Ōkyo, whom Sadanobu admired but did not use, was all self. Bunchō was an encyclopaedia of pictorial manner, and there was no mode he could not undertake impartially. This was Bunchō's skill, but it was also his public hallmark. The *Record of Master Tani Bunchō (Tani Bunchō no ki)*, by his student Nomura Bunshō, stated he excelled in 'the styles of Kose [no Kanaoka], Satakuma, Sumiyoshi, Soga, Nikaidō, Murasaki, Kōgen and Sesshū, and in modern times of Nanpin [i.e. Nagasaki School], Kōetsu and Kōrin'. He could do everything and 'while rooting himself in the manners of high antiquity, he did not neglect those of our debased present'. He was not a jack-copyist because, with each style he took, 'he exhausted it to its profundities.'[138] This was the circulated Bunchō image.

Whereas most artists gave their studios flowery names, such as Taiga's Hall of Great Elegance (Taiga-dō), or Jakuchū's Mansion Where the Heart is Distant (Shin'en-kan), Bunchō's work space was called Study Where Painting is Learned (Gagaku-sai). His was a clearing house for the imagery of the Tenka to be sorted and filed. The one known picture of the studio shows it as an unremittingly public arena, with crowds who have come to commission or look; with arrant self-promotion, the picture is entitled 'Showing the multitudes that daily come up'; the space is topped by an exaggerated sign reading 'Place to choose pictures' (*senga-jo*) (illus. 103). Unlike Ōkyo's self-projection, in which the continuum of style and self was stressed, all becoming part of *his* 'new concept' with nothing learned and all derived from looking, Bunchō created himself as a transparent entity that produces in any manner.

Bunchō's students were many (several have appeared above), and many used the *bun* element of his name. However, only Ōkyo's sons were allowed to use his ō- (Ōzui and Ōjū). Ōkyo kept a tight rein on what was his – to his ultimate cost when Goshun expropriated his thinned-out line. Bunchō's pupils saturated Edo and beyond with *bun*s. If the records are accurate, the preponderance (some 55 per cent) of his students were shogunal employees. His concern with efficiency, even over taboo, is revealed in his taking on women students when they showed promise (ten per cent).[139] Bunchō's followers cannot be recognized by any stylistic means, and the most unlikely figures turn out to have worked under him (Tanomura Chikuden, Kanwatei Onitake). With him, they learned an attitude towards style rather than a style itself.

This was a time when the notion of the 'work of art' emerged. Things were isolated and circulated, pulled away from the circumstances of their first commissioning and cut from habits of veneration and heirloom fetishization. Provenance is important for a 'work of

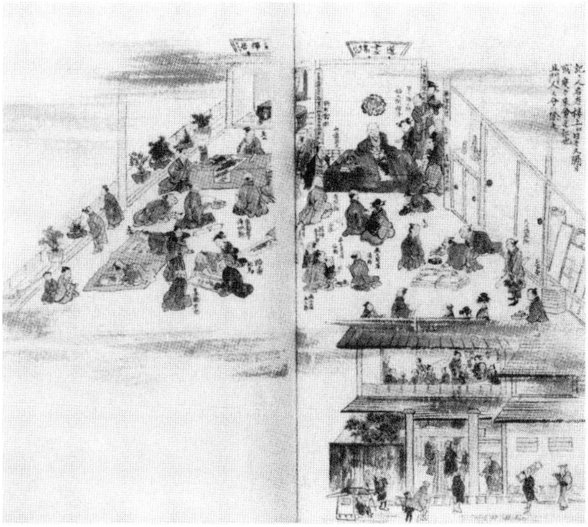

103 Nomura Bunshō, from his *Shazanrō no ki*, *c.* 1810, manuscript with sketches in light colour. Bunchō's studio with purchasers.

art', because this assures value while allowing a piece to move away to a new owner. The issue is too large to cover adequately here, but it is necessary to note in passing that a new market for paintings emerged in Kyoto after the fire. From 1790 biannual exhibitions were held, organized by Ōkyo's friend Minagawa Kien, and at these artists in all styles worthy of the past were invited to display. Bunchō's school was much in evidence, as it could supply anything desired. The only school denied admission was that of the Floating World.[140] Good modern works judiciously adapted from the old stimulated historical styles into new relevance. Degraded styles only cheapened.

Magical aura was significantly eroded by Sadanobu and his entourage as a matter of policy. Many works were so venerated they were never actually seen. Wonder-working capacities had to be denied if the hands-on work of preservation, copying and restoring could begin. Bunchō learned old styles to replicate damaged pieces as well as to make new pictures in old manners. On Sadanobu's orders, he went to the Temple of Ninna ('Ninna' was the era of its foundation, 885–89) in Kyoto to copy a portrait of the great statesman of that period, Ono no Takamura, made by the venerated prelate Kōbō Daishi. There, a modern *episteme* of 'art' collided with the old dispensation of ritual imagery. To Sadanobu, the picture was too important to be sequestered, but to the monks it was too holy to be replicated. They warned Bunchō: 'Anyone who copies it will forthwith begin to choke and find their eyes go dim, and they will die'. Moreover, 'never once has anyone traced it', and no one was about to now.[141] Bunchō had a rationalizing riposte:

I said, 'Why do you think the image was made in the first place if not to pass on [Takamura's] appearance to later ages? Soot has made it less distinct than it once was, and in another hundred years time it will be even more damaged, and probably impossible to discern at all. I shall make one [extra] replica to present to this temple. It will further the intentions of the original painter. Why is this worthy of death?'

The monks conceded the logic. One copy stayed at the Ninna-ji, and one went to Edo.

The sense that magic had to be planed off materials in order to ensure their preservation was a discourse of some strength, given the coefficient of loss that occurred at the end of the eighteenth century and the feeling that this was the brink of a time when objects would no longer exist. The state of mind is clear across many areas, and this was a discourse that went beyond painting. We may cite the case of gardens again.[142] The chief groundsman of Edo Castle came upon the new thinking and was shocked by it. A splendid old maple grew in the castle's central enceinte, planted by Yoshimune. It was too revered to be touched and had never once been pruned. By the 1790s the alarm at loss, and its attendant demythologization, spread to this tree, and voices were heard that if it were not dealt with it would die. The tree was some half-century old. The gardener would not let it be touched because of the ritual niceties. Ieharu stepped in and commanded a lopping of the branches. Genuine continuity of the past required abrupt action to prevent bonds snapping altogether. This was a late eighteenth-century preoccupation. The gradual accumulation of markers of age was stopped, and living history was stilled to avert its going clean away; this created the 'work of art'.

Sadanobu's ultimate purpose in the many copyings was compilation of a complete archive of the visual deposit of history, ordered and made available as an archive of the Tenka. This was to be called *Collected Antiquities in Ten Categories (Shūko jusshū)*. It cut out all aura-related issues, like whether an object had mysterious qualities. It also ignored tourist contexts, like what else was to be seen nearby and how to get there. It informed about who owned what. The book was illustrated, and the pictures did not deny their status as copies (illus. 104, 105). They referred to something else, namely the originals as constituents of 'Japanese culture'. The *Ten Categories* bears a preface dated 1799, but it took another decade for all 85 volumes to be completed.[143] The categories are bells (usually inscribed with historical records), steles, bronzes, musical instruments, framed inscriptions, stationery equipment, seals, calligraphy and painting. The last, largest section was separately entitled *Survey of Old Pictures (Koga ruijū)* and has some 2600 images reproduced, including of course the Ninna-ji portrait. Sadanobu provided a small number of colour painted versions for those whom he felt needed them and then had the entire work printed in monochrome; every home could possess the shogun's culture (illus. 106). The huge compendium was the summation of Sadanobu's urge to reify and restore, but also to leave intact the Tenka's historic artefacts. It was a paper archive of the states.

Bunchō's Boundless Painting

Bunchō achieved fame equal to Ōkyo's but of a different kind. Ōkyo was 'of Heian', and he monopolized the creativity of that revived city. Bunchō had no place. Sadanobu said one reason he admired Bunchō was that the artist had travelled 'throughout the states and mountains that lie within the Tenka, excepting only four or five he has yet to visit'.[144] Bunchō was perpetually passing through spaces, literally and figuratively, as he moved over style, unlodged anywhere within the official establishment. Once the Tenka's borders had been set, nothing internal constituted a block, and Bunchō exemplified this. He often turned to print, replicating in multiple clusters the Tenka's natural or human-made rarities. One of his more famous compilations was the *Famous Illustrated Mountains of Japan (Nihon meizan zue)*, covering the entire land.

Many legends associate Bunchō with passing and repassing, and a breaching of lines of demarcation. He overcame barriers both temporal (with the Ishiyama scrolls) and psychological (the Takamura portrait), and he slid across the division of reality and fake, geography and more cognitive conditions. In later life he became a heavy drinker and a brand of *sake* was named after him; this was not inapt, for drunkenness was the quintessential state of mental cross-over – of being both lucid and fuddled, waking and sleeping. There was a wide literature on this. A witty *senryū* captured another sense of Bunchō's liminality:

Sweating it out over
Zhuangzi's dream –
Tani Bunchō.[145]

The Dream of Zhuangzi was often painted, although there is no evidence Bunchō ever did it. The subject adheres to him for another reason. The third-century-BC sage had dreamt he was a butterfly, but on waking he realized he might now be a butterfly asleep and dreaming it was a man. This existential conundrum placed Zhuangzi hovering

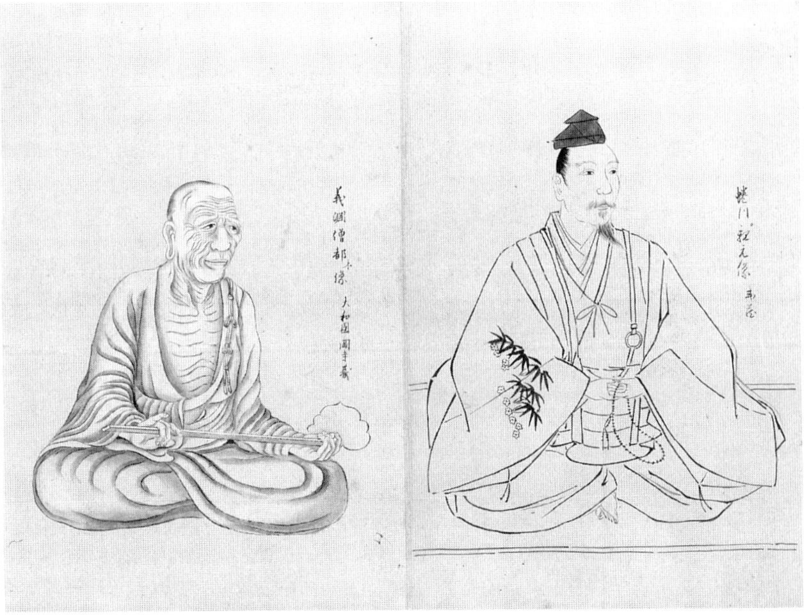

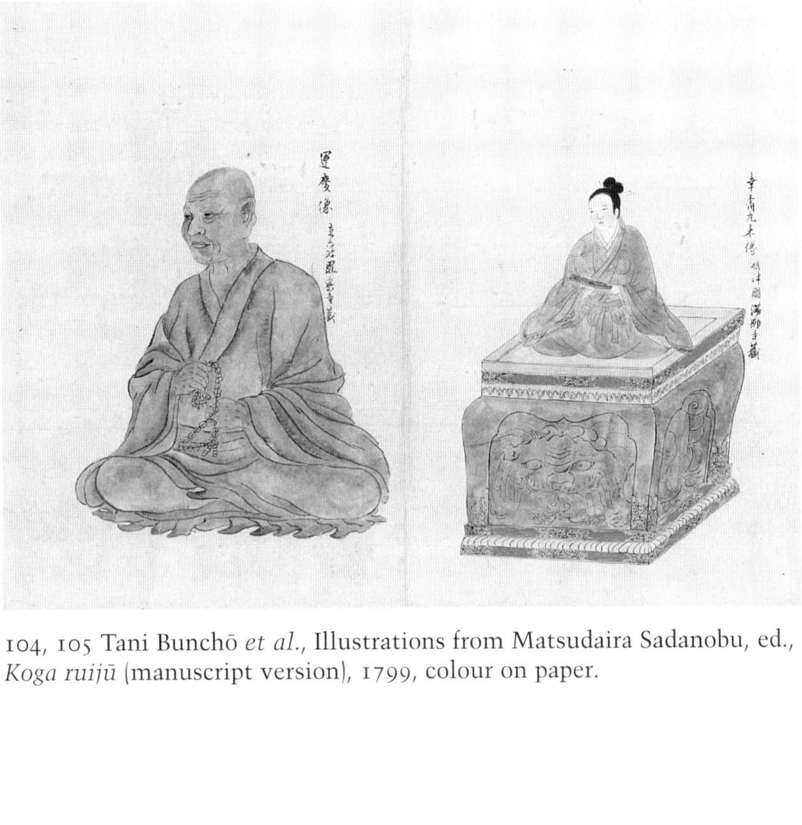

104, 105 Tani Bunchō *et al.*, Illustrations from Matsudaira Sadanobu, ed., *Koga ruijū* (manuscript version), 1799, colour on paper.

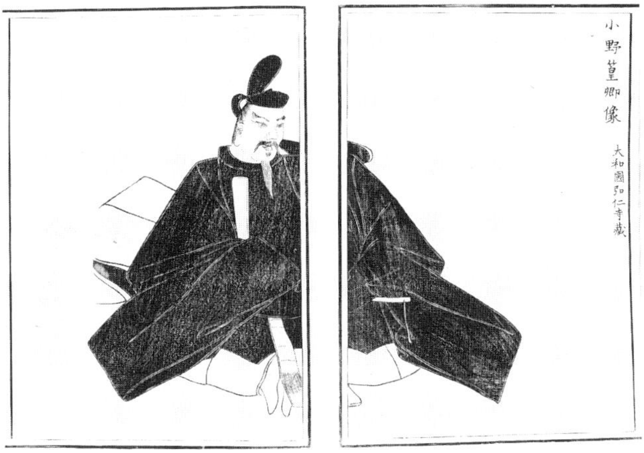

106 Tani Bunchō *et al.*, 'Ono no Takamura by Kōbō Daishi', *c.* 1815, from Matsudaira Sadanobu, ed., *Koga ruijū* (printed version), monochrome woodblock prints. The compendium of the state was eventually published in a modestly priced edition.

eternally at the ultimate division. When Bunchō attacked this theme, he did so as the workaholic he was, sweating, but he was an artist whose presence was existentially vapid. Chikuden condemned Bunchō as a stylistic butterfly, superficial in his mastery of so many styles and 'applying his brush with confidence, using strong colour and deep hues, but unable in his mind [*i*] to call the past back to us'.[146] But in fact Bunchō's motion was his core, not just a surface quality.

An episode linking the Bunchō circle to a capacity to override boundaries, here those of cultural geography, is emblematic too. It centres on Hakone, eleventh of the fifty-three stations of the Tōkaidō and the most intimidating. This was the station of which a traveller recorded early in the nineteenth century that 'there is not a person alive whose hair does not stand on end out of fear when passing through Hakone for the first time'; when Thunberg crossed he found it 'like a frontier'.[147] This was the prime shogunal checkpoint for those entering the Edo region and was sturdily manned. Hakone marked a major cultural rift, that between the Edo region (Kantō) and Kyoto–Osaka (Kansai), so it was a caesura which any postulating of a shared 'Japanese culture' had to sew shut. The story tells of a second generation pupil of Bunchō, who had studied under the master's pupil Bunzan but is not himself named: this is a generic star in Bunchō's orbit. This man arrived at Hakone only to find he had lost his papers. This was enough to thwart all hope of passage, but the man tried to get across three times. The number is significant, for two attempts after initial denial came within the bounds of the crime of 'barrier-breaking' (*sekisho yaburi*), for which the penalty was death.[148] But not for someone with the free-range, 'open sesame' Bunchō talisman. The following exchange between painter and officer ensued:

'Who do you think you are?'
'A painter.'
'Who is your teacher?'
'I am taught by Bunzan, a pupil of Tani Bunchō.'
'Well, in that case, I'll only need a few fans off you!'[149]

And the guard let him through, only extorting a few paintings produced spontaneously on paper fans. Bunchō-style pictures are passports, and his name is a *passe-partout*. The guard decided he would have yet more pictures, but a woman's voice from inside ('Would it have been the guardsman's wife?') called out 'Let him through!' The truth of the story is not relevant, but it is pertinent that it was found revealing enough to remain in the Bunchō lore.

A further anecdote bears a heavier load of signification. The protagonists this time are Yashiro Hirokata and Shibano Ritsuzan, part of the same Sadanobu entourage; Bunchō himself is not named, but his presence is implicit. The location is somewhat further on, beyond Hakone. Dispatched by Sadanobu late in 1792, Hirokata and Ritsuzan hardly noticed Hakone, so easily did they slip through, in Hirokata's account of the trip, guards unopposing, and they soon arrived at a village that lay at the exact midpoint between Edo and Kyoto. This was not a historically sanctioned 'famous place'; poetic travellers seem never to have noticed the salience of its location. There are no verses on it, neither was it hailed pictorially.[150] Here, though, Ritsuzan and Hirokata mused on the single step that would take them from one half of the Tenka to the other. They denied the border of Hakone, which posed cultural and political rifts, and selected for prominence a purely mathematical point which proclaimed the new emplottedness of the Tenka's vastness. This node was an odd one, for it was not quite land or water but a small island caught between the two streams of the river Tenryū. The village was called Naka-no-Machi ('the place between') because of its island situation, but it was also in the middle of the Japanese states. Betweenness was written on the ground as mythical beings (Tenryū is literally 'heavenly dragons') soared aloft. For Sadanobu's emissaries this was hugely significant. They were at the vacant point at the epicentre of the shogun's painted world. As they crossed to the island, Hirokata reached down and picked up a flat pebble, which, he declared, would be the inkstone on which he would copy the artefacts of the Tenka, as was his task, for he and Ritsuzan were bound for Kansai to record objects to take back to Sadanobu. The inkstone's non-participation in any previous enscripting, and its emergence from a wet vacuum 'in between', ensured it a claim to objectivity that carried over to the images made with it, which would posit a culture. Ritsuzan gave the stone a name – Dragon's Footprint (Ryōtei) – and memorialized it in verse:

The flying dragon is in the Heavens,
But it has left behind a footprint, as a gift for you, my Lord.
As you grind your ink in contemplation,
Five[-coloured] clouds will spring into life.

''Five-coloured clouds' was a literary cliché for wondrous visions. That was what Hirokata would have, as he took copies for Sadanobu's *Collected Antiquities*. Interestingly, though, this was one of the few verses Ritsuzan composed *en route* in Chinese. Some proposition of otherness was imbricated in the confabulations of 'Japanese culture'.

The Sound and Sight of Continuity

The centrality of painters to projects involving plotting the lie of the cultural land and the objects scattered through it made it likely that the barriers themselves would figure as a source of subject matter. The historic barriers became inspirations for new pictures, with Shirakawa a ripe candidate. The tradition emerged, although when is unclear, of showing Shirakawa together with Nakoso and Nezu; these were called the 'three barriers of Mutsu' and had occasionally been linked in verse. The trio also worked as a painted triptych – display in threes being common. But triptychs generally consisted of a figure painting hung between two landscapes and, if this were applied to barriers, Nezu, which had the lowest poetic profile, could be dropped, leaving Shirakawa and Nakoso flanking some appropriate personage. This binary formulation heightened ambivalence, for Shirakawa, with its problematization of culture, met Nakoso, which was homophonous with the phrase 'do not come' (*nakoso*). Bunchō painted a *Nakoso Barrier*, although if it had a pendant (Shirakawa?) this is no longer extant (illus. 107).

Bunchō illustrated Nakoso's most famous poetic referent, Minamoto no Yoshiie, the great eleventh-century general, on his horse. Cherry blossoms were said to have fallen as Yoshiie passed the barrier, making him think of the harshness of warfare: at the time he was bound (pertinently for Sadanobu and Bunchō) to subdue the Ainu of Ezo. It was these juxtapositions that became the subject of the verse, which is itself inscribed above the painting in Sadanobu's hand:

In the blowing wind,
Though I remember
The Barrier of Nakoso/To which I do not come,
Along the narrowness of the pathway,
Petals of mountain cherry fall.[151]

The poet is lost in a hinterland wilderness deep in the windswept mountains whose beauty is receding around him.

The troubling feelings of any Shirakawa–Nakoso pairing would have made it fairly undisplayable in most formal contexts. It seems to have been at this time that Shirakawa (for which Sadanobu had an understandable predilection) was given a new partner. This arrangement lacked justification by any of the normal rules (poetic, punning or geographical), but it was decidedly not chosen at random. Whether it was at Sadanobu's instigation or not is uncertain, Shirakawa began to be put with Mt Ashigara. This second place was known as the spot where in the thirteenth century Toyohara no Tokiaki had taught the secret melodies of the *shō* (a classical mouth-organ) to Minamoto no Yoshimitsu, the warrior by whose efforts the shogunate had been

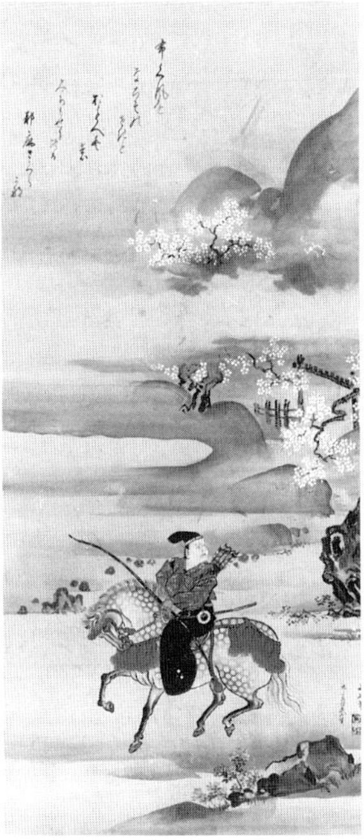

107 Tani Bunchō, inscribed by Matsudaira Sadanobu, *Nakoso Barrier, c.* 1810, hanging scroll, colour on silk. The pendant (Shirakawa?) is lost; Sadanobu inscribed Minamoto no Yoshiie's famous verse on crossing the barrier as cherry blossoms fell.

preserved; transmission took place as battle raged below. The secret melodies were saved by the skin of their teeth. Emblematically, by means of music, Tokiaki and Yoshimitsu had rescued culture in its dying gasp and ensured 'tradition' could survive. If Shirakawa sounded alarms, Ashigara rang out assurances.

The choice of music to exemplify cultural transmission was not peculiar. In Confucian thought, instruments were central to proper rituals. Regulation of music was a government duty. Melodic sound attuned the earth and planets, and a decline in music was often spoken of as a weighty portent. In the eighteenth century, the lowering level of musical taste was repeatedly inveighed against. When the great scholar Ogyū Sorai practised his archetypally lofty *shō* at home, the neighbours complained; instead of revelling in its ethereal sound, they objected that it made the cat go berserk.[152] The danger was not in the loss of skill but in a preference for vulgar cacophonies over august tunes, and this was particularly so in the Tenka where, scholars were wont to claim, classical music – uniquely – had survived, having been lost in China and Korea. The scholar Kumazawa Banzan proposed in 1709 that 'the music of the ancients remains only in this land; should a wise ruler appear on the Continent in later ages, he will come here to study the music of the ancients'.[153] Musical rupture was loss indeed. As eroticized pictures of the Floating World were ousting 'real painting', theatre and brothel music, as typified by the *shamisen*, was pushing court melody from samurai households. A whole moral order was slipping. Moriyama Takamori recorded that the *shamisen* became extremely popular at this time 'and the children of samurai families – even the heir – began learning it, so that from morning to night the noise was always with you'; in the end other theatre music caught on too, until lords 'were laying on complete accompanied dramatic performances'. Woe betide an elite whose sons 'hung out all day with such cacophonous friends'.[154]

When Sadanobu gave parties in his Garden of Bathing in Obligation, he was particular to ensure refined music, often indeed played on the *shō*. He recorded one such event in the 1780s:

> We relaxed by singing antique court melodies [*saibara*] as the cups went round and round, and when we were feeling fairly well roused the moon appeared from behind the Mountain of Sage-Play, bathing our minds in its silvery waves. All agreed it was a rare sight to see, and so we went out to the verandah to enjoy the view better. Players of the classical *koto*, the *shō* and reed pipe [*hichiriki*] boarded a small craft and rowed out into the Willow Pond.[155]

Ashigara illustrated how elegant distractions of this sort had been secured for the future in extremis.

Foreign states had music, although it was different. The way in which they formulated sound gave clues as to how their culture worked. Daikoku-ya Kōdayū was taken to concerts in Moscow and St Petersburg, and to the opera, and he noted the existence of instruments, masques and castrati.[156] Sadanobu was quite moved by such Western music as he heard played on stringed instruments, and pictures of the European contingent in Nagasaki made by those friendly to the foreigners' cause always show them enjoying orchestral performances, confirming the contention that European culture was not a contradiction in terms (illus. 108).[157]

Isaac Titsingh was overheard playing the mouth-organ in 1780.[158] If a harmonica was not quite a *shō*, the Nagasaki governor was nevertheless struck by the haunting timbre. He suggested Titsingh make a present of it to Ieharu's new heir-apparent, the boy Ienari. A box was made and the instrument sent off, and Ienari presumably learned how to play it. Some years later, Ienari married the daughter of Shimazu Shigehide, daimyo of Satsuma and an enthusiast for Western music. Baron van Reede, then in charge of the Dutch East India Company in Japan, brought from Europe for Shigehide a 'beautiful, large, standing street organ'.[159] The political wrangle this charming instrument caused is remarkable. Unstated bureaucratic obstructions forestalled handing the present over in either Nagasaki or Satsuma, and van Reede had to lug it up to Edo the following spring, 1789. By that time Sadanobu had taken over the shogunal counsel and did not want foreign music beguiling people; he forbade presentation of the organ, obliging van Reede to remove it. The instrument's final resting place is not revealed. Perhaps it was realized this was an instrument of the street, not the court, and so was improper, but then so was a harmonica. In general, between 1780 and 1789 the harmonies of Europe had come to sound wrong in the Tenka's air, which was a space for the *shō*.

There was a problem with the *shō* too. Although indigenized, it harked back to the Continent and was common to all north-east Asian states, so the pretence that it was specifically 'Japanese' would not do, for all that some aspects of its performance had only survived in Japan. This was compensated for instrumentally and also, noteworthily, pictorially. Another painting theme was devised to supplement Tokiaki and Yoshimitsu, and this might be placed alongside Ashigara instead of Shirakawa. Continuity in both Continental and indigenous music was thereby displayed for the new theme was Hakuga of the Third Rank learning the secret *biwa* melody. The *biwa* was a Japanese

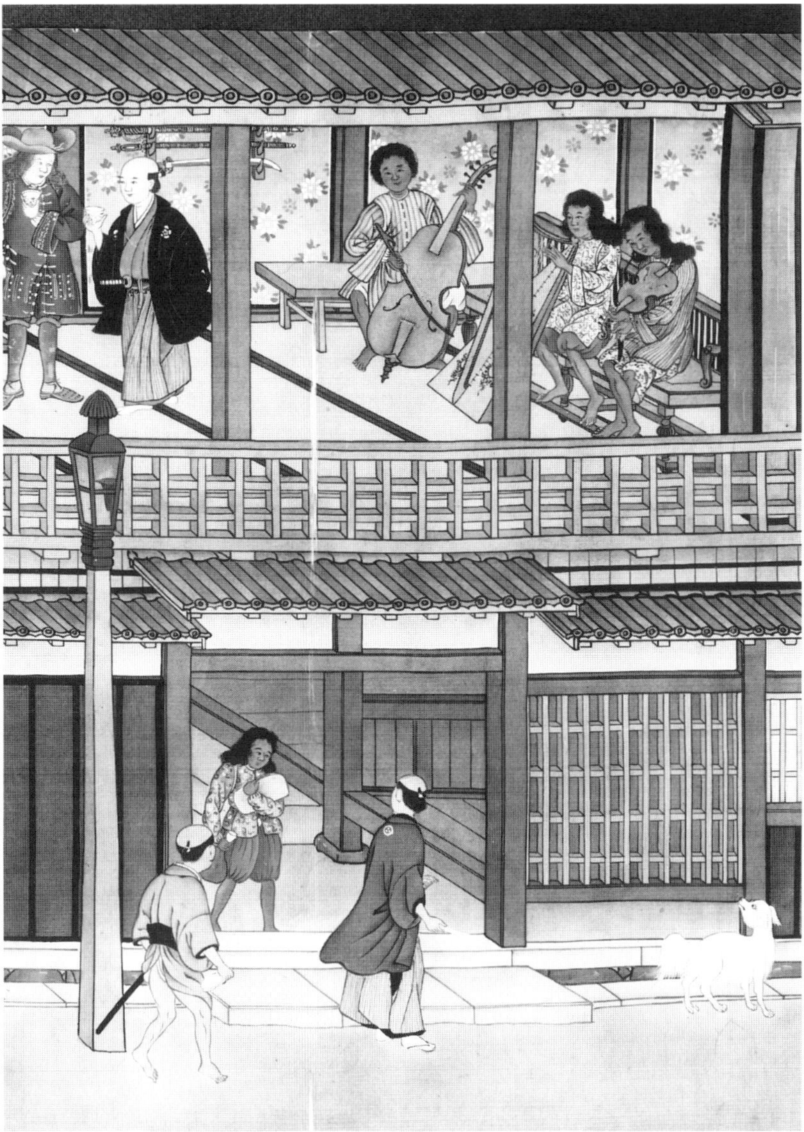

108 Section depicting Western music being played, from *Life on Dejima*, *c.* 1810, handscroll, colour on paper.

instrument and, although it resembled the Continental *pipa*, it had evolved independently. Hakuga, otherwise known as Minamoto no Hiromasa, was the grandson of the shujo Atsugimi (posthumously, Daigo); he had learned consummate *biwa* music, which was on the brink of extinction, from its sole surviving practitioner, Semimaru.[160]

Semimaru was old and blind. This happened in the tenth century and so pre-dated the *shō* transmission story. By placing the two together, culture was shown preserved in the shogunal realm, in both its Continental and local forms. Together, in pictures, these represented the shogun's painted culture, which in its diverse plaits was 'Japanese'.

The much-delayed arrival of ambassadors from Sunjo, *wang* of the Chosŏn, in 1811 offered an opportunity to produce, as always happened, several pairs of screens to reciprocate the Korean gifts. Production began three years in advance, and it was for the head of the Kano School to parcel out, and their leader was now Eisen-in's son Korenobu (many assisted, including Hiroyuki [see illus. 4]). As part of a wider reduction of diplomatic expenses, the number of screens was halved to ten: they were fantastically costly and could run to 37 *ryō* apiece.[161] The 44-year interval since the last disastrous embassy left room for a manipulation of precedents. Subjects were always auspicious, but the shifts in the Tenka's painting meant the old themes of birds and flowers were cleared out to make way for 'revived' ones. These were selected to indicate that, although it had undeniably gone through vicissitudes, shogunal culture was now alive and well. One pair of screens showed antique courtiers and scenes from *The Tale of Genji (Genji monogatari)*, which had been deployed before, but another pair showed *Hakuga of the Third Rank*.

It is not recorded how Shunjo reacted to this theme. Subsequently, Hakuga was to become a standard subject in the school calling itself 'revived *yamato-e*' (*fukkō yamato-e*). With Sadanobu long deceased, it was generally paired with the Nakoso Barrier (illus. 109).

The End

Some months before this diplomatic retinue arrived, one of Edo's prime festivals, interrupted for twelve years, was 'revived'. It had been suppressed by Sadanobu on account of rioting.[162] The festival was associated with the Hachiman Shrine in Fukagawa, which had now been rebuilt and looked splendid. Torrential rains fell, delaying festivities for several days, until the happy, if bedraggled, floats finally set off. They were adorned with montages representing scenes from legend, like the dragon king's palace and the clam's dream, and everything was in the spirit of good omen. The crowds crossed the Bridge of Eternal Generations (Eitai-bashi), which formed the ceremonial link from Fukagawa to Edo proper, and the bridge was also new, having been reconstructed at great cost in 1792.[163] Suddenly, as the maximum number of people were on it, the central section dropped out. Those

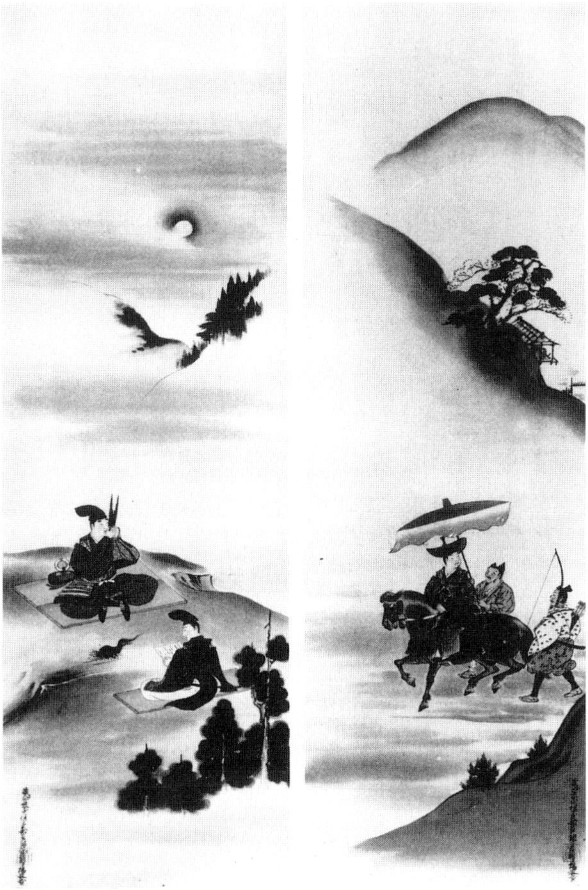

109 Reizei Tamechika, *Nakoso Barrier* and *Ashigara*, c. 1850, pair of hanging scrolls, colour on paper. Minamoto no Yoshiie crosses Nakoso Barrier; Toyohara no Tokiaki learns the *shō* from Minamoto no Yoshimitsu.

behind pushed those in front, who tumbled into the water, 'like rice through a hopper' (illus. 110). 1,500 people died in minutes.[164] All the surrounding bridges became jammed, threatening similar disasters. It was tragic. Saitō Hikomaro, who had witnessed Asama's eruption as a child, recorded seeing festal clothes, floral hats and picnic boxes floating in the river, a girl of sixteen, caught in the folds of her coloured dress, drowned, with her mother weeping beside her, and a lifeless girl of just five in the hands of her father. 'For people in their hundreds to die in the twinkling of an eye', he thought, 'is a tragedy unequalled in past or present'.[165] The shogunate sensed the portents veering sideways again. Their reaction was rapid. 'Under strict instructions from the authorities, [corpses] were lain out along the main road, without regard to age or sex, to be claimed by kin.' The bodies were disposed of with a speed some thought incompatible with sympathetic bereavement.

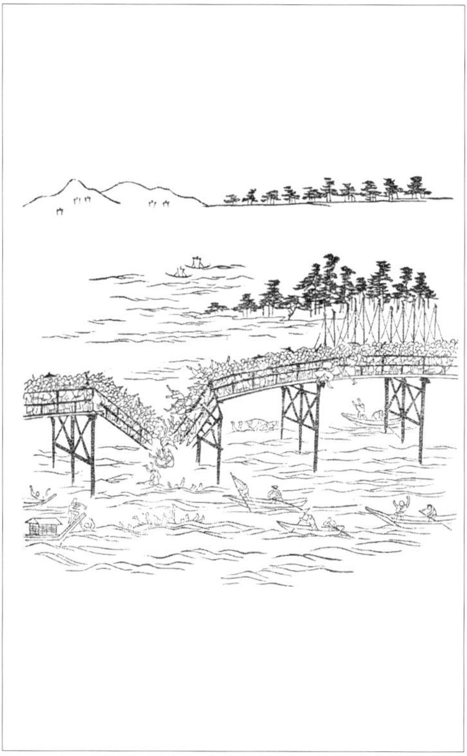

110 Toyoshima-ya Jūzaemon, Illustration from his *Yume no ukihashi furoku*, 1808, from Ichijima Kaneyoshi *et al.*, eds, *Enseki jusshū* (Kokusho Kankōkai, 1907), monochrome woodblock. Collapse of the Eitai Bridge during the Fukagawa Festival.

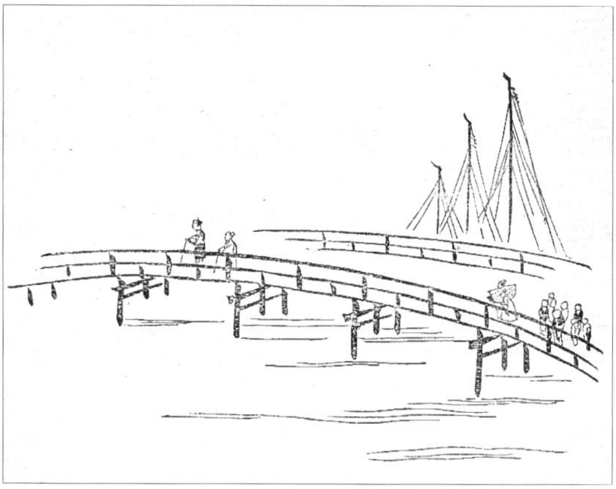

111 Ōta Nanpo, Illustration from his *Yume no ukihashi*, 1808, from Ichijima Kaneyoshi *et al.*, eds, *Enseki jusshū* (Kokusho Kankōkai, 1907), monochrome woodblock. Edo's oldest couple cross Eitai Bridge.

The Bridge of Eternal Generations was reopened the following year. Edo's oldest living couple – a man of 83 and a woman of 106 – were given the honour of being the first to walk across (illus. 111). Their age reaffirmed that the structure was indeed there for 'eternal generations'.

References

1 Matsudaira Sadanobu and the Domestic Dilemma

1 The persona of Sadanobu, as presented in this book, is unlike that in other studies, but see Herman Ooms, *The Charismatic Bureaucrat: A Political Biography of Matsudaira Sadanobu* (Chicago and London, 1975), and Haruko Iwasaki, 'Portrait of a Daimyo: Comic Fiction by Matsudaira Sadanobu', *Monumenta Nipponica*, 38 (1983), pp. 1–48; the standard biography is Shibusawa Eiichi, *Rakuō-kō den* (Iwanami, 1983), followed more recently by Fujita Satoru, *Matsudaira Sadanobu: seiji kaikaku ni idonda rōjū* (1993).

2 Yoshida Shigefusa, *Tenmei kibun kansei kibun*, in *Mikan zuihitsu hyakushū* (1976), vol. IV, p. 262; citing an unnamed official document.

3 Matsudaira Sadanobu, *Ōmu no kotoba*, in *Misonoya*, ed. Ōta Nanpo (1917), vol. III, pp. 436–37; this metaphor structures the section entitled 'On Ruling' (*sei no koto*).

4 Paul van der Velde and Cynthia Viallé, eds, *Deshima Dagregisters* (hereafter abbreviated as DDR), vol. VIII, p. 68, and vol. IX, ed. Viallé and Leonard Blussé, p. 204.

5 The other famous riposte was attributed to Ōta Nanpo (although he denied writing the verse): *Yononaka ni ka hodo urusaki mono wa nashi bunbu to iute yo mo nerarezu*. See Hamada Giichirō, *Ōta Nanpo* (1963), pp. 130–31. It was Matsura Seizan who put it about that Nanpo was the author, see *ibid.*

6 Koikawa Harumachi, *Ōmu-gaeshi bunbu no futamichi*, in *Kibyōshi, senryū, kyōka* (Iwanami, 1971), p. 176. The men are said to have bought a book called *Kyūkanchō no kotoba* ('Words of a Myna Bird').

7 For sales figures, see Matsuki Hiroshi, *Tsutaya Jūzaburō: Edo geijutsu no enshutsuka* (1988), p. 83; for Sadanobu's response, see Chapter Two below.

8 It was customary for shoguns and shujo and their relatives to be referred to by posthumous names (*ingō*); in modern Japanese shujo continue to be so designated, while shoguns are called by their living names. I have rectified this anomaly by referring to all rulers by their living names (where necessary with the posthumous name in parenthesis). Also I give 'shogun' and 'shujo' without macrons. Until the early twelfth century the shujo had been called *tennō*, which term was to be revived by Tomohito; see Fujita Satoru, *Bakumatsu no tennō* (1994) pp. 129–33.

9 *Ibid.*, p. 112.

10 Georg Langsdorff, *Voyages and Travels* (London, 1817), p. 37; the German version *Bemerkungen auf eine Reise* had appeared five years earlier.

11 Matsudaira Sadanobu, *Kan naru amari*, in *Nihon zuihitsu taisei: 2* (1974), vol. IV, p. 331; see also ibid., pp. 329–38.

12 The other two 'princes' were the Hitotsubashi and Shimizu; the *go-sanke* had the family name Tokugawa. The *go-sanke* grouping was old, but *sankyō* had been established only in Munetake's time. See, inter alia, John Whitney Hall, *Tanuma Okitsugu: Forerunner of Modern Japan* (Cambridge, MA, and London, 1955), p. 23. Hall has a chart of families and offices, see pp. 28–29.

13 There are several versions of this painting. The original is in a private collection. For a reproduction see *Sadanobu to Bunchō: Matsudaira Sadanobu to shūhen no gajintachi*, exh. cat., Fukushima Prefectural Museum (1992), no. 119, but the scene is strongly occluded by clouds and the version used here is among the clearest.

14 Matsudaira Sadanobu, *Taikan zakki*, in *Zoku nihon zuihitsu taisei* (1988), vol.

VI, p. 133; the *locus classicus* of literary lists was Sei Shōnagon, *Makura no sōshi*, known in English as the *Pillow Book of Sei Shōnagon* (*c.* 1000).

15 Yuasa Akiyoshi, *Tenmei taisei-roku*, in *Nihon keizai daiten* (1927), vol. XXII, p. 230; the actual book is undated.

16 Matsudaira Sadanobu, *Daigaku keibun kōgi*, quoted in Ōjima Yasunori, 'Jugaku no shakaika', in *Nihon no kinsei* (1993), vol. XIII, pp. 170–71.

17 Matsudaira Sadanobu, *Seigo*, in *Nihon shisō taikei* (Iwanami, 1976), vol. XXXVIII, p. 267.

18 Matsudaira Sadanobu, *Kagetsu sōshi*, in *Nihon zuihitsu taisei: 3* (1976), vol. I, p. 420.

19 Yamada Shinsukei, on Sadanobu's collection of reproductions, *Komonjo burui*, cited in Tokyo National Museum, ed., *Koga ruiju: chōsa kenkyū hōkokusho* (1990), vol. I, p. 77.

20 DDR, vol. IX, pp. 204 and 222.

21 DDR, vol. X, p. 50.

22 DDR, vol. VIII, p. 68, and vol. IX, p. 204.

23 Isaac Titsingh, *Secret Diary of Opperhoofd Isaac Titsingh*, in DDR, vol. IX, pp. 237–50; p. 239. Titsingh diplomatically recorded a different opinion in his *Illustrations of Japan*, trans. F. Shoberl (London, 1822), p. 87, noting Ieharu 'enjoys the reputation of being a good prince'.

24 Yoshida Shigefusa, *Tenmei kibun kansei kibun*, p. 261.

25 Okitsugu had been head of the commission appointed to find Ieharu's successor and had selected Ieharu in the mistaken belief he was controllable: see Hall, *Tanuma Okitsugu*, p. 38. Okitsugu was arrested in 1785 and died in 1788. For an overview see Tsuji Tatsuya, 'Politics in the Eighteenth Century' in *Cambridge History of Japan* (Cambridge, 1991), vol. IV, pp. 425–77.

26 Yoshida Shigefusa, *Tenmei kibun kansei kibun*, p. 261; Hall, *ibid.*, p. 38 and *passim*, misreads 'Okitomo' as 'Mototomo'.

27 Hall, *ibid.*, pp. 39–40. Titsingh, *Illustrations of Japan*, p. 101.

28 Yoshida Shigefusa, *Tenmei kibun kansei kibun*, p. 261.

29 Titsingh, *Illustrations of Japan*, p. 102. Sano Zenzaemon's formal name was Masakata; Titsingh spells him 'Sanno Jinzaemon'.

30 *Azuma-ji no sano no watari mizu mashite tanuma mo kirete otsuro yamashiro.* Quoted in *ibid.*, p. 149. I have modernized the romanization.

31 DDR, vol. IX, p. 62; Titsingh, *Illustrations of Japan*, p. 101.

32 DDR, vol. IX, pp. 120, 132. For a more positive interpretation of Ienari, based on surviving letters, see Mori Senzō, 'Shōgun Ienari no jinbutsu' in *Mori Senzō chosaku shū: zokuhen* (1992), vol. I, pp. 58–63.

33 For a translation and analysis see Joyce Ackroyd, *Told Around a Brushwood Fire: the Autobiography of Arai Hakuseki* (Princeton and Tokyo, 1979). Ienobu died in 1712 and was replaced by Ietsugu; by the time of Hakuseki's writing, Yoshimune was shogun.

34 Arai Hakuseki, *Oritaku shiba no ki*, in *Nihon koten bungaku taikei* (1964), vol. XCIV, pp. 240–41; actually the figure was 8,301 amnesties.

35 Moriyama Takamori, *Ama no takumo no ki*, in *Nihon zuihitsu taisei: 2* (1974), vol. XXII, p. 256.

36 For Hiroyuki's biography, see Yokota Tadashi, 'Sumiyoshi Hiroyuki: denki kenkyū: Yashiro Kōkei-sen "michi no sachi" to kanren shite', *Bijutsushi kenkyū*, 10 (1977), pp. 31–47.

37 Moriyama Takamori, *Ama no takumo no ki*, in *Nihon zuihitsu taisei*: 2 (1974), vol. XXII, pp. 200–263.

38 Arai Hakuseki, *Oritaku shiba no ki*, p. 166.

39 For the incipient shogunal navy, see Adachi Hiroyuki, *Iyō no fune: yōshikisen dōnyū to sakoku taisei* (1995), pp. 128–41.

40 *Ibid.*, pp. 146–50 (illustration p. 147).

41 Moriyama Takamori, *Ama no takumo no ki*, p. 263.
42 *Ibid., loc. cit.*
43 *Ibid.*, p. 246.
44 The compilation, *Ensei gunki-kō*, was compiled from Western sources by the Nagasaki translator Ishii Shōsuke, see Fukui Kyūzō, *Shodaimyō no gakujitsu to bungaku no kenkyū*, 2nd edn (1976), vol. I, p. 324; for Europe, see Ken Alder, *Engineering the Revolution: Arms and Enlightenment in France, 1763–1815* (Princeton, 1997), p. 25.
45 Aoki Okikatsu, *Tōmon jussaku* (1804), in *Nihon keizai daiten* (1928), vol. XX, pp. 371–2 and 384.
46 Moriyama Takamori, *Ama no takumo no ki*, pp. 243–44.
47 Fujita, *Matsudaira Sadanobu*, pp. 203–10.
48 Moriyama Takamori, *Ama no takumo no ki*, pp. 244–45, and *passim*.
49 Frank Chance, 'Tani Bunchō and the Edo School of Japanese Painting', PhD thesis, University of Washington, Seattle, 1986, p. 75; Bunchō's first major teacher was Katō Bunrei.
50 Suganuma Teizō, 'Shibun-ō no kōyo tanshō-zu', in his *Kazan no kenkyū* (1969), pp. 280–89; the set was a copy by the Osaka artist Ueno Kōkyō.
51 There is debate on this point as Bunchō's original for this scene is lost and exists only in a copy by Nomura Bunsei: see Hosono Masanobu, ed., *Tani Bunchō hitsu 'kōyo tanshō zu'* (1975), p. 86 (with illustration).
52 Matsudaira Sadanobu, *Taikan zakki*, p. 25; the journal covers 1794–97.
53 For Yoshiyasu and Tsunayoshi, see Harold Bolitho, *Treasures among Men* (New Haven and London, 1974), pp. 157–58; Bolitho ahistorically condemns Yoshiyasu as 'pandering to [the shogun's] grosser vices'.
54 *Nanga* ('southern painting') is also referred to as *bunjinga* ('literati painting'); for Sadanobu's opinions on it, see his *Taikan zakki*, p. 35.
55 Yanagisawa Kien, *Hitorine*, p. 207; the page length refers to the Iwanami edition used here.
56 Yagi Kōji, 'Wa to yō no katachi', in *Mado: nihon no katachi* (Flat Glass Association of Japan, 1997), pp. 170–84, esp. p. 170. Yagi notes one previous instance of glass windows in Edo, those of Date Tsunamune, daimyo of Sendai, in his mansion in Shinagawa, *c.* 1710; however, that site was removed from the centre of the city. The date of Sadanobu's installation is not stated, but it is said to have been done when he was an old man.
57 Timon Screech, 'Glass, Painting on Glass, and Vision in Late-Eighteenth-Century Japan', *Apollo* (1998), pp. 28–32.
58 Egbert Buys, *Nieuw en volkomen woordenboek van kunsten en weltenschappen*, 'perspective', q.v. I have used the bilingual Dutch–English version, *A New and Complete Dictionary of Terms of Art* (Amsterdam, 1768). For his reading of Buys, see Matsudaira Sadanobu, *Taikan zakki*, p. 45.
59 See for example Katsuragawa Hoshū's comments in *Hokusa bunryaku* (1970), pp. 74, 120, 205 and 221. The verse is entitled 'Glass Windows' (*Boli chuang*).
60 Guoli Gugong Bowuyuan, ed., *Qing gaozong yuzhi shiwen quanhi*, vol. I, section 15 (unpaginated). For my full translation, see Timon Screech, *The Western Scientific Gaze and Popular Imagery in Later Edo Japan: The Lens Within the Heart* (Cambridge and New York, 1996), pp. 135–36.
61 DDR, vol. IX, p. 76. Before this, panes were sometimes given but seem to have been for painting on, not looking through.
62 DDR vol. IX, pp. 184–90.
63 Screech, *Western Scientific Gaze*, p. 135.
64 Ooms, *Charismatic Bureaucrat*, p. 34.
65 Shimizu Kyōkō, 'Matsudaira Sadanobu no shinkoku shisō', in Umehara Tetsuo, ed., *Tennōsei kokka no tōgō to shihai* (1992), pp. 99–124.
66 For Koshōken's spying, see Chapter 5 below. For his pornography (written

under the name of Kibi Sanjin), see Timon Screech, *Sex and the Floating World: Erotic Images in Japan, 1700–1820* (London, 1999). p. 189.

67 Matsudaira Sadanobu, *Taikan zakki*, p. 28; for the library, see Yoshida Shigefusa, *Tenmei kibun kansei kibun*, p. 269.

68 Yoshida Shigefusa, *ibid.*, p. 270; see also Shibusawa, *Rakuō-kō den*, pp. 201–3.

69 Matsudaira Sadanobu, *Taikan zakki*, p. 28.

70 The 1749 edition was published by Yoshida Zengorō of Kyoto, see Andrew Markus, 'Representations of *Genji Monogatari* in Edo Period Fiction' (unpublished paper presented at the Eighth Oriental–Western Literacy and Cultural Relations Conference, Indiana University, 1981), p. 3.

71 Hagiwara Hiromichi, *Genji monogatari hyōshaku* (1854), quoted in Thomas Harper, '"The Tale of Genji" in the Eighteenth Century', in *18th Century Japan*, ed. C. Andrew Gerstle (Sydney, 1989). p. 108.

72 For this series of transcriptions see Shibusawa, *Rakuō-kō den*, pp. 381–87.

73 Shibano Ritsuzan, *Jisha hōmotsu kaisetsu kokuroku*, in *Zoku-zoku gunsho ruiyū*, vol. XVI (Kokusho Kankōkai, 1909), p. 157.

74 *Ibid.*, p. 158.

75 Sugita Genpaku, *Nochimigusa*, in *Nihon shomin seikatsu shiryō shūsei* (1976), vol. VII, p. 74.

76 Matsudaira Sadanobu, *Taikan zakki*, p. 56.

77 A selection of building models made for Sadanobu has recently been discovered in the Tokyo National Museum.

78 Yoshida Shigefusa, *Tenmei kibun kansei kibun*, p. 270.

79 For Buys's book (published 1769–79) see note 58 above; Shiba Kōkan said he was inspired by Buys's account of printing, see his *Seiyō gadan*, in Naruse *et al.*, eds, *Shiba Kōkan zenshū* (1994), vol. III, p. 142.

80 Matsudaira Sadanobu, *Taikan zakki*, pp. 185–86.

81 *Ibid.*, p. 45.

82 This claim is written on Kōkan's etching, 'Artist in His Studio' (1794); for a convenient reproduction see Naruse Fujio *et al.*, eds, *Shiba Kōkan zenshū*, vol. IV, p. 180.

83 Nagata Sakichi, *Nagata yūi sho*, quoted in Hosono Masanobu, *Kōkan to Denzen*, vol. CCXXXII of *Nihon no bijutsu* (1985), p. 61.

84 Shiba Kōkan, *Seiyō gadan*, p. 142; Kōkan does not date the anecdote but says it was told him by Hiraga Gennai, who died in 1779.

85 DDR, vol. IX, p. 17.

86 Sugita Genpaku, *Rangaku kotohajime*, in *Nihon koten bungaku taikei* (1964), vol. XCV, p. 478.

87 For Chūryō's entry into Sadanobu's service, see Tozawa Yukio, *Katsuragawa-ke no sekai*, (1994), p. 311. Morishima Chūryō, *Kōmō zatsuwa*, in *Bunmei genryū sōsho* (1913), vol. I, pp. 479–80.

88 Udagawa Genzui, *Ihan teikō*; this was an anatomical study based on Stephan Blankaart's *Anatomia reformata* (1687), from which the pictures were also taken. For a reproduction, see Nihon Ishi Gakkai, ed., *Zuroku nihon iji Bunka shiryō shūsei* (1977), vol. II, pp. 182–99.

89 For Tairō's life, see Katagiri Kazuo, 'Yōfū gaka Ishikawa Tairō to edo no rangakkai', pt 1, *Museum*, 227 (1970), p. 4.

90 Morishima Chūryō, preface to *Shūchin gachō*, quoted in *ibid.*, p. 14. The collection belonged to the late artist Suzuki Rinshō, whose son, Rinkō, commissioned publication.

91 Tani Bunchō, *Honchō gasan* (undated), in *Nihon garon taikan*, ed. Sakazaki Tan (Arusu, 1927), vol. II, p. 1536.

92 Rembrandt's portrait is now in the Metropolitan Museum of Art, New York; for a reproduction, see Lyckle de Vries, *Gérard de Lairesse: An Artist Between Stage and Studio* (Amsterdam, 1998), p. v.

93 For use of the *Groot schilderboek*, see Morishima Chūryō, *Kōmō zatsuwa*, p. 479, which includes figures taken from de Lairesse (omitted in edition cited here); Tani Bunchō, *Bunchō gadan*, in *Nihon shogaen* (1915), vol. II, p. 232; for Denzen, see Isozaki Yasuhiko, *Aōdō Denzen no kenkyū* (1980), fig. 108; Shiba Kōkan, *Seiyō gadan*, p. 141. For a summary of the *Groot Schilderboek* and comparison with other works of the period, see de Vries, *Gérard de Lairesse*, pp. 98–134, and Alain Roy, *Gérard de Lairesse (1640–1711)* (Paris, 1992), pp. 88–104.
94 Gérard de Lairesse (John Fitsch, trans.), *The Art of Painting in All its Branches* (London, 1783), p. 630–31.
95 Matsudaira Sadanobu, *Taikan zakki*, p. 70.
96 The robe is now in the Okura Museum; an inscription on the box states the daimyo, Ikeda Harumasa, secretly wore it for this purpose. I am grateful to Nicole Rousmaniere for alerting me to this document.
97 Matsudaira Sadanobu, *Taikan zakki*, p. 182–83. The pictures referred to are *gaku* (plaques).
98 Documents relating to the garden are reproduced in Tokyo City, ed., *Tōkyō shishi-kō, Yūen-hen* (Tokyo, 1923–8), vol II, pp. 885–97; the garden name may also be pronounced Rokuen or Rikuen. As far as I am aware, no depiction of it exists.
99 Ki Yorisuke, *Mutsu no sono hanami no ki* (1834), in *ibid.*, p. 894.
100 *Ibid.*, p. 892.
101 For the restoration of the temple, see Yashiro Hirokata, *Michi no sachi* (1885), p. 17; Hirokata had been sent there (with Shibano Ritsuzan) to inspect the temple for Sadanobu. See also Akiyama Terukazu, *Byōdō-in taikan* (Iwanami, 1992), vol. III, pp. 18–22.
102 Ki Yorisuke, *Mutsu no sono hanami no ki*, p. 892.
103 For Ōkyo and his name, see Chapter Four below.
104 Matsudaira Sadanobu, *Taikan zakki*, p. 38.
105 Fujita, *Matsudaira Sadanobu*, p. 36; the examinations were intended to be annual but lapsed in 1792.
106 Moriyama Takamori, *Ama no takumo no ki*, pp. 235–36.
107 *Mokuzu kaku shiwaza mo kyoi arawarete tsuki ni kashikoku miru me o zo moro.*
108 Titsingh, *Illustrations of Japan*, p. 149.
109 Charles Thunberg (F. and C. Rivington, trans.), *Thunberg's Travels* (London, 1795), vol. III, pp. 49, 284–85.
110 Matsudaira Sadanobu, *Taikan zakki*, pp. 29, 34.
111 Guoli Gugong Bowuyuan, ed., *Qing gaozong yuzhi shiwen quanhi*, vol. I, section 15 (unpaginated). For my full translation see Screech, *Western Scientific Gaze*, p. 159.
112 See, for example, Satō Narihiro's discussion of Western pictures in his *Chūryō manroku*, in *Nihon zuihitsu taisei: 3* (1976), vol. III, pp. 74–6.
113 For portraiture in the Dutch compound, see Shiba Kōkan's illustration in his *Saiyū ryōtan* (1794), for a convenient reproduction, see Screech, *Western Scientific Gaze*, p. 18.
114 Tani Bunchō, *Bunchō gadan*, p. 235. Note that de Lairesse was also opposed to over-prominence of portraiture: see his *Art of Painting*, pp. 146, 362.
115 Shibusawa, *Rakuō-kō den*, pp. 109–110. Osanobu's name was properly read Takenobu, but he deferentially altered it when the shogun had a son named Takechiyo.
116 *Saru ya saru, koe ni hibiku no taninaka ni utsusu sugata o saranu kage to wa.* In Matsudaira Sadanobu, *Seki no akikaze*, quoted in Ema Masamizu, ed., *Rakuō-kō isho* (1993), vol. I, p. 5. This is the version of the poem that Sadanobu recorded for posterity, and it is slightly different from that inscribed on the illustration given here. A repost verse is also recorded, *ibid.*:

Mizukagami utsuseba utsurusareta saru ono ga sugata o maitsu ni miruran.

2 Sugita Genpaku and the Dismemberment of the Present

1 Kuranari Ryōsho, *Shunsui tōroku* (1793), quoted in Rai Kiichi, 'Kinseijin ni totte no gakumon to jissen', in *Nihon no kinsei* (1993), vol. XIII, p. 32. Rai makes the link with Marie-Antoinette's notorious statement. The bird is properly the wild goose (*gan*).
2 This work has been largely forgotten in Genpaku's oeuvre; for an exception see Mori Senzō, '*Nochimigusa* wo tōshite mita Sugita Genpaku', in *Mori Senzō chosaku shū* (1989), vol. V, pp. 154–61.
3 The author is named as Kameoka Iwami, called the Lay Monk Shūzan.
4 Sugita Genpaku, *Nochimigusa*, p. 69.
5 *Ibid.*, p. 75. The traveller is described as a *gyōnin* (religious mendicant).
6 *Ibid.*, *loc. cit.*.
7 *Ibid.*, p. 65.
8 In common with other north-east Asian countries, Japan counted inclusively, with a child being one at birth.
9 For a more extended discussion of the medical discourse of this book see Timon Screech (trans. Takayama Hiroshi), *Edo no shintai o hiraku* (1997).
10 For the publishing history, see A. M. Luendijk-Elshout, '"Ontledinge" (Anatomy) as Underlying Principle of Western Medicine in Japan', in *Red-hair Medicine: Dutch–Japanese Medical Relations*, ed. H. Beukers *et al.* (Amsterdam and Atlanta, GA, 1991), pp. 27–36.
11 Sugita Genpaku, *Rangaku kotohajime*, p. 504.
12 For the pictorial sources, see Sugita Genpaku (*et al.*, trans.), *Kaitai shinsho*, in *Yōgaku* (Iwanami, 1972), vol. I, pp. 216-17.
13 Shiba Kōkan, *Shunparō hikki* (1811), p. 55; *Dokushō bōgen*, p. 24; and letter to Kaihō Seizō, dated 27/8 probably 1813, in Naruse *et al.*, eds, *Shiba Kōkan Zenshū*, vol. 2, p. 353. Kōkan criticizes Udagawa Genshin's *Ihan teikō* for the same reason. On the other hand, the famous doctor Koishi Gensui said he was first converted to Western medicine by reading the *Kaitai shinsho*, as claimed in Sugita Genpaku, *Rangaku kotohajime*, p. 506–7.
14 Sugita Genpaku, *ibid.*, p. 504. For Sukehira and Sadanobu, see Fujita, *Matsudaira Sadanobu*, pp. 137–45. Note that the dating given by Genpaku does not quite fit: see Sugita Genpaku, *ibid.*, p. 504, note 13. The term rendered 'regent' is *kanpaku*.
15 Sugita Genpaku, *ibid.*, p. 496.
16 Yōrō Takeshi, *Nihonjin no shintaikan no rekishi* (1996), especially pp. 48–68.
17 Yuasa Genzō, *Kokui-ron*, in *Nihon keizai daiten* (1928), vol. XXII, pp. 3–48.
18 Sugita Genpaku, *Rangaku kotohajime*, p. 474.
19 Sugita Genpaku, *Nochimigusa*, p. 75. He gives this figure for 1783 (during the Tenmei Famines).
20 DDR, vol. IX, pp. 40, 63; see also p. 37; rice was imported on other occasions, e.g. in 1793, see *ibid.*, vol. X, p. 48.
21 Sugita Genpaku, *Nochimigusa*, p. 75.
22 *Ibid.*, p. 65; one *shō* = 1.8 litres.
23 *Ibid.*, p. 79.
24 *Ibid.*, p. 65.
25 Moriyama Takamori, *Shizu no odamaki*, in *Nihon zuihitsu taisei: 3* (1976), vol. IV, p. 232. The epistemology of fear surrounding thieving is discussed in Fujita, *Matsudaira Sadanobu*, pp. 10–12.
26 Matsudaira Sadanobu, *Uge no hitokoto* (1942), p. 120.
27 Quoted in Fujita, *Matsudaira Sadanobu*, p. 30 (no source given). Nobuaki and Sadanobu co-held *rōjū* positions, although the former was under the latter's

orders.
28 Sugita Genpaku, *Nochimigusa*, p. 66.
29 Titsingh, *Illustrations of Japan*, p. 97; Titsingh was in Edo barely two months after the eruption.
30 *Ibid.*, pp. 71–4. Yuasa Genzō, *Kokui-ron*, p. 39. Matsudaira Sadanobu, *Taikan zakki*, p. 114.
31 Denzen's painting is undated but is almost identical to the depiction of Mt Asama in Tani Bunchō, *Meizan zufu* (1804). Two other versions also exist; for convenient reproductions see *Sadanobu to Bunchō*, exh. cat., p. 35.
32 The fullest first-hand record is that of Meishū Chōemon, *Asama-zan daishō ikken-gen*, in *Nihon shomin seikatsu shiryō shūsei* (1970), vol. VII, pp. 121–82. See also Ōishi Shinzaburō, *Tenmei sannen: asama no funkatsu* (1986).
33 Sugita Genpaku, *Nochimigusa*, p. 71.
34 Saitō Hikomaro, *Kamiyo yawa*, in *Enseki jusshū* (1987), vol. III, p. 125.
35 *Ibid.*
36 For the new shogunal observatory, see Screech, *Western Scientific Gaze*, pp. 235–39 and Watanabe Toshio, *Kinsei nihon tenmon gaku-shi* (1994), vol. II, pp. 475–85. Many Western theories were known via Chinese writings. Lalande's book was published in French in 1771 but entered Japan in the Dutch edition of four years later (entitled *Astronomia*); it is only known to have been read in detail from 1800 and was most influential in the early nineteenth-century calendrical revisions, see Nakayama Shigeru, *A History of Japanese Astronomy: Chinese Background and Western Impacts* (Cambridge, MA, and London, 1969), pp. 174, 194–5.
37 DDR, vol. IX, p. 99. Only 1/16th of the sun appeared.
38 *Ibid.*, p. 103.
39 Certainly El Niño hit in 1789–93; the intriguing possibility of a link to the French Revolution has been discussed by Richard Grove (Australian Institute of Advanced Studies): see John and Mary Gibbin, 'Weatherwatch', *Guardian*, 10/8/98, p. 15.
40 Matsudaira Sadanobu, *Taikan zakki*, p. 114.
41 Sugita Genpaku, *Nochimigusa*, p. 76.
42 See note 1 above.
43 DDR, vol. X, p. 3. For the position of the Nagasaki governor, see Toyama Mikio, *Nagasaki bugyō* (1998).
44 DDR, vol. X, p. i. For more general issues of Tokugawa international diplomacy see Ronald Toby, *State and Diplomacy in Early Modern Japan* (Stanford, 1991), and Timon Screech, *O-edo ijin ōrai*, trans. Takayama Hiroshi (Maruzen, 1995).
45 Takafuji Harutoshi, *Nikkō tōshōgū no nazo* (1996), pp. 163–65.
46 DDR, vol. VIII, p. 29, and vol. IX, pp. 64–65, 236–37.
47 DDR, vol. IX, p. 30.
48 Haga Tōru, *Hiraga Gennai* (1989), pp. 364–78.
49 Conrad Totman, *Origin of Japan's Modern Forests* (Ithaca, NY, 1989), p. 44 (quoting an unnamed source of 1785).
50 Watanabe Keiichi, *Kubota-jō monogatari* (Mumeisha, 1989), pp. 97–100.
51 DDR, vol. VIII, pp. 29, 48. The Dutch believed exhaustion of the copper supply was due to embezzlement, see *ibid.*, p. 66.
52 Titsingh, *The Secret Diary*, p. 237, in DDR, vol. IX (pp. 237–48), and *Illustrations of Japan*, p. 183.
53 Titsingh, *The Secret Diary*, *loc. cit.*
54 DDR, vol. IX, p. 149.
55 Sekio Seiichi, ed., *Oranda fūsetsu-gaki shūsei* (1977), pp. 48–49.
56 For the Circular Note (or Declaration) of Kew, see, Jonathan Israel, *The Dutch Republic: Its Rise, Greatness and Fall, 1407–1806* (Oxford, 1995), p. 1127.
57 DDR, vol. IX, p. 141.

58 For the *Phaeton's* construction, see note 59 below.

59 W. G. Aston, '"HMS Phaeton" at Nagasaki in 1808', *Transactions of the Asiatic Society of Japan*, 7 (1879), pp. 326, 328, quoting 'the official diary kept by Government House at Nagasaki', compiled by one Tokuemon, see *ibid.*, pp. 323, 326.

60 Hayashi Hikaru *et al.*, eds, *Tsūkō ichiran* (1913), vol. IV, pp. 398–408.

61 DDR, vol. X, p. 94; the American ships were not government-sponsored.

62 *Ibid.*, pp. 139, 130; the Nagasaki governor bought the watches at the knock-down price of 30 taels apiece.

63 *Ibid.*, pp. 119 and 132, note 1; the date was 1799.

64 M. Nepveu's preface to Titsingh, *Illustrations of Japan*, p. x.

65 Ibid., p. 81. The date was 1785; the Dutch refused but donated Tomohito 27 pieces of silk.

66 Shiba Kōkan was also there and recorded the event, see *Saiyū nikki*, p. 400. The cash was 100 *mon* for an adult and 50 *mon* for a child – equivalent to about a week's labouring wage; the year was 1787. This was the first such act.

67 *Ibid.*, pp. 100, 151; highly irregularly, the official Dutch log for November 1797–May 1798 was not kept (or deliberately lost), and it picks up again with Hemmij leaving Edo; he died three weeks later.

68 For Raffles in Japan, see Nigel Barley, 'White Elephants and Cannibals', in *The Golden Sword: Stamford Raffles and the East*, ed. Nigel Barley (London, 1999), pp. 77–86, and S. T. Raffles, *Raffles' Report on Japan to the Secret Committee for the English East India Company* (Kōbe, 1929). The Dutchman was Willem Wardenaar, see DDR, vol. X, pp. x–xiii. For the elephant's (non-)reception in Japan, see Screech, *Western Scientific Gaze*, p. 39, and Barley, *ibid.*, plate 7.

69 For another significant intrusion, that of the Russians, see Chapter Five below.

70 Thunberg, *Thunberg's Travels*, vol. III, p. 107. Thunberg was in Japan in 1776. He says in Europe only Dutch roads were a match.

71 DDR, vol. VIII, p. 40.

72 Sugita Genpaku, *Nochimigusa*, p. 64. DDR, vol. VIII, pp. 43–45. The ambassador was Hong Kyehui.

73 DDR, vol. X, p. 85

74 *Ibid.*, pp. 87–88.

75 DDR, vol. VIII, pp. 175, 189; Romberg would have gone anyway in his original capacity as scribe.

76 One such was Takizawa Bakin: *Kiryo manroku*, in *Nihon zuihitsu taisei: 1* (1975), vol. I, p. 152. Shiba Kōkan drew Duurkoop's grave for his *Saiyū ryōtan*; for a reproduction see Screech, *Ō-edo ijin ōrai*, pp. 82–83.

77 DDR, vol. X, p. 101; see also *ibid.*, p. 104. The substitute leader said he heard rumours of the fire while still in Edo.

78 DDR, vol. VIII, p. 176; Feith noted, 'the Japanese seem to like the look of it'.

79 *Ibid.*, p. 180.

80 Morishima Chūryū, *Kōmō zatsuwa*, p. 464. Chūryō says the information devived from his brother Hoshū (referred to as Kuniakira Hōgen); Iemoto is referred to by the posthumous name, Kōkyō-in.

81 DDR, vol. IX, p. 232.

82 Shibusawa Eiichi, *Rakuō-kō den*, p. 172.

83 DDR, vol. X, pp. 1–3. The Dutch were not averse to this arrangement since they saw the trips as expensive and useless. They nevertheless continued to come every three years, not every five.

84 Nakai Chikuzan, *Sōbō kigen* (1789), quoted in Fujita, *Matsudaira Sadanobu*, p. 165.

85 Fujita, *ibid.*, p. 170.

86 For several illustrations (including that given here), see Hamada Giichirō, *Kibyōshi edaisen shū* (1979), pp. 129–130.

87 Tōrai Sanna, *Tenka ichimen kagami umehachi*, in *Edo no gesaku ehon*, ed. Koike Masatane *et al.* (1982), vol. III, p. 206–7. The text also appears here (illus. 35). Sanna also parodied other disasters (urban revolts and eruption of Mt Asama). The publisher is presumed to be Tsutaya, although this is unsure; see Tanahashi Munehiro, *Kibyōshi sōran* (1989), vol. II, p. 47.

88 For the publishing history of the story, see Tanahashi, *ibid.*, p. 48.

89 Ōtsuki Gentaku, *Rangaku kaitei*, in *Yōgaku: 1* (Iwanami, 1976), vol. LXIV, p. 340. Gentaku transliterated the proverb without using Roman letters. Shiba Kōkan's Dutch reads: *men moet eeten om te leeven maar nie [leeven] om te eeten*. Kōkan also recorded this in *Dokushō bōgen* (1810), p. 23, correcting '*eeten*' and '*leeven*' to '*eten*' and '*leven*'. If Kōkan's painting is from 1783, there may be a political message, since the failure of a Dutch ship to arrive in 1782 with a new leader led to cancellation of the trip to Edo, and, if so, the two men are Romberg and Petrus Chassé (leader and physician to the embassy of 1784).

90 Titsingh, *Illustrations of Japan*, p. 86.

91 Bolitho, *Treasures Among Men*, p. 191; DDR, vol. VIII, p. 103, and vol. IX, p. 240. Note, however, Titsingh, *ibid.*, p. 86.

92 Yuasa Akiyoshi, *Tenmei taisei-roku*, p. 153; DDR, vol. X, p. 27. The sugar ban was announced after Ieharu's death.

93 Sugita Genpaku, *Nochimigusa*, p. 80.

94 Uchiyama Mikiko, 'Engeki-shi no naka no tennō', in *Nihon no kinsei* (1991), vol. II, pp. 298–99; Thunberg, *Thunberg's Travels*, vol. III, p. 207; Bolitho, *Treasures*, p. 194; *Tokugawa jikki*, vol. VI, pp. 497–99.

95 Sugita Genpaku, *Nochimigusa*, p. 69.

96 *Ibid., loc. cit.*

97 *Ibid.*, p. 77.

98 DDR, vol. VIII, p. 188.

99 *Ibid.*, p. 193.

100 In 1784 this resulted in postponement of the Dutch reception in Edo, see DDR, vol. ix, p. 53.

101 Sugita Genpaku, *Nochimigusa*, pp. 79–80.

102 *Ibid.*, p. 64. This was not in fact one of Edo's worst fires.

103 For these two events, see *ibid.*, pp. 64, 69; the earlier occurrence was in 1764.

104 Buyō Inshi, *Seiji kenbunroku*, quoted in Takeuchi Makoto, 'Festivals and Fights: The Law and the People of Ido', in *Edo and Paris: Urban Life and the State in the Early Modern Era*, ed. James McClain *et al.* (Ithaca and London, 1994), pp. 404–5.

105 Yuasa Genzō, *Kokui-ron*, p. 6.

106 Sugita Genpaku, *Nochimigusa*, p. 82.

107 Shiba Kōkan, *Mugen dōjin hikki*, in *Shiba Kōkan Zenshū*, ed. Naruse Fujio *et al.* (Yasaka Shobō, 1993), vol. II, p. 117.

108 Takeuchi, 'Festivals and Fights', pp. 387–97.

109 Yuasa Akiyoshi, *Tenmei taisei-roku*, quoted in Fujita, *Matsudaira Sadanobu*, p. 111. Akiyoshi cites this as verbatim from Sadanobu. Note that there is no connection between Yuasa Genzō and Yuasa Akiyoshi.

110 Mizuno Tamenaga, *Yoshi no zasshi*, (*c.* 1790), quoted in Takeuchi, 'Festivals and Fights', p. 402. For the law on delinquency, see *ibid.*, p. 401.

111 For a general treatment, see Tsunoyama Sakae, *Tokei no shakaishi* (1984), pp. 103–18.

112 Ōta Nanpo, *Ichiwa ichigon*, supplementary vol. IV of *Nihon zuihitsu taisei* (1978), p. 197. This enormous work was compiled over many years but completed in 1820.

113 Su Koppei, *Myōmyō kidan*, in *Nihon zuihitsu taisei: 3* (1976), vol. XI, p. 370.

114 Matsudaira Sadanobu, *Seigo*, p. 257.

115 Sugita Genpaku, *Nochimigusa*, p. 66.

116 *Ibid., loc. cit.*
117 Hakuseki's deposition is translated in Ryusaku Tsunoda (*et al.*), *Sources of Japanese Tradition*, Introduction to Oriental Civilizations (New York and London, 1958), p. 475–76; for Kyōsō's opposite view, see Kate Nakai, *Shogunal Politics: Arai Hakuseki and the Premises of Tokugawa Rule*, Harvard East Asian Monographs (Cambridge, MA, and London, 1988), p. 216. The earlier use was Shōhō (1644–48).
118 *Nengō wa yasuku nagashi to kawaredomo shoshoku kōchi ima ni meiwaku*, quoted (anonymously) in Sugita Genpaku, *Nochimigusa*, p. 68.
119 *Ibid.*, p. 69.
120 Saitō Gesshin, ed., *Bukō nenpyō*, vol. XII of *Edo sōsho* (1964), p. 184. The anniversary of an era's beginning was not the same as the first day of year two: eras did not necessarily begin on the first day of the first month.
121 Imadegawa Sanetane, *Sanetane kō ki*, quoted in Fujita, *Matsudaira Sadanobu*, p. 151.
122 Santō Kyōden, *Kōshijima toki ni aizome* (1798), illustrated by the author (signing Masanobu). For a reproduction, see Koike Masatane *et al.*, eds, *Edo no gesaku ehon* (1984), supp. vol. II, pp. 129–60.
123 Yoshida Shigefusa, *Tenmei kibun kansei kibun*, pp. 255, 258, 269, 271.
124 DDR, vol. IX, pp. 204, 222; vol. X, p. 50.
125 Matsudaira Sadanobu, *Taikan zakki*, p. 43.
126 Kimuro Bōun, *Mita kyō monogatari*, in *Nihon zuihitsu taisei: 3* (1976), vol. VIII, p. 8.
127 *Ibid.*, p. 20.
128 Shiba Kōkan, *Saiyū nikki*, pp. 78, 195–204; this quotation, p. 202.
129 This time sequence follows that given in Fujishima Munenobu, *Tenmei taika no ki*, in *Kansei bungaku-sen*, ed. Fujishima Masao (Kyoto, 1974), v. 141–44; this is a section of his larger *Munenobu no nikki*.
130 Kimuro Bōun, *Mita kyō monogatari*, p. 8.
131 Fujishima Munenobu, *Tenmei taika no ki*, p. 154.
132 Yuasa Akiyoshi, *Tenmei taisei-roku*, p. 261; the original units of measurement are 5 *ri* in 1 *koku* 6 *bu*.
133 DDR, vol. IX, p. 153.
134 Titsingh, *Illustrations of Japan*, p. 101. Published in 1812.
135 DDR, vol. IX., p. 154, and City of Kyoto, ed., *Kyōto no rekishi* (1973), vol. VI, p. 63; see *ibid.* for a modern map of the fire.
136 Tachibana Nankei, *Hokusō sadan*, in *Tōzai yūki, hokusō sadan* (Yūhōdō, 1913), p. 207.
137 Fujishima Munenobu, *Tenmei taika no ki*, pp. 141–44.
138 Tachibana Nankei, *Hokusō sadan*, p. 174.
139 *Kaeri kite kiki mo sen ni some-tsukashiki kemuri no moreshi ya to no uguisu.* Ban Kōkei, *Yagutsuchi no arabi: Tenmei hachi-nen ni-gatsu shojun*, in *Kansei bungaku-sen*, ed. Fujishima Masao (Kyoto, 1974), p. 126.
140 *Moto no iro ni haya fuki-kaese haru no kaze hana no miyako mo chiri-chiri no yo. Ibid., loc. cit.*
141 *Kesa mireba yakeno no hara to narinikeri koko ya kinō no tamashiki no tei. Ibid., loc. cit*, and Tachibana Nankei, *Hokusō sadan*, p. 202; Nankei's phrase is *kangai no amari*.
142 Machijiri Ryōgen, *Tenmei uutsu kōki*, in *Kansei bungaku-sen*, ed. Fujishima Masao (Kyoto, 1974), p. 119.
143 Ueda Akinari, *Kyōto taika no ki*, in *Kansei bungaku-sen*, ed. Fujishima Masao (Kyoto, 1974), p. 138.
144 Machijiri Ryōgen, *Tenmei uutsu kōki*, in *Kansei bungaku-sen*, ed. Fujishima Masao (Kyoto, 1974), pp. 119–25.
145 DDR, vol. IX, p. 155.

146 Matsura Seizan, *Kasshi yawa* (1977 edn), vol. I, p. 126. Seizan says the ball was 3–4 *shaku* (about 2 m).
147 City of Kyoto, ed., *Kyōto no rekishi*, vol. VI, p. 64.
148 For Tomohito's childhood period at the Shōgo-in, see Fujita, *Bakumatsu no tennō*, p. 47; for his feet, see DDR, vol. IX, p. 155 (wrongly stating no shujo's feet had ever previously touched the ground).
149 DDR, vol. IX, p. 153. The Dutch record states Tomohito went on to take refuge on Mt Hiei but later realizes this was a rumour; he had moved to the Shōren-in, see p. 154.
150 For details of the temporary residences, see Yuasa Akiyoshi, *Tenmei taisei roku*, pp. 261–62. The ex-shujo's suite at the Shōren-in is extant; she then moved to the Rinkaku-ji.
151 Yoshida Shigefusa, *Tenmei kibun kansei kibun*, p. 269.
152 DDR, vol. IX, pp. 159–60.
153 Ban Kōkei, *Yagutsuchi no arabi*, p. 127; Sugita Genpaku, *Nochimigusa*, p. 2.
154 Kamo no Chōmei, *Hōjō-ki*, translated by A. L. Sadler, *The Ten Foot Square Hut and the Tales of the Heike* (Tokyo and Rutland, VT, 1972) p. 1.
155 Ban Kōkei, *Yagutsuchi no arabi*, p. 130.
156 See City of Kyoto, ed., *Kyōto no rekishi*, vol. VI, p. 124. Outlying temples were saved, notably Kiyomizu-dera and Kōdai-ji, and most of Nijō Castle was saved, thanks to its moat.
157 Kamihira Chie, 'Kyōto oranda-juku no shokumu', in *Ronshū nihon no yōgaku*, ed. Arizaka Takamichi *et al.* (Osaka, 1995), vol. III, p. 156. Shiba Kōkan, *Saiyū nikki*, p. 384 (Kōkan miswrites the name as 'gleaming generations', not 'high terraces').
158 DDR, vol. IX, p. 186; the Dutch stayed at the Hōrin-ji, see Kamihira, 'Kyōto oranda-juku', p. 156 (their compound was not rebuilt until 1806). Romberg refers to the Kōdai-ji only as the 'burial place of Taiko sama' (Hideyoshi).
159 Yoshida Shigefusa, *Tenmei kibun kansei kibun*, p. 269.
160 Yuasa Akiyoshi, *Tenmei taisei-roku*, pp. 220–21. DDR, vol. IX, pp. 154, 158.
161 DDR, *ibid.*, p. 163.
162 For this opinion of the Hōkō-ji, see DDR, vol. X, p. 109.
163 Ōta Kinjō, *Gosō manpitsu*, in *Nihon zuihitsu zenshū* (1928), vol. XVII, p. 32.
164 The Great Buddha of Nara is 16 m, and that of Kamakura 11.5 m in height.
165 Yoshida Shigefusa, *Tenmei kibun kansei kibun*, p. 283. Shigefusa took the fireballs as accompaniments to the Kyoto fire.
166 A more finished version of the work is preserved in the Mitsui Bunko, Tokyo.
167 Anon., *Heike monogatari*, trans. by Helen Craig McCullough, *The Tale of the Heike* (Stanford, 1988), pp. 195–6 (adapted). The Nara hall and statue were rebuilt, and they existed in the late eighteenth century (as they do today).

3 Image Management for Royal Power

1 Thunberg, *Thunberg's Travels*, vol. III, p. 198.
2 *Ibid.*, p. 210, Thunberg gives the shogun his court family name, Minamoto. For Iemoto's name (Saijō-dono), see Matsudaira Sadanobu, *Uge no hitokoto*, p. 44.
3 For exhumed skeletons, see Suzuki Hisashi, *Zōjō-ji: Tokugawa shōgun hi to sono zuihin, zuitai* (Tokyo, 1967).
4 DDR, vol. IX, pp. 102, 132, 187.
5 Narishima Morimichi *et al.*, eds, *Tokugawa jikki* (1976), vol. X, p. 499.
6 DDR, vol. IX, p. 161.
7 I have laid out some thoughts on this subject in Timon Screech, 'Shogun no zuzō o utsusu', trans. Takayama Hiroshi, in *Edo no kirikuchi*, ed. Takayama Hiroshi (Maruzen, 1994), pp. 259–73.
8 For the importance of gates, see William H. Coaldrake, *Architecture and*

Authority in Japan (London and New York, 1996), pp. 193–207.

9 Anon., *Nihongi*, W. G. Aston (trans.), *Nihongi: Chronicles of Japan from the Earliest Times to AD 697* (Rutland, VT, and Tokyo, 1972), p. 279.

10 Coaldrake, *Architecture and Authority*, p. 132; 58.4 m to be exact.

11 *Ibid.*, p. 136; Coaldrake sees non-rebuilding as 'new pragmatism'.

12 Ōta Kinjō, *Gosō manpitsu* (1823), in *Nihon zuihitsu zenshū* (1928), vol. XVII, pp. 32–3. Geomancy is *ekiri*; the palaces were Jianzhan and Yuqingzhaoying.

13 Coaldrake, *Architecture and Authority*, p. 143.

14 T. Fujitani, *Splendid Monarchy: Power and Pageantry in Modern Japan* (Berkeley, CA, and London, 1996). pp. 66–8; Fujitani does not discuss Edo precedents.

15 Moriyama Takamori, *Ama no takumo no ki*, pp. 237–8.

16 William Coaldrake, 'Architecture and Tokugawa Law', p. 253–61.

17 Moriyama Takamori, *Ama no takumo no ki*, p. 243.

18 Thunberg, *Thunberg's Travels*, vol. III, p. 144.

19 Moriyama Takamori, *Ama no takumo no ki*, p. 244.

20 *Ibid.*, *loc. cit.*

21 Ōta Nanpo, *Ichiwa ichigon*, p. 197.

22 *Ibid.*, *loc. cit.*

23 DDR, vol. IX, p. 206; mercury mirrors were called *unubore* ('vanity') mirrors.

24 Sugita Genpaku, *Nochimigusa*, p. 81.

25 *Ibid.*, p. 80.

26 Screech, *Sex and the Floating World*, pp. 116–17.

27 Moriyama Takamori, *Shizu no odamaki*, p. 240.

28 See Chapter Two above.

29 Shiba Kōkan, *Oranda tsūhaku*, in Naruse *et al.*, eds., *Shiba Kōkan zenshū* (1994), vol. III, p. 164.

30 Hosono Masanobu, in *Kōkan to Denzen*, p. 6120, also discusses the origin of this print, which is actually a mirror-image, with minor alterations, of Robert Sayer and John Bowles's *Rome in Its Original Splendour* (c. 1770).

31 Anon., *Katsuragawa kafū*, quoted in Tozawa Yukio, *Katsuragawa-ke no sekai*, p. 210. Kōdayū was allowed out of confinement once annually, see Reinier Hesserlink, 'A Dutch New Year at the Shirandō Academy; 1 January 1795', *Monumenta Nipponica*, 50 (1995), pp. 198–223. Notably, in 1793 Sadanobu enlisted Morishima Chūryō on to his staff.

32 For Hoshū and Thunberg, see Thunberg, *Travels*, vol. III, p. 206, and Morishima Chūryō, *Hōgu-kago* (undated), in *Zoku enseki jusshū* (1980), vol. II, p. 172.

33 Katsuragawa Hoshū, *Hokusa bunryaku*, pp. 90–91.

34 *Ibid.*, p. 82. See also Anne Betty Weinshenker, *Falconet: His Writings and His Friend Diderot* (Geneva, 1996), pp. 2–5, 28–29.

35 Katsuragawa Hoshū, *Hokusa bunryaku*, p. 92; 'Peter's Court' is given by Hoshū in a Japanese transliteration of the Dutch 'Petershof'.

36 Katsuragawa Hoshū, *Hokusa bunryaku*, p. 86.

37 *Ibid.*, *loc. cit.*

38 Ōtsuki Gentaku was assisted by Shimura Kōkyō.

39 Shiba Kōkan, *Oranda tsūhaku*, p. 155.

40 Tachihara Suiken, *Yūrin zatsuwa*, in *Nanban kōmō shiryō* (1930), vol. I, p. 31.

41 The sale of Western coins is attested in Koikawa Yukimachi, *Sakaemasu megane no toku* (1790), p. 14 *verso*; for a reproduction, see Screech, *Western Scientific Gaze* (Cambridge and New York, 1996), fig. 105.

42 Morishima Chūryō, *Hōgu-kago*, pp. 168–69; anecdote undated.

43 For the daimyo's collecting, see Tōno Haruyuki, 'Kahei shūshū-ka no Kutsuki Masatsuna', in his *Kahei no nihonshi* (1997), pp. 211–27. Masatsuna also collected Japanese coins, and this portion of his holdings has recently (January, 1999) been discovered in the British Museum (identified as the Tanba

Collection: that being the province of Fukuchiyama). Titsingh collected coins, and Thunberg's inaugural lecture to the Swedish Royal Academy (1779) was on that subject (he gave several coins to King Gustav III): see Katarina Blomberg, 'Carl Peter Thunberg', in *Contemporary European Writing on Japan*, ed. Ian Nish (Ashford, 1988), p. 21. Satō Narihiro also noted that the material of European coins (silver, not copper as in Japan) looked odd: see his *Chūryō manroku*, p. 49.

44 Hattori Nankaku, 'Gotōshi-jo', in *Nankaku-sensei bunshū*, vol. VII of *Kinsei juka bunshū shūsei* (1985), p. 64; I am grateful to Timothy Barrett for the Confucian observation.

45 Peter Jay, *Downcast Eyes: The Denigration of Vision in Twentieth-Century French Thought* (Berkeley, CA, and London, 1993), p. 94; Jay mistakenly has the king's face on paper currency.

46 Shiba Kōkan, *Saiyū nikki*, p. 398.

47 Ieharu died on twenty-third day of the eighth month, and was buried on the fourth of the tenth; his death was announced in Edo on the eighth of the ninth, but only fully proclaimed after the burial; Ienari was inducted on the fifteenth of the fourth month 1787, and Ieyasu's feast day was the seventeenth. See DDR, vol. IX, pp. 120–23 and 136.

48 Morishima Chūryō, *Keirin manroku*, in *Nihon zuihitsu taisei: 2* (1975), vol. I, p. 656.

49 Motoori Norinaga, *Naobi no mitama* (1771, in *Readings in Tokugawa Thought*, Selected Papers, vol. IX, Center for East Asian Studies, University of Chicago (Chicago, 1993), p. 126.

50 See Sawada Akira, *Nihon gaka jiten* (1987), vol, I, pp. 1, 471; Toshimoto flourished from 857 to 859. For the early history of the Tosa, see John M. Rosenfield, 'Japanese Studio Practice: the Tosa Family and the Imperial Painting Office', in *The Artist's Workshop*, ed. Peter Lukehard, Studies in the History of Art, 38 (Washington, DC, 1993), pp. 79–101.

51 The principal recent sources on the Kano School are Takeda Tsuneo, *Kano-ha kaiga shi* (1995), and Matsuki Hiroshi, *Kano-ke no chi to katana* (1994).

52 Matsudaira Sadanobu, *Uge no hitokoto*, p. 31.

53 For the Kyō–Kano, see Takeda, *Kano-ha*, pp. 274–300; Tan'yū's grandfather, Kano Eitoku, adopted Sanraku.

54 Takeda, *Kano-ha*, p. 292; this did not last, however, for under the ninth head they stopped, although continuing to work for courtiers, particularly the Kujō.

55 *Ibid.*, p. 295; Fujioka Sakutarō, *Kinsei nihon kaiga-shi* (Seidosha, 1967), p. 40. Tansō died in 1797, aged 25.

56 Sakakibara Satoru, 'Kano-ha goyō eshi no koto', *Kobijutsu*, 100 (1991), pp. 41–42; the rules date from 1858. The Kano in Chikuzen were called the Kuroda School.

57 Kobayashi Tadashi, 'Gazoku no kōō: honga to ukiyo-e', in *Nihon no kinsei* (1993), vol. XII, pp. 351–57.

58 Kano Yasunobu, *Gadō yōketsu*, in *Nihon kaigaron taisei* (1997), vol. IV, p. 10.

59 *Ibid., loc. cit.*

60 For another discussion of this work see Kobayashi, 'Gazoku no kōō', pp. 370–73.

61 Yanagisawa Kien, *Hitorine*, in *Kinsei zuisō-shū* (Iwanami, 1965), vol. XLVI, p. 164.

62 Daiten Tōjō, *Koun-rō kō*, quoted in Satō Yasuhiro, 'Jūhasseiki no zen'ei shinwa', in *Edo bunka no hen'yō: jūhasseiki nihon no keiken*, ed. Momokawa Takahito *et al.* (1994), p. 122.

63 This painting is now in the Etsuko and Joe Price Collection; for a convenient illustration and discussion, see Money Hickman and Yasuhiro Satō, *The Paintings of Jakuchū* (New York, 1989), pp. 46–47.

64 Tanomura Chikuden, *Sanchūjin jōsetsu*, in *Nihon garon taisei*, ed. Kobayashi Tadashi *et al.* (1966), vol. VII, p. 35.
65 Morishima Chūryō, *Keirin manroku*, p. 656; 'make fools out of' is *azamuku*.
66 Nakabayashi Chikutō, *Chikutō garon*, in *Nihon garon taikan*, ed. Sakazaki Tan (Arusu, 1927), vol. I, p. 204.
67 Anon., *Kanpo enkyō fūzokushi*, quoted in Kobayashi Tadashi, 'Akedemizumu no kōzai: kano-ha no baai', in his *Edo kaiga shiron* (1983), p. 32.
68 Ueda Akinari, *Tan daishō shinroku*, in *Ueda Akinari shū* (Iwanami, 1959), vol. LVI, p. 291.
69 See note 5 above.
70 Yanagisawa Kien, *Rikyō nikki danpen*, quoted in Satō Yasuhiro, 'Jūhasseiki no zen'ei shinwa', p. 137.
71 Mitsui Takafusa, *Chōnin kōken roku*; see E. S. Crawcour (trans.), 'Some Observations on Merchants: A Translation of Mitsu Takafusa's "Chōnin Kōken Roku"', *Transactions of the Asiatic Society of Japan: Series 3* (1961), vol. VIII, p. 62. The work was compiled in 1727 or 1728, but this episode appears only in the late eighteenth-century edition, see *ibid.*, p. 61; one million *ryō* is an impossibly vast sum.
72 *Zashikimochi nise Tan'yū o kakete oki*. Okada Hajime, ed., *Haifū yanagi-daru* (1978), 21/3; see also 2/168.
73 *Shittaburi oya-Hōgen wa motsu to ii. Ibid.*, 12/181.
74 Note that the triptych was a luxury format in the eighteenth century but barely existed in Ko-Hōgen's day; use of a large motif with no background is post-Tan'yū.
75 Takeda, *Kano-ha*, p. 344. Ambassadors came to congratulate Ieshige on his elevation to shogun in 1745; the *wang* was Yongjo. The previous embassy was in 1719. I follow the pronunciation 'Terunobu', given in Kobayashi Tadashi, 'Gazoku no kōō', p. 351, although Sawada, *Nihon gaka jiten*, vol. I, p. 534, gives 'Hidenobu'.
76 *Ibid.*, pp. 245, 249, 344; Eisen-in the Elder is also called Hisanobu, Jusen-in and Harunobu.
77 Narishima *et al.*, eds, *Tokugawa jikki*. The passage is difficult as names are given inaccurately; I follow Matsuki, *Kano-ke*, p. 194.
78 Ueda Akinari, *Tan daishō shinroku*, p. 291.
79 Nakabayashi Chikitō, *Chikutō garon*, p. 204.
80 Nakayama Kōyō, *Gadan keiroku*, in *Nihon zuihitsu taisei: 1* (1975), vol. IV, pp. 194–95.
81 Narishima *et al.*, eds, *Tokugawa jikki*, quoted in Matsuki, *Kano-ke*, p. 194; the term rendered 'teaching treatise' is *kyōron*.
82 See *ibid.*, pp. 153, 195. The secondary sources are not in agreement: that Takegawa became Kobikichō is sure, although once the latter name was coined, it was retrospectively applied to Takegawa painters (and is still in modern scholarship), so that Eisen-in is sometimes called the fifth, not first, Kobikichō head; the Takegawa founder, Naonobu, is then the 'first'. The atelier certainly relocated to Kobikichō under Eisen-in, and it would hardly have used that toponym before.
83 Takeda, *Kano-ha*, p. 383.
84 Matsuki, *Kano-ke* p. 195; these words were inscribed on Eisen-in's grave.
85 Takeda, *Kano-ha*, p. 258.
86 Matsudaira Sadanobu, *Uge no hitokoto*, p. 31.
87 Matsudaira Sadanobu, *Taikan zakki*, p. 135.
88 Moriyama Takamori, *Shizu no odamaki*, p. 261.
89 For Eishi, see Chapter Two above. For Rinshō, see Moriyama Takamori, *Shizu no odamaki*, p. 251. Eisen-in's son and successor Yōsen-in Korenobu (also pronounced Tadanobu) was nevertheless regarded as a serious painter.

90 The work, *Waka ebisu*, is a *kyōka* book of five pages, each done in a different style (Tosa and *ukiyo-e* are included). It closes with a screen 'by Eisen'; see Roger Keyes, 'Envisioning the Past: Utamaro's Album "Waka ebisu"', in *A Sheaf of Japanese Papers: In Tribute to Heinz Kaempfer on his 75th Birthday*, ed. Matthi Forrer *et al.* (The Hague, 1979), p. 89.
91 Donald Shiveley, 'Bakufu versus Kabuki', *Harvard Journal of Asiatic Studies*, 18 (1955), pp. 326–56.
92 Andrew Gerstle, 'Flowers of Edo: Kabuki and its Patrons in the Eighteenth Century', in *18th Century Japan*, ed. C. Andrew Gerstle (Sydney, 1989), pp. 33–50.
93 See Hanasaki Kazuo, *Edo no kagama-jaya* (1992), pp. 32–7.
94 Sugita Genpaku, *Nochimigusa*, p. 74.
95 Matsura Seizan, *Kasshi yawa* (1930 edition), vol. VII, pp. 31–2.
96 Kitamura Kashiro, *Satsuki ame jisshū* (1868), in *Shin enseki jusshū* (1982), vol. II, p. 110; although this source is late, Kashiro cites it as the testimony of Okitsugu's doctor, Chiga Dōyū.
97 Hall, *Tanuma Okitsugu*, p. 39.
98 Moriyama Takamori, *Shizu no odamaki*, p. 261.
99 Matsuki, *Kano-ke*, p. 194.
100 *Urimono ni yoshichō ura omote aru to ii*. This *senryū* is quoted without source in Hiratsuka Yoshinobu, *Nihon ni okeru nanshoku no kenkyū* (1987), p. 31.
101 Tachibana Nankei, *Hokusō sadan*, p. 335.
102 *Ibid.*, p. 38.
103 *Ibid.*, p. 50; Nankei confusingly refers to both Hiroyuki and his father as 'Sumiyoshi Naiki' (the name was used hereditarily).
104 For Suiken's career, see Victor Koschmann, *The Mito Ideology: Discourse, Reform, and Insurrection in Late Tokugawa Japan, 1790–1868* (Berkeley, CA, and London, 1987), p. 36; note that Koschmann mistakenly gives Suiken's birthdate as 1774 rather than 1744.
105 Tachihara Suiken, Shikundō kōsodan (undated), p. 4; this MS work is unpaginated, and the page numbers here refer to sheets in the National Diet Library's copy.
106 *Ibid.*, pp. 29, 33.
107 Kyōsho's career is little studied, but see *Gaka to tabi: egakareta shizen 2*, exhib. cat., Suntory Museum, Tokyo (Tokyo, 1990), p. 69.
108 Kano Einō, *Koga biko*, quoted in Money Hickman, 'The Paintings of Soga Shōhaku', PhD diss. (Harvard, 1976), p. 25 (adapted).
109 *Koma tomete sode uchiharau kage mo nashi sano no watari no yuki no yūgure*. The verse is no. 671 in Fujiwara Teika, ed., *Shin kokinshū* (1306).
110 Motoori Norinaga, *E no koto*, in *Nihon garon taikan*, ed. Sakazaki Tan (Arusu, 1927), vol. I, p. 190.
111 *Ibid.*, p. 191.
112 Sadanobu recorded this as a preface to the scrolls, quoted in Takasu Toyomori, 'Rakuō-kō to koga no mōsha ni tsuite', *Chūō bijutsu*, 38 (1936), pp. 9–10.
113 Matsudaira Sadanobu, *Taikan zakki*, p. 72.
114 *Ibid.*, p. 35.
115 *Ibid.*, *loc. cit.*
116 For Eishi's biography, see Naitō Masato, 'Chōbunsai Eishi no iwayuru "yoshiwara-gayoi zukan" ni tsuite', *in Nikuhitsu ukiyo-e taikan*, ed. Kobayashi Tadashi (1996), vol. III, and Screech, *Sex and the Floating World*, pp. 57, 73.
117 Naitō, *ibid.*, p. 240.
118 Kobayashi Tadashi, '"Sumidagawa ryōgan zukan" no seiritsu to tenkai', *Kokka*, 1172 (1993), pp. 5–22.
119 The retired shujo, Toshiko (posthumously, Go-Sakuramachi), was in office

1762–70; for her character, see Fujita, *Bakumatsu no tennō*, pp. 51–52. For the title *tenran*, see Naitō, 'Chōbunsai Eishi', p. 240, where Toshiko is referred to as *sentō* (i.e. ex-shujo).

120 See Chapter One above.

121 For Keisai/Masayoshi's life, see Uchida Kinzō, 'Kuwagata Keisai kenkyū: okaka-eshi jidai no katsudō o megutte: 2', *Kokka*, 1159 (1992), pp. 9–21.

122 *Ibid., loc. cit.* The scroll is called *Tōshōgū engi emaki*.

123 Matsudaira Sadanobu, *Taikan zakki*, p. 35.

124 Moriyama Takamori, *Shizu no odamaki*, pp. 251–52; the term rendered 'illustrated stories of the Floating World' is *kusazōshi*.

125 *Ibid., loc. cit.*

126 Sugita Genpaku, *Nochimigusa*, p. 46.

127 Julie Nelson Davis, 'Drawing his Own Ravishing Features: Kitagawa Utamaro and the Construction of a Public Identity in Ukiyo-e Prints', PhD thesis, University of Washington, Seattle, 1998, pp. 337–38.

128 There is some uncertainty about the exact details: see Shugo Asano and Timothy Clark, *The Passionate Art of Utamaro* (London, 1995), vol. II, pp. 243–44. For convenient reproductions, see *ibid. loc. cit.*, and Screech, *Sex and the Floating World*, illus. 131 and 132.

129 Takizawa Bakin, *Iwademon-ki* (1819), quoted in Sakai Gankow, *Utamaro* (Matsumoto, 1992), p. 78. For a discussion of this event, see Davis, 'Drawing his Own Ravishing Features', pp. 337–47. (Davis mistakenly attributes the book to Shikitei Sanba.)

130 For details of the events, see Kumakura Isao, *Go-Mizunoo tennō* (Iwanami, 1994), pp. 109–25 and Akita Shōtei and Higo Kazuo, eds, *Tennō rekidai zukan* (1975). Okiko was the niece of the second shogun, Hidetada.

131 Kuroda Hideo, 'Kinsei no tennō to shōgun no shozōga', in his *Ō no shintai ō no shōzō* (1993), pp. 286–7.

132 For shujo ages, see table in *ibid.*, p. 285.

133 Ichijō Teruyoshi, *Teruyoshi-kō ki*, quoted in Fujita Satoru, 'Kokusei ni taisuru chōtei no sonzai', in *Nihon no kinsei* (1991), vol. II, p. 328.

134 *Ibid., loc. cit.*

135 Akita and Higo, *Tennō rekidai zukan*, pp. 157, 223. Several shoguns were adopted by a previous incumbent (e.g. Tsunayoshi, Ienobu, Yoshimune), but the shujo-ship had to go from blood father to son, although brothers could inherit laterally before passing to the next generation.

136 Fujita, *Bakumatsu no tennō*, p. 49.

137 *Ibid.*, p. 79; by the modern count, he was the 119th.

138 James McMullen, 'Non-Agnatic Adoption as a Confucian Controversy in Seventeenth and Eighteenth-Century Japan', *Harvard Journal of Asiatic Studies*, 35 (1975), pp. 133–48.

139 Fujita, *Bakumatsu no tennō*, p. 50; Kannin can also be read Kan'in.

140 *Ibid.*, pp. 103–4. This was requested to avoid Tomohito taking priority over his father; the term rendered 'retired shujo' is *daijō-tennō*. This is known as the Title Incident (*songō jiken*).

141 For the locking up, see Fujita, *Matsudaira Sadanobu*, p. 145; for the feigned illness and death, see DDR, vol. X, p. 54.

142 Titsingh, *Illustrations of Japan*, pp. 113–14.

143 DDR, *loc. cit.*

144 Much of the scholarship behind the rebuilding was contributed by Uramatsu Mitsuyo, and his collossal *Dai-dairi zukōshō* was underway before the fire; see Fujioka Michio, *Kyōto gosho* (1987), pp. 141–43, and Fujita Satoru, 'Kansei dairi zōei o meguru chōbaku kankei', *Nihon rekishi*, 517 (1991), p. 2.

145 Fujita, *ibid., loc. cit.*

146 DDR, vol. IX, p. 195; Sadanobu's letter to the *kanpaku* (regent), in *Matsudaira*

Teikyō bunshō, quoted in Fujita, *Matsudaira Sadanobu*, p. 127.
147 Matsudaira Sadanobu, *Uge no hitokoto*, p. 83.
148 *Ibid., loc. cit.*
149 Fujioka, *Kyōto gosho*, Chapter 10, is the source of the facts cited here and below.
150 DDR, vol. IX, p. 160.
151 *Ibid.*, p. 195.
152 *Ibid., loc. cit.*; Fujita, 'Kansei dairi', p. 10.
153 Matsudaira Sadanobu, *Seigo*, pp. 256–57.
154 Kimuro Bōun, *Mita kyō monogatari*, p. 5.
155 Since the *Unjō meikan* was published in the twelfth month, the 1788 edition would have appeared after the fire; this edition is only some third the length of preceding ones.
156 For a list of editions, see *Kokusho sōmokuroku*, q.v; it seems as though a shortened edition was printed in 1790, but I have been unable to verify whether it contained the picture. One other view of the earlier Dairi is to be found in Akizato Ritō, *Shūi miyako meisho zue* (1780); for a convenient reproduction see Takemura Hidenori, ed., *Nihon meisho fūzoku zue* (1981), vol. VIII, p. 9.
157 DDR, vol. IX, pp. 92, 99.
158 Koikawa Harumachi, *Ōmu-gaeshi bunbu no futamichi* (1789), p. 172. Atsugimi's reputation is based on his issuing of the *Records of the Engi Era* (*Engi-shiki*). Interestingly, this same year Ienari appeared as Atsugimi in Tōrai Sanna, *Tenka ichimen kagami.* (Sanna calls him 'Daigo tennō'; Harumachi says 'Engi tei'.)
159 *Toribeno wa kyosei no hoka no kemuri tachi*, in *Haifū yanagi-daru*, 6/154.
160 Fujita, *Matsudaira Sadanobu*, p. 102; the garden was at the Rozan-ji, next to the Dairi.
161 DDR, vol. IX, p. 163.
162 The history of usage has not been proven. I offer the suggestion tentatively.
163 Matsudaira Sadanobu, *Uge no hitokoto*, p. 143; the term rendered 'famous sites' is *meisho.*
164 *Sōji* is the antique name for what are now called *fusuma*, that is, sliding doors.
165 For an eighteenth-century articulation of this belief, see Nakayama Kōyō, *Gadan keiroku*, p. 177.
166 Kawamoto Shigeo (*et al.*), 'Kenjō sōji no kenkyū', pt 1, pp. 10–15; eight sets were made in the Edo period. See also Shimada Takehiko, *Kinsei fukkō seiryōden no kenkyū* (Shibunkaku, 1987), p. 34ff.
167 Matsuki, *Kano-ke*, p. 209.
168 Kawamoto (*et al.*), 'Kenjō shōji', pt 1, p. 21.
169 Takeda, *Kano-ha*, pp. 328–31; Eisen-in died in 1790.
170 Yashiro Hirokata, *Michi no sachi*, p. 1 *recto*; Hirokata is also called Kōken.
171 For Kairyō's 'untrammelled' image, see Stephen Addiss, *Tall Mountains and Flowing Waters* (Honolulu, 1987), p. 14; Addiss omits to mention Kairyō's covert activities.
172 Mori Senzō, 'Kairyō hōshi', in *Mori Senzō chosaku shū* (1988), vol. III, p. 156–7.
173 Yashiro Hirokata, *Michi no sachi*, p. 16 *recto.*
174 Narishima, ed., *Tokugawa jikki*, quoted in Yokota, 'Sumiyoshi Hiroyuki', p. 43; see also Fujioka, *Kyōto gosho*, p. 152. Ritsuzan composed a study of the sages' costumes, *Kenjō sōji meshin kanpuku kōtō.*
175 This circular of 18/3/1789 was entitled *Go-zōgū goyō shōki*; it is quoted in Fukioka, *Kyōto gosho*, p. 149. What follows is indebted to *ibid.*, pp. 149–53.
176 Shimada, *Kinsei fukkō seiryōden*, p. 82; this last screen was by Sugiyama Genshun.
177 The precise architecture of the hall is unknown; this analysis is based on the

reconstruction found in Chino Kaori, 'Kensetsu no naibu kūkan to shōhekiga', in *Nihon bijutsu zenshū* (1991), vol. XVI, pp. 158–65.

178 The fullest original account is anon., *Jōkyū-ji*, quoted in Edward Kamens, *Utamakura: Allusion and Intertextuality in Traditional Japanese Poetry* (New Haven and London, 1997), p. 177; for the paintings and verses, see *ibid.*, pp. 168–221. These were not installed in the Dairi (which Takahira had vacated on retirement) but at the Saishō Shitennō-ji; for a plan, see *ibid.*, fig. 37.

179 The Suruga sites were Mt Utsu, Tago Bay, Ukijimabara and Fuji, see Chino, 'Kensetsu no naibu kūkan', p. 165.

180 Such screens had existed in older Dairi, but expunging of other Continental themes created a new polarity.

181 Kanai Ujū, *Musei shiwa* (1853), in Hugh Wylie, ed. and trans., 'Nanga Treatises of Nineteenth Century Japan', PhD thesis, University of Kansas, 1991, p. 191; Ujū cites a set of 1837, which appears to be inextant. The exact nature of the commission and the significance of the dates are unclear.

182 Fujita, *Bakumatsu no tennō*, pp. 131–5.

183 Reizei Tamechika, *Kōkaku tennō satsureishi emaki*; for a partial reproduction, see Nakamura Tanio, *Reizei Tamechika to fukkō yamato-e*, vol. CCLXI of *Nihon no bijutsu* (1988), fig. 22. Tamechika was nineteen.

4 Ōkyo's 'New Concept'

1 Tachibana Nankei, *Hokusō sadan*, p. 187.

2 Oku Bunmei, 'Sensai Maruyama-sensei den', *Bijutsu kenkyū*, 36 (1934), p. 591.

3 *Ibid.*, p. 591.

4 Motoori Norinaga, *E no koto*, p. 192.

5 Minagawa Kien, *Kien bunshū*; quoted in Satō Yasuhiro, 'Jūhasseiki no zen'ei shinwa', p. 123.

6 *Ibid.*, p. 194.

7 *Ibid.*, pp. 192–4.

8 Yūjō, *Banji*, quoted in Sasaki Jōhei and Sasaki Masako, *Maruyama Ōkyo kenkyū* (1996), vol II, p. 441; see also Shirai Kayō, *Gajō yōryaku* (1831), in *Nihon garon taisei* (1996), vol. IV, p. 49, and Anzai Un'en, *Kinsei meika shoka dan* in *Nihon garon taikan*, ed. Sakazaki Tan (Arusu, 1927), vol. I, p. 441.

9 Su Koppei, *Myōmyō kidan*, p. 377.

10 Kōkan obfuscated his chronology in his own writings, but this is resolved in Naruse Fujio, 'Shiba Kōkan no ukiyo-eshi jidai ni tsuite', *Ukiyo-e geijutsu*, 73 (1982), pp. 3–23.

11 Sawada Akira, *Nihon gaka jiten*, vol. I, p. 85; the painting is inextant.

12 Satake Yoshiatsu (Shozan), *Gahō kōryō*, in *Nihon garon taikan*, ed. Sakazaki Tan (Arusu, 1927), vol. I, pp. 101–2.

13 The works are *Gahō kōryō* and *Gazu rikai*, both of *c.* 1775.

14 Satake Yoshiatsu (Shozan), *Gahō kōryō*, p. 102; *Gazu rikai*, p. 102.

15 Shiba Kōkan, *Seiyō gadan*, p. 141.

16 Timon Screech, 'The Meaning of Western Perspective in Edo Popular Culture', *Archives of Asian Art*, 47 (1994), pp. 58–69.

17 Makoto Ueda, *Literary and Art Theories in Japan*, (Cleveland, OH, 1967), pp.132–3.

18 Shirai Kayō, *Gajō yōryaku*, p. 49.

19 Motoori Norinaga, *E no koto*, p. 194.

20 Matsudaira Sadanobu, *Taikan zakki*, p. 35.

21 Anzai Un'en, *Kinsei meika*, pp. 386–7; Minagawa Kien, *Shahon Kien bunshū*, in *Kinsei jukan bunshū shūsei* (1988), vol. IX, p. 329; it cannot conclusively be said the verse refers to this painting, although Kien calls it verse 'on a submerged carp'.

22 This painting is signed *hōgen* Terunobu (i.e. it is post-1742); he died in 1763. Un'en's book was issued from 1830. For an Ōkyo carp flying out of the water, see Sasaki and Sasaki, *Maruyama Ōkyo kenkyū*, p. 95, although this is early (1774); the image given as illus. 66 has a pendant, see *ibid.*, p. 263, and a second version exists as a single painting, see *ibid.*, vol. I, pp. 210–11; see also note 75, p. 280.
23 Matsudaira Sadanobu, *Taikan zakki*, p. 35.
24 Su Koppei, *Myōmyō kidan*, p. 377.
25 The fullest extant example of Ōkyo working as a Tsuruzawa artist is in the commission of 1765 for the Onjō-ji: see Takeda Tsuneo, *Kano-ha*, p. 296. For Yūtei's son, see Mori Senzō, 'Okyo den tōki', *Bijutsu kenkyū*, 36 (1934), p. 585.
26 This motive is claimed by Sasaki Jōhei, in *Ōkyo shasei gashū*, p. 36.
27 I have also proposed that these optical views might be later, see, Screech, *Western Scientific Gaze*, pp. 94–132.
28 See, *ibid.*, p. 103 and pl. 6; Kōkan produced views of Edo, although of Floating World, not poetic, sites.
29 The Kamo Festival was revived under the name Aoi Matsuri in 1694; it is still held annually on May 15.
30 *Tan'yū wa iya yo to Maruyama no jorō*: Okada Hajime, ed., *Yanagidaru, waki 2/7 verso.*
31 Anzai Un'en, *Kinsei meika*, pp. 441–3; Un'en calls Gantai 'Takudō'.
32 Tachibana Nankei, *Hokusō sadan*, pp. 187–8.
33 Anzai Un'en, *Kinsei meika*, p. 361.
34 Shiba Kōkan, *Shunparō hikki*, p. 62.
35 Ueda Akinari, *Tan daishō shinroku*, p. 291.
36 Oku Bunmei, *Sensai Maruyama-sensei den*, p. 591.
37 For the *Peacock and Peony*, see Oku Bunmei, *Sensai Maruyama-sensei den*, p. 593; the Minamoto name was probably awarded for the work (or awarded before to give Ōkyo the status to present a painting). For the brothel, see Shiba Kōkan, *Saiyū nikki*, p. 283 (Kōkan calls him only 'Maruyama'). For the singing brush, see the *senryū* verse, *Utau no mo toki ni Ōkyo no fude no myō*, *Yanagidaru*, no. *Ume/yanagi* 23/32 *recto*.
38 Ōkyo painted under his 'real name' (*honmyō*) rather than a variable studio name; initially he occasionally signed Isshō and was later known as Mondo (but did not paint under that name). 'Ōkyo' is occasionally glossed to be read 'Masataka': see Sasaki and Sasaki, *Maruyama Ōkyo*, pp. 124–5. As a peasant he had no family name, but his mother is thought to have been ex-samurai, entitling him to one.
39 *'Nakazukasa Hōgen Kano Eisen Fujiwara Michinobu'.*
40 Tsuji Nobuo, *Kisō no keifu* (1988), p. 83.
41 See Chapter Three above.
42 Sasaki and Sasaki, *Maruyama Ōkyo*, p. 67. Calvin French, *The Poet Painters: Buson and his Followers*, University of Michigan Art Museum (Ann Arbor, MI, 1974), pp. 32–40.
43 Sasaki Jōhei, 'Sanji Chion-ji no fusuma-e ni tsuite', *Kyōto daigaku bungakubu bijutsu gaku bijutsu shigaku kenkyūshitsu kenkyū kiyo*, 10 (1989), pp. 6–10.
44 Sadanobu had ten days in Keishi but was busy most of the time; for his schedule, see Fujita, 'Kansei dairi zōei', p. 4. He spent only three days sight-seeing and meeting people.
45 Yashiro Hirokata, *Michi no sachi*, p. 22 *verso*; Ōkyo is referred to as 'Mondo'. I have been unable to identify Sumino Tōshirō. The (lost) *Nightingale Leaving a Springtime Valley* was recorded in a verse by Minagawa Kien, see Mori, 'Ōkyo den', p. 587; the college was the Yushima Seidō. For Bunchō's meeting, see Frank L. Chance, 'Tani Bunchō', p. 89.
46 For a reproduction and discussion, see Kyoto National Museum, ed., *Nihon no*

shōzō (Chūō Kōronsha, 1978), pp. 201–2 and 301-2, and Ueno Keiji, 'Den Tani Bunchō hitsu "Kinsei meika shozō zukan" ni tsuite', *Tochigi kenritsu bijutsukan kiyo*, 7 (1979), pp. 73–80. Some contest the attribution to Bunchō.

47 Sasaki and Sasaki, *Maruyama Ōkyo kenkyū*, pp. 74–82.

48 Mori, 'Ōkyo den', p. 586. 1795 was the year of Ōkyo's death: he was ailing.

49 Ueda Akinari, *Tan daishō shinroku*, p. 291. See Philip Harries, '*Fūryū*: a Concept of Elegance in Pre-Modern Literature', in *Europe Interprets Japan*, ed. Gordon Daniels (Tenterden, 1984), pp. 137–44, and Gunji Masakatsu, *Fūryū no zuzōshi* (Sanshōdō, 1987).

50 The party took place in the first month of 1788, just after the fire. In his *Fushimi kanbai ka* Tekien makes no reference to Ōkyo, whereas Minagawa Kien's record of the same event, *Baikei kikō*, includes him: see Mori, 'Ōkyo den', p. 586.

51 *Ibid.*, p. 587.

52 *Ibid.*, pp. 589–90. Ōkyo was summoned on the seventeeth day of the fifth month of 1787 but came on the twelfth of the seventh; the enquirer was his patron Myōhō-in no Miya Shinmi (Ippin Shinmi): see Oku Bunmei, *Sensai Maruyama-sensei den*, p. 592. Ōkyo's son, Ōzui, is also called Ukon.

53 The verse, 'Sō Minamoto chūsen', appears in Minagawa Kien, *Kien bunshū*, p. 66.

54 For Jakuchū, see Hiraga Hakusan, *Shōsai hikki* (*c.* 1800), quoted in Money Hickman and Yasuhiro Satō, *The Paintings of Jakuchū*, p. 18. For Shōhaku, see Morishima Nagashi, *Hanpakuzawa* (*c.* 1825), quoted in Money Hickman, 'The Paintings of Soga Shōhaku', PhD thesis, Harvard University, 1976, p. 17. For Taiga, see Melinda Takeuchi, 'Ike Taiga: A Biographical Sketch', *Harvard Journal of Asiatic Studies*, 43 (1983), p. 145.

55 Oku Bunmei, *Sensai Maruyama-sensei den*, p. 593.

56 The record is dated the ninth month of 1801, Ōkyo having died in 1795.

57 Oku Bunmei, *Sensai Maruyama-sensei den*, p. 592.

58 *Ibid.*, p. 592.

59 Ueda Akinari, *Tan daishō shinroku*, pp. 291–2. Kano Hiroyuki has argued the term means stingy: see his 'Ōkyo danshō: hito to shigoto', in *Maruyama Ōkyo*, exh. cat., Kyoto National Museum (Kyoto, 1995), p. 5.

60 French, *Poet Painters*, pp. 32–40.

61 Buson is today usually known as Yosa (not Taniguchi) Buson. See Okada Rihei, *Haiga no bi: Buson, Gekkei* (Osaka, 1973), p. 269.

62 Goshun's new name was acquired before he met Ōkyo in the early 1780s; it was formed from the place where he was then living, Kureha (*kure* is also pronounced *go*) and 'spring' (*shun*). The period between Buson and Ōkyo is called Goshun's Ikeda period (Kureha being in Ikeda).

63 Tanomura Chikuden, *Sanchūjin jōzetsu*, p. 22.

64 *Ibid.*, *loc. cit.*; the editor, Shinozaki Shōchiku (1781–1851), refers to Shukuya as Shuntō.

65 Quoted without a source in C. H. Mitchell, *The Illustrated Books of the Nanga, Maruyama-Shijō and Related Schools of Japanese Art – A Biographical Bibliography* (Tokyo, 1971), p. 54.

66 Mori, 'Ōkyo den', p. 587.

67 *Zeni-game ya aosoko mo shiranu yamakiyomizu*. Quoted in *ibid.*, p. 587.

68 *Shirakawa no kiyoraki nagare ni sumekanete iketa wa iken* Ōta Nanpo. Interestingly, Buson also wrote a verse on Shirakawa, 'clear waters dried up' (*shimizu kare*); see Donald Keene, *World Within Walls: Japanese Literature of the Pre-Modern Era, 1600–1868* (New York, 1976), p. 345.

69 *Ono ga mi no yami yori hoete yahan no aki*. Quoted in Mori, 'Ōkyo den', p. 587.

70 Satō, 'Juhasseiki', p. 153.

71 Anzai Un'en, *Kinsei meika shoga dan*, p. 357.
72 Nakabayashi Chikutō, *Gadō kongōshō*, in *Nihon garon taikan*, ed. Sakazaki Tan (Arusu, 1927), vol. I, p. 184; Ōkyo occupies this category with Sō Shiseki and Shōkadō Shōjō.
73 Nakabayashi Chikutō, *Chikutō garon* (1804), pp. 208–9; the terms are *akudō* and *gayō*.
74 Anzai Un'en, *Kinsei meika*, p. 441.
75 Tanomura Chikuden, *Sanchūjin jōzetsu*, p. 42; Chikuden adapts the Ming critic Yi Dongyong's statement that it was harder to select a poem than to write one.
76 For reproductions of Okyo's sketches, see Sasaki Jōhei, *Ōkyo shasei gashū* (1981), pp. 120–45; for these comments, see *ibid.*, p. 150.
77 Yūjō, *Banji*, quoted in Sasaki and Sasaki, *Maruyama Ōkyo kenkyū*, pp. 134, 450.
78 Yūjō's diary, *Banji*, covers 1761–73 (Yūjō's death); it is partially reproduced in *ibid.*, pp. 447–60.
79 *Ibid.*, pp. 134, 445; Sasaki renders *chika-magane* as 'mirror brought up close', instead of 'lenses for close viewing' (spectacles).
80 Motoori Norinaga, *E no koto*, p. 195.
81 See Sasaki and Sasaki, *Maruyama Ōkyo kenkyū*, pp. 295–9
82 Oku Bunmei, *Sensai Maruyama-sensei den*, p. 593.
83 Sasaki, *Ōkyo shasei gashū*, p. 149.
84 Yūjō, *Banji*, quoted in Sasaki and Sasaki, *Maruyama Ōkyo kenkyū*, pp. 135, 454–44.
85 Minagawa Kien, *Baikei kikō*, in Mori, 'Ōkyo den', p. 586; Sasaki and Sasaki, *Maruyama Ōkyo*, pp. 128, 447.
86 Yūjō, *Banji*, quoted in Sasaki and Sasaki, *ibid.*, pp. 124, 447.
87 Yūjō, *ibid.*, quoted in *ibid.*, pp. 125, 447, 138 and 454.
88 For a convenient reproduction, see Timon Screech, *Shunga: katate de yomu edo no e* (Heibonsha, 1999), p. 32. The terms rendered 'powdered and crystalline white' are *hakufun* and *unmo*.
89 Yūjō, *Banji*, quoted in Sasaki and Sasaki, *Maruyama Ōkyo kenkyū*, pp. 124, 447.
90 Yūjō, *ibid.*, quoted in *ibid.*, pp. 100–5.
91 Morishima Chūryō, *Kōmō zatsuwa*, p. 479.
92 For example, Nakayama Kōyō, *Gadan keiroku*, p. 192. Kōyō's term of praise is *shōutsushi* 'copying from life'.
93 Sasaki and Sasaki, *Maruyama Ōkyo kenkyū*, pp. 95–9.
94 Fully reproduced in Nihon Ishi Gakkai, ed., *Zuroku nihon iji bunka shiryō shūsei*, vol. II, pp. 37–52. For Ranshū, see Fukuoka Sakutarō, *Kinsei nihon kaigashi* (1982), p. 40.
95 Nihon Ishi Gakkai, ed., *ibid.*, pp. 53–59.
96 Nakayama Kōyō, *Gadan keiroku*, p. 169.
97 Yūjō's preface to the scrolls is quoted in Doi Tsuguyoshi, *Kinsei nihon kaiga no kenkyū* (1970), p. 613.
98 Oku Bunmei, *Sensai Maruyama-sensei den*, p. 592.
99 Takizawa Bakin, *Kiryo manroku*, p. 205; Bakin calls Goshun 'Gekkei'.
100 Kano Yasunobu, *Gadō yōketsu*, pp. 16–17.
101 Anzai Un'en, *Kinsei meika*, p. 443.
102 Quoted in Kano Hiroyuki, 'Ōkyo danshō' (Chishin Kōgei, 1994), p. 11; the verse is from the year after Ōkyo's death.
103 Yūjō, *Banji*, quoted in Sasaki and Sasaki, *Maruyama Ōkyo kenkyū*, pp. 135, 454–44.
104 Rai San'yō (unsourced), quoted in Satō, 'Jūhasseiki', p. 156.
105 *Fusō ni mo kakau on-e o miru koyo yo kumadori to ii irodori to ii.* Quoted in

Hirafuku Hyakusui, *Nihon yōga no shokō* (1930), p. 16. Heikaku is usually known from his pen-name as Hōseidō Kisanji.

106 Screech, *Western Scientific Gaze*, pp. 52–4.

107 Satake Yoshiatsu (Shozan), *Gahō kōryō*, p. 101.

108 Matsudaira Sadanobu, *Taikan zakki*, p. 73; Sadanobu generalizes from the case of Mi Fu.

109 Motoori Norinaga, *E no koto*, p. 191; Satake Yoshiatsu, *Gahō kōryō*, p. 101.

110 Shiba Kōkan, letter to Yamaryō Kazuma, dated 25th day of 2nd month (year unknown); reproduced in Naruse Fujio *et al.*, eds, *Shiba Kōkan zenshū* vol. II, p. 342; Satō Narihiro, *Chūryō manroku*, p. 70 (Narihiro, also called Chūryō, is not to be confused with Morishima Chūryō).

111 Timon Screech, 'The Strangest Place in Edo', *Monumenta Nipponica*, 48 (1993), pp. 407–28, including Edo-period copies of the now inextant paintings.

112 Satō Narihiro, *Chūryō manroku*, pp. 74–5; the term rendered 'European painting' is *ranga*.

113 Kōkan apparently had to repair his 'mud paintings' after completion, see Calvin French, *Shiba Kōkan: Artist, Innovator and Pioneer in the Westernization of Japan* (New York and Tokyo, 1974), p. 103; illustrations, *ibid.*, pls 6–8 and figs 75–7.

114 Matsudaira Sadanobu, *Taikan zakki*, pp. 27–8.

115 Nishina Yūsuke, *Edo bijutsu kōgengaku* (1988), pp. 148–64.

116 Satō Narichiro, *Chūryō manroku*, p. 70; Satake Yoshiatsu (Shozan), 'Tansei bu', in Tamamushi Satoko, ed., *Edo meisaku gachō zenshū* (1995), vol. VIII, pp. 142–4

117 DDR, vol. VIII, p. 189; Gennai's name is spelt 'Gennij'.

118 Hiraga Gennai, *Butsurui hinshitsu* (1763), vol. XVI of *Nihon koten zenshū: 3* (1927), p. 27. Several recent studies on Berlin blue exist, but they omit many of the data given here: see Higuchi Kazuya, 'Aizuri ukiyo-e hanga ni kansuru ikkōsatsu', *Idemitsu bijutsukan kanpō*, 90 (1995), pp. 4–20; Henry Smith, 'Hokusai's "Thirty-six Views of Mt Fuji" and the "Blue Revolution" in Edo Prints', in Gian Carlo Calza and John Carpenter, eds, *Hokusai and His Age* (Venice, forthcoming).

119 *Encyclopaedia Britannica* (London, 1711), 'Berlin blue', q.v.

120 Tachihara Suiken, Shikundō kōsōdan (ms), p. 14.

121 For a convenenient reproduction, see Melinda Takeuchi, *Taiga's True Views: The Language of Landscape Painting in Eighteenth-Century Japan* (Stanford, 1992), fig. 29.

122 Satake Yoshiatsu, 'Tansei bu', in Tamamushi, ed., *Edo meisaku gachō*, p. 142.

123 For Chinese imports, see Miyashita Saburō, 'Jinkō konjō (purushian buruu) no mozō to yunyū', in *Ronshū nihon no yōgaku*, ed. Arisaki Takamichi and Asai Mitsuaki (Osaka, 1995), vol. III, pp. 131–4; for the Dutch, see DDR, vol. VIII, p. 178, and vol. IX, p. 89 (the text refers to 1 catty = 625 g). For the hatred, see *ibid.*, p. 231; the recipient of the 1790 request was again Romberg.

124 J. Mac Lean, 'The Introduction of Books and Scientific Instruments into Japan, 1712–1854', *Japanese Studies in the History of Science*, 13 (1974), pp. 22–4; Chalmot was an expansion of Abbé Chomel (1743), known in Japan in the Dutch version, *Woordenboek*. Chomel's original did not include Berlin blue.

125 Ōta Nanpo, *Ichiwa ichigon*, pp. 943–4.

126 Carmine was first imported to China in 1582, see Craig Clunas, *Art in China*, Oxford History of Art (Oxford and New York, 1997), p. 187. However, Toyama Usaburō – *Nihon shoki yōga shikō* (1965), pp. 120–21 – suggests *gōrudo* is either umber or 'Van Dyke brown'; it may be linked to the red iron crystals mentioned in Mac Lean, 'Introduction of Books', p. 24. For *shamudei*, see Ōta Nanpo, *ibid.*, *loc. cit.*, and Hiraga Gennai, *Butsurui hinshitsu*, p. 39. For *shōdo*, see Yokoi Kinkoku, *Kinkoku shōnin on-ichdai ki* (undated), see abridged

edition in *Mori Senzō chosaku shū*, vol. III, pp. 500–01.

127 Hiraga Gennai, *ibid., loc. cit.*

128 Kano Yasunobu, *Gadō yōketsu*, p. 17. The prime minister, Phaulkom, was in office in the 1680s, see David K. Watt, *Thailand: A Short History* (New Haven and London, 1982), p. 116. For closure of the Siamese station and reactions in Japan, see DDR, vol. VII, p. 39.

129 Yūjō, *Banji*, quoted in Sasaki and Sasaki, *Maruyama Ōkyo kenkyū*, p. 447; regrettably, Sasaki and Sasaki fail to comment on this passage (see lacuna, pp. 129–30). Yokoi Kinkoku, *Kinkoku shōnin*, says it was Dutch (*kōmō*), quoted in *Mori Senzō chosakushū* vol. III, p. 500.

130 *Fudetsute mo aki wa enogu o sutetayō*. Okada, ed., *Yanagidaru*, *Shin* 17/*aki* 5 *recto*.

131 Yokoi Kinkoku, *Kinkoku shōnin*, quoted in Mori Senzō, 'Kairyō hōshi', in *Mori Senzō chosaku shū*, vol. III, p. 161; Kinkoku calls Sadanobu 'Matsudaira Etchū-no-kami'.

132 Mori Senzō, 'Kairyō hōshi', *loc. cit.*

133 The village was in Ōmi, see *ibid.*, p. 159.

134 *Ibid.*, p. 162.

135 *Iro ao sameshi Ōkyo ga enoguzara*. Okada, ed., *Yanagidaru*, *Shin-shin* 3/40 *verso*; literally, people go 'blue-green' (*ao*).

5 Boundaries for a Centre

1 Since few records of the Yoku'on-en exist, my interpretation relies on the image reproduced here (illus. 14) and Anon., *Yokuon-en kana no ki*, in Ema Masamizu, ed., *Rakuō-kō ishō* (Yao, 1893), vol. III, pp. 1–24.

2 See Arthur Waley, *Introduction to Chinese Poetry* (London, 1956), pp. 172–6.

3 Matsuo Bashō, *Oku no hosomichi*, in *Bashō bunshū* (Iwanami, 1959), vol. XLVI, p. 70.

4 Ōta Kinjō, Yū kōrakuen ki narabi ni jo (1795), unpaginated MS in National Diet Library, Tokyo; see sections on Little Mt Lu and the Octagonal Hall. I am grateful to Gotō Seiko for alerting me to this MS.

5 Ukai Nobunori, Kōraku-en kiji (1736), unpaginated MS in National Diet Library, Tokyo. I am grateful to Gotō Seiko for alerting me to this MS. The event is said to have taken place in Genroku (1688–1703) and, if in 1703, the lady Mitsuko (better known as Keishō-in) would have been over 70 years old; the shogun was Tsunayoshi.

6 See Kodera Takehisa, *Owari-han Edo shimo-yashiki no nazo* (1989), pp. 53–60; Shirahata Yōzaburō, *Daimyō teien* (1997), p. 240.

7 Bunchō's 31 paintings, *Toyama zansō emaki*, are reproduced in Ueno Kenji, ed., *Edo meisaku gachō zenshū* (1995), vol. III, pp. 34–175, and in Sakakibara Satoru, 'Tani Bunchō hitsu, "Aoyama ensō zukō", "Toyama zansō zukō"', *Kokka*, 1148 (1991), pp. 33–41.

8 See, generally, Günther Nitschke, *Japanese Gardens* (Cologne, 1991).

9 The finest official work on this theme is by Kano Sansetsu; for a convenient reproduction, see Hosono Masanobu, *Edo no kano*, (vol. CCLXII of *Nihon no bijutsu* (1988), p. 20–21.

10 Anon., *Wada toyama onari-ki*, quoted in Kodera, *Owari-han*, p. 119.

11 Ōta Kinjō, Yū Kōraku-en ki narabi no jo (unpaginated MS). The temple of Wen *wang* is the Octagonal Hall (Happō-dō), mentioned above, note 4.

12 Hama goten is now Hama Rikkyū and the Ōkubo's Rakujūen is now Shiba Rikkyū.

13 *Hito sumanu Fuwa no sekiya no itahisashi are ni shi nochi wa tada aki no kaze*. In Fujiwara no Teika, ed., *Shin kokin-shū* (1205), p. 328, where Ryōkyō is called Sessei Taisei Daijin; the place first appears in *Man'yōshū* (no. 4372).

14 Anon., *Yokuon-en kana no ki*, p. 20.
15 Anon., *Kii akasaka o-yakata on-tei no ki*, in *Edo sōsho* (1964), vol. I, p. 36.
16 For a translation, see A. R. Davis, *T'ao Yuan-ming: His Works and Their Meaning* (Cambridge and New York, 1983), vol. I, p. 195ff.
17 Craig Clunas, *Fruitful Sites: Garden Culture in Ming Dynasty China* (London, 1996) p. 100. For Dong's rapacity, see Celia Reily, 'Tung Ch'i-ch'ang's Life', in *The Century of Tung Ch'i-ch'ang*, ed. Wai-kam Ho (Kansas City, 1992), vol. II, pp. 415–19 (N.B.: Tung Ch'i-ch'ang = Dong Qichang).
18 Matsuo Masanobu (Karyō), *Karyō kikō* (transcription of a lost record by Sano Yoshiyuki), see Kodera, *Owari-han*, p. 155.
19 For example, Ōta Kinjō, Yū Kōrakuen ki narabi ni jo (unpaginated ms).
20 *Ibid., loc, cit.*
21 Shirahata, *Daimyō teien*, p. 131; dating uncertain and previous park name unsure.
22 Not visible here (illus. 14), but see Anon., *Yokuon-en kana no ki*, p. 2.
23 Shirahata, *Daimyō teien*, pp. 100-2, 110–11. The criteria were: expansiveness, mysterious recesses, visible human labour, ancient plant life, waterworks and wide views.
24 Hamada Giichirō, ed., *Edo bungaku chimei jiten* (1972), p. 18.
25 Shirahata, *Daimyō teien*, p. 151.
26 *Ibid., loc. cit.*
27 Kodera, *Owari-han*, pp. 114–18.
28 *Ibid.*, p. 116.
29 Narishima *et al.*, eds, *Tokugawa jikki*, quoted in *ibid.*, p. 53 (not direct speech).
30 Hirose Ten, *Shirakawa fūdo-ki*, quoted in Satō Yōichi, 'Matsudaira Sadanobu no ryōnai junken: zuikō suru bunjin to gajin', in *Sadanobu to Bunchō: Matsudaira Sadanobu to shūhen no gakatachi*, ed. Prefectural Museum, Fukushima (Fukushima, 1992), p. 103.
31 Yamamoto Toshio, *Matsudaira Sadanobu: sono hito to shōgai*, (Shirakawa, 1983), pp. 175–6.
32 *Shirakawa no sekiya o tsuki no morukage wa hito no kokoro o tomuru narikeri.* Saigyō, *Saigyō hōshi kashū* (*c.* twelfth century), in *Shinpen: kokushi taikei*, vol. III/1, p. 608. The text states Saigyō's thought of Nōin's earlier verse as he composed.
33 For a treatment of this issue, see Kamens, *Utamakura: Allusion and Intertextuality*.
34 Haruo Shirane argues that Bashō preferred new sites to old: see his *Traces of Dreams: Landscape, Cultural Memory, and the Poetry of Bashō* (Stanford, 1988), p. 237.
35 Matsuo Bashō, *Oku no hosomichi*, pp. 75–6. The last phrase, *kaikyū ni harawata o tachite*, is literally 'fond remembrances severed my bowels'.
36 Sora, *Sora zuikō nikki*, vol. VI of *Kōhen: Bashō zenshū* (1989), p. 248.
37 *Ibid., loc. cit.*, and headnote 8.
38 Furukawa Koshōken, *Tōyū zakki*, vol. XII of *Kinsei shakai keizai sōsho* (1927), p. 9; he especially chides the famous *Wakan sansai zue* and an unidentified book he refers to by the author's surname, 'Okamoto'.
39 Yamamoto, *Matsudaira Sadanobu*, pp. 176–7 (with illustration).
40 *Hakodate no seki no fusemori kokoro seyo nami nomi yosuru yo ni shi araneba*. Quoted in George Lensen, *The Russian Push Towards Japan* (New York, 1971), p. 181 (translation mine); Lensen calls Harumori 'Mito Rekkō'.
41 For the Korean 'island', see DDR, vol. IX, p. 192. For the Russians, see Lensen, *ibid.*, pp. 150–7; the Russian base (which lasted only weeks) was called 'Russian Dejima'.
42 The cannonball had been fired on shogunal behalf by the Dutch and originally served as a lesson against Iberian Catholicism; for an illustration, see Ishizaki

Yūshi, *Nagasaki kokon shūran meisho zue* (1842), in *Nagasaki bunken sōsho: 2* (Nagasaki, 1975), vol. I, pp. 182–3.

43 Lensen, *Russian Push*, p. 171.

44 Amenomori Hoshū, *Kōrin taisei* (1728); verbal communication from James Lewis and see his 'Across the Straits: Frontier Contact between Chosŏn Korea and Tokugawa Japan', PhD thesis, University of Honolulu, 1994. See also note 43 above.

45 Matsudaira Sadanobu, *Kan naru amari*, p. 334.

46 DDR, vol. VIII, pp. 149–53.

47 For this ship, *Sankoku-maru*, and its absurd construction, see DDR, vol. VIII, pp. 127–39; for its encounter with the French, see Adachi Hiroyuki, *Iyō no fune*, pp. 114–16.

48 Lensen, *Russian Push*, p. 127; for Tolstoi see *ibid.*, p. 134, note 30.

49 The log was closed in 1853; see Hayashi *et al.*, eds, *Tsūkō ichiran*.

50 Matsudaira Sadanobu, *Taikan zakki*, p. 195.

51 *Ibid.*, pp. 172–3.

52 *Ensai gunsho kō* was compiled for Sadanobu by Ishii Shōsuke: see Fukui Kyūzō, *Shodaimyō no gakujitsu to bungaku no kenkyū*, vol. I, p. 324.

53 Nakamura Shin'ichirō, *Kakizaki Hakyō no shōgai* (1989), pp. 78–85.

54 Horiya Fumi, in his *Oranda-bumi* (1825), in *Hyōryu kidan zenshū* (1900), vol. XXII, pp. 997–1000, confuses both places. The authenticity of this letter is debated: see Andrew Cobbing, 'The First Japanese Woman in Europe?', *Proceedings of the Japan Society*, 132 (1999), pp. 34–42; pp. 35, 40.

55 Isozaki Yasuhiko, *Matsumae-han no gajin to kinsei kaigashi* (1986), p. 59; Hirotoshi or Hakyō's first teacher, Takebe Ryōtai, died when he was only ten.

56 *Ibid.*, pp. 69 and 72, and Suganuma Teizō, *Kazan no kenkyū*, pp. 280–9.

57 Tachibana Nankei, *Tōyūki*, in *Tōzai yūki, hokusō sadan* (Yūhōdō, 1913), pp. 195–6.

58 *Ibid.*, p. 73.

59 *Ibid.*, p. 75.

60 For the Russians and their charts, see DDR, vol. X, pp. 42, 59; Mannevillette, *Neptune Oriental* (Brest and Paris, 1775, supplement ditto). There is some confusion here. The Dutch refer to the 'corrected version' of Mannevillette (DDR, vol. X. p. 42), presumably meaning the supplement, but this contains no map of Ezo; the nearest is that given here as illus. 87. I have not had access, however, to the Russian edition. For the British, see Adachi, *Iyō no fune*, p. 15.

61 Matsudaira Sadanobu, *Taikan zakki*, p. 185.

62 *Ezo oshi* (Ezo invasion) puns on *ezōshi* (picture book); *hiiki* (favouritism) refers to *hōgan-biiki* (sticking up for the under-dog), literally for Hōgan (Yoshitsune), who was said to have travelled to Ezo in medieval times.

63 Nakamura, *Kakizaki Hakyō*, p. 90.

64 Aoki Okikatsu, *Tōmon jussaku*, pp. 383–4.

65 Beatrice Bodart-Bailey, ed. and trans., *Kaempfer's Japan: Tokugawa Culture Observed* (Honolulu, 1999), p. 138; DDR, vol. X, p. v.

66 C. C. Krieger, *The Infiltration of European Civilisation in Japan during the Eighteenth Century* (Leiden, 1940), pp. 81–2.

67 Hayashi Shihei, *Kaikoku heidan*, quoted in Kagawa Takayuki, *Kuzure-yuku sakoku*, vol. XIV, *Nihon no Rekishi* (Shūeisha, 1992), p. 104. For Sadanobu, see Mori Senzō, 'Kaikoku heidan sagon', in *Mori Senzō chosaku shū* (1988), vol. VII, pp. 147–8.

68 Lensen, *Russian Push*, p. 140.

69 Juppō-an, *Yūreki zakki*, vols III–VII of *Edo sōsho* (1964), p. 146–7. Tange Slope was the original name; after abolition of Christian Slope (and Christian Mansion by it), the old name was re-used; see Hamada Giichirō, ed., *Edo bungaku chimei jiten*, pp. 138–9.

70 Isozaki Yasuhiko, *Aōdō Denzen no kenyū*, p. 58.
71 For the cultural significance of the device, see Steven Shapin and Simon Schaffer, *Leviathan and the Air-Pump* (Princeton and London, 1985).
72 Mac Lean, 'Introduction of Books', p. 37; 'planetarium' must mean orrery, for which see Screech, *Western Scientific Gaze*, pp. 247–53.
73 DDR, vol. X, p. 40. The book's subtitle is *Beschryving der nieuwe en onlangs uytgevonden luchtpompen* (Leiden, 1736). The full book was by Petrus, and the pump section by Jan van Musschenbroek. The original appeared in Latin: *Descriptio antliae pneumaticae* (Leiden, 1730).
74 Ōtsuki Gentaku and Arima Genchō, *Ransetsu benwaku*, in *Edo kagaku koten sōsho* (1979), vol. XVII, p. 45; the book was completed twelve years before publication.
75 DDR, vol. IX, p. 173. For Hoshū (quoting Satake Yoshiatsu), see Screech, *Western Scientific Gaze*, pp. 142–43.
76 Hiraga Gennai, *Butsurui hinshitsu*, p. 99.
77 Matsudaira Sadanobu, *Taikan zakki*, p. 32.
78 *Ibid.*, p. 45.
79 Tani Bunchō, *Bunchō gadan*, pp. 182–235 and p. 189.
80 For a general treatment, see Melinda Takeuchi, *Taiga's True Views.*
81 Shiba Kōkan, letter to Yamaryō Kazuma; see Naruse Fujio *et al.*, eds, *Shiba Kōkan zenshū*, vol. 2, p. 351.
82 Shiba Kōkan, *Shunparō hikki*, p. 61.
83 Saitō Gesshin, ed., *Bukō nenpyō*, p. 193.
84 Matsudaira Sadanobu, *Taikan zakki*, p. 185.
85 DDR, vol. IX, p. 127; Romberg recognized the daimyo's face (ordinary Edoites would not have done).
86 Hattori Nankaku, *Nankaku-sensei bunshō*, Naoki Sakai (trans.) in Tetsuo Najita, ed., *Readings in Tokugawa Thought*, Select Papers, vol. 9, Center for East Asian Studies, University of Chicago (Chicago, 1993), p. 40. See also Luke Roberts, *Mercantilism in a Japanese Domain: The Merchant Origins of Economic Nationalism in 18th-Century Tosa* (Cambridge and New York, 1998), p. 118, note 44.
87 DDR, vol. IX, p. 84.
88 *Ibid.*, pp. 191, 193–4.
89 Yuasa Genzō, *Kokuiron*, p. 15.
90 Shiba Kōkan, *Saiyū zakki*, p. 316.
91 DDR vol. IX, p. 200.
92 Shibusawa Eiichi, *Rakuō-kō den*, pp. 136–7.
93 Furukawa Koshōken, *Tōyū zakki*, pp. 5–6.
94 *Ibid.*, p. 1.
95 Furukawa Kōshōken, *Saiyū zakki*, vol. IX of *Kinsei shakai keizai sōsho* (1927), p. 64. I have been unable to trace this book.
96 *Ibid.*, p. 72.
97 *Ibid.*, p. 65.
98 Munesaka Isoo, 'Tachibana Nankei "Tōyū-ki" to Edo kōki no kikō bungaku', in *Shin-nihon bungaku taikei* (Iwanami, 1991), vol. XCVIII, pp. 437–55; p. 445.
99 Shiba Kōkan, *Shunparō hikki*, pp. 95–6.
100 Robert Campbell, 'Poems on the Way to Yoshiwara', in *Imaging/Reading Eros: Proceedings for the Conference, Sexuality and Edo Culture, 1750–1850*, ed. Sumie Jones (Bloomington, IN, 1996), p. 96.
101 Akimoto Norio, 'Kinsei nikkō tōshōgū to minshū no sanshi: sono ikkōsatsu', *Utsunomiya daigaku kyōiku kenkyū hōkoku*, 8 (1965), pp. 1–29; Moriyama Takamori, *Ama no takumo no ki*, p. 257; Saitō Gesshin, *Bukō nenpyō*, p. 184 (the famous and extant five-storey pagoda was built in 1792).
102 Tachibana Nankei, *Hokusō sadan*, p. 126.

103 Yashiro Hirokata, *Michi no sachi*, p. 21 *verso*.
104 *Natsugusa ya tsuwamonodomo ga yume no seki*. Matsuo Bashō, *Oku no hosomichi*, p. 84; Bashō refers to 'two halls' (the Golden Hall and Sutra Repository) of 1124.
105 Yuasa Akiyoshi, *Tenmei taisei-roku*, p. 244. Shiba Kōkan, *Saiyū nikki*, p. 399.
106 *Sabitaredo jigō wa kakari kin to gin*. Okada Hajime, ed., *Haifū yanagi-daru*, vol. VII, p. 88; in English they are often called 'pavilions'.
107 Tachibana Nankei, *Tōyūki*, pp. 89, 94.
108 *Kyō no tera ryōgae o shite edo ni tatsu*. Okada, ed., *Haifū yanagidaru*, vols III, p. 91, and XXXII, p. 8.
109 Kan Tenjū (attrib.), *Sangaku kikō nikki*. Tenjū travelled with Bashō and the sums are collated from his diary, see the edition of Suganuma Teizō, 'Taiga no *Sangaku kikō*', in his *Ike Taiga hito to geijutsu* (Nigensha, 1977), pp. 20–6.
110 Shiba Kōkan, *Saiyū nikki*, p. 399, and Takizawa Bakin, *Kiryo manroku*, p. 201; Bakin called the fee *haikenryō* ('viewing charge').
111 Matsuo Bashō, *Oku no hosomichi*, p. 70; Bashō specifies Dōsojin, god of travellers.
112 *Fudesuteta yama meishoki ni hiroage*. See *Yanagidaru*, no. *Ansei 4/ma i 2 omote*.
113 Ban Kōkei, *Kinsei kijin-den*, pp. 152–9. For illustration, see *ibid.*, p. 157, or Melinda Takeuchi, *Taiga's True Views*, p. 76.
114 Ritsujō-tei Kiran, *Tōkaidō jinbutsu-shi*, in Kasuya Hideki, *Tōkaidō meisho' zue o yomu* (1997), pp. 235–67.
115 Kairyō Hōshi, *Musashiburi*, quoted in Mori Sensō, 'Kairyō Hōshi', p. 153.
116 Jurgis Elisonas, 'Notorious Places: A Brief Excursion into the Narrative Topography of Early Edo', in James McClain *et al.*, eds, *Edo and Paris: Urban Life and the State in the Early Modern Period* (Ithaca and London, 1994), pp. 253–91.
117 Akizato Ritō, *Shūi miyako meisho zue*, prologue (*hanrei*), p. 209.
118 *Nadokoro wa kore o miyako no annaisha zue wa shiradomo omou utsushi-e*.
119 Jippensha Ikku, *Tōkaidōchū hizakurige*, vol. LXVIII of *Nihon koten bungaku taikei* (Iwanami, 1958), p. 68.
120 For a table of Ritō's books and illustrators, see Takemura Takanori, 'Akizato Ritō to "miyako meisho zue"', in *Nihon meisho fūzoku zue* (Kadokawa, 1981) vol. VIII, pp. 516–20, and the same author's 'Nakagawa Kiun to "Miyako-warabe", "Miyako-warabe sekitsui"', in *Nihon meisho fūzoku zue* (Kadokawa, 1981), vol. VII, p. 470.
121 The illustrations to Ritō's book were undertaken by Nishimura Chūwa and Sakuma Sōen as well as Bunmei; while it is impossible to assign images, I think it reasonable to attribute this idea to Bunmei on account of his connection to Ōkyo.
122 See Stephan Oettermann, *Panorama: The History of A Mass Medium* (New York, 1997), p. 6.
123 Henry Smith, 'World Without Walls: Kuwagata Keisai's Panoramic Vision', in *Japan and the World*, ed. Gail Bernstein and Haruhito Fukui (London, 1988), pp. 3–19.
124 There is controversy over the dating of Ōkyo's optical paintings, with most scholars placing them *c.* 1755–65, and there is internal evidence for this. However, external evidence suggests this is too early, since using pictures with optical machines (which alone justifies reverse painting) began only in the late 1760s: see Sasaki and Sasaki, *Maruyama Ōkyo kenkyū*, vol. I, pp. 279–83, and Screech, *Western Scientific Gaze*, pp. 102 and 270, notes 28 and 29.
125 I am grateful to Henry Smith for drawing my attention to Bunmei's alterations, although he assumes some forty years between the two works.
126 Also called the Bridge Temple (Hashidera) and properly the Jōkō-ji; its monks

were responsible for maintaining the bridge structure.

127 Akizato Ritō, *Miyako meisho zue*, pp. 162–4.

128 Matsudaira Sadanobu, *Taikan zakki*, p. 35.

129 Shiba Kōkan, *Saiyū nikki*, p. 391.

130 Matsudaira Sadanobu, *Uge hitokoto*, p. 157.

131 Hitomaro, in *Man'yō-shū* (no. 11/2430); Teika, *Shin-Kokinshū* (no. 420).

132 Umehara Takeshi, *Kyōto hakken: chirei chinkon* (1997), p. 220. The inscription matched that in *Teiō hen nenki*: see *ibid., loc. cit.*

133 Takizawa Bakin, *Kiryo manroku*, p. 200.

134 Mitsui Takafuda, *Chōnin kōken roku* (*c.* 1720), see Crawcour, ed. and trans., 'Some Observations on Merchants', pp. 123, 59.

135 Aimi Kōu, 'Ishiyama-dera engi hoshū tenmatsu', in *Aimi Kōu-shū*, Nihon shoshigaku taikei, vol. XLV/2 (1986), pp. 397, 394–402; Umezu Jirō, 'Ishiyama-dera e kō', *Bijutsushi*, 19 (1952), pp. 35–48.

136 Matsudaira Sadanobu, *Tokugyō*, quoted in *ibid.*, p. 399; this section of *Tokugyō* is a transcription of Jishō's account, *Kantoku-roku*.

137 Takasu Toyomori, 'Rakuō kō to koga no mosha ni tsuite', pp. 3–4.

138 Nomura Bunshō, *Tani Bunchō-ō no ki* (also known as *Shazanrō no ki*) (undated), in *Enseki jusshū* (1988), vol. V, pp. 47–58; p. 49.

139 *Ibid., loc. cit.*; 82 pupils of whom 45 were shogunal officials and eight were women.

140 Timothy Clark, *Ukiyo-e Paintings in the British Museum* (London, 1992), p. 31.

141 Tani Bunchō, *Yamato junga nikki*, see Tōno Hiroshi, '"Koga ruijū" no seiritsu', in *Koga ruijū* (1990), pp. 82–91; p. 88. The anecdote was circulated by Kimura Kenkadō in *Kenkadō zatsuroku* (1856), pp. 438–41 (with illustration).

142 Yuasa Genzō, *Kokuiron*, p. 148.

143 Hoshino Kuniya, '"Koga ruijū" ni tsuite', in *Koga ruijū*, ed. Tokyo National Museum, 1990), pp. 76–81.

144 Matsudaira Sadanobu, *Taikan zakki*, p. 128.

145 *Bunchō wa sōshi ga yume ni hone wo oru*. See Okada, ed., *Haifū yanagi daru*, vol. VII, p. 35.

146 Tanomura Chikuden, *Sanchūjin jōzetsu*, p. 21; Chikuden supports the criticism while attributing it to Kitayama Kangan.

147 Kiyokawa Hachirō, *Saiyūsō*, quoted in Constantine Vaporis, *Breaking Barriers: Travel and the State in Early Modern Japan* (Cambridge, MA, and London, 1994), p. 160. Thunberg, *Thunberg's Travels*, p. 165.

148 Vaporis, *Breaking Barriers*, pp. 126 and 182.

149 Su Koppei, *Myōmyō kidan*, pp. 160–68. Bunzan was active in the late 1840s to 1850s.

150 Its mathematical centrality was noted, for example, by Engelbert Kaempfer, who broke his narrative there: see Bodart-Bailey, trans. and ed., *Kaempfer's Japan*, p. 336.

151 *Fuku kaze wo Nakoso no seki to omoedomo michi mo sema ni chiru yamasakura hana*. In *Senzai-shū* (1187), see *Shinpen: kokushi taikei*, vol. I/1, p. 187.

152 Ōgyū Sorai, letter to Irie Jakusui, quoted in Kate Wildman Nakai, 'The Naturalization of Neo-Confucianism in Tokugawa Japan: the Problem of Sinocentrism', *Harvard Journal of Asiatic Studies*, 40 (1980), p. 176.

153 Kumazawa Banzan, *Shūgi gaisho*, quoted in *ibid.*, p. 176 (adapted).

154 Moriyama Takamori, *Shizu no odamaki*, pp. 242, and the same author, *Ama no yakumo no ki*, p. 253. More generally, see Andrew Gerstle, 'Amateurs and the Theatre: The So-called Demented Art of Gidayū', in *Japanese Civilization in the Modern World*, ed. Umesao Tadao, Senri Ethnological Series: 40, National Museum of Ethnology (Osaka, 1995), vol. IX, pp. 37–57.

155 Matsudaira Sadanobu, *Taikan zakki*, p. 197; the party recreated the Four Accomplishments (*shigei*), of which one is music (with painting, calligraphy and board-gaming).
156 Katsuragawa Hoshū, *Hokusa bunryaku*, Yoshikawa Kōbunkan edition, pp. 205, 238, 253.
157 Matsudaira Sadanobu, *Taikan zakki*, p. 111. He refers to *mokuchin* (wooden *qin*).
158 DDR, vol. IX, p. 8.
159 *Ibid.*, pp. 159–60.
160 From *Konjaku monogatari*, see Susan Matisoff, *The Legend of Semimaru* (New York and London, 1978), pp. 63–8.
161 Not all costs are recorded, but one pair was over 37 *ryō*: see Katō Hideyuki, 'Sumiyoshi Hiroyuki hitsu "shunjū dōjō hōyō no zu byōbu" shita-e', *Bijutsu kenkyū*, 27, (1970), p. 20.
162 Tokyo City, ed., *Tokyo shishi: Sangyō hen*, vol. XXXVIII, p. 683.
163 *Ibid.*, pp. 684–707.
164 For this and below, see Toyoshima-ya Jūzburō, *Yume no ukihashi: furoku*, in *Enseki jusshū* (1988), vol. V, pp. 335–84.
165 Saitō Hikomaro, *Kumo no ito maki*, in *ibid.*, vol. V, p. 297.

Select Bibliography

Ackroyd, Joyce, *Told Around a Brushwood Fire: the Autobiography of Arai Hakuseki* (Princeton and Tokyo, 1979)

Adachi Hiroyuki, *Iyō no fune: yōshikisen dōnyū to sakoku taisei*, Heibonsha (1995)

Addiss, Stephen, *Tall Mountains and Flowing Waters: The Arts of Uragami Gyokudō* (Honolulu, 1987)

Aimi Kōu, 'Ishiyama-dera engi hoshū tenmatsu', in *Aimi Kōu-shū*, Nihon shoshigaku taikei, vol. XLV/2, Seishōdō (1986), pp. 394–402

Akimoto Norio, 'Kinsei nikkō tōshōgū to minshū sanshi: sono ikkōsatsu', *Utsunomiya daigaku kyōiku kenkyū hōkoku*, 8 (1965), pp. 1–46

Akita Shōtei and Higo Kazuo, eds, *Tennō rekidai zukan*, Heibonsha (1975)

Akizato Ritō, *Shūi miyako meisho zue*, in *Nihon meisho fūzoku zue*, ed. Takemura Hidenori (Kadokawa, 1981), vol. VIII, pp. 207–385

Anon., *Kii akasaka o-yakata on-tei no ki*, in *Edo sōsho*, Meicho Kankōkai (1964), vol. I, pp. 6–36

Anzai Un'en, *Kinsei meika shoga dan*, in *Nihon garon taikan*, 2 vols, ed. Sakazaki Tan (Arusu, 1927), vol. I, pp. 327–460

Aoki Okikatsu, *Tōmon jussaku*, in *Nihon keizai daiten*, Keimeisha (1928), vol. XX, pp. 367–86

Arai Hakuseki, *Oritaku shiba no ki*, in *Nihon koten bungaku taikei* (Iwanami, 1964), vol. XCIV, pp. 146–426

Asano, Shugo, and Timothy Clark, *The Passionate Art of Utamaro* (London, 1995)

Aston, W. G., '"HMS Phaeton" at Nagasaki in 1808', *Transactions of the Asiatic Society of Japan*, 7 (1879), pp. 323–36

Ban Kōkei, *Kinsei kijin-den*, in *Kinsei kijin-den, zoku-kinsei kijin-den*, Tōyō bunko, Heibonsha (1972)

——, *Yagutsuchi no arabi: Tenmei hachi-nen ni-gatsu shojun*, in *Kansei bungaku-sen*, ed. Fujishima Masao, Private Press (Kyoto, 1974), pp. 126–36

Barley, Nigel, 'White Elephants and Cannibals', in *The Golden Sword: Stamford Raffles and the East*, ed. Nigel Barley (London, 1999), pp. 77–86

Berry, Paul, 'Tanomura Chikuden, 1777–1835: Man Amidst Mountains', PhD thesis, University of Michigan, 1985

Blomberg, Katarina, 'Carl Peter Thunberg: A Swedish Scholar in Tokugawa Japan', in *Contemporary European Writing on Japan*, ed. Ian Nish (Ashford, Kent, 1988), pp. 16–22

Blussé, Leonard, Paul van der Velde and Cynthia Viallé, eds, *The Deshima Dagregisters: Their Original Tables of Contents* (Leiden, 1996–97), 10 vols

Bodart-Bailey, Beatrice, ed., *Kaempfer's Japan: Tokugawa Culture Observed* (Honololu, 1999)

Bolitho, Harold, *Treasures Among Men: The Fudai Daimyo in Tokugawa Japan* (New Haven and London, 1974)

Campbell, Robert, 'Poems on the Way to Yoshiwara', in *Imaging/Reading Eros: Proceedings for the Conference, Sexuality and Edo Culture, 1750–1850*, ed. Sumie Jones (Bloomington, IN, 1996), pp. 95–97

Chance, Frank L., 'Tani Bunchō (1763–1841) and the Edo School of Japanese Painting', PhD thesis, University of Washington, Seattle, 1986

Chino Kaori, 'Kensetsu no naibu kūkan to shōhekiga', in *Nihon bijutsu zenshū*, Kōdansha (1991), vol. XVI, pp. 158–65

Clark, Timothy, *Ukiyo-e Paintings in the British Museum* (London, 1992)

Clunas, Craig, *Art in China*, Oxford History of Art (Oxford and New York, 1997)
——, *Fruitful Sites: Garden Culture in Ming Dynasty China* (London, 1996)
Coaldrake, William H., *Architecture and Authority in Japan* (London and New York, 1996)
——, 'Edo Architecture and Tokugawa Law', *Monumenta Nipponica*, 36 (1981), pp. 235–84
Cobbing, Andrew, 'The First Japanese Woman in Europe?', *Proceedings of the Japan Society*, 132 (1999), pp. 34–42
Crawcour, E. S., 'Some Observations on Merchants: A Translation of Mitsui Takafusa's "Chōnin Kōken Roku', *Transactions of the Asiatic Society of Japan: Series 3*, 8 (1961), pp. 31–139
Davis, A. R., *T'ao Yuan-ming: His Works and Their Meaning*, 2 vols (Cambridge and New York, 1983)
Davis, Julie Nelson, 'Drawing His Own Ravishing Features: Kitagawa Utamaro and the Construction of a Public Identity in Ukiyo-e Prints', PhD thesis, University of Washington, Seattle, 1998
Doi Tsuguyoshi, *Kinsei nihon kaiga no kenkyū*, Bijutsu Shuppan-sha (1970)
Elisonas, Jurgis, 'Notorious Places: A Brief Excursion into the Narrative Topography of Early Edo', in *Edo and Paris: Urban Life and the State in the Early Modern Period*, ed. James McClain *et al.* (Ithaca and London, 1994), pp. 253–91
Ema Masamizu, ed., *Rakuō-kō isho*, 2 vols (Yao, 1993)
French, Calvin, *The Poet Painters: Buson and his Followers*, University of Michigan Art Museum (Ann Arbor, MI, 1974)
——, *Shiba Kōkan: Artist, Innovator and Pioneer in the Westernization of Japan* (New York and Tokyo, 1974)
Fujioka Michio, *Kyōto gosho (shinchō)*, Chūō Kōron Bijutsu Shuppan (1987)
Fujishima Munenobu, *Tenmei taika no ki*, in *Kansei bungaku-sen*, ed. Fujishima Masao, Private Press (Kyoto, 1974), pp. 141–4
Fujita Satoru, *Bakumatsu no tennō*, Kōdansha Mechie, Kōdansha (1994)
——, 'Kansei dairi zōei o meguru chōbaku kankei', *Nihon rekishi*, 517 (1991), pp. 6–32
——, 'Kokusei ni taisuru chōtei no sonzai', in *Nihon no kinsei*, Chūō Kōronsha (1991), vol. II, pp. 307–58
——, *Matsudaira Sadanobu: seiji kaikaku ni idonda rōjū*, Chūō Shinsho, Chūō Kōronsha (1993)
Fujitani, T., *Splendid Monarchy: Power and Pagentry in Modern Japan* (Berkeley, CA, and London, 1996)
Fukui Kyūzō, *Shodaimyō no gakujitsu to bungaku no kenkyū*, 2nd edn, Hara Shobō (1976)
Fujioka Sakutarō, *Kinsei nihon kaiga shi*, 2nd edn, Perikan-sha (1982)
Furukawa Koshōken, *Saiyū zakki*, vol. IX of *Kinsei shakai keizai sōsho*, Kaizōsha (1927), pp. 140–67
——, *Tōyū zakki*, vol. XII of *Kinsei shakai keizai sōsho*, Kaizōsha (1927)
Gaka to tabi: egakareta shizen 2, exh. cat.; Suntory Museum of Art, Tokyo (Tokyo, 1990)
Gerstle, Andrew, 'Amateurs and the Theatre: The So-Called Demented Art of Gigadyū', in *Japanese Civilization in the Modern World*, ed. Umesao Tadao, Senri Ethnological Series: 40, National Museum of Ethnology (Osaka, 1995), vol. IX, pp. 37–57
——, 'Flowers of Edo: Kabuki and its Patrons in the Eighteenth Century', in *18th Century Japan*, ed. C. Andrew Gerstle (Sydney, 1989), pp. 33–50
Gunji Masakatsu, *Fūryū no zuzōshi*, Sanshōdō (1987)
Haga Tōru, *Hiraga Gennai*, Asahi Sensho, Asahi Shinbun (1989)
Hall, John Whitney, *Tanuma Okitsugu: Forerunner of Modern Japan* (Cambridge, MA, and London, 1955)

Hamada Giichirō, *Kibyōshi edaisen shū*, Yumani Shobō (1979)
——, *Ōta Nanpo*. Jinbutsu sōsho, Yoshikawa Kōbunkan (1963)
——, ed., *Edo bungaku chimei jiten*, Tōkyōdō (1972)
Hanasaki Kazuo, *Edo no kagama-jaya*, Miki Shobō (1992)
Harper, Thomas, '"The Tale of Genji" in the Eighteenth Century', in *18th Century Japan*, ed. C. Andrew Gerstle (Sydney, 1989), pp. 106–23
Harries, Phillip, '*Fūryū*: a Concept of Elegance in Pre-Modern Literature', in *Europe Interprets Japan*, ed. Gordon Daniels (Tenterden, 1984), pp. 137–44
Hattori Nankaku, *Nankaku-sensei bunshū*, vol. VII of *Kinsei juka bunshū shūsei*, Perikan-sha (1985)
Hayashi Hikaru *et al.*, eds, *Tsūkō ichiran*, 16 vols, Kokusho Kankōkai (1913)
Hesserlink, Reinier, 'A Dutch New Year at the Shirandō Academy: 1 January 1795', *Monumenta Nipponica*, 50 (1995), pp. 189–234
Hickman, Money, 'The Paintings of Soga Shōhaku', PhD thesis, Harvard University, 1976
—— and Yasuhiro Satō, *The Paintings of Jakuchū* (New York, 1989)
Higuchi Kazuya, 'Aizuri ukiyo-e hanga ni kansuru ikkōsatsu', *Idemitsu bijutsukan kanpō*, 90 (1995), pp. 4–20
Hirafuku Hyakusui, *Nihon yōga no shōkō* (Iwanami, 1930)
Hiraga Gennai, *Butsurui hinshitsu*, vol. XVI of *Nihon koten zenshū: 3*, Nihon Koten Zenshū Kankōkai (1927)
Hiratsuka Yoshinobu, *Nihon ni okeru nanshoku no kenkyū*, Ningen no Kagakusha (1987)
Horiya Fumi, *Oranda-bumi*, in *Hyōryo kidan zenshū*, Teikoku bunko, Hakubunkan (1900), vol. XXII, pp. 997–1000
Hoshino Kuniya, '"Koga ruijū" ni tsuite', in *Koga ruijū*, ed. Tokyo National Museum, Mainichi Shinbunsha (1990), pp. 76–81
Hosono Masanobu, *Edo no kano*, vol. CCLXII of *Nihon no bijutsu*, Shibundō (1988)
——, *Kōkan to Denzen*, vol. CCXXXII of *Nihon no bijutsu*, Shibundō (1985)
——, ed., *Tani Bunchō hitsu 'kōyo tanshō zu'*, Meicho Shuppan (1975)
Ishizaki Yūshi, *Nagasaki kokon shūran meisho zue*, in *Nagasaki bunken sōsho: 2*, Bunken-sha (Nagasaki, 1975), vol I, pp. 71–350
Isozaki Yasuhiko, *Aōdō Denzen no kenkyū*, Yūshōdō (1980)
——, *Matsumae-han no gajin to kinsei kaigashi*, Keisuisha (1986)
Israel, Jonathan, *The Dutch Republic: Its Rise, Greatness and Fall, 1477–1806*, Oxford History of Early Modern Europe (Oxford, 1995)
Iwasaki, Haruko, 'Portrait of a Daimyo: Comic Fiction by Matsudaira Sadanobu', *Monumenta Nipponica*, 38 (1983), pp. 1–48
Jay, Peter, *Downcast Eyes: The Denigration of Vision in Twentieth-Century French Thought* (Berkeley, CA, and London, 1993)
Jippensha Ikku, *Tōkaidōchū hizakurige*, vol. LXVIII of *Nihon koten bungaku taikei* (Iwanami, 1958)
Juppō-an, *Yūreki zakki*, vols III-VII of *Edo sōsho*, Meichō Kankōkai (1964)
Kamens, Edward, *Utamakura: Allusion and Intertextuality in Traditional Japanese Poetry* (New Haven and London, 1997)
Kamihira Chie, 'Kyōto oranda-juku no shokumu', in *Ronshū nihon no yōgaku*, ed. Arizaka Takamichi *et al.*, Seibundō (Osaka, 1995), vol. III, pp. 137–68
Kano Yasunobu, *Gadō yōketsu*, in *Nihon kaigaron taisei*, Perikan-sha (1997), vol. IV, pp. 7–30
Kasuya Hideki, *'Tōkaidō meisho' zue o yomu*, Tōkyōdō (1997)
Katagiri Kazuo, 'Yōfū gaka Ishikawa Tairō to edo no rangakkai: 1', *Museum*, 227 (1970), pp. 4–17
——, 'Yōfū gaka Ishikawa Tairō to edo no rangakkai: 2', *Museum*, 228 (1970), pp. 16–28
Katō Hideyuki, 'Sumiyoshi Hiroyuki hitsu "shunjū dōjō hōyō no zu byōbu" shita-e

oyobi "chōsen shinshi raihei ikken shorui"', *Bijutsu kenkyū*, 27 (1970), pp. 191–201
Katsuragawa Hoshū, *Hokusa bunryaku*, Yoshikawa Kōbunkan (1970)
——, *Hokusa bunryaku*, Iwanami bunko (Iwanami, 1990)
Kawamoto Shigeo, Kawamoto Keiko, Miura Masayaki, 'Kenjō sōji no kenkyū: Ninna-ji zō keichō-do kenjō sōji o chūshin ni', *Kokka*, 1028 (1979), pp.7–31; 1029 (1979), pp. 9–28.
Keene, Donald, *World Within Walls: Japanese Literature of the Pre-Modern Era, 1600–1868* (New York, 1976)
Keyes, Roger, 'Envisioning the Past: Utamaro's Album "Waka ebisu"', in *A Sheaf of Japanese Papers: In Tribute to Heinz Kaempfer on his 75th Birthday*, ed. Matthi Forrer *et al.* (The Hague, 1979)
Kimura Kenkadō, 'Kenkadō zatsuroku', in *Nihon zuihitsu taisei: 1*, Yoshikawa Kōbunkan (1975), vol. VII
Kimuro Bōun, *Mita kyō monogatari*, in *Nihon zuihitsu taisei: 3*, Yoshikawa Kōbunkan (1976), vol. VIII, pp. 565–81
Kitamura Kashiro, *Satsuki ame jisshū*, in *Shin enseki jusshū*, Chūō Kōronsha (1982), vol. II
Kobayashi Tadashi, *Edo kaiga shiron*, Ruri Shobō (1983)
——, 'Gazoku no kōō: honga to ukiyo-e', in *Nihon no kinsei*, Chūō Kōronsha (1993), vol. XII, pp. 351–76
——, '"Sumidagawa ryōgan zukan" no seiritsu to tenkai', *Kokka*, 1172 (1993), pp. 5–22
Kodera Takehisa, *Owari-han Edo shimo-yashiki no nazo: gikō no machi wo motsu daimyō teien*, Chūkō shinsho, Chūō Kōronsha (1989)
Koikawa Harumachi, *Ōmu-gaeshi bunbu no futamichi*, in *Kibyōshi, senryū, kyōkka*, Nihon koten bungaku taikei (Iwanami, 1971), pp. 159–98
Koike Masatane *et al.*, eds, *Edo no gesaku ehon*, 6 vols, Kyōiku Bunko, Shakai Shisōsha (1984)
Kokaen, *Yume no ukihashi: furoku*, in *Enseki jusshū*, Chūō Kōronsha (1988), vol. V
Kokushi Taikei Henshū Iinkai, ed., *Shinpen: kokushi taikei* (Kadokawa, 1985)
Kornicki, Peter, *The Book in Japan: A Cultural History from the Beginnings to the Nineteenth Century* (Leiden, Boston and Cologne, 1998)
Koschmann, Victor, *The Mito Ideology: Discourse, Reform, and Insurrection in Late Tokugawa Japan, 1790–1868* (Berkeley, CA, and London, 1987)
Kreiger, C. C., *The Infiltration of European Civilisation in Japan during the Eighteenth Century* (Leiden, 1940)
Kumakura Isao, *Go-mizunoo tennō*, Dōjidai Raiburii (Iwanami, 1994)
Kuroda Hideo, *Ō no shintai ō no shōzō*, Imeji riideingu, Heibonsha (1993)
Kyoto, City of, ed., *Kyōto no rekishi*, Gakugei Shorin (1973)
de Lairesse, Gérard, *The Art of Painting in All its Branches*, trans. John Fitsch (London, 1783)
Lensen, George, *The Russian Push Towards Japan: Russo-Japanese Relations, 1697–1875* (New York, 1971)
Lewis, James, 'Across the Straits. Frontier Contact between Chosŏn Korea and Tokugawa Japan', PhD thesis, University of Honolulu, 1994
Luendijk-Elshout, A. M., '"Ontledinge" (Anatomy) as Underlying Principle of Western Medicine in Japan', in *Red-hair Medicine: Dutch–Japanese Medical Relations*, ed. H. Beukers *et al.* (Amsterdam and Atlanta, GA, 1991), pp. 27–37
Mac Lean, J., 'The Introduction of Books and Scientific Instruments into Japan, 1712–1854', *Japanese Studies in the History of Science*, 13 (1974), pp. 9–68
Machijiri Ryōgen, *Tenmei uutsu kōki*, in *Kansei bungaku-sen*, ed. Fujishima Masao, Private Press (Kyoto, 1974), pp. 119–25
Maruyama Ōkyo, exh. cat.; Kyoto National Museum (Kyoto, 1995)
Matisoff, Susan, *The Legend of Semimaru: Blind Musician of Japan* (New York and

London, 1978)
Matsudaira Sadanobu, *Kagetsu sōshi*, in *Nihon zuihitsu taisei: 3*, Yoshikawa Kōbunkan (1976), vol. I
——, *Kan naru amari*, in *Nihon zuihitsu taisei: 2*, Yoshikawa Kōbunkan (1974), vol. IV, pp. 329–38
——, *Ōmu no kotoba*, in *Misonoya*, ed. Ōta Nanpo, Kokusho Kankōkai (1917), vol. III, pp. 433–38
——, *Seigo*, in *Nihon shisō taikei* (Iwanami, 1976), vol. XXXVIII, pp. 249–78
——, *Taikan zakki*, in *Zoku nihon zuihitsu taisei*, Yoshikawa Kōbunkan (1998), vol. VI, pp. 11–253
——, *Uge no hitokoto*, in *Uge no hitogoto/Shugyō-roku*, Iwanami Bunko (Iwanami, 1942)
Matsuki Hiroshi, *Kano-ke no chi to katana*, Kōdansha Mechie, Kōdansha (1994)
——, *Tsutaya Jūzaburō: Edo geijutsu no enshutsuka*, Nihon Keizai Shinbunsha (1988)
Matsuo Bashō, *Oku no hosomichi*, in *Bashō bunshū*, Nihon koten bungaku taikai (Iwanami, 1959), vol. XLVI, pp. 69–100
Matsura Seizan, *Kasshi yawa*, vol. VII of *Nihon zuihitsu taisei: 3*, Yoshikawa Kōbunkan (1930)
——, *Kasshi yawa*, Tōyō bunko, Heibonsha (1977)
McCullough, Helen Craig, ed., *The Tale of the Heike* (Stanford, 1988)
McMullen, I. James, 'Non-Agnatic Adoption as a Confucian Controversy in Seventeenth and Eighteenth-Century Japan', *Harvard Journal of Asiatic Studies*, 35 (1975), pp. 133–48
Meishū Chōemon, *Asama-zan daishō ikken-gen*, in *Nihon shomin seikatsu shiryō shūsei*, San'ichi Shobō (1970), vol. VII, pp. 141–82
Minagawa Kien, *Kien bunshū*, in *Kinsei jukan bunshū shūsei*, Perikan-sha (1988), vol. IX
——, *Shahon Kien bunshū*, in *Kinsei jukan bunshū shūsei*, Perikan-sha (1988), vol. IX
Miyajima Shin'ichi, 'Garyū no keisei to keishō: maruyama, shijō to hara, kishi ha', in *Nihon byōbu-e shūsei*, Kōdansha (1978), vol. VIII, pp. 141–49
Miyashita Saburō, 'Jinkō konjō (purushian buruu) no mozō to yunyū', in *Ronshū nihon no yōgaku*, ed. Arisaki Takamichi and Asai Mitsuaki, Seibundō (Osaka, 1995), vol. III
Mori Senzō, 'Kaikoku heidan sagon', in *Mori Senzō chosaku shū*, Chūō Kōronsha (1988), vol. VII, pp. 147–51
——, 'Kairyō hōshi', in *Mori Senzō chosaku shū*, Chūō Kōronsha (1988), vol. III
——, *Mori Senzō chosaku shū*, 12 vols, Chūō Kōronsha (1988)
——, '*Nochimigusa* wo tōshite mita Sugita Genpaku', in *Mori Senzō chosaku shū*, Chūō Kōronsha (1989), vol. V, pp. 154–61
——, 'Ōkyo den tōki', *Bijutsu kenkyū*, 36 (1934), pp. 584–94
——, 'Shōgun Ienari no jinbutsu', in *Mori Senzō chosaku shū: zokuhen*, Chūō Kōronsha (1992), vol. I, pp. 58–63
Morishima Chūryō, *Hōgu-kago*, in *Zoku enseki jusshū*, Chūō Kōronsha (1980), vol. II, pp. 167–78
——, *Keirin manroku*, in *Nihon zuihitsu taisei: 2*, Yoshikawa Kōbunkan (1975), vol I
——, *Kōmō zatsuwa*, in *Bunmei genryū sōsho*, Kokusho Kankōkai (1913), vol. I, pp. 454–86
Moriyama Takamori, *Ama no takumo no ki*, in *Nihon zuihitsu taisei: 2*, Yoshikawa Kōbunkan (1974), vol. XXII, pp. 199–264
——, *Shizu no odamaki*, in *Nihon zuihitsu taisei: 3*, Yoshikawa Kōbunkan (1976), vol. IV, pp. 225–67
Motoori Norinaga, *E no koto*, in *Nihon garon taikan*, ed. Sakazaki Tan (Arusu,

1927), vol. I, pp. 190–95
Munesaka Isoo, 'Tachibana Nankei "Tōyū-ki" to Edo kōki no kikō bungaku', in *Shin-nihon bungaku taikei* (Iwanami, 1991), vol. XCVIII, pp. 437–55
Naitō Masato, 'Chōbunsai Eishi no iwayuru "yoshiwara-gayoi zukan" ni tsuite', in *Nikuhitsu ukiyo-e taikan*, ed. Kobayashi Tadashi, Kōdansha (1996), vol. III
Najita, Tetsuo, ed., *Readings in Tokugawa Thought*, Selected Papers: Center for East Asian Studies, University of Chicago (Chicago, 1993)
Nakabayashi Chikutō, *Chikutō garon*, in *Nihon garon taikan*, ed. Sakazaki Tan (Arusu, 1927), vol. I, pp. 199–222
——, *Gadō kongōshō*, in *Nihon garon taikan*, ed. Sakazaki Tan (Arusu, 1927), vol. I, pp. 171–88
Nakai, Kate Wildman, 'The Naturalization of Neo-Confucianism in Tokugawa Japan: the Problem of Sinocentrism', *Harvard Journal of Asiatic Studies*, 40 (1980), pp. 157–99
——, *Shogunal Politics: Arai Hakuseki and the Premises of Tokugawa Rule*, Harvard East Asian Monographs (Cambridge, MA, and London, 1988)
Nakamura Shin'ichirō, *Kakizaki Hakyō no shōgai*, Shinkosha (1989)
Nakamura Tanio, *Reizei Tamechika to fukkō yamato-e*, vol. CCLXI of *Nihon no bijutsu*, Shibundō (1988)
Nakayama Kōyō, *Gadan keiroku*, in *Nihon zuihitsu taisei: 1*, Yoshikawa Kōbunkan (1975), vol. IV, pp. 159–96
Nakayama, Shigeru, *A History of Japanese Astronomy: Chinese Background and Western Impact* (Cambridge, MA, and London, 1969)
Narishima Morimichi *et al.*, eds, *Tokugawa jikki*, Kokushi taikei, Yoshikawa Kōbunkan (1976)
Naruse Fujio, 'Shiba Kōkan no ukiyo-eshi jidai ni tsuite', *Ukiyo-e geijutsu*, 73 (1982), pp. 3–23
Naruse Fujio *et al.*, eds, *Shiba Kōkan Zenshū*, 8 vols (Yasaka Shobō, 1992)
Nihon Ishi Gakkai, ed., *Zuroku nihon iji bunka shiryō shūsei*, 5 vols, San'ichi Shobō (1977)
Nishina Yūsuke, *Edo bijutsu kōgengaku: ukiyo-e no hikari to kage*, Gabundō (1988)
Nomura Bunshō, *Tani Bunchō-ō no ki*, in *Enseki jusshū*, Chūō Kōronsha (1988), vol. V
Oetterman, Stephan, *Panorama: The History of a Mass Medium* (New York, 1997)
Ōishi Shinzaburō, *Tenmei sannen: asama no funkatsu* (1986)
Ojima Yasunori, 'Jugaku no shakaika: seiji kaikaku to sorai ikō no jugaku', in *Nihon no kinsei*, Chūō Kōronsha (1993), vol. XIII, pp. 123–74
Okada Hajime, ed., *[Haifū]yanagi-daru zenshū*, Sanshōdō (1978)
Okada Rihei, *Haiga no bi: Buson, Gekkei* (Osaka, 1973)
Oku Bunmei, '*Sensai Maruyama-sensei den*', *Bijutsu kenkyū*, 36 (1934), pp. 548–93
Ooms, Herman, *The Charismatic Bureaucrat: A Political Biography of Matsudaira Sadanobu* (Chicago and London, 1975)
Ōta Kinjō, *Gosō manpitsu*, in *Nihon zuihitsu zenshū*, Kokumin Tosho (1928), vol. XVII, pp. 1–330
——, Yū kōrakuen ki narabi ni jo, MS [1795], National Diet Library, Tokyo
Ōta Nanpo, *Ichiwa ichigon*, supplementary vol. IV of *Nihon zuihitsu taisei*, Yoshikawa Kōbunkan (1978)
Ōtsuki Gentaku, *Rangaku kaitei*, in *Yōgaku: 1*, Nihon shisō taikei (Iwanami, 1976), vol. LXIV, pp. 317–372
—— and Arima Genchō, *Ransetsu benwaku*, in *Edo kagaku koten sōsho*, Inawa Shoten (1979), vol. XVII, pp. 133–319
Raffles, S. T., *Raffles' Report on Japan to the Secret Committee for the English East India Company* (Kōbe, 1929)
Rai Kiichi, 'Kinseijin ni totte no gakumon to jissen', in *Nihon no kinsei*, Chūō Kōronsha (1993), vol. XIII, pp. 7–34
Reily, Celia, 'Tung Ch'i-ch'ang's Life', in *The Century of Tung Ch'i-ch'ang*, ed. Wai-

kam Ho (Kansas City, 1992), vol. II, pp. 385–458
Roberts, Luke, *Mercantilism in a Japanese Domain: The Merchant Origins of Economic Nationalism in 18th-Century Tosa* (Cambridge and New York, 1998)
Rosenfield, John M., 'Japanese Studio Practice: the Tosa Family and the Imperial Painting Office', in *The Artist's Workshop*, ed. Peter Lukehard, Studies in the History of Art, 38 (Washington, DC, 1993), pp. 78–102
Roy, Alain, *Gérard de Lairesse (1640–1711)* (Paris, 1992)
Sadanobu to Bunchō: Matsudaira Sadanobu to shūhen no gajintachi, exh. cat.; Prefectural Museum, Fukushima (Fukushima, 1992)
Sadler, A. L., trans. and ed., *The Ten Foot Square Hut and the Tales of the Heike* (Tokyo and Rutland, VT, 1972)
Saitō Gesshin, ed., *Bukō nenpyō*, vol. XII of *Edo sōsho*, Meicho Kankōkai (1964)
Saitō Hikomaro, *Kamiyo yawa*, in *Enseki jusshū*, Chūō Kōronsha (1987), vol. III, pp. 111–48
——, *Kumo no ito maki*, in *Enseki jusshū*, Chuo Kōronsha (1988), vol. V
Sakai Gankow, *Utamaro*, Sanyō Press (Matsumoto, 1992)
Sakakibara Satoru, 'Kano-ha goyō eshi no koto', *Kobijutsu*, 100 (1991), pp.12–43
——, 'Tani Bunchō hitsu, "Aoyama ensō zukō", "Toyama zansō zukō"', *Kokka*, 1148 (1991), pp. 33–41
Sasaki Jōhei, *Ōkyo shasei gashū*, Kōdansha (1981)
—— and Sasaki Masako, *Maruyama Ōkyo kenkyū*, 2 vols, Chūō Kōronsha (1996)
Satake Yoshiatsu (Shozan), *Gahō kōryō*, in *Nihon garon taikan*, ed. Sakazaki Tan (Arusu, 1927), vol. I, pp. 100–102
——, *Gazu rikai*, in *Nihon garon taikan*, ed. Sakazaki Tan (Arusu, 1927), vol. I, pp. 102–3
Satō Narihiro, *Chūryō manroku*, in *Nihon zuihitsu taisei: 3*, Yoshikawa Kōbunkan (1976), vol. III, pp. 1–362
Satō Yasuhiro, 'Jūhasseiki no zen'ei shinwa', in *Edo bunka no hen'yō: jūhasseiki nihon no keiken*, ed. Momokawa Takahito *et al.*, Heibonsha (1994), pp. 119–62
Satō Yōichi, 'Matsudaira Sadanobu no ryōnai junken: zuikō suru bunjin to gajin', in *Sadanobu to Bunchō: Matsudaira Sadanobu to shūhen no gakatachi*, ed. Prefectural Museum, Fukushima (Fukushima, 1992), pp. 98–112
Sawada Akira, *Nihon gaka jiten*, 2nd edn, 2 vols, Daigakudō (1987)
Screech, Timon, *Edo no shintai o hiraku*, trans. Takayama Hiroshi, Sakuhinsha (1997)
——, 'Glass, Painting on Glass, and Vision in Late-Eighteenth-Century Japan', *Apollo*, 433 (1998), pp. 28–32
——, 'The Meaning of Western Perspective in Edo Popular Culture', *Archives of Asian Art*, 47 (1994), pp. 58–69
——, *Ō-edo ijin ōrai*, trans. Takayama Hiroshi, Maruzen Books (Maruzen, 1995)
——, *Sex and the Floating World: Erotic Images in Japan, 1700–1820* (London, 1999)
——, 'Shōgun no zuzō o utsusu', trans. Takayama Hiroshi, in *Edo no kirikuchi*, ed. Takayama Hiroshi, Maruzen Books (Maruzen, 1994), pp. 259–73
——, 'The Strangest Place in Edo: The Temple of the Five-hundred Arhats', *Monumenta Nipponica*, 48 (1993), pp. 407–28
——, *The Western Scientific Gaze and Popular Imagery in Later Edo Japan: The Lens within the Heart* (Cambridge and New York, 1996)
Sekio Seiichi, ed., *Oranda fūsetsu-gaki shūsei*, Yoshikawa Kōbunkan (1977)
Shapin, Steven, and Simon Schaffer, *Leviathan and the Air-Pump: Hobbes, Boyle and the Experimental Life* (Princeton and London, 1985)
Shiba Kōkan, *Dokushō bōgen*, in *Shiba Kōkan zenshū*, Naruse Fujio *et al.*, eds, Yasaka Shobō (1993), vol. II, pp. 1–28
——, *Oranda tsūhaku*, in *Shiba Kōkan zenshū*, Naruse Fujio *et al.*, eds, Yasaka Shobō (1994), vol. III, pp. 147–92

——, *Saiyū nikki*, in *Shiba Kōkan zenshū*, Naruse Fujio *et al.*, eds, Yasaka Shobō (1993), vol. I, pp. 223–404
——, *Seiyō gadan*, in *Shiba Kōkan zenshū*, Naruse Fujio *et al.*, eds, Yasaka Shobō (1994), vol. III, pp. 137–46
——, *Shunparō hikki*, in *Shiba Kōkan zenshū*, Naruse Fujio *et al.*, eds, Yasaka Shobō (1993), vol. II, pp. 29–114
Shibusawa Eiichi, *Rakuō-kō den*, 2nd edn (Iwanami, 1983)
Shimada Takehiko, *Kinsei fukkō seiryōden no kenkyū*, Shibunkaku (1987)
Shirahata Yōzaburō, *Daimyō teien: Edo no kyōen*, Kōdansha sensho mechie, Kōdansha (1997)
Shirai Kayō, *Gajō yōryaku*, in *Nihon garon taisei*, ed. Kobayashi Tadashi *et al.*, Perikan-sha (1996), vol. IV, pp. 9–88
Shirane, Haruo, *Traces of Dreams: Landscape, Cultural Memory, and the Poetry of Bashō* (Stanford, 1988)
Shiveley, Donald, 'Bakufu versus Kabuki', *Harvard Journal of Asiatic Studies*, 18 (1955), pp. 326–58
Smith, Henry, 'World Without Walls: Kuwagata Keisai's Panoramic Vision', in *Japan and the World*, ed. Gail Bernstein and Haruhito Fukui (London, 1988), pp. 3–19
Sora, *Sora zuikō nikki*, vol. VI of *Kōhen: Bashō zenshū*, Fujimi Shobō (1989)
Su Koppei, *Myōmyō kidan*, in *Nihon zuihitsu taisei: 3* (1976), vol. XI, pp. 353–403
Suganuma Teizō, *Kazan no kenkyū*, Mokiji-sha (1969)
Sugita Genpaku, *Nochimigusa*, in *Nihon shomin seikatsu shiryō shūsei*, San'ichi Shobō (1976), vol. VII, pp. 57–86
——, *Rangaku kotohajime*, in *Nihon koten bungaku taikei* (Iwanami, 1964), vol. XCV, pp. 473–516
—— *et al.*, trans., *Kaitai shinsho*, in *Yōgaku*: 1, Nihon shisō taikei (Iwanami, 1972), vol. LXIV, pp. 207–218
Suzuki Hisashi, *Zōjō-ji: Tokugawa shōgun hi to sono zuihin, zuitai*, Tokyo University Press (Tokyo, 1967)
Tachibana Nankei, *Hokusō sadan*, in *Tōzai yūki, hokusō sadan*, Yūhōdō bunko, Yūhōd (1913), pp. 1–208
——, *Saiyūki*, in *Azumaji no ki, kishikikō, saiyūki*, Shin-nihon koten bungaku taikei (Iwanami, 1991), vol. XCVIII, pp. 174–390
——, *Tōyūki*, in *Tōzai yūki, hokusō sadan*, Yūhōdō bunko (Yūhōdō, 1913), pp. 1–200
Tachihara Suiken, *Yūrin zatsuwa*, in *Nanban kōmō shiryō*, Shinbundō (1930), vol. I, pp. 1–46
——, Shikundō kōsōden, MS [n.d.], National Diet Library, Tokyo
Takafuji Harutoshi, *Nikkō tōshōgū no nazo*, Kōdansha Gendai Shinsho, Kōdansha (1996)
Takasu Toyomori, 'Rakuō-kō to koga no mōsha ni tsuite', *Chūō bijutsu*, 38 (1936), pp. 1–26
Takeda Tsuneo, *Kano-ha kaiga shi*, Yoshikawa Kōbunkan (1995)
Takemura Hidenori, ed., *Nihon meisho fūzoku zue*, Kadokawa (1981)
Takemura Takanori, 'Akizako Ritō to "miyako meisho zue"', in *Nihon meisho fūzoku zue*, Kadokawa (1981), vol. VIII, pp. 510–26
——, 'Nakagawa Kiun to "Miyako-warabe", "Miyako-warabe sekitsui"', in *Nihon meisho fūzoku zue*, Kadokawa (1981), vol. VII, pp. 467–77
Takeuchi, Melinda, 'Ike Taiga: A Biographical Sketch', *Harvard Journal of Asiatic Studies*, 43 (1983), pp. 141–86
——, *Taiga's True Views: The Language of Landscape Painting in Eighteenth-century Japan* (Stanford, 1992)
Takeuchi Makoto, 'Festivals and Fights: The Law and the People of Edo', in *Edo and Paris: Urban Life and the State in the Early Modern Era*, ed. James McClain *et al.* (Ithaca and London, 1994), pp. 384–406

Takizawa Bakin, *Kiryo manroku*, in *Nihon zuihitsu taisei: 1* (1975), vol. I, pp. 137–256
Tamamushi Satoko, ed., *Bunchō, Kazan, Chinzan*, vol. 3 of *Edo meisaku gachō zenshū*, Shinshindō (1995)
Tanahashi Munehiro, *Kibyōshi sōran, Nihon shoshigaku taikei: 48*, 4 vols, Seishōdō (1989)
Tani Bunchō, *Bunchō gadan*, in *Nihon shogaen*, Kokusho Kankōkai (1915), vol. II, pp. 182–235
——, *Honchō gasan*, in *Nihon garon taikan*, ed. Sakazaki Tan (Arusu, 1927), vol. II, pp. 1533–58
Tanomura Chikuden, *Sanchūjin jōzetsu*, in *Nihon garon taisei*, ed. Kobayashi Tadashi *et al.*, Perikan-sha (1966), vol. VII, pp. 9–48
Thunberg, Charles, *Thunberg's Travels*, trans. F. and C. Rivington, 4 vols (London, 1795)
Titsingh, [Isaac], *Illustrations of Japan: Consisting of Private Memoires and Anecdotes of the Reigning Dynasty of the Djogouns, or Sovereigns of Japan*, trans. Frederick Shoberl (London, 1822)
Toby, Ronald, *State and Diplomacy in Early Modern Japan: Asia in the Development of the Tokugawa Bakufu*, 2nd edn (Stanford, 1991)
Tokyo, City of, ed., *Tōkyō shishi-kō*, 2 vols (Tokyo, 1923–8)
Tokyo National Museum, ed., *Koga ruijū: chōsa kenkyū hōkokusho*, Mainichi Shinbun (1990)
Tōno Haruyuki, *Kahei no nihonshi*, Asahi Shinbun-sha (1997)
Tōno Hiroshi, '"Koga ruijū" no seiritsu', in *Koga ruijū*, Mainichi Shinbunsha (1990), pp. 82–91
Tōrai Sanna, *Tenka ichimen kagami umehachi*, in *Edo no gesaku ehon*, ed. Koike Masatane *et al.*, Kyōiku Bunko, Shakai Shisōsha (1982), vol. III, pp. 181–208
Toyama Mikio, *Nagasaki bugyō, Chūkō Shinsho*, Chūō Kōronsha (1988)
Toyama Usaburō , *Nihon shoki yōga shikō*, Zenkoku Shobō (1965)
Tozawa Yukio, *Katsuragawa-ke no sekai: Edo geien no kiun*, Chikuma Shobō (1994)
Tsuji Nobuo, *Kisō no keifu*, Perikan-sha (1988)
Tsunoda, Ryusaku, *et al.*, *Sources of Japanese Tradition.* Introduction to Oriental Civilizations (New York and London, 1958)
Tsunoyama Sakae, *Tokei no shakaishi*, Shuko Shinsho, Chūō Kōronsha (1984)
Uchida Kinzō, 'Kuwagata Keisai kenkyū: okaka-eshi jidai no katsudō o megutte: 1', *Kokka*, 1158 (1992), pp. 11–30
——, 'Kuwagata Keisai kenkyū: okaka-eshi jidai no katsudō o megutte: 2', *Kokka*, 1159 (1992), pp. 9–24
Uchiyama Mikiko, 'Engeki-shi no naka no tennō', in *Nihon no kinsei*, Chūō Kōronsha (1991), vol. II, pp. 251–306
Ueda Akinari, *Kyōto taika no ki*, in *Kansei bungaku-sen*, ed. Fujishima Masao, Private Press (Kyoto, 1974), pp. 112–18
——, *Tan daishō shinroku*, in *Ueda Akinari shū*, Nihon koten bungaku taikei (Iwanami, 1959), vol. LVI, pp. 249–382
Ueda, Makoto, *Literary and Art Theories in Japan* (Cleveland, OH, 1967)
Ueno Kenji, 'Den Tani Bunchō hitsu "Kinsei meika shozō zukan" ni tsuite', *Tochigi kenritsu bijutsukan kiyō*, 7 (1979), pp. 73–85
——, ed., *Edo meisaku gachō zenshū*, Shinshindō (1995)
Ukai Nobunari, Kōraku-en kiji, MS [1737], National Diet Library, Tokyo
Umehara Takeshi, *Kyōto hakken: chirei chinkon*, Shinkosha (1997)
Umehara Tetsuo, ed., *Tennōsei kokka no tōgō to shihai*, Bunri-kaku (1992)
Umezu Jirō, 'Ishiyama-dera e kō', *Bijutsushi*, 19 (1952), pp. 35–48
Vaporis, Constantine, *Breaking Barriers: Travel and the State in Early Modern Japan*, Council of East Asian Studies (Cambridge, MA, and London, 1994)
de Vries, Lyckle, *Gérard de Lairesse: An Artist Between Stage and Studio*

(Amsterdam, 1998)
Warnke, Martin, *Political Landscape: The Art History of Nature*, trans. David McLintock (London, 1995)
Watanabe Keiichi, *Kubota-jō monogatari*, Mumeisha (Akita, 1989)
Watanabe Toshio, *Kinsei nihon tenmon gaku-shi*, 2 vols, Kōseisha Kōseikaku (1984)
Watt, David K., *Thailand: A Short History* (New Haven and London, 1982)
Weinshenker, Anne Betty, *Falconet: His Writings and His Friend Diderot* (Geneva, 1966)
Wylie, Hugh, 'Nanga Treatises of Nineteenth Century Japan: Translation, Commentary and Analysis', PhD thesis, University of Kansas, 1991
Yamamoto Toshio, *Matsudaira Sadanobu: sono hito to shōgai*, Private Press (Shirakawa, 1983)
Yanagisawa Kien, *Hitorine*, in *Kinsei zuisō-shū*, Nihon koten bungaku taikei (Iwanami, 1965), vol. XLVI, pp. 25–208
Yashiro Hirokata, *Michi no sachi*, Sonsai sōsho, Kondō Keizō (1885)
Yasuoka Shigeaki, 'Maruyama Ōkyo to kyōto chōnin', in *Nihon byōbu-e shūsei*, Kōdansha (1978), vol. VIII, pp. 150–56
Yokota Tadashi, 'Sumiyoshi Hiroyuki: denki kenkyū: Yashiro Kōken-sen "michi no sachi" to kanren shite', *Bijutsushi Kenkyū*, 10 (1977), pp. 31–47
Yōrō Takeshi, *Nihonjin no shintaikan no rekishi*, Hōzōkan (1996)
Yoshida Shigefusa, *Tenmei kibun kansei kibun*, in *Mikan zuihitsu hyakushū*, Chūō Kōronsha (1976), vol. IV, pp. 255–98
Yuasa Akiyoshi, *Tenmei taisei-roku*, in *Nihon keizai daiten*, Obunsho (1927), vol. XXII, pp. 145–364
Yuasa Genzō, *Kokui-ron*, in *Nihon keizai daiten*, Hōbunkan (1928), vol. XXII, pp. 3–48

Photographic Acknowledgements

Following are the locations of artworks illustrated in this volume, together with the names of owning bodies and other individuals and institutions who have supplied their own or other picture material and/or permission to reproduce it (and to whom the author and publishers owe their thanks):

Formerly Azabu Museum of Arts and Crafts, present location unknown: 19; British Museum, London: 48, 50, 85, 108; Daijō-ji, Hyōgo: 29, 74–5; Fukushima Prefectural Museum: 17; Hakodate Municipal Library: 31; Ishiyama-dera, Omi: 33; Itsuo Museum, Osaka: 72; Kanagawa Prefectural Museum of History: 52; Keiō University Library, Tokyo: 9; Kobe City Museum: 32; Kongō-ji, Hyōgo: 69–70; Kuwana Museum: cover, 10; Kyoto National Museum: 77; Manno Museum, Osaka: 79–80; Mitsui Bunko, Tokyo: 83; Musée de Nancy: 42; Museum of Fine Arts, Boston (Fenellosa-Weld Collection; photo courtesy of the Museum of Fine Arts, reproduced with permission; © 1999 Museum of Fine Arts, Boston; all rights reserved): 22–4; National Diet Library, Tokyo: 2–3, 13–14, 44, 46, 56, 81–2, 97, 103; National Museum of Poland, Krakow: 20; National Museums and Galleries on Merseyside, Liverpool: 67; Nihon Iji Bunka Shiryō Shūsei Henshū Iinkai: 30, 78; Ninna-ji, Kyoto: 57; Osaka City Museum: 107; Kimiko and John Powers Collection, Colorado: 36, 96; Enzan Memorial Museum, Saitama: 65; Etsuko and Joe Price Collection, Los Angeles: 21; School of Oriental and African Studies, University of London: 5, 11, 43, 45; Sendai City Museum: 51; Shinkoku Morikani Shrine, Kuwana, Mie: 1, 16; Sukagawa City Museum, Fukushima: 7; Tenri University Library: 76; Tokyo National Museum: 6, 12, 15, 62, 71, 101, 104–5; Tokyo University Library: 55; Waseda University Library, Tokyo: 4, 8; John Webber collection, New York: 66; Yamato Bunkakan, Nara: 106; private collections: 18, 25–8, 30, 34–5, 37–41, 47, 49, 63–4, 68, 73, 78, 84, 86–95, 98–100, 102, 109.

Index

Pages on which illustrations appear are shown in *italic*.